DO NOT REMOVE
CARDS FROM POCKET

ALLEN COUNTY PUBLIC LIBRARY

FORT WAYNE, INDIANA 46802

You may return this book to any agency, branch,
or bookmobile of the Allen County Public Library.

DEMCO

ISTVAN ANHALT is a member of the Department of Music at Queen's University.

Istvan Anhalt, himself a composer of many vocal works, has written an interdisciplinary study of the innovative vocal and choral music that has emerged in Europe and North America since the Second World War. This music has amazed, confused, sometimes shocked, and often deeply moved its listeners, and the author probes its very roots.

Anhalt sketches briefly the antecedents of this revolutionary music and then illustrates the subject by looking closely at works by three of the greatest composers of modern vocal and choral music: Luciano Berio's *Sequenza III* for female solo voice, György Ligeti's *Nouvelles Aventures* for three solo voices and small instrumental ensemble, and Witold Lutosław-ski's *Trois Poèmes d'Henri Michaux* for large chorus and orchestra.

The author next seeks to formulate a conceptual framework to explain post-war vocal composition. He discusses relationships between poetry and music, speaking and singing, theatre and music, and composers and performers. He identifies and examines recurring themes in this corpus, including hallowed and cursed names, repetition as a mythical and/or mystical technique, the arcane, magical elements in music and language, and music as spectacle or celebration and as a search for the past. Anhalt also considers the structural elements and compositional procedures used in creating this type of music.

The complex associations with other creative activities that typify modern vocal composition help to make it, as Anhalt shows clearly, an extraordinarily rich mosaic of alternative voices.

'*Alternative Voices* is broad-ranging, imaginative, stimulating, and provocative ... Everything discussed has become a source of great illumination for me.' R. Murray Schafer

ISTVAN ANHALT

Alternative voices:
Essays on contemporary vocal
and choral composition

UNIVERSITY OF TORONTO PRESS
Toronto Buffalo London

© University of Toronto Press 1984
Toronto Buffalo London
Printed in Canada

ISBN 0-8020-5531-1

Canadian Cataloguing in Publication Data

Anhalt, István, 1919–
Alternative voices

Bibliography: p.
Includes index.
ISBN 0-8020-5531-1

1. Vocal music – 20th century – History and criticism.
2. Berio, Luciano, 1925–   Sequenza III.
3. Ligeti, György, 1923–   Nouvelles aventures.
4. Lutoslowski, Witold, 1913–   Poèmes d'Henri
Michaux. I. Title.

ML1406.A53   784'.09'04   C83-098290-6

This book has been printed on acid-free paper.

MUSICAL EXAMPLES: Example 2.1: Luciano Berio *Sequenza III* used by permission of Universal
Edition (London) Ltd; Examples 3.1–3.16: György Ligeti *Nouvelles Aventures* Copyright (©)
1966 by Henry Litolff's Verlag, Frankfurt; Examples 4.1–4.17: Witold Lutosławski *Trois Poèmes
d'Henri Michaux* Copyright 1963 by Polskie Wydawnictwo Muzyczne, Kraków, Poland, used by
kind permission of J&W Chester/Edition Wilhelm Hansen London Ltd who control the rights in
the Western World; Example 5.2: Peter Maxwell Davies *Eight Songs for a Mad King* copyright
1971, Boosey & Hawkes Ltd

To my wife, Beate,
and
to John Beckwith

Contents

viii Contents

Preface

These essays have grown out of a desire fourteen years ago better to understand a number of contemporary compositions that employ the human voice in what seemed an innovative manner. I still think that much innovative activity has taken place in this area during the past quarter-century, but the word innovative has considerably changed its meaning for me. I regard this change as one of the most interesting and rewarding aspects of this project.[1]

The book's central topic is Western vocal and choral composition since 1945. While most works discussed in the text belong to this domain, I have mentioned also, on occasion, works composed before that date and examples of other genres, including some from related fields, wherever such references contributed to a better understanding of some aspect of the main theme.

The three studies constituting part I reached their present state the earliest: that of chapter 2 in 1972, and those of chapters 3 and 4 in 1976. Parts of chapters 1 and 5 were written in the fall of 1977, after I returned from a half-year stay in Cambridge, where I also attended Professor J.L.M. Trim's classes in articulatory phonetics. The remainder of the text I wrote during the summer of 1981.

I offer my thanks to Professor Trim, from whom I learned more about phonetics during my all too brief stay in his classes than I can give account of here; and also for his many kindnesses.

Dr Francis J. Nolan of Cambridge University, who was a post-graduate student of Professor Trim's in 1977, gave generously of his time and helped me by making spectrograms and phonetic transcriptions.

Dr John Laver of the Department of Linguistics at the University of Edinburgh provided, through his writings and through direct exchanges, the ideational framework that helped me first to recognize the full scope of the dimension of voice quality, and then to think about it, with respect to music, in a coherent way. Several stimulating conversations with Professor David Crystal, of Reading University, put into perspective certain aspects of prosody and speech intonation and suggested ideas on their applicability to vocal music. To all three I wish to express my thanks and appreciation.

I am deeply grateful to Professor Roman Jakobson for providing valuable information about V. Sereznikov related to collective recitation. I also much appreciate the help I received from Professor James A. Leith on the topic of revolutionary festivals.

Colleagues who have read the manuscript in its various stages – John Beckwith, R. Murray Schafer, and (one chapter) Dr Beverley Cavanagh, as well as others whose identity I do not know – have greatly helped with their criticism to sustain my continuing work on this project. I claim sole responsibility for all errors and mistaken views that remain in the text.

To my students and colleagues at Queen's University, at McGill University, and at the State University of New York at Buffalo,[2] as well as to all the helpful librarians at these institutions (to Eve Albrich, Margaret Webster, and Marcia Weese, especially), I would like to offer my warm thanks for stimulating and facilitating in uncounted ways the work related to this book. Among them are my former students David Colwell, Robin Elliott, and David McIsaacs, who helped me to assemble the bibliography. Robin Elliott also did most of the work on the indexes. He also helped me most effectively in many other ways, including searching for data and proof-reading, which responsibilities he shared with Lesley Higgins, who was equally painstaking and pleasant to work with. Keith Hamel, another former pupil, and Donald McKenzie drew most of the figures and several examples with a fine hand. I am grateful to them. I want to express my gratitude to my former secretary, Mrs Terrie Sheen, as well as to Ms Marsha Hartley, for their patience and cheerfulness while typing from a manuscript that was difficult to decipher and for bearing with me through numerous different versions of the text.

I wish to say special thanks to Dr R.M. Schoeffel of University of Toronto Press for his stimulating interest in, and helpful assistance to, this project, ever since I first spoke to him about it, and to John Parry, whom I had the good fortune to have as an exacting and very understanding copy-editor who significantly contributed to the present shape of the text. I acknowledge with appreciation the permissions kindly granted by the following to quote from scores under their copyright: Universal Edition (London) Ltd; Henry Litolff's Verlag, Frankfurt; Polskie Wydawnictwo Muzyczne, Kraków; J&W Chester / Edition Wilhelm Hansen London Ltd; Boosey & Hawkes Ltd; and Edition Gallimard, Paris, for permission to quote from the work of Henri Michaux.

I wish to express my appreciation for various other kinds of assistance: a generously granted sabbatical leave by Queen's University in Kingston, Ontario; research grants from the Canada Council and from the Queen's University Advisory Committee on Research; a Leave Fellowship for 1976–7 from the Canada Council; and a grant from the Ontario Arts Council.

This book has been published with the help of a grant from the Canadian Federation for the Humanities, using funds provided by the Social Sciences and Humanities Research Council of Canada, and a grant from the Andrew W. Mellon Foundation to the University of Toronto Press.

Istvan Anhalt
Kingston, Ontario
January 1983

ALTERNATIVE VOICES

1

Theme and recent background

THEME

A trend has been noticeable in music since the mid-1950s: the appearance of a succession of new compositions for the voice that use it in ways other than exclusively in the 'usual singing mode' (see note 1 to the preface). Spoken, whispered, murmured, and hummed delivery is combined in these works with normal singing and with such marginal sounds as coughing, sighing, audible breathing. While some pieces use a syntactically correct text, others employ language in different kinds of construction. With respect to treatment of texts, some works emphasize, or at least preserve, intelligibility; others reduce it to a greater or lesser extent by various means and for diverse compositional purposes. Certain works use a single language; others employ more than one, even many. Some works are composed using a new language invented for the purpose, while others just use seemingly meaningless buccal noises.

This repertoire contains also works that exist only on tape and that were composed by the use of what we regard today as routine techniques of recording and tape-manipulation. In some of these the voice is combined with other recorded sounds, mechanical and/or electronic. Other works are composed with live and tape-recorded sounds, creating a blend of the two.

One encounters unaccompanied solo pieces and works for smaller or larger unaccompanied choir. Some works use a few instruments, or even tape accompaniment only; others require a larger complement (that might include tape-recorders) or a full orchestra.

Given the continuing growth of this repertoire, and its very considerable diversity, do we have in it a development of lasting importance? The principal purpose of this study is to find a reasoned answer to this question. I shall look at a number of individual works and shall also try to identify the broad characteristic features, as well as the underlying ideas, that support this body of work.

In the late 1940s Pierre Boulez composed two major works for orchestra and voices, *Le Visage nuptial* (1946–7) and *Le Soleil des eaux* (1948), in which he used, in addition to singing, a variety of different speaking modes; in so doing he continued to develop the idea of Schoenberg's *Sprechstimme*. The melodic structures in these pieces feature the frequent use of wide intervals; subtle declamatory rhythms notated with great precision; non-measured passages; a mechanical, rapid, and monotone parlando; difficult transitions from one type of utterance into another; and an obvious striving for intelligibility of the text, emphasizing the exaggerated prosodic designs of the sentences and within them the intonation curves of the individual words. *Le Marteau sans maître* (1954) poses lesser demands from the vocal point of view. The solo soprano voice, which is accompanied by a small, instrumental ensemble, uses a somewhat simplified palette for the transitional area between singing and parlando. As in the two earlier works, the syntactic and prosodic logic is derived from declamatory models that are approximated as much as the self-imposed, purely musical exigencies have allowed for (Stockhausen 1960).

Karlheinz Stockhausen's *Gesang der Jünglinge* (1955–6), one of the most outstanding tape compositions ever made, is a combination of a large variety of recorded utterances sung and spoken by a boy-soprano and an equally large assortment of electronically generated sounds (Stockhausen 1960). The boy's voice seems to be an embodiment of human reality in one of its symbolically purest representations, and the electronic layer, an expression of the physical, the cosmic, and perhaps the mystical. The two types are blended through a finely differentiated spectrum of micro-structures, allowing for subtle transitions of various kinds.

Mauricio Kagel's *Anagrama* (1957–8), through the medium of four vocal (singing) soloists, a speaking choir, and an instrumental chamber ensemble, introduces a number of procedures, for possibly the first time in real-time performance. The composition atomizes the text into its phonemic components and then either assembles these (with certain liberties as to allophonic relationships) into new words in French, German, Italian, and Spanish or uses them as phoneme-chains, with or without morphemic meaning. Copious instructions define the manner of speech, articulation, phonation, and voice qualities such as stuttering, vibrato, tremolando, ingressive phonation, guttural, nasal, falsetto, breathy, or whispery voice, or a quasi-whistle.

Such marginal sounds as laughter, click, and cough are also called for to serve expressive purposes, as are nasalization, dentalization, or labialization (Schnebel 1970: 15–26; Klüppelholz 1976: 85–125).

John Cage's slight piece *Solo for Voice 1* (1958) is flexible in construction and desirous of accommodating the performer. The notation of the score is not so much prescriptive as suggestive, aiming at drawing out a proven, or presumably latent, potential for improvisation from the interpreter.

In Luciano Berio's *Circles* (1960) the solo soprano is the dominant component of the piece, and the three instrumentalists support her in a remarkably flexible, yet closely controlled interplay made possible by an ingeniously conceived performance process and a matching notation. In this setting the emphasis is on the sonic elements and on the onomatopoeic connotations of the text. The constantly changing character of the voice part contains the following modalities of delivery: singing, speech, speech-song, low (quasi-secretive) whisper, shout, audible sigh, typical lip-spreadings and glides of a North American female popular vocalist, a disjointedness (emphasizing the pseudo-meaninglessness indicated in, and by, the text), an occasional slangy utterance, nervous giggling, isolated syllables, and pure buccal play. When this stage is reached, the voice and the instruments become a homogeneous blend, giving the impression that the performers are enacting a magic ritual, in which the singer is the celebrant, and the three instrumentalists her acolytes. Thus the piece spans a trajectory that begins here and now and progresses, by implication, into a layer far removed from the surface of the actual (Hoenle and Lanoix 1974).

Stockhausen completed in 1962 the first version of his *Momente*, in which he employed many of the formal procedures developed by himself and his colleagues during the preceding half-decade or so. It is a large-scale work, aiming at a broad and somewhat rough affective appeal, scored for a solo soprano, four choirs, and a middle-sized instrumental ensemble. The new feature in this work is its modular construction. The piece consists of a number of more or less invariant portions that can be assembled according to certain rules (Smalley 1974).

In the same year (1962) György Ligeti completed his *Aventures*, which uses only chains of phonetic sounds that are not derived from any meaningful text, but taken from the International Phonetic Alphabet for their articulatory and acoustical characteristics as well as for their affective connotations. With this work, the process of removing oneself from the implications of a 'thematic' and syntactic-semantic domain, and a related sense of alienation, have been seemingly totally achieved. However, the rich musical, affective, and paralinguistic layers of the piece provide points of orientation and thus forcefully prove the compositional and communicative importance of these layers (Klüppelholz 1976: 160–99).

In 1963 Witold Lutosławski's *Trois Poèmes d'Henri Michaux* for large chorus, winds, percussion, and two pianos had its première. It is one of the first works, if not the first, that uses with telling effect mass-design as a dominant structural type in choral music. The work became a prototype for numerous other works that came to form the Polish school of choral composition of the 1960s. In this piece Lutosławski gave voice to certain mass (even mob) effects, like those that occurred during some of the sordid and tragic scenes of the Second World War (see chapter 4).

In the same year Roger Reynolds composed *The Emperor of Ice Cream* for eight speaking, declaiming, or singing solo voices with piano, percussion, and contra-bass. This work is to be performed according to a scenario that requires the displacement of the vocalists during the performance. These movements, and a related lighting plan, constitute intrinsic elements of the score.

Pauline Oliveros's *Sound Patterns* (1964) employs an unaccompanied group of four vocalists, or a chorus. Her text consists of buccal sounds children like to produce. Some are auto-erotic in nature; others are of the type one encounters in comic strips.

By the mid-1960s the new repertoire had gained momentum. In Italy, Berio, Giacinto Scelsi, Luigi Nono, and Sylvano Bussotti continued to produce new works of this type; in Holland, Joep Strasser; in Denmark, Per Nørgård; in Sweden, Jan Bark, Arne Mellnäs, Bernhard Lewkowitch, and several composers of the Fylkingen group, including Sten Hanson and Bengt Emil Johnsson; in Germany, Stockhausen, Herbert Eimert, Kagel, Dieter Schnebel, Ligeti, Hans Werner Henze, Helmut Lachenmann, and Erhard Karkoschka, among others; in Austria, Roman Haubenstock-Ramati; in Belgium, Leo Küpper and Henri Pousseur; in France, Boulez, Ivo Malec, Vinko Globokar, François-Bernard Mache, Luc Ferrari, Iannis Xenakis, Betsy Jolas, Marius Constant, and Claude Ballif; in Switzerland, Wladimir Vogel and Heinz Holliger; in Britain, David Bedford, Peter Maxwell Davies, Harrison Birtwistle, John Tavener, Alexander Goehr, Trevor Wishart, John Paynter, and Giles Swayne; in Poland, Lutosławski, Kazimierz Serocki, Krzysztof Penderecki, and Tadeusz Baird; in Canada, John Beckwith, Harry Somers, Udo Kasemets, Bruce Mather, R. Murray Schafer, Istvan Anhalt, Gilles Tremblay, and Claude Vivier; and in the United States, Cage, Milton Babbitt, Salvatore Martirano, George Crumb, Reynolds, Lejaren Hiller, Robert Ashley, Steve Reich, Lukas Foss, George Rochberg, Oliveros, Charles

Dodge, Alvin Lucier, Philip Glass, and Kenneth Gaburo. There is nothing to indicate that this trend is slowing down: new works appear in considerable numbers each year by the composers mentioned, as well as by others.[1] Some of the recent works are of monumental dimensions: Schafer's *In Search of Zoroaster* (1971) lasts well over an hour, and his *Apocalypsis* (1977) about two hours; Berio's *Coro* (1975–6) is about an hour long; and Giles Swayne's unaccompanied *Cry* (1979) takes seventy minutes to perform.[2]

The last-mentioned work, in its total effect a major composition, contains thematic and stylistic elements and an overall compositional approach shared by a number of works in this repertoire. These include the theme of Creation itself (the same theme informs part II of Schafer's *Apocalypsis* and seems to be related to those of Stockhausen's *Sternklang*, his *Atmen gibt das Leben*, and possibly also his *Licht*); the use of a non-verbal text, consisting of abstract phoneme-sequences, such as rapid and spoken iterations of consonant-vowel duplets, or pairs of duplets, in which the consonants are different, but the vowels the same (||:sa:||, ||:wē:||, ||:bē:||, etc; ||:taka:||, ||:kūnū:||, ||:mēlē:||, ||:fiti:||, etc), vowel series, sustained fricatives, and tongue-trills. The work makes frequent use of quasi-static, or mobile, mass-structures and exhibits catholicism in its choice of materials.

RECENT BACKGROUND

It seems almost self-evident that one would begin to look for the antecedents of this repertoire in Schoenbergian *Sprechstimme*, used for the first time in a fully developed form in *Pierrot lunaire* (1912) (Crawford 1963; Klüppelholz 1976: 25–35). Schoenberg composed this work after completing *Gurre-Lieder* (1900–1), *Fifteen Poems from 'Das Buch der hängenden Gärten' by Stefan George* (1908–9), and *Erwartung* (1909). There were, however, other models for *Pierrot lunaire*: Schoenberg could look at an unbroken tradition of melodrama that reached back to J.J. Rousseau's *Pygmalion* (1772) (Van Der Veen 1955) and was able to witness also the flourishing of the genre in his own time. Whether by a great composer, or by a lesser one, these melodramas were engendered by a yearning for certain kinds of expression, by a love for the beauty of the speaking, declaiming voice, by a desire for a heightened intelligibility of text, as well as by the wish to create a more subtle interpretation than was thought possible through a *bel canto* delivery.

From Max Steinitzer's excellent monograph *Zur Entwicklungsgeschichte des Melodrams und Mimodrams* (1918) one learns a wealth of detail about nineteenth- and early-twentieth-century melodrama, in its dramatic, epic, and lyric manifestations. A few works and dates of composition or of première performances give an idea of the currency of this genre during the twenty-three years that preceded the composition of *Pierrot lunaire*: Hans Pfitzner's *Das Fest auf Solhaug* (1889–90), Adalbert Goldschmidt's selections from *Grimms Märchen* (1896), Richard Strauss's *Enoch Arden* (1898), Engelbert Humperdinck's *Die Königskinder* (1898), Max von Schilling's *Das Hexenlied* (1902), Theodor Gerlach's *Liebeswogen* (1903), August Bungert's melodramatic music for both parts of Goethe's *Faust* (1903), Wilhelm Brandes's *Die Jüdin von Worms* (1911), Paul Colberg's *Der gläserne Berg* (1911), and in the year of the première of *Pierrot lunaire* Hans Sommer's *Waldschratt* (Steinitzer 1918: 33–6).

There were a variety of ways in which the composers of melodramas correlated the declaimer's part with the instrumental part(s). Between the so-called 'free' melodrama, which gave a continuous text, without special markers added above the score, and the strict (*gebundenes*) variety, there were transitional types of various kinds (Steinitzer 1918: 45–9; Schuhmacher 1967). The notation of the voice part in *Pierrot lunaire* represented, of course, a commitment to precision, thus curtailing the performer's scope for interpretative decision-making, in the interest of keeping performances close to the composer's own conception of the work.

There were numerous artists, *recitants*, declaimers, and *diseurs* or *diseuses* who specialized in this genre. One of them, Albertine Zehme of Leipzig, who commissioned *Pierrot lunaire*, gave a performance of a work consisting of a recitation of poems by Ujejski with music selected from Chopin's piano works by Richard Burmeister (Steinitzer 1918: 41). The art of the declaimer remained in fashion throughout Europe through the 1920s and 1930s, and I remember some examples of it in Budapest at that time.

In France this genre took on a special character with the great *diseuse* Yvette Guilbert (1867–1944), who in her interpretations of popular French *chansons* combined the sung and spoken delivery in a hitherto unexperienced, subtle, manner. Her art elicited serious commentary (predominantly by German critics) (Guilbert 1929: 186–7), and she sustained a long friendship with Freud, who was an admirer of her art (Guilbert 1929, 1946; Knapp and Chipman 1964).

The emergence of the expressionist melodrama of Schoenberg was not a creation *ex nihilo*, but rather a logical development resulting from a tradition, and from a new motivic-contrapuntal-harmonic, atonal language that Schoenberg was instrumental in bringing about. He worked in response to some inner necessity that probably had as much to do with his genius and personality as with the cultural, social, and political forces in central Europe. That he worked for a year, in 1901, as a conductor, arranger, and composer, in the

Berlin Kabaret Überbrettl of Ernst von Wolzogen, where *diseurs, recitants,* and *chansoniers* were also employed, could have played some part in the development towards *Pierrot lunaire* and *Die glückliche Hand*. It is likely, however, that Schoenberg had ample opportunities to hear melodrama, or dramatic and other types of recitation, in other circumstances as well.

The expressionist melodrama, and the expressionist melos in general, continued to develop after 1912, principally through the work of Schoenberg and Alban Berg.[3] They came to play important roles in *Moses und Aron* (1930–2) and Schoenberg employed *Sprechstimme* also in *Kol Nidre* (1938), *Ode to Napoleon* (1942), and *A Survivor from Warsaw* (1945). Berg used solo *Sprechstimme* extensively, and to great effect, in both his great operas, *Wozzeck* and *Lulu*. Their expressionist melos, including the use of *Sprechstimme*, also influenced greatly the evolution of post-1945 vocal music, as did Webern's jagged, and angular, melodic designs.

The practice of spoken solo and/or choral recitation (measured or unmeasured) with musical accompaniment was adopted by a number of other composers (Milhaud, Stravinsky, Honegger, Toch, Vogel, and Walton, among others) during the decades between the two world wars, but with none of them did it attain the sophistication of Schoenberg's usage.

In 1909, the year *Erwartung* was composed, a new voice appeared – dynamic and enthusiastic, albeit in a disturbing way. Filippo Tommaso Marinetti, the founder of the futurist movement in Italy and a noted *diseur*, was sounding off through the first *Manifesto of Futurism* (1909) (Flint 1972). This document speaks, nay, shouts, of risk-taking, of the love of danger, of courage and revolt. A new demon has been elevated to a pedestal – speed – and an automobile with a powerful engine has become its sculpted symbol. With callousness and ignorance the manifesto pledges itself to the glorification of war and calls it 'the world's only hygiene' (42), knowing not at all that two world conflagrations would render these words grotesque, obscene, and cruel.

Through a disjointed, feverish, and posturing language Marinetti was able to capture something of the mood of a human crowd in motion, one of his claimed objectives. He thrived on excitement and wanted to 'sing of great crowds excited by work, by pleasure and by riot' (42). His prose sounds like a free poem, the text of a poster, a proclamation, or a series of headlines. It is a throbbing, aggressive, insistent language, brooking no dissent, dismissing the need for reflection, intolerant, and destructive. Yet it caught something of the essence of the constructivist mood that informed some of the designers and producers of machines that have changed twentieth-century society. As a declaimer (*diseur*) Marinetti must have been quite effective; his style probably influenced the Dada movement and even the neo-Dadaists of our day.

Our interest in Marinetti concerns his comments on the art of declamation. In an article published in 1916, 'Dynamic and Synoptic Declamation,' he describes in some detail the style of performance he considers to be superior. At the outset he speaks of 'the deficiencies of declamation as it has been understood up to now' (142). He then describes the style of the 'new Futurist lyricism' in terms of how the person ought to speak, stand, move his arms and hands; his facial expressions; his displacement in space during the recitation; the use of several declaimers at the same time; the employment of design; and the instrumental accompaniment. In suggesting the use of other declaimers, 'equal, or subordinate, mixing or alternating their voices with his' (144), he may have envisaged a special kind of vocal (spoken) polyphony different from the expressionist *Sprechstimme* of Schoenberg. He demanded that the vocalist 'completely dehumanize his voice, systematically doing away with every modulation and nuance' (144). 'Metallize, liquify, vegetalize, petrify, and electrify his voice, grounding it in the vibrations of matter itself as expressed by words in freedom' (144). Whatever these impressionistic allusions may have meant for him, he wanted the use of the voice to be different from 'normal' prosody or from its expressionistically intensified variants. He probably wanted various kinds of artificial or even abstract vocal utterances or delivery styles. In advocating the use of a certain number of 'elementary instruments such as hammers, ... tables, automobile horns, drums, ... saws, and electric bells, to produce precisely ... the different simple or abstract onomatopoeias and different onomatopoeic harmonies' (144), he was probably aiming at certain noises that were to blend with orally produced onomatopoeic sounds, a compositionally innovative concept at that time. By advocating the use of non-harmonic spectra, he anticipated and influenced (together with Russolo) the emergence since the 1920s[4] of percussion instruments as a major instrumental family in avant-garde music, with an important role as complementary sounds to vocal ones in the new repertoire we are considering.

Although both men were deeply interested in the voice, Schoenberg and Marinetti apparently had no interest in each other. This is hardly surprising in view of their antithetical outlooks on ethics and aesthetics. One wonders if Marinetti even knew of *Pierrot lunaire*.

The almost unprecedented intellectual ferment between 1900 and 1914 produced and/or sustained a great variety of artistic movements: symbolism, fauvism, expressionism, conditionalism, cubism, vorticism, imagism, impersonalism, acmeism, nihilism, occultism, primitivism, simultaneism, suprematism, syncretism, hybridism, and others (Poggioli 1960, 1968; Shattuck 1961; Kirby and Nes Kirby 1971; Gillmor 1972; Barooshian 1974; Kruchenykh 1971; Schwitters 1973–7; Tisdall and Bozzolla 1978; Barron and Tuchman 1980). Artists, composers, and writers not only showed a vivid interest in each other's work, but also crossed media boundaries and worked in sister domains and/or wrote about such activities. As Schoenberg had a professional's affinity for painting, so the painter Kandinskij showed an uncommon sensitivity to the musical potential of the spoken word and to the incantational character of repetition: 'The apt use of a word (in its poetic sense), its repetition, twice, three times, or even more frequently ... will not only tend to intensify the internal structure but also bring out unsuspected spiritual properties in the word itself ... Frequent repetition ... deprives the word of its external reference. Similarly, the symbolic reference of a designated object tends to be forgotten and only the sound is retained. We hear this pure sound unconsciously perhaps, in relation to the concrete or immaterial objects. But in the latter case pure sound exercises a direct impression on the soul' (*Concerning the Spiritual in Art* [1912: 34]).

When war broke out, many of the contacts between artists of different countries were interrupted. Even within countries artistic activity was inhibited. A number of artists left their homelands and took refuge in Switzerland, which offered them peace, shelter, and an opportunity for free exchange of ideas. A group, in 1916, formed in Zürich a movement that was to be known as Dada.

In the words of one of its founders, Richard Huelsenbeck, Dada was meant to be principally a focus for an abstract art, the character of which was to reflect the world-view of its founders, who were convinced 'that the war had been contrived by the various governments for the most automatic, sordid and materialistic reasons' (Motherwell 1951: 23).

Another face of Dada was its absurd expression. Another of its founders, Tristan Tzara, wrote: 'Dada is our intensity: it sets up inconsequential bayonets the sumatran head of the german baby; ... It is for and against unity and definitely against the future' (Motherwell 1951: 75). We shall see later how expressions of suggestive unintelligibility and absurdity such as these were made into powerful artistic expressions by such composers as John Cage and Mauricio Kagel a half-century later.

One of the most original of the Dada poets was Hugo Ball, who in 1915 invented poems without words or sound poems, in which he composed with the sonic qualities of vowels and consonants as the composer does with tones and instrumental timbres. One of his poems begins:

gadji beri bimba
glandridi lauli lonni cadori
gadjama bim beri glassala
glandridi glassala tuffm i zimbrabim
blassa galassasa tuffm i zimbrabim   (Ball 1974: 70).

A few months after writing this poem, Ball observed: 'Language as a social organ can be destroyed without the creative process having to suffer. In fact, it seems that the creative process even benefits from it' (76). This idea came to generate the 'texts' of many recent compositions for the voice. Ball knew that poems such as the one quoted do not constitute only pretty and 'empty' sounds, but can penetrate deeply into man's consciousness or, even more probably, into his unconscious (Ellenberger 1970). They are 'magical floating words ... word images,' which, when 'successful, are irresistibly and hypnotically engraved on the memory' (Ball 1974: 66–7).

The repetitive poems, in an abstract phonemic language (see page 228), of Kurt Schwitters, another Dada painter and poet, forecast the present-day incantational text-sound compositions of a Steve Reich, a Brion Gysin, or a Charles Amirkhanian; his collages (as do some works of Charles Ives) anticipate another trend that functions with vitality in our days (Schwitters 1973–7, 1975). (Recent manifestations of this approach include Stockhausen's *Telemusik* and *Hymnen*, Hiller's *An Avalanche*, and Kagel's *Recitativarie*.)

During the 1910s and 1920s members of a group of poets in Russia, who came to be known by the appellation *cubo-futurists* (Poggioli 1960; Markov 1968; Woroszylski 1970; Kruchenykh 1971; Barooshian 1974; Barron and Tuchman 1980), were also engaged in linguistic experimentation aimed at renewing poetical language in response to what they saw to be changing sociopolitical realities. The most adventurous among them were Velimir Xlebnikov, Aleksej Kruchenykh, and Vasilij Kamenskij. Their work was supported by fellow poets, scholars, and critics such as Roman Jakobson, Viktor Sklovskij, Sergej Bernštejn, and V. Serežnikov (Stempel and Paulman 1972). One of the earliest, and still most significant, apologias for these experiments, Viktor Sklovskij's *The Awakening of the Word*, was first read in a St Petersburg cabaret, in 1914 (418). It begins with the clarion call: 'The oldest creative act of man was the creation of words. Now the words are dead, and language resembles a cemetery.' Viktor Serežnikov wrote *The Music of the Word* (Serežnikov 1923). S. Bernštejn wrote on the aesthetics and theory of declamation (Stempel and Paulman 1972: 339–85). Roman Jakobson, today one of the greatest living linguists, wrote on the work of Xlebnikov (ibid) and other related topics (Barron and Tuchman 1980: 18). All this activity has a close bearing on the present study, as we shall see.

In contrast to the relative ease with which the emergence of the various forms of solo utterance can be traced, that of group utterances is more difficult to follow. It is almost certain that in 1916, when his 'Dynamic and Synoptic Declamation' was published, Marinetti was unaware of Schoenberg's *Die glückliche Hand*, as the work received its première only in 1924. But he had been in correspondence with Tristan Tzara, who was the first to introduce the *poème simultané* in the Cabaret Voltaire (Motherwell 1951: 24–5).

The cubo-futurists in Russia, possibly influenced by Marinetti, who visited that country in 1910 and 1914 (Poggioli 1960), became interested in the genre of simultaneous recitation. In 1919 Viktor Serežnikov thought it warranted to organize in Moscow an Institute of Collective Recitation![5]

Darius Milhaud's *Les Choéphores* and *Les Euménides*, to Aeschylus's text in Paul Claudel's French translation, contain group-declamations. They were composed during 1915–16 and 1921, respectively, which suggests that models for Schoenberg's and Milhaud's group-utterances might be also found in the performances of the choruses in classical drama at the turn of the century and during the two decades following.

Earlier precedents might be looked for in French revolutionary festivals between 1789 and 1799, and in 1848; in popular theatre in Switzerland and Germany; and in socialist drama in the late nineteenth and early twentieth centuries, principally in France, Belgium, and Russia (Rolland 1901; 1913: 125–9; Füllöp-Miller 1927; Herbert 1961; Ozouf 1976: 28–30, 49–50; Agulhon 1977; Barron and Tuchman 1980). During those events there were probably spontaneous group responses from the audience. In Paris, during the opening performance of the Théâtre de l'Art social, in March 1893, 'a program composed exclusively of revolutionary poems and short plays,' the audience was reported to be 'enthusiastic and could not restrain cries of "Down with *La Patrie!*" "Vive l'anarchie!" and the like' (Herbert 1961: 37).

According to an account during the 1905–6 upheavals in Russia 'over 5,000 clubs and theatrical organizations of a revolutionary character were established' (Carter 1929: 11–12). In the years following the Bolshevik revolution, several trends in theatre competed with each other, including that advocated by the futurists, who believed that the opportunity had finally come for the realization of their ideas. In the turbulent world of the early years of the Russian revolution, theatre life, and political theory often merged into a single experience. 'As the Revolution improvised on the social life, so the theatre reflected it through mass improvisation' (34). 'Festival processions, parades and mass celebrations generally were theatricalised' (34). The proletcult theatre that evolved had probably only the revolutionary theatre of 1905–6 to model itself on. The movement 'had no plays, no established technique, no organization' (123). It was conditioned by the desire *actively* to engage the mass – *mass* meaning individuals untrained in acting, who might be effectively employed as members of a chorus. It was demanded that these representations 'should express a mass-personality, a human collectivism' (Woroszylski 1970: 124). It was held that in these events 'the personality of the mass must predominate ... The Mass must form a Greek chorus resembling the ancient Greek chorus to express misery and triumph, social and political' (124–5).

Similar theatrical developments also took place in Germany after the 1918 revolution there. As in Russia, the two forces behind this movement were the 'workers' organizations and the theatre-experiments of the leftist intelligentsia' (Hoffmann and Hoffmann-Ostwald 1961: 32). 'The most notable results of these efforts were the mass-play and the speech-choir. They prevailed until ca 1924 as 'typical proletarian artforms,' as the dawn of a new 'collective culture' and the direct expression of the 'revolutionary mass-feeling' (32). In these accounts we have the first unequivocal information of the speech-choir as an organized, autonomous, and significant performing medium. 'Between 1922 and 1923 communist speech-choirs came into existence in many cities' (32). 'Between 1924 and 1925 most of the communist speech-choir groups transformed themselves into theatrical groups ... although the chorus format retained its place during the festive occasions, or feasts of the workers' (32).

What were the performances of these speech-choirs like? We might get an idea of this from the preface to *Chorus of Work* (Chor der Arbeit) by Gustav von Wangenheim, written for the speech-choir of the Communist party organization in Berlin, in 1923. It specifies the exclusive use of workers (*Proletarier*) for the choir, but allows, as an exception, the use of trained actors ('of revolutionary disposition') for the difficult solos (128). Wangenheim indicates that 'in general the chorus does not recite more than two to three consecutive words. The collision of the diverse voices and choir-segments, as well as the mechanically imitated short and long syllables, attenuations, intensifications, provide the effect ... The chorus might speak in its totality, and it can divide itself into a larger or smaller number of high and low voices, men and women; the tone might come from various places in the hall, different tones might create the effect of confusion ... The absolute precision and stillness during pauses and then the unified attack is of decisive importance; this can be achieved by the adoption of numbers, words or sentences, which are to be spoken in the mind only' (126–7).

During the early 1920s, the speech-choir movement spread. In Scotland it was initiated by Marjorie Gullan, who brought it into the schools of Glasgow (Gullan 1929). After Gullan used a speech-choir in a performance of Euripides' *The Trojan Women* at the Glasgow Musical Festival of 1923, the use of the medium spread to numerous British and American universities (Gullan 1929).

In Czechoslovakia Emil František Burian developed a voice band for choral recitation[6] in 1927, and at about the same time the celebrated Hungarian *diseur* Oszkár Ascher organized a speech-choir in Budapest.

In the late 1920s and the early 1930s, as the leftist parties, and those on the far right, competed for power in Germany, Austria, and Hungary, choral speech was employed by both sides. It was gradually drowned out by or taken over in the form of the shrill and cruel utterances of a political environment that was inexorably lurching towards catastrophe.

It is difficult to recall these efforts in controlled collective recitation without wondering about the relationship between the medium and its social milieu or thinking about the carefully composed vocal mass-structures of a Ligeti, a Xenakis, or a Lutosławski. There seems to be a link between the central European speech-choirs of the early 1920s and these recent works.

Reading the score of Swayne's monumental *Cry*, I had the impression of having encountered the piece before. But where? I re-read this instruction in the score: 'It is essential that *Cry* should completely envelop its listeners, creating a sound-world which surrounds them on all sides, and which sets the entire air-space and the building itself in vibration. The voices are amplified and the sound spread around the auditorium.' Suddenly the concluding section of Baudelaire's 'Les Phares' (*Les Fleurs du mal*, 1857) came to mind:

> These maledictions, these blasphemies, these complaints,
> These ecstasies, these cries, these tears, these *Te Deums*,
> Are an echo reverberating in a thousand labyrinths ...

and then:

> ... a cry repeated by a thousand sentinels,
> A command returned by a thousand megaphones ...

and:

> This, indeed, is the best evidence, O Lord,
> Which we are able to give of our dignity,
> That intense sobbing that rolls through the ages
> And dies at the threshold of your eternity.

There are other works in this repertoire that were also influenced by writers, such as Baudelaire, Rimbaud, Mallarmé, Joyce, Kafka, Artaud, and Beckett. Let us think, for example, of the childhood fantasy that is Claude Vivier's *Chants*, or of Beckwith's remembrances of adolescence in *The Trumpets of Summer*, or of the echoes from early childhood that appear in profusion in Jolas's *Sonate à 12*. A similar spirit breathes from Rimbaud's 'Le Buffet,' or from his 'À la musique,' or even from his still puzzling 'Voyelles.' The merging of the categories of poetry and prose, the symbolic tone and the elliptical syntax that at times veers towards the surreal or the absurd, in *Les Illuminations* and *Une Saison en Enfer*, and his avowed aim of developing into 'a seer by a long, immense and rational *disordering* of *all the senses*' (Rimbaud 1972: 251) sound all too familiar today. With these tendencies young Rimbaud anticipated a number of attitudes and means of expression that have become commonplace and that have found expression in all the arts.

Mallarmé stretched the structure of meaningful language yet avoided snapping the syntactic thread; showed great sensitivity for the phonaesthetic qualities of words; indicated intonation, degree of emphasis, and other prosodic features, by composing the 'mise-en-page' of a poem;[7] and experimented with a variable poetic structure. Roger Shattuck pointed out: 'Mallarmé's work comes close to violating our normal powers of thinking' (Shattuck 1961: 334). Indeed, Mallarmé seems to ask the very question: what is meaning? In this way, and also through what Charles Chassé calls his 'hesitation between mysticism and positivism' (Chassé 1954: 15–16), Mallarmé is still very much one of us and seems to be present whenever a composer or poet tries to penetrate into the magical layer of language.[8]

Another *fin-de-siècle* voice whose echo still resonates today is that of Alfred Jarry. Behind the mockery and the grotesque façade of his *Ubu Roy* pieces, or in the absurdity of his pseudo-scientific texts, of 'pataphysics,' one senses the serious satire of Ionesco and that of several of the works of Cage, Kagel, and Ligeti and of Schnebel's *Glossolalie*.

André Breton's experiments with automatic writing secularized a centuries-old Kabbalistic mystical technique. (See also Ellenberger 1970 for numerous psychiatric references.) Of the results so obtained he observed:

'Poetically speaking, what strikes you about them above all is their *extreme degree of immediate absurdity*, the quality of this absurdity, upon closer scrutiny, being to give way to everything admissible, everything legitimate in the world is the disclosure of a certain number of properties and of facts no less objective in the final analysis, than the others' (Breton 1972: 24). His findings called into question the exclusive validity of form-building procedures in poetry (and by extension in other arts as well) based on the principle of teleology: the implication being that reality is so vast that one must do everything possible to prevent (supposedly ingrained) prejudices from curtailing one's imagination through confining it to rational goal-directed thinking. (Beckett has pointed out a related view, held by Proust: 'Voluntary memory is of no value as an instrument of evocation, and provides an image as far removed from the real as the myth of our imagination or the caricature furnished by direct perception' [Beckett 1931: 4]).

It is readily evident that the ideas of these men influenced the emergence of such intuitive compositional approaches as indeterminacy and to an extent also the orientation that regards music as a process.

If it is relatively easy to trace some of the more superficial aspects of Joyce's influence on a number of composers and poet-composers of contemporary music for the voice (Hans Helms is one of them), Kafka's impact is more difficult to identify. It is nevertheless there, for example in the insane asylum of Schafer's *Patria II – Requiems for the Party Girl*, and perhaps even more strongly in his *Patria I – The Characteristics Man*, in which the conflict between an individual and a society is the principal theme. One also senses Kafka's influence in Berio's *Passaggio*.

The visionary conceptions of Artaud, relating to the use of language in the theatre, came to fruition only after the end of the Second World War. In 1930, in *Theatre of Cruelty (First Manifesto)*, he wrote: 'What the theatre can still take over from speech are its possibilities for extension beyond words, for development in space, for dissociative and vibratory action upon the sensibility. This is the hour of intonations, of a word's particular pronunciation' (Artaud 1958: 89–90). He asks for the incorporation of cries and onomatopoeia into the language of the stage and for the inclusion of Oriental expressions that change 'words into incantations' (91). In his expectation, this usage will succeed in breaking away 'from the intellectual subjugation of the language by conveying the sense of a new and deeper intellectuality' (91).

The writers mentioned here, and some others, helped to redraw man's image of himself, of his fellow beings, of society, and of the world they live in. Their instrument – language – underwent a momentous change in the process.

One cannot help but sense also the extent and complexity of nineteenth-century political, social, and cultural history, which forms a vast background to the activities and contributions of these men. The temptation to refer in some detail to the achievements of the period in the physical, biological, and social sciences, in the humanities, including philosophy, must be resisted. (Ellenberger 1970 gives a concise account.[9]) If we recall the contrast between the positivism of Auguste Comte and the pessimism of Schopenhauer, we do it only because a similar dichotomy exists between certain recurring artistic stances represented by compositions in our repertoire.

One is similarly compelled to pass by George Büchner, as significant for twentieth-century opera as for political history, and the great expansion of interest in, and studies of, the great Eastern religions and their literatures. (C.G. Jung's interest in these are echoing in R. Murray Schafer's œuvre, for example.)

The linguistic innovations of the poets just mentioned, and the spirit and ideas these symbolized, have found little echo in the major choral and vocal works of the 1920s and 1930s. The concerns expressed through works such as *Le Roi David* (1921) by Honegger, *Psalmus Hungaricus* (1923) by Kodály, *Oedipus Rex* (1926–7) and *Symphony of Psalms* (1930) by Stravinsky, *Cantata Profana* (1930) by Bartók, *Belshazzar's Feast* (1931) by Walton, and *Mathis der Maler* (1934–5) by Hindemith reside in realms far removed from those of a Rimbaud or a Mallarmé, let alone those of a Ball, a Joyce, or an Artaud (though see p 206). Even the expressionistic melos, and the *Sprechstimme* of Schoenberg, remained closer to the prosody that could be heard in Vienna's *Burgtheater*, than to the more esoteric ones implied by the works of the poets referred to. However, one senses a deep understanding of certain absurdities in the social environment in Berg's two operas, similar to the vision in Kafka's works. For this reason, I would like to suggest that the members of the new generation of composers who came into their own at about mid-century were principally those who first succeeded in absorbing fully into their music the fruits of the thought and aesthetics of Mallarmé, Joyce, Ball, Pound, Breton, and Artaud. If I am correct, then there was a delay of a generation, or a generation and a half, between these writers and the composers who came to address themselves, with comparable intensity and concentration, to similar themes and problems.

While a study of the reasons for this delay is best left for another occasion, it is necessary to mention here briefly those post-war compositional trends that preceded and influenced the rebirth of interest in innovative composition for the voice that began in the late 1940s. It is important to keep in mind that innovative composition for the voice did not develop in a musical vacuum, independently from other compositional endeavours. The same composers who composed innovatively for instruments and in the electronic studio were also often composing for the voice with similar attitudes and objectives in mind.

The first significant change in composition in the early post-war years was an upsurge of interest in twelve-tone music. This paved the way for relatively short-lived attempts at general serialism, involving several, or even all, parameters. The same period witnessed the continuation of the absorption of non-Western musical elements (timbres, structures, and, later, procedures) into Western musical practice, and the beginnings of *musique concrète*, tape-music, and (in the early 1950s) electronic music. In the late 1940s Harry Partch's micro-tonal music, and the instruments he built for its performance, began to attract attention. In the early 1950s Cage introduced chance procedures (later called indeterminate) into musical composition.

It was not accidental that the first work in the 1950s to use the voice in a truly novel way, Stockhausen's *Gesang der Jünglinge* (1955–6) was a hybrid, born in an electronic music studio. It seems that the acquisition of tape-composition techniques, in addition to studies in linguistics, was necessary before Stockhausen could produce that piece. He had to learn to think in terms of different parameters: of acoustical data, instead of notes, and, most importantly, of durations in terms of chronometric units and/or tape-lengths, instead of beats, measures, tempi, and rhythms. The new approach liberated him sufficiently for the effort of composing the work. Working with musical materials in terms of these, and other, new concepts, as well as the changes that resulted from these in the practice of musical notation in general, has had a strong influence on innovative composition by numerous composers.

In the mid-1950s Xenakis introduced into music the idea of statistical organization, which came together with the concept of mass-structure. He, Ligeti, and several of the Polish school of composers (led by Lutosławski) have continued to develop this orientation ever since. Their compositional objectives have included also work with spoken and sung choral mass-structures, which again made use of the concept of time-field, expressible through a given time-span, or in some composite fashion.

In the late 1950s composers began to include spatial distribution among the structural features that had to be determined in the course of composition. The use of percussion instruments came also to be further emphasized. Innovative vocal and choral composition, especially in Germany, was beginning to attract serious attention.

In the early 1960s innovative composition for the voice assumed a dominant place and held this position throughout the decade and beyond. Together with it came the interest in novel ways of playing standard instruments and in high virtuosity in performance. Modular form (called by some moment form) and its corollary, variable macro-structure, were developed in this period, as were some of the early instances of mixed-media performances. The first attempts at various approaches to the use of digital computers for the generation of musical structure and/or musical sound took place at this time.

The idea of inter-musical borrowing was reintroduced during the mid-1960s. Instrumentation in electronic music studios underwent a considerable change, and more and more of its practitioners moved away, either to live-performance electronic music or to the computing facilities of various institutions. Repetitive, minimal music, or static music, made its first appearance.

In the late 1960s process music and environmental music were initiated, and the theatrical aspects of musical performance received additional attention. In the 1970s bio-feedback control of musical signals, concept musics, all kinds of hybrid structures and events involving sound and silence, renewed interest in improvisation, and diverse kinds of intuitive sound-making found practitioners and adherents. Some of these orientations were compatible with certain jazz practices or with interest in the antecedents of jazz (such as ragtime). Inter-musical borrowing during the late 1960s and the 1970s contributed to the emergence of a new romanticism.

All, or almost all, the orientations listed are still being practiced. Some seem to be flourishing, while others are in decline or in the process of disappearing. Composition for the voice seems to command continuing strong interest among composers with a wide variety of aesthetic orientations, and this has resulted in a steady succession of new works.

The years since the end of the Second World War constitute a period of intensive experimentation in music. This spirit has affected composition for the human voice. The result is a repertoire of remarkable, not to say bewildering, diversity. One is spurred on to try to identify the multitude of vocal techniques and devices used and is challenged by the numerous other new structural features found in these works. One asks: Why do composers compose this way? What does this pseudo-language sample mean? Why use such extremities of expression? What is the place of marginal sounds in a musical work? Why did the composer destroy his text? Does the piece mean anything? If yes, what? Is there a message? Where did the idea come from? Are there any precedents for this?

I suggest that we should now study three seminal works in this repertoire: Berio's *Sequenza III*, Ligeti's *Nouvelles Aventures*, and Lutosławski's *Trois Poèmes d'Henri Michaux*. These studies constitute part I of this book, in the course of which I shall ask questions similar to those just listed and seek answers to them and to others as well. From this process we can expect to obtain a considerable amount of information, both technical and ideational, related not only to the works in question, but also to other works, with similar features, in the repertoire.

Following these studies, we shall be ready to undertake, in part II, a search for ideas that might be found to characterize groups of compositions, for large-scale patterns in this body of works, and for indications of how these may relate to wider contexts.

PART ONE

2

Berio's *Sequenza III*:
A portrait

In *Sequenza III* Luciano Berio has created a vocal portrait of a woman,* probably North American, who goes through a series of puzzling and disturbing vocal behaviours, making us wonder why she expresses herself in this manner and what she wants to convey to us. It seems that she is in no mood to address us through a coherent discourse, spoken or sung, and perhaps she is incapable of doing so. She seems, during much of her delivery, to be oblivious to our presence and to her environment. The thought may occur to us that she is acting in a dream. She reveals what might appear to one as a great variety of feelings, highly unstable moods, anxieties, neurosis, and psychosis, and she is quite unconcerned with these and possibly unable to conceal them. In some ways she acts like a young child, or like an adult who has regressed to childhood, and her account gushes forth with great intensity. We sense that she may be a person whose thinking and perceiving are regulated more by irrepressible desires or needs, than by an awareness of any objective reality around her. Her changes of mood occur erratically and, at times, rapidly. We have no clues as to the psychic triggers that set off her vocal actions, and she seems to relate to no outside trigger at all. The impression that she exists in, and speak-sings from, a dream world persists, but on occasion we may discern an inflection of appeal in her voice, as if she is calling out of the dream, addressing people 'on the outside.' These appeals do not last long, though, and she soon relapses into her dreamlike world.

As contrast follows contrast in her delivery we wonder what is taking place in her mind. What are the sources of her anxiety? Whom is she fighting? From whom is she fleeing?

---

* The analysis in this chapter first appeared, in a slightly more extensive version, in *Canada Music Book* autumn–winter 1973.

In *The Language and Thought of the Child* Jean Piaget describes research concerning vocal and verbal behaviour of children of six years of age and above. He reports that children often engage in thinking aloud, without directing the utterance to anyone. He calls such utterances monologues. If the child feels that he is of interest to other persons around him, his speech may change. Piaget calls the resulting soliloquy collective monologue. (Other authors, for example P.J. Moses, use the term appeal for such utterance.) Piaget reports also that senseless repetitions are characteristic of a child's speech. Other studies (for example, Jakobson 1968) investigated the nature of infant babble and its role in the development of child language. Babble is also noted as a form of auto-erotic behaviour.[1]

These ideas are relevant to the understanding of *Sequenza III*. They point, in fact, to the considerable literature on language behaviour, and to research on the relationship between language behaviour and psychopathology, as further sources of help in this respect.

While the researches of F. de Saussure, P.J. Moses, K.L. Pike, G.L. Trager, I. Fónagy, K. Magdics, R.E. Pittenger, C.F. Hockett, J.J. Danehy, and many others, do not explain *Sequenza III*, they do contribute relevant and important information. A further note of caution is necessary. It is widely recognized by linguists and psychiatrists that much basic research remains to be done before it will be possible to relate, with reasonable probability, a certain pattern of prosodic behaviour to a specific psychic state. D. Crystal states the matter with clarity: 'In the field of psycho-therapy, personality adjustment and so on, the importance of non-verbal aspects has been clearly realised, but little has been done' (Crystal 1969: 66). He quotes Dell Hymes: 'At present the focus of this work is chiefly on identifying and describing the relevant features. How these features occur relative to each other, how their distribution of occurrence interrelates with such things as situation, role, personality ... is yet to be determined' (66).

Crystal adds: 'Much of the experimentation took place on the assumption that for given emotional states or personality traits *one* vocal measure could provide sufficient indication. The possibility of a complex of vocal parameters producing a final effect (and modifying each other in the process) is rarely discussed, though we now know, thanks to progress in synthetic speech, that for adequate specification of voice-quality we do need this extra complexity' (68).

Some authors, for example Moses, are less hesitant. In *The Voice of Neurosis* (Moses 1954), he describes what he perceives to be the characteristics of the schizophrenic voice. Other authors have a different approach. Pittenger, Hockett, and Danehy devoted an entire book to a linguistic-psychiatric analysis of the first five minutes of a therapeutic interview (Pittenger, Hockett, and Danehy 1960).

While it helps to read this literature in search of clues to *Sequenza III*, each of us possesses, from experience, a store-house of information about oral behaviour and its relationship to mental states. This knowledge seems to be the most useful for composers and audiences alike. Trust in one's experience seems to me an indispensable attitude in the search for the personality of Berio's protagonist. Reference to the literature on prosody and the psychopathology of the voice will only confirm what common sense suggests. This thought gives me support to present here a hypothesis about the substance and form of this work.

Berio portrays a woman who reveals, it seems, a syndrome of psychic ailments that contains elements of schizophrenia. The seemingly unwarranted series of contrasts in the piece and the fracturing of the words (and when they are uttered intact the syntax is often warped) assume an air of authenticity if we assume we are seeing a complex sample of the turbulent inner life of a person either psychotic or having a severe nightmare. Her behaviour then assumes a very special kind of logic of its own and also reveals the structure of the work itself, in its remarkable combination of simplicity and complexity.

Sequenza III lasts eight minutes and forty seconds (see excerpts in Example 2.1), but seems to last longer, perhaps because of the large variety of expressions, the structure of their succession, and our response to these. G.J. Whitrow notes: 'Our conscious awareness of time depends on the fact that our minds operate *by successive acts of attention*; in particular, it is influenced by the tempo of our attention. This tempo depends both on the subject matter attended to and our own physical and mental condition, including our memory and expectation' (Whitrow 1961: 72).

It is useful to reduce this profusion of affects to more general categories. Five classes of oral expression may be discerned, and each class will be described in terms of the following, wherever applicable, under an umbrella label for the class itself:

1 *subtypes* (often described by the affective labels prescribed by the composer, as aids to the performance)
2 *range, register, directionality*, and their prosodic implications
3 *intensity* (implied in the score by affective labels and not by the customary dynamic marks), and its prosodic role
4 *duration*, and its prosodic role
5 *affective labels*, indicated in the score[2]

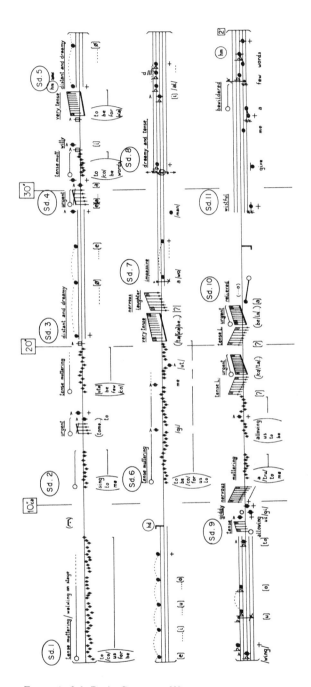

Example 2.1 Berio *Sequenza III*

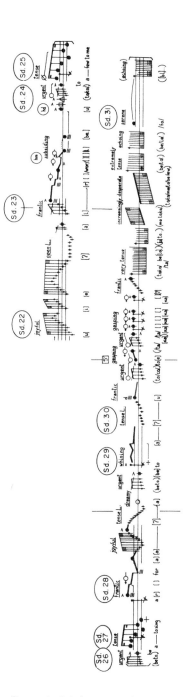

Example 2.1 (continued)

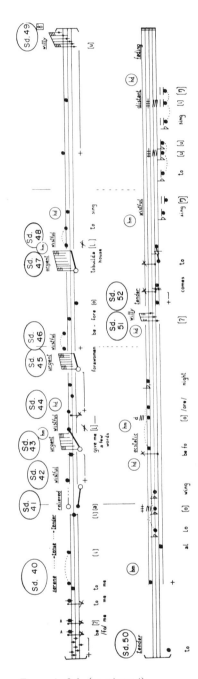

Example 2.1 (continued)

6 *text-use* (rearrangement of the text; the various levels of coherence; the intelligibility achieved)

7 *psycholinguistic connotations* (including terms for denoting psychopathological phenomena in the use of language and in oral behaviour, implied psychopathological conditions, 'normal' psychic phenomena, and paralinguistic phenomena [English and English 1958; Trager 1958; Robbins 1963; and Vetter 1970]).

CLASS ONE: RAPID, WELL-ARTICULATED, PERIODIC UTTERANCES

1 *Subtypes*: Muttering, breathy whispering, whimpering, articulated humming, laughter, articulated rapid singing

2 *Range, register, directionality*: *Range*: narrow, wide, very wide (implying monotony, unpredictable, temporary, abandonments of, and returns to, a dominant range, and other prosodic affects;[3] *register*: low, middle, high, very high, changing; *directionality*: random distribution within a narrow range, rising, descending, rising-descending, descending-rising, more complex designs (A change of direction is often accompanied by a change in the text, or in the paralinguistic affect used.)

3 *Intensity*: From very soft to very loud; stable, changing

4 *Duration*: A variety between about one and ten seconds. (An event may be ended by [a] a shorter, or longer pause for breath, or hesitation, or [b] a change to another type of utterance. The rate of breathing, and the rate of switching from affect to affect, have strong prosodic implications.)

5 *Affective labels*: Tense muttering, urgent, very tense, nervous laughter, tense, nervous, tense laughter, whimpering, witty, joyful, frantic, increasingly desperate, extremely tense, echoing, very excited, etc

6 *Text-use*: Words, morphemes, syllables, vowels, in various combinations. Notable are the frequent consonant-vowel pairs where the consonant is a plosive. Semantic intelligibility is low, syntactic constructs are absent.

7 *Psycholinguistic connotations*: Agitolalia[4] (cluttered and excessively rapid speech with sounds slurred, omitted, or distorted), automatic speaking (speaking without voluntary control), compulsiveness, egocentric speech (speech having no social reference: speech controlled by one's own needs and insensitive to the needs of others), embololalia (the interpolation of superfluous sounds, words, etc), fidget (oral), filled pause, giggling, logorrhoea (excessive and often incoherent talkativeness), obsessive-compulsive reaction, repetition compulsion (an irrational need to repeat some behaviour pattern – here oral – over and over in an effort to allay anxiety), schizophrenic speech[5]

CLASS TWO: PAUSES (Crystal 1969: 166)

1 *Subtypes*: Shorter or longer pauses for breathing (pauses due to biological necessity), hesitation phenomena (unfilled pauses) (Crystal 1969: 168). The context of the pause is important – what precedes, and what follows it. (Is the affect following the pause the same as that which preceded it, or is it different? In the first instance an interruption has taken place. In the second instance the mental activity during the pause may have a causal relationship to the new affect that follows.)

7 *Psycholinguistic connotations*: Aphemia (knowing what one wants to say, but being unable to utter the words), aposiopesis (a breaking of speech suddenly, as if unwilling, or unable, to state what was in one's mind), inhibition, internal speech, speech block (momentary inability to continue speaking, usually accompanied by anxiety and tension), etc

CLASS THREE: VOCAL TICS, AND OTHER INTERJECTIONS
(SINGLE EVENTS, OR A BRIEF SEQUENCE OF THE SAME)

1 *Subtypes*:[6]

TONGUE CLICK (中), BRIEF SUNG OR WHISPERED SOUNDS (♦, ◊),
BRIEF HUMMED NOTE (♦), COUGH (⚠), SIGH (♋), WHINE (?♦)
GASP (◄○), FINGER SNAP (Ш).

2 *Register*: Most often high or low
3 *Intensity*: Unspecified (left for the performer's decision)
4 *Duration*: Most are very short
5 *Affective labels*: Urgent, witty, giddy, relieved, frantic, gasping, etc
6 *Text-use*: Single vowels, consonant-vowel pairs, marginal sounds (such as cough) not indicated in the text
7 *Psycholinguistic connotations*: Apnea (partial privation of breath; breathlessness caused by forced respiration), compulsiveness, embololalia, filled pauses, inhibition, mannerism, obsessive-compulsive reaction, regression, repetition compulsion, spasmodic articulation, vocal tic

CLASS FOUR: SUSTAINED SINGING

1 *Subtypes*: (a) bocca aperta, bocca chiusa, breathy; (b) as to intonation: precisely prescribed intervals, approximately described intervals, and glides; (c) as to intervals: the minor third interval predominates, and the semitone has the next highest frequency.

2 *Range, register, directionality*: *Range*: Very wide over-all range, of about 2½ octaves. The sub-ranges within breath-groups are often narrow. *Register*: A great variety is employed. *Directionality*: From the monotone to the highly inflected (There is a great variety of pitch-changes within breath-groups, ranging from a single pitch to as many as eighteen.)

3 *Intensity*: Very wide range; from almost inaudible to very loud (left to the interpreter's discretion who may take her cues from the affective labels)

4 *Duration*: A variety between about 2 and 35 seconds

5 *Affective labels*: Distant and dreamy, impassive, dreamy and tense, wistful, bewildered, coy, tender, etc

6 *Text-use*: Sentences, fragments of sentences, words, morphemes, syllables, phonemes, in various combinations (The text is used most intelligibly in this class of delivery.)

7 *Psycholinguistic connotations*: Appeal, bradylalia (slowness of speech), drawl, hyperbole, slur, etc

CLASS FIVE: TIMBRE MODIFICATIONS

1 *Subtypes*: Trills, tremolos (lip, tongue, dental, with jaw quivering, with hand or fingers tapping against the mouth, moving hand cupped over mouth as a mute [wa-wa effect])

4 *Duration*: From brief to very brief

5 *Affective labels*: Ecstatic, apprehensive, tender, frantic, etc

6 *Text-use*: Syllables, vowels, semi-vowels

7 *Psycholinguistic connotations*: Babble, dysphonia (impairment of voice quality), etc

NB It is possible to regard these modified sounds as dysphonic variants of class 4 events.

Hereafter, the classes will be referred to as, respectively, C1, C2, C3, C4, and C5.

Before we begin a detailed study of the score, we must analyse the text and the way Berio treated it. We shall also have a closer look at some of the affective fields suggested by Berio's labels, printed in the score as aids to the performer.

The text (a poem by Markus Kutter) is on a page appended to the score:

give me	a few words	for a woman
to sing	a truth	allowing us
to build a house	without worrying	before night comes

How is one to read it? – horizontally, by complete lines, or vertically, according to the line segments and the columns? Perhaps we should read it diagonally, or according to other patterns? All seem possible and Berio uses many readings, some quite intelligible, some not at all so, at least according to normal syntactic and semantic usages of meaning.

The poem is powerful and sophisticated in its theme, in its mood, and in its choice of words and elisions. Most of the words denote basic and symbolically charged concepts, such as house, truth, night, woman, to build, worrying. The text abounds in linguistic universals, of both the sortal variety (those that group individuals into classes) and the characterizing variety (that refer to qualities, states, actions, etc [Lyons 1969: 377–8]). The words add up to a complex semantic field (429–31) of intimacy, of inner life filled with I-you relationships, allusions to sex, desire for expression of self ('to sing,' 'a few words,' 'truth'), and anxiety ('without worrying,' 'before night comes,' 'allowing us'). The brevity of the text (its type/token ratio is 19/23) (Vetter 1970: 7–8), given the work's considerable length, allows us to recognize, and to recall, these words even in their fractured state, after only a few listenings. But we should be careful with such a concern for intelligibility. I believe it is not Berio's intention that we should constantly search for syntactic or semantic meaning. The isolated morphemes, syllables, and phonemes, in the worked text often assume a musical significance that transcends syntactic and semantic meanings. (Berio well knows that information about a speaker's emotional state is carried more by non-verbal features – prosodic and paralinguistic – than by verbal. This recognition is of central importance in understanding this work.)

The following variety of language use (oral behaviour) can be observed in Berio's setting: 1 / two–three–four–five-word continuities taken from a normal reading of the text ('give me a few words,' 'to build a house,' etc); 2 / two (or more) words that establish additional patterns of coherence ('sing to me,' 'to be,' 'allowing us to be,' etc); 3 / breaking up of a word into its phonemic components ([t] [r] /uth/); 4 / construction of words not in the text from phonemes in the text (we, sin); 5 / mixtures of words and non-word syllables:

$$
\left\{ \begin{array}{l} \text{[uta]} \\ \text{be} \\ \text{few} \\ \text{/co/} \end{array} \right\} \quad \left\{ \begin{array}{l} \text{to} \\ \text{/co/} \\ \text{be} \\ \text{words} \end{array} \right\}
$$

(these sounds and words to be repeated quickly in a random and slightly discontinuous way); 6 / combination of syllables without semantic meaning

(/ta/ ka be ...); 7 / vowel modulations (+ ---- [ø] [e] --- [i] - [u] ---- [o] +); 8 / vocalizations on a single vowel; 9 / auto-erotic sounds ([bl]); and 10 / vocal characterizers (laughter, gasping, whimpering, clicks, muttering, etc) – many of these added by Berio. (With respect to the origin of this text I offer here a conjecture: perhaps Markus Kutter received a letter from Berio asking for a few words for a woman to sing and conveying a few other ideas, and in response Berio received the poem that he set to music.)

The affective fields suggested by Berio's labels are best surveyed by arranging them in so-called bi-polar series, which allow for semantic-differential rating (Crystal 1969: 79). The leftmost and rightmost members of a series represent a pair of contrasting terms. Those between represent intermediate degrees. Each series constructed may be regarded as a band in the total affective fabric of the work. Here are three such series:

1

Whining   Whimpering   Sigh   Gasping   Joyful   Laughing   Frantic laughter

2

Very excited and frantic		Very tense	Intense	Apprehensive, anxious, urgent
	Extremely intense	Increasingly desperate		Accusing

2 (cont'd)

Dreamy and tense	Relieved	Tender	
	Subsiding	Noble	Serene	Calm

3

Ecstatic	Joyful	Coy	Giddy	Witty	Wistfully dreamy	Languorous, distant, and dreamy	Impassive

Berio refrains from the use of such extreme affects as that of crying, which could have been a logical leftmost member in the series no. 1. He kept away from this, and from other affects, such as shouting, moaning, groaning, belching, that would have been inconsistent with certain character traits (a fundamental dignity, among others, perhaps) of the person depicted.[7]

The next step is to find criteria for understanding the articulatory process in the piece, showing the boundaries of the formal divisions.

Figure 2.1

Subdivision	Duration (seconds)	Affect classes				
		1	2	3	4	5
1	12	1	1	–	–	–
2	9	3	2	2	–	–
3	9	–	–	–	1	–
4	8	3	1	4	–	–
5	15	–	1	–	1	–
6	12	3	–	3	–	–
7	5	–	–	–	1	–
8	15	–	–	3	2	1
9	16	8	3	4	–	–
10	6	–	1	1	–	–
11	22	–	–	1	2	3
22	7	1	1	–	–	–
23	7	1	–	4	–	3
24	3	1	–	3	–	–
25	3	–	–	–	1	–
26	1	1	–	–	–	–
27	3	–	–	–	1	–
28	9	3	–	2	3	2
29	3	–	–	–	4	–
30	20	5	–	5	–	1

In locating the beginnings and endings of the minor subdivisions, two conditions are indicative: a pause larger than needed for a quick breath, and a change from an event of the type of c_1 and/or c_3 to one of c_4 (or vice-versa). Often both conditions are found.

At the level of the larger divisions (sections) of the piece such changes may, or may not, have articulatory functions. For example I regard the first occurrence, at 0'20'', of singing (c_4) after a series of c_1 and c_3 events as a major articulation point. The brief, and gradually less and less frequent, appearances of c_1 events between subdivision 40 and the end of the piece, however, do not create major breaks.

What is the nature of the individual subdivisions? What superordinate tendencies can be observed from the succession of these?

Figure 2.1 describes two longer successions of subdivisions of the work, in terms of the five oral expression classes, and indicates the respective durations. From a study of the score, and with the use of the figure, a number of generalizations can be made. 1 / Normally, a subdivision has either c_1 events or c_4 events. The two appear very seldom in the same subdivision.

2 / c3 events appear together with c1, and also with c4 events, in one and the same subdivision. 3 / c5 events usually co-exist with c4 events in a subdivision. (In most cases they constitute only dysphonias of c4 sounds.) 4 / c2 events occur during seven of the first twelve subdivisions, but only during four others for the rest of the piece. (Delivery, thus, becomes more continuous, and the breathing more rapid.)

Of these four gross characteristics of relationships between class types, the first, that is the mutual exclusion of c1 and c4, is of great importance. It represents a key not only to the large-scale form of the work, but also to the personality of the singer/speaker.[8] But more of this later on; let us turn to the score and Figure 2.2 for a closer look.

Subdivision 1 is a c1 event followed by a pause. The performer walks onto the stage, oblivious of the audience and muttering incoherently, in a low, soft, and breathy voice. Her oral behaviour may be denoted as a word salad, automatic speaking, logorrhoea, or cluttered and excessively rapid speech with sounds omitted, distorted as in agitolalia. It is an egocentric monologue with monotonous delivery, suddenly inhibited, voluntarily, or involuntarily, indicative, perhaps, of autism. (During the silence, the performer reaches her place on the stage where she will remain until the end of her soliloquy.)

In subdivision 2 she utters three patterns similar to that of the previous subdivision. The second of these is unidirectional, implying some feeling of purpose. These are separated by brief spells of silences (hesitation phenomena) and such spasmodic tics as a single, short, high hummed sound ($\frac{\bullet}{+}$) and a tongue click ($\boxplus$). Both of these will prove to be important mannerisms.

In subdivision 3 she suddenly begins with a hum, which gradually changes into singing on two vowels and then returns to the bocca chiusa; all this is on a high monotone. The $(+)$ ----- $(\emptyset)$ ----- (e) ----- $(+)$ sequence may also be regarded as an instance of the 'MAMA' affect (the imitation of sucking the breast), thus infantile, and regressive behaviour.

Subdivision 4 brings a sudden change again; we are back in the world of c1 and c3 sounds, broken up by a silence (c2) of about two seconds.

Subdivision 5 brings another change. It is a c4 structure, again with the 'MAMA' effect, but longer in duration. It ends with c2 (silence).

Subdivision 6 quite expectedly brings back a series of c1 and c3 events, sustained longer than before.

Subdivision 7 also quite expectedly returns to the expression of the c4 type (coloured by a c5 modifier). This event is also the longest of its kind, so far.

The tendency is becoming clear: this woman oscillates between two psychic states; one is characterized by c1 and c3 events, and the other by c4 events. Whatever the psychic correlates of these affects, the large-scale musical form unfolds through them with predictability. This predictability also includes the tendency of a gradual loss of the initial speech block. This may indicate that an inhibitory tendency has been overcome.

Between subdivisions 11 and 22 the weight gradually shifts from C1 and C3 events to C4 events with a parallel increase in intelligibility during the C4 events.

The passage between subdivisions 22 and 30 comprises the most powerful expression of C1, C3, and C5 types in a profusion of affects and contrasts, the performance of which demands a staggering degree of vocal virtuosity.

In this series the C4 type utterances are inhibited. They come to the surface only in subdivisions 25, 27, 28, and 29, and only for very brief durations. This frantic piling of contrast on contrast, the lack of intelligibility of text in the C1, C3, C5 events, the relative emphasis on a specific C3 type affect – the gasp – the spasmodic delivery of nervous laughter, the sudden breaks, the very rapid breathings, and the lack of pauses all convey the impression of a mind in an extremely agitated oscillation between certain psychic states, of a person searching frantically for something. This passage constitutes one of the most gripping parts of the piece.

Figure 2.2 shows the distribution of the major sections of the work, with durations and commentaries. How to interpret the large-scale structure?

One may say that after an introductory section (I) there comes another (II), in which two mutually incompatible structures (or psychic states to which they give voice) compete for dominance. One of these traits almost succeeds in suppressing the other. It asserts itself with great effort, but nevertheless there are intrusions from the suppressed trait (section III).

Suddenly the suppressed trait surfaces, and almost completely obliterates, at least temporarily, the trait that was dominant in the previous section. (We are now considering the turbulent section IV.) In section V the cantilena type (C4) reasserts itself, suppressing the C1 and C3 traits almost completely, but at the cost of a considerable physical and psychological effort (note the very high register, the loud delivery, and Berio's accompanying labels). It is not possible to sustain this for a very long time. An attack of C1 and C3 traits breaks through again at subdivision 37 and constitutes the next section (VI). The final section (VII) is a gradual subsiding of tension; the finding of some sort of peace of mind is expressed through song, lowering of register, and decreasing intensity. It seems that the few brief, and immediately interrupted, flurries of C1, C3, and C5 behaviours in this section represent a final, or at least temporary, overcoming of certain inner tendencies embodied in these affects. The singing mode becomes victorious. The character portrayed

Figure 2.2

Section and subdivision	Affect classes	Duration (seconds)	Comments on affect classes and text-use	General comments
I				
1	1, 2	12	Entrance ($c1$). Intelligibility of	Entrance
2	1, 2, 3	9	text low	
Total		21		
II				
3	3, 4	9	Two types ($c1$, 2, 3 and $c4$)	Oscillation between
4	1, 2, 3	8	alternate. Both gain in duration.	two moods
5	2, 4	15	Intelligibility of text low	
6	1, 3	12		
7–8	3, 4, 5	20		
9–10	1, 2, 3	22		
Total		86		
III				
11–21	{ 4, 5	141	$c4$, occasionally coloured by $c5$,	Singing, with inter-
	{ 1, 3	13	dominates. $c1$, 3 appear as brief	ruptions caused by a
Total		154	interruptions or even as filled	disturbance factor
			pauses (embolophrasias). Intelli-	
			gibility of text varies	
IV				
22–30	{ 1, 3	47	$c1$, 3 suddenly regain domi-	First attack of
	{ 4, 5	9	nance. $c4$, 5 are relatively fast	anxiety
Total		56	and sometimes gliding. A high	
			plateau of $c1$, 3 layers. Text	
			incoherent	
V				
31	4, 5	12	Rather rapid calming down.	Calming down a bit,
32–6	{ 4	72	Some auto-erotic lip-play. $c4$	followed by an
	{ 1, 2, 3	8	dominates, with smaller and	approach to climax.
Total		92	larger interruptions by $c1$, 2, 3.	Declamation (high
			Intelligibility low at outset, but	plateau of the $c4$, 5
			gradually increases	layers)
VI				
37–9	1, 3	36	A second high plateau of $c1$, 3	Second attack of anxiety
VII				
40–52	{ 4	69	Suddenly again melodic; slowly	A return to a (tem-
	{ 1, 3	8	descending and subsiding occa-	porary, precari-
Total		77	sionally, and less and less fre-	ous?) peace of mind
			quently interrupted by $c1$, 3	

seems to have found a state of precarious inner stability, which she partly expresses through the words: 'be-fore night – comes to sing – to – sing –,' ending with a nasal sound, full of appeal.

How can we understand *Sequenza III* in the framework of our musical culture, and culture in general?

Berio has been quoted (Cadieu 1967) as having said: 'Je tente de délivrer la voix de ce qui la limitait, faire qu'il n'y ait plus de frontières entre le *parlé* et le *chanté*. La composition pour voix devient la structure de "significations articulées."'

Cathy Berberian, the close collaborator (one is tempted to say co-creator[9]) with Berio, said that *Sequenza III* is 'like an X-ray of a woman's inner life.'[10]

The protagonist is truly a child of our time and society (with its strong interest in the workings of the mind and related behaviour), called into being by Berio's insight, intuition, and mastery of portrayal through sound. She is also out-of-time, since what she struggles with is not limited to any one era. She conceals little, and stands, figuratively speaking, naked before us, in this quasi-clinical, albeit abstracted reconstruction. Berio did not create a new *verismo* with this piece. His heroine's utterances differ just as much from reality as *gidayu* declamation differs from normally emotive Japanese prosody. There is hope for Berio's woman, whose experience might have been but a nightmare, a night mirror, perhaps, held in front of our own faces.[11] The final result, then, for both performer and listener is catharsis.[12] Emotional tensions are relieved by having been expressed through an aesthetic experience and sublimated by artistic portrayal, thus by universalization.[13]

3

Ligeti's *Nouvelles Aventures*: A small group as a model for composition

György Ligeti's *Nouvelles Aventures* is a story in music, vocal and instrumental, about three people. The language used is artificial, invented by the composer himself. Far from sounding like gibberish, it appears as a pseudo-language possessing clearly observable properties such as a limited phonemic repertoire, restricted assemblies of phonemic dyads and longer chains providing structure and order, as if it were the language of a newly discovered tribe or perhaps an enactment of the linguistic evolution of such a group. Such a supposition may suggest certain Jungian echoes, resonances from a shared phylogenetic past or from the early history of the species. This strange-sounding language, complemented with facial and other gestures, seems to tell us about certain basic situations in a social setting as old, if not older, than the ochre bulls on the walls of the caves of Lascaux, yet also as fresh and topical as yesterday's contest among rivals for power and as timeless as a courtship ritual or a family scene.

Ligeti seems to have two concerns here. As the piece unfolds we are learning about the personalities of the three protagonists, and about the syntality[1] of the group. Of the three vocalists, two sustain at times what one is led to identify as roles. In the first of the two parts of the work the baritone appears as an initiator of actions that reinforce the cohesive tendencies of the group. The other role-player, the soprano, assumes the character of a person with a disruptive influence (this emerges in the second part of the piece). Apart from these relatively stable character traits, the moods of the three protagonists shift frequently, and often surprisingly. There is no plot. The composer suggests that we observe the unfolding of emotive curves, surges of affects and energies, that engage us in empathy or aversion. As the piece begins, we are trying to guess the nature of the affective states portrayed and their causes, the changes of moods, the patterns of interaction, and the environment. Despite, or perhaps because of, the largely a-semantic pseudo-speech, we find it possible to identify group attitudes, such as agreement, disagreement, dominance, submissiveness, sincerity, lying, persistence, hesitation, fatigue. Certain sustained group attitudes and tendencies can also be sensed. These emerge in the course of the work and indicate the macro-structure of the composition. This structure depends on the energy generated by the group and on the succession of such patterns of energy. These energy packages are divided between those that are aimed at the formation and maintenance of the group itself and those that constitute action directed towards the external world. The various ways of apportioning the available group energy constitute one of the deepest strata of the work. Ultimately the work appears as an enactment of the emergence of a small society, its evolution, and its eventual decay.

This drama has two parts of approximately the same duration. The first part begins with what appears to be a chance encounter of the three individuals and shows the group's evolution from a less to a more complex state. The second part depicts the group as it destroys itself through aggression conveyed through speech acts and kinesics. (It is a progression from a more complex to a less complex state.) Increasingly strong centrifugal tendencies come to dominate and gradually outmatch the dwindling residue of the energy that earlier provided cohesion. Ligeti tells this intricate tale in about twelve and a half minutes, a remarkably short duration, given its content and impact.

Language and speech, together with a kinesic layer, form the major dimensions of the work, and certain ideas in Merleau-Ponty's *Phenomenology of Perception* can help us gain insight into the piece. Merleau-Ponty comments on the relationship between the visible gesture and the invisible, or partly visible, oral gesture (Lewis 1970). He suggests that some facets of this relationship must be approached from an anthropological point of view. 'The meaning of a gesture intermingles with the structure of the world that the gesture outlines' (19). Merleau-Ponty chides 'psychologists and linguists who put aside the problem of language's origin in the name of positive knowledge, [and] contends that it may be profitably reviewed once we recognize that the mental landscape related by verbal gesticulation does not really separate the linguistic gesture from the physical one' (19). Merleau-Ponty carries this idea further by introducing the aesthetic dimension: 'We would then find that words, vowels, and phonemes are all just various ways of singing the world, and that they are destined to represent objects, not as the naive theory of onomatopoeia supposed, by virtue of an objective similarity, but because they extract and, in the literal sense of the word, express its psychical essence' (20).

Where shall one look for better proof of the expressive power residing in the phonetic-phonemic layer of language than in a 'naive theory of onomatopoeia'? Can phonemes, in fact, carry meaning? This is a crucial question since Ligeti invests much of the burden of his work in phonemes either in isolation or in sequences that are words in no known language.

In *Die Metaphern in der Phonetik*[2] (Metaphors in Phonetics) Iván Fónagy presents a wealth of information about the alleged metaphorical power of phonemes and the provenance of these attributes. He demonstrates that various generations of people in a wide range of cultures have believed in the associative and metaphorical powers of phonemes. The reported connections include allusions to darkness and light, to various degrees of sharpness, to femininity and masculinity, to hardness, softness, or strength, to fineness or roughness, to being high or low, clear or opaque, aggressive or reserved, and so on. I shall cite from Fónagy's book a few examples:

'The full sounding English dipthong /ai / is, according to Richard Mulcaster a masculine sound in contrast to its female variant /ei /: "Ai, is the man's dipthong, & soundeth full: ei, the woman's, and soundeth finish in the same both sense, and use, a woman is deintie, and fainteth soon, the man fainteth not bycause he is nothing daintie"'' (18).[3]

'The designations masculine, feminine are more developed in the phonetic literature of the Far East. The concepts of maleness and femaleness, *yang* and *yin* are also applied to speech sounds in China. One considers syllables with a dominant /a/ vowel as being masculine, and those with either /ø/ or /oe/ as feminine' (18).[4]

'In the old-mongolian grammar the velar vowels /a/, /o/, /u/ are regarded as being masculine (ere egesig), and the palatal ones /e/, /oe/, /y/ as being feminine (eme egesig)' (18).

'In the Arab grammar the stops and affricates /ʔ/, /q/, /k/, /ṭ/, /t/, /d/, /ḍ/, /b/, /dʒ/ are regarded as being hard' (26).[5]

'According to Dionysios Halikarnasseus, the /l/ is the softest, sweetest of the semi vowels' (27).[6]

'In the production of the /l/ sound the tongue sweetly touches the palate ('lingua palatoque dulcescit')' (27).

'Of the fricatives /s/ is sharper than /ʃ/. The speech sounds that are considered to be sharp have only one common attribute: they are – in contrast to the soft ones – characterized by higher partial tones. Their dominant partials are, therefore, closer to the threshold of pain (the register where the sounds evoke unpleasant sensations), and are, thereby, perceived as sharp objects that are penetrating the organ of hearing' (51).

'[As in the language of many human groupings] even in the 'speech' of the chimpanzees the bilabial nasal plosive appears in various combinations of sound sequences, or in isolation often in connection with feeding, the mother's breast, and longing' (71). 'It is, therefore, no sheer coincidence that in the Tibetan the suffix -ma serves to denote female occupations and activities, and the prefix m- sound is regarded by grammarians as having a strongly female character' (71).

'It is often emphasized that women prefer the more closed variants (of vowels) ... But why would /ei / be perceived as being more refined than /ai / ... Henri Estienne knows here again for certain. Because the ladies this way can open their mouths to a lesser extent' (75).[7]

'The word *lip* is one of those words that have numerous secondary meanings, and are displaced in many various directions. For example, the vocal chords are also called vocal lips [Stimmlippen in the German] and the word is also used with respect to the female genitals' (76).

'The overly strong closure of the vocal chords which produces a tense vocal delivery, or hinders the voice-production lends to the expression a harsh character. In general the forces that delay and withhold (the air-flow) are the ones that lend to the speech sounds their harshness. The velar plosives /k/, /q/ and the laryngeal plosive /ʔ/ are perceived as especially harsh' (77–8).[8]

Since *Nouvelles Aventures* tells a story about three interacting persons, another key may be looked for in sociological theory. Certain ideas of Leonard Cottrell jr appear to be of particular interest in this regard (Cottrell 1942).

Ligeti's three people interact with each other in a variety of ways and at least two of them assume identifiable roles in certain parts of the work. Cottrell's definitions of what constitutes interaction and role will prove helpful.

When human organisms respond to each other over a period of time, the activity of each becomes the stimulus pattern for a more or less stabilized response pattern in the other(s), assuming that the motivational components remain essentially unchanged.

Definition 1 A series of conditioned acts comprising the reciprocal responses of all members of a social situation is referred to as an interact pattern.

Definition 2 An internally consistent series of conditioned responses by one member of a social situation which represents the stimulus pattern for the similarly internally consistent series of conditioned responses of the other(s) in that situation is called a role. (Cottrell 1942: 374)

In the course of this analysis we shall have occasion to see various 'interact patterns,' and we shall observe numerous 'internally consistent series of conditional responses' expressed in musico-linguistic terms that evoke similar or different series in the other participants.

Cottrell notes that we are committed to respond not only to our interlocutor but also to our inner voice (perhaps even more strongly to the latter than to the former): 'Each member of an interpersonal relationship is not only conditioned to respond to the acts of the other(s) with his own act series but is conditioned to respond to his own response series as a stimulus series with actions he incorporates from the other(s)' (374). The process 'of responding by reproducing the acts of the other(s) has been referred to by various writers as taking the role of the other, identification, introjection, sympathy, empathy, imitation ... This process of double conditioning is referred to as the incorporation or internalization of an interact pattern' (374). Cottrell conceives a social act to be 'a series of reciprocally related acts by units called selves, which series forms a dynamic perceptual unit' (379). He perceives the general form of such acts as consisting of 'a beginning or precipitating condition, the definition of goals or end relations toward which the interacting units conceive themselves to be moving, a series of relevant intermediate activities, and finally, some kind of end-state of relationship of the implicated selves' (379). These insights proved to be helpful to me in my study of *Nouvelles Aventures*.

For purposes of description, I have segmented the work into parts and scenes. All of these will bear a title, some given by the composer, and others made up by me, on the basis of the suggestive qualities of the music. (The composer's titles are used in part I for scenes 4, 7, and 8 and in part II for the hysterical scenes, the chorale, the daemonic clocks, and the coda.) Examples 3.1–3.9 show those parts of the score of part I that will be discussed in detail; Examples 3.10–3.16 do the same for part II.

PART ONE

Scene 1: 'Signalling' (measures 1–14)
Nouvelles Aventures begins with a short but mighty yell emitted by the baritone (see measure 1 in Example 3.1). Its characteristics are as follows: high-pitched, loud, short, emphatic, on the vowel /a/, a typically male open-mouthed sound, according to sources listed by Fónagy (see page 43). This

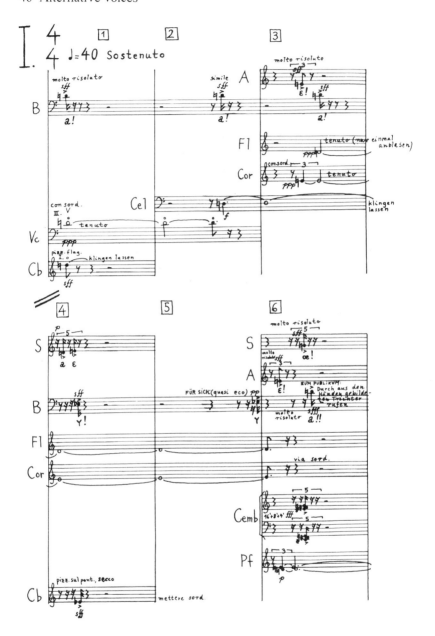

Example 3.1 Ligeti *Nouvelles Aventures*

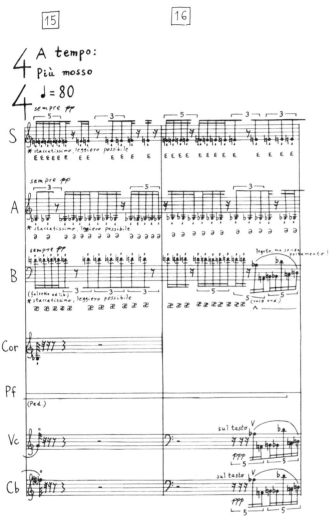

Example 3.2 Ligeti *Nouvelles Aventures*

Example 3.3 Ligeti *Nouvelles Aventures*

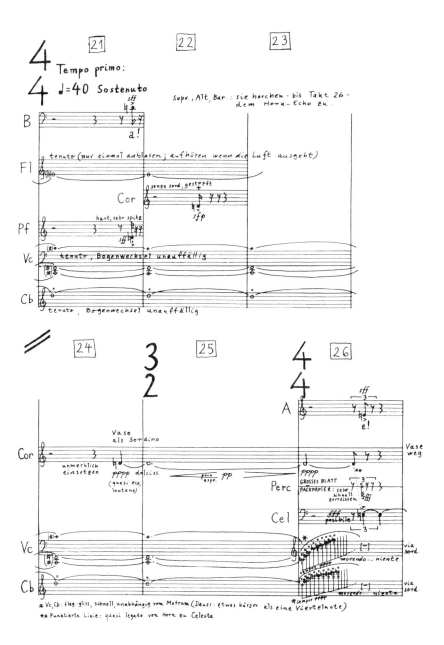

Example 3.4 Ligeti *Nouvelles Aventures*

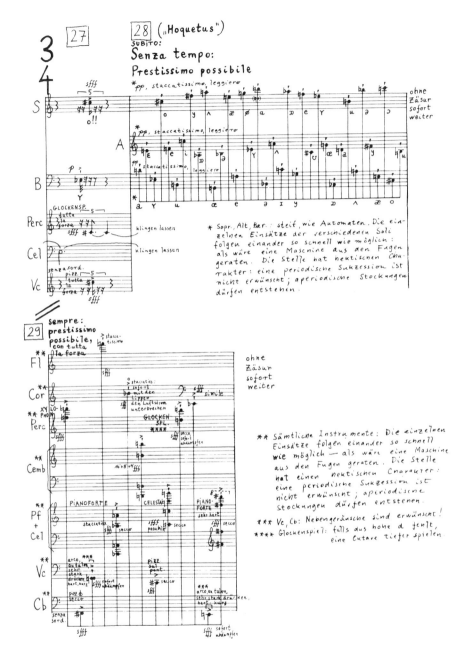

Example 3.5 Ligeti *Nouvelles Aventures*

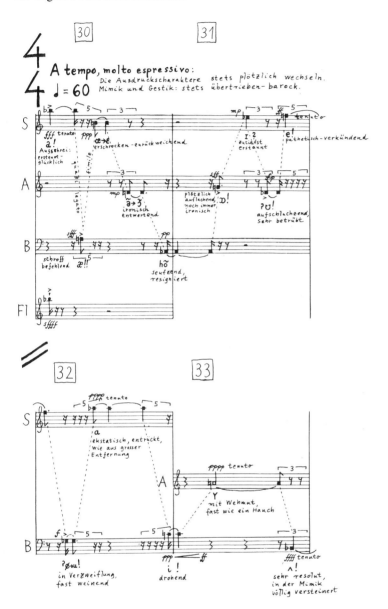

Example 3.6 Ligeti *Nouvelles Aventures*

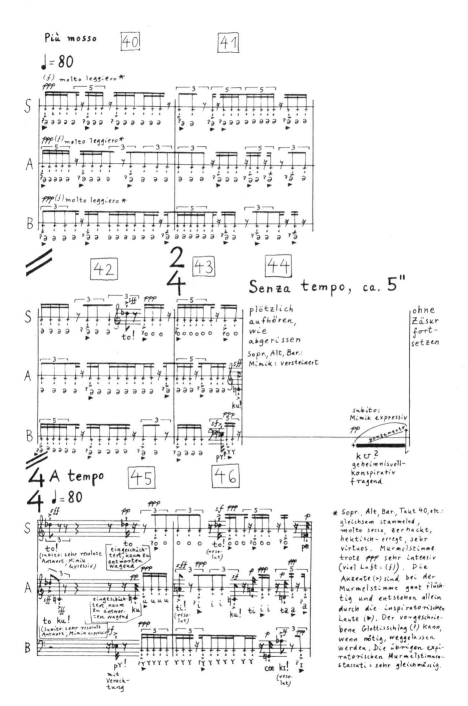

Example 3.7 Ligeti *Nouvelles Aventures*

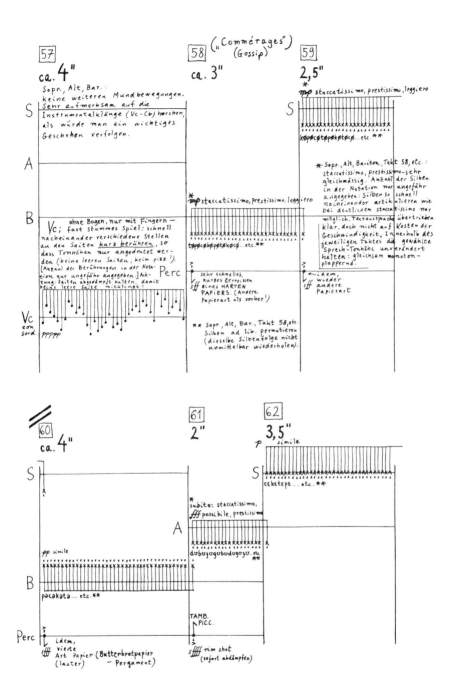

Example 3.8 Ligeti *Nouvelles Aventures*

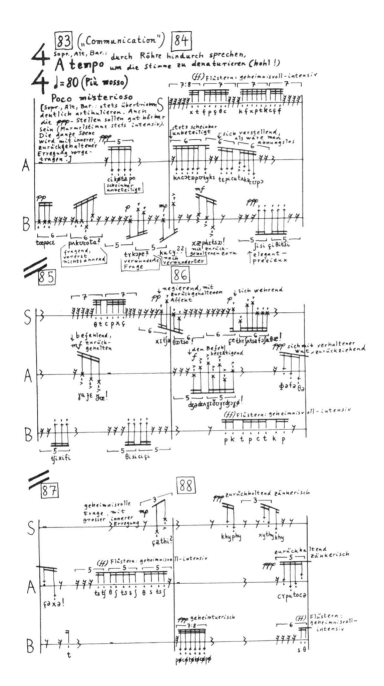

Example 3.9 Ligeti *Nouvelles Aventures*

sound, the result of a brief burst of powerful sound energy, is an optimal signal for relatively long-distance communication. It may be a command message, or an appeal perhaps.[9] The silence of the baritone that follows, lasting about nine seconds, constitutes a period of waiting. It is a pause of expectation, questioning, as if saying (at least here) 'Is anyone else around?' or 'I see you ... who are you?' This signal is stated four more times in this scene and seven more times in the course of part I. (It does not return in part II.) It is the stablest and most redundantly used sound-signal of part I. In its later appearances it may suggest, as we shall see, a different meaning than in the opening scene. Whenever it appears, it is a signal for some action aimed at strengthening the bond among the three participants. It remains invariant throughout part I.

To this pitch-vowel couple the alto responds in measure 3 (after a silence of about three and a half seconds) by another invariant pitch-vowel couple. This signal has the briefness, resoluteness, and loudness of the baritone's signal. It differs in register (middle, instead of high), in pitch, and in the vowel. It is uttered with a medium opening of the mouth, on a vowel that Fónagy's sources label feminine. The identical features indicate a matching of message with the baritone. The differing features in the two signals may indicate provisionally asserted sex roles. We shall observe the persistence, or ephemerality, of these components.

The third entry, that of the soprano, follows in measure 4 with an even shorter delay: about two and a half seconds. This double utterance has the novel feature of repetition of components of two earlier utterances. It indicates a careful attention paid to the two preceding signals and suggests caution (note the dynamics), empathy, introjection, learning, and/or agreement. The soprano begins signalling with pitch-vowel couples initiated by (belonging to or characteristic of) the two other singers. Her utterance may be regarded as a brief summing-up of what has already been stated. While the baritone's signal may precipitate a whole chain of events (the entire work, and what it suggests), the alto's utterance indicates a willingness to respond to an appeal, and the soprano takes stock of the situation as it emerges, perhaps as a result of a pseudo-chance encounter.

The baritone is the next to signal, in measure 4. This is a new pitch-vowel couple, in the middle register. Ten seconds later the baritone repeats it as an echo. The composer prescribes the affect: 'to himself.' This is, thus, the first instance of introspection. It comes after a long silence in the vocal parts and thus suggests a 'thinking silence.'

Within the next three seconds (measure 6) three non-synchronous vocal events occur: the alto restates its pitch-vowel couple; the soprano utters a new signal that shares some obvious characteristics with preceding signals; and the baritone states (for the third time) his opening call. In this group of signals the signalling has become more intense (there is less silence between the succeeding calls); the protagonists have reverted to previously used signals, showing a reliance on memory, a certain limitedness of invention, persistence, and similar manifestations of stability and order (this suggests either a conservative tendency and an avoidance of change or an enlargement of signal repertoire); and the soprano has asserted its personality: it uses a new pitch-vowel couple, feminine in nature, according to Fónagy's sources.

The scene, so far, has an overpowering air of deliberateness, and control. The next two utterances, in measure 7, by the baritone and soprano, contain further restatements of characteristic signals by those singers who uttered them originally. A new element occurs in measure 8. While all the preceding signals were very short, single-pitch calls, the one uttered here by the alto is a slow, ascending glide, of about two seconds' duration. It has the connotation of a hesitant, puzzled question. While all the previous sounds signified assertions, or echoes of assertions, this sound introduces an element of wonderment, perhaps doubt – a pensive affect that indicates that coming events may be less predictable than all the earlier assertive statements might have led one to believe.

After a few more assertions and borrowings (the baritone borrows an utterance from the soprano, falsetto *pp*, and loses, for a moment, its male identity), all three converge on a single pitch-vowel couple (ε) on E in measure 13. This melding strongly suggests a further stage of attention to the 'other selves,' learning, and a strong degree of agreement and indicates that the three protagonists have agreed to merge their identities, at least provisionally. The last utterance by the alto (the originator of this pitch-phoneme couple) is almost jubilant and proudly emphatic: *sff*, 'ancora piu risoluto.'

We have concentrated on the relay of these 'minimal' signals. Reference was made to silences in the vocal parts between the utterances. Further comment is necessary about the relative frequency of the signals, the pitch organization, and the accompaniment of quasi-environmental sounds.

Of the three vocalists, the baritone is the most active here. He not only took the initiative in launching the chain of events, but is also a dominant figure in this scene. His initial call signal could even be perceived as the 'tone-giving' appeal of part I, an appeal to come together, to co-operate. The pitches of the first signals of the baritone, of the alto, and of the soprano constitute a characteristic trichord that appears in many primitive and folk music: D, E, G.

Figure 3.1

Is there an allusion to ancient tone systems in this feature? Ligeti has studied ethnomusicology, and particularly Hungarian music. It seems probable that he had repeated contact with Bence Szabolcsi, the author of *A History of Melody* (Szabolcsi 1950), who for many years was deeply concerned with the pre-history of melos and with the pattern of geographical propagation of various idioms of traditional melody. I believe it is no coincidence that Ligeti began with these three pitches and not with others. His choice reinforces the character of the piece, as described earlier. The pitch succession D, E, E flat (a paradigm of the 0 + 1 + 1 semitone aggregate) is another structural constituent. As a composite melodic succession, in the voice parts (see measure 4 for example), it constitutes the first three notes of a twelve-tone row that will first appear in its basic shape in measure 28. Harmonically, it, and its subsequent derivatives, function as abstractions of 'noise' events.

The instrumental accompaniment is provided by seven instrumentalists playing the flute, horn, percussion, harpsichord, piano, violoncello, and double-bass. The main functions of the accompaniment in this scene is to sustain pseudo-echoes and strengthen the *sff* attacks in the vocal parts. The busy horn solo (measure 14) stands in contrast to what preceded it. It is an extravagant gesture, saturated as to twelve-tone chromatic content and rapid in delivery. It bridges scenes 1 and 2; it appears to be triggered by the agreement reached in measure 13, and, in turn, launches the nervous stammer that signals the beginning of the next scene. The first twelve notes of this hyperbole announce the three unordered tetrachords of 1P of the twelve-tone row that will return on a number of occasions (see Figure 3.1).

Scene 2: 'Stammer Melisma' (measures 15–20)
At the outset all three voices break simultaneously into a rapid and quasi-mechanical stammer. According to the composer's instructions, miming must accompany it, 'as though one wanted by all means to explain something without being able to find the words to do so' (see Example 3.2). We are faced either with speech impediment or, more probably, with the predicament of insufficiently developed speech-capability. The passage also points to the complementarity between the vocal and the kinesic gesture. (See Merleau-Ponty *Phenomenology of Perception*.) The implication is that we are watching people whose spoken language is rudimentary and who complement it forcefully in the kinesic domain. All three stammer rapidly, still only using vowels. Their repertoire is /ɛ/, /ə/, and /ae/, on the pitches G flat, E, F:

(Note that it is the same pitch aggregate – as to intervals – that was used in scene 1.) The phoneme-vowel couple of the soprano is a carry over from the previous scene; the other two singers introduce new couples.

This combination of new features with previously used ones suggests that the individuals in the group are able to draw on past experience; can generate new responses to meet new stimuli, challenges, etc and can incorporate these into their behaviour; and are capable of responding to an outside stimulus as a group (note especially the baritone's effort to blend with the others, through falsetto.) The expression of anxiety through the stammer is probably caused by wanting to convey a sense of frustration due to difficulties in a normal process of learning.

We have heard so far seven phonemes, all vowels. Is Ligeti positing here a hypothesis about the chronology of evolution of natural languages? I shall return to this possibility later.

In the course of measures 16–18, this group stammer gradually changes into a polyphony of melismas, each sung on a single vowel. These are supported in unison or at the interval of one, or two, octave(s), by the instruments. These melodic lines are characterized by a variety of interval sizes, a wide gamut in all the parts, frequent direction changes, pianissimo delivery, and chromatic saturation (Example 3.3). The three-to-four-note, or longer, melodic successions show only a tenuous affinity to the twelve-tone row stated by the horn solo in measure 14. One can observe, however, a pattern of redundancy of certain trichord groups: 011, 022, 013, 031, 046, and 064.[10] There is a buildup of density in the accompaniment paralleling the modulation from the group stammer to the polyphony of melismas.

The pianissimo performance of the melismas is a strain on the singers. Accuracy of intonation is difficult to achieve, and the overall effect is a mix between emotive glides and whimpering. As the passage reaches a state of saturation in the rhythmic, intervalic, and vocal-instrumental domains without producing an increase of loudness, a sudden break occurs, perhaps as a result of the implied tension and fatigue.[11] This scene considerably enlarges the phonemic repertoire of the group: it adds eleven new vowels to the earlier five.

The sudden break after measure 20 could also be interpreted as an instance of group aposiopesis (a sudden break in the flow of speech – a figure in rhetoric), as a moment of inhibition or of suspense, or as a sudden cessation of activity as a result of the recognition that certain goals are not attainable with these means and a modification is necessary.[12]

Scene 3: 'Retrogression' (measures 21–7)
The instrumental residue echo that follows the cut-off of the melismatic passage consists of a small cluster, C sharp, D, E flat:

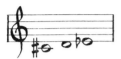

It is comprised of the last three tones sung by the singers before the sudden break and is also a transposition of the pitch-class aggregate of the stuttering that began scene 2. It is one of the numerous pseudo-echoes in the work that make allusion to an environment. This residue, one notes, includes the notes D and E♭ that were sung by the baritone in scene 1. They imply that an earlier state of mind reoccurs in this scene (see measures 21–6 in Example 3.4). The restatement of the opening call by the baritone occurs in measure 21. This is briefly echoed by the muted horn in the following measure, eliciting a pantomime from the three singers who listen to this (and the following, second) echo for about twenty-two seconds (the first echo is delayed about three and a half seconds, and the second, about seventeen and a half, both implying features of an imagined space). Measure 26 brings two important instrumental events: the glissando harmonics in the strings and the sound of paper being torn. These dissolve and tear apart the concentration of the three singers. The result is the quick succession of the three pitches E, E♭, and C♯, which, together with the earlier D, form a 0111 aggregate; this aggregate appeared in measures 1–6 and will begin the next scene.

Scene 4: 'Hoquetus' (measures 28–9)
The title is apposite for this structure: a relay of thirty-six short, single, pitch-vowel couples, performed very softly, lightly, and as fast as possible (Example 3.5). The instructions are intended to produce a totally chromatic machine that wobbles slightly, as perfect periodicity of rhythm is not achievable and not even to be attempted. Conception, structure, and notation co-operate perfectly here to bring about the desired effect. The internal structure of this event displays a sudden leap in syntactical sophistication. The thirty-six notes are evenly distributed among the three parts. Each part contains the

Figure 3.2

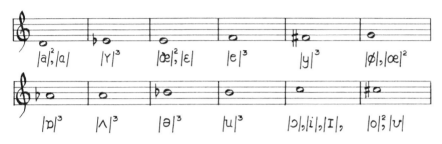

Figure 3.3

total chromatic collection of the twelve pitch-classes (each part is a twelve-tone row). These horizontal rows share certain melodic features but are not derivable from a single row. The first twelve tones of the thirty-six constitute the twelve-tone row from which the initial twelve tones of the horn solo are derived, and to which the opening passage (measures 1–6) has a strong affinity, too (see Figure 3.2). Altogether there are eighteen different phonemes used here, and they are still only vowels. All three voices observe a certain structural principle of invariance: each of these eighteen vowels appears with only one pitch-class. In view of the non-identical numbers of pitch-classes and vowels there cannot be a perfect pitch-phoneme invariance here (see Figure 3.3). (Note the pitch-vowel invariances between this distribution and that in measures 1–6.)

The awkwardness of this passage raises questions about the effectiveness of its construction. The procedure is an instance of structural sophistication, but, at the same time, it violates the principle of least effort in endeavouring to achieve effective co-ordination. As a construct it is too laboured, and this mode of exchange will not be used again in this work.[13]

The repetition of the hocket process by the instruments, in measure 29, may be understood as a quasi-mechanization of a process too difficult to be performed by humans. Its pitch-content consists of the total chromatic plus one additional F♯. The succession shows the typically Bartókian combination of direct and indirect chromatic progression, consisting of a succession of only one or two equitempered semitones.

If the piece is a simulation of phylogenesis, two conclusions may be drawn now. The major goal of the group seems to be to evolve effective linguistic vehicles. These vehicles are being tested, and those features that prove effective are retained and incorporated in subsequent stages, while ineffective features are discarded.

To the first (effective) category belong the enriched pitch and vowel repertoires and the dynamic range. To the second (ineffective) one belong the rapid melismas, covering a wide gamut, and the hocket process.

After this experiment the group is ready to begin its next adventure.

Scene 5: 'Miming-Gestures-Affects' (measures 30–9)
The idea behind this scene is interesting: the singers are to utter highly expressive isolated notes, first one singer at a time, then all together, in a homophonic manner, and later, accompanied by an exaggerated and baroque miming and gesticulation (Example 3.6). The scene displays clearly the difference between speech and song on the one hand and language on the

other. The latter includes forms of communication other than those produced by the vocal tract, and this dimension is probably the central issue here. The singers struggle to develop still another mode of communication, this time markedly two-dimensional, in which the vocal element is matched, if not outweighed, by the visual, kinesic domain. Every note sung-enacted seems to be an affect-packed bundle of concentrated message, and the relay of such events makes us wonder what they are conversing about. The nature of the isolated bundles is such that it is difficult to perceive appeal-response, question-answer, or some other identifiable cause-effect-like relationship between the statements. Are we facing here a series of irrational conjunctions or *non sequiturs*? Is Ligeti positing a series of subtle ellipses the meanings of which have escaped me despite dozens of listenings? My conjecture is that we have here an urge to exercise an exaggerated expressive potential. One may exercise one's muscles because it 'feels good,' and so one may exclaim, make faces, and gesticulate, because one knows how to do so and because doing so relieves tension. One may also wish to engage a neighbour in an exchange, trying to elicit a response. In other words, it may be a heightened form of 'phatic communion.'[14]

Let us look a bit closer at this sequence of thirty-six affect-bundles (Figure 3.4). This list can be read vertically, thus informing us about the changing emotive state of the individuals, and diagonally descending, in the order of the utterances, thus showing affective interchange, action-reaction chains of shorter or more extended length. There are holes in the succeeding interventions. For example, what has happened internally (at the moment of action or, alternatively, in the memory of the participants) that brought forth a response by the baritone, labelled 'gruffly commanding,' right after the soprano's 'astonished, happy outcry' (measure 30)? Why is the alto 'ironically deprecating' right after the soprano sang softly the diphthong /oe→ɛ/ in a 'frightened shrinking back' manner? There may be a host of reasons for such seemingly elliptic responses, which make little sense on first hearing to the outsider-listener as the members of the group communicate through abbreviated chains of expression, perhaps to imply that they know each other intimately.[15] In trying to discern here a quasi-sensible, if not wholly predictable, behaviour, we might find it useful to look at a typological framework consisting of the affects and affect groups used.

The thirty-six affects can be classed in three groups. In group 1 (G1) are affects of dominance, hostility, aggression (to this class also belong outbursts, signals of disapproval, and releases of emotion). The affects in group 2 (G2) are affects of uncertainty, expressions of female sexuality, and com-

Figure 3.4

Event	Soprano	Alto	Baritone
1	Outcry: astonished-happy		
2			Gruffly commanding
3	Frightened – shrinking back		
4		Ironically deprecating	
5		⎰ Suddenly bursting out laughing,	Sighing, resigned
6		⎱ still ironical	
7	Profoundly amazed		
8		Sobbing loudly, very distressed	
9	Pathetic – proclaiming		⎰ In desperation,
10	⎧ Ecstatically, withdrawn		⎱ almost weeping
11	⎨ as though from		
12	⎩ a great distance		Threatening
13		Wistfully, almost like a breath	⎧ Very resolutely,
14			⎨ facial expression
15	Short cry, sensually		⎩ utterly frozen
16		With disgust	
17	Expressionless, puppet-like		
18			Diabolically laughing
19	Grave listening -		
20	Quasi echo, but very distant -		
21			Angrily
22			Pained
23	Coquettish	- -	
24		Deceitfully	- - - - - - - - - - - - - - -
25			Affirmatively
26	Sweeping theatrical gesture -		
27	Innocently		
28		Submissively -	
29	Shamelessly – cheerful -		
30	Sentimentally -		
31	Capricious -		
32	Sensuously -		
33	Quasi echo -		
34	⎰ Enthusiastically radiant		
	⎱ with delight -		
35	Clowning -		
36	As though ill -		

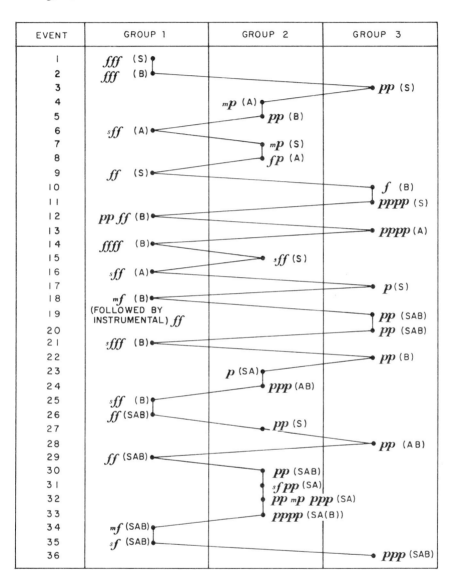

Figure 3.5

pound non-aggressive/non-repressive (or borderline) affects. Group 3 (G3) includes affects of repression, withdrawal, tension, fear, and anxiety.

The succession of the thirty-six utterances shows a pattern of oscillation that appears in Figure 3.5. One can draw the following information from this model:

1 The distribution of the 36 events into three groups favours slightly G1 (14 events) and G2 (12 events) over G3 (10 events). The overall character of the scene is determined by this weighted distribution.

2 The characteristic dynamic ranges are G1: ff and louder; G2: pp to mp, with a few fp and sf events; and G3: pp and softer.

3 Of the 14 G1 events, 6 are male, 4 female, and 4 mixed. Of the 12 G2 events, 8 are female, 1 is male, and 3 are mixed. (If we count the falsetto of the baritone in event 33 as a quasi-female sound the distribution is 9-1-2.) Of the 10 G3 events 4 are female, 2 male, and 4 mixed. This distribution shows a clear, but not overwhelming, propensity for the enactment or habitual manifestation of sexual prototypes.

4 The scene begins with a G1 event and after thirty-five changes of affect, concludes with a G3 one. The moves from group to group show three types: the 'big swing' (from G1 to G3, and its converse); the 'small swing' (from G1 to G2, from G2 to G3, and their converse movements); and 'no swing,' two successive events belonging to any one of the three groups. This constitutes the pattern of possibilities in Figure 3.6.[16] According to this model, there are 12 big swings (in a 7+5 distribution), 12 small swings (9 between G1 and G2, and the remaining 3 between G2 and G3), and 11 no-swing events, of which 6 occur in G2, 3 in G1, and 2 in G3. This almost symmetrical distribution (12-12-11) seems to suggest a lack of predictability. However, the sum of *all* the swings outweighs by a big margin the no-swing moves. Furthermore, one observes certain concentrations such as the group of 7 G3 events between event 10 and event 22 and the 7 G2 events between event 24 and event 33, in contrast to the almost predictable occurrences of G1 events (1 out of 2 or 3) between event 6 and event 21. These add up to a gradual, and subtle, shift from aggressive utterances first, towards non-aggressive types later, and, following this, to a kind characterized by capriciousness, sensuality, and clowning, all leading to a collectively expressed nausea.

5 The first eighteen utterances are by individuals. In contrast, the last nine are group utterances. Thus one is led from highly individualistic, perhaps idiosyncratic, statements to a series of simultaneous expressions of identical affects.

6 Instrumental accompaniment is absent at first, but intervenes in measure 34. There follow fourteen such interventions, of which twelve are

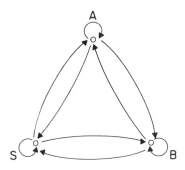

Figure 3.6

independent – they do not coincide with a vocal attack. The vocal and instrumental strata complement each other in measures 34–9. This interplay is underlined by the last affective label in measure 34, 'grave, listening,' which follows the first of the fourteen instrumental interventions and is the work's first SAB event (uttered synchronously) on one and the same vowel.

A less systematic analysis may take a simple descriptive shape. The initial outburst of the soprano may have been elicited by the 'magnificent hocket machine' of measure 29; the baritone reproves this outcry (events 1–2). Understandably, the soprano may get frightened by the baritone's gruff command to 'shut up' (?), and consequently 'shrinks back' to molto pianissimo (events 2–3). The alto, after having observed this exchange, comments with irony; the baritone, realizing how he has hurt the soprano, and hearing the alto's comment, sighs and withdraws with resignation (events 4–5). The alto maintains her previous ironical stance, this time accompanied by laughter, which causes in the soprano profound amazement (events 6–7).

The earlier spasmodic act of laughing by the alto turns into another spasmodic act: sobbing, which elicits from the soprano a loud pathetic statement; thus ends a brief dialogue between the two female vocalists (events 8–9). The baritone, after witnessing this exchange, responds with an expression of desperation, weeping (event 10).

If such an account is reasonable, we have witnessed a series of logical successions of affect, without, however, knowing their cause. Must we find an explanation? I do not think so. These affects in their generality, as universals, stand for any, and all, reasons, that could call them forth. As such, they constitute a true abstractly musical, non-referential symbolic system. (Ligeti later wrote a libretto for the work, which is designed to give visible, quasi-explicit, if at times absurd, causes for this succession of affects. In doing so, he displayed a lack of confidence in the evocative power of his music. Later he stopped insisting on this scenic presentation – rightly so, since such a presentation limits the imagination of the spectator/listener and reduces the power of generality of the work. (See also 92.)

All my comments on this scene are based on a subjective interpretation of Ligeti's thirty-six labels. How relevant may my account be for other listeners? How reliable are Ligeti's labels for obtaining the desired execution of the work? What are the physiological correlates of the labels, and how useful is the labelling process itself?

These labels (constituting what D. Abercrombie calls 'indexical information'[17]) are alluring because they are economical and can be expected to be effective most of the time. Given a sensitive, and culturally competent interpreter, they often work well. The labels will permit the interpreter to produce an affect that a similarly competent hearer may be capable of identifying (with the help of the accompanying gestures) at least approximately. According to Laver, 'We all act, as listeners, as if we were experts in using information in voice quality to reach conclusions about biological, psychological and social characteristics of speakers. Long experience of inferring such characteristics from voice quality presumably often successfully confirmed by information from other levels, inverts our implicit ideas about the correlations between voice quality and indexical information with an imagined infallibility. It is worth questioning the validity of this judgement process. We make judgements, and we act on them, but is the information we infer accurate, or is there a possibility that it is quite false?'[18] Ligeti has taken a considerable risk, which he could not avoid as long as he used this mode of expression, consisting of single tones, each using a single vowel or diphthong, each of which has to carry a considerable affective load, with the help of dynamics, register, and, of course, kinesics.

I was unable to derive all the pitch-succession of measures 30–9 from the row first stated in its entirety in measure 28. However, there are strong connections, easy to identify. For example, the passage beginning on the fourth beat of measure 34 and ending during beat 3 of measure 35 uses the retrograde of 1P (see Figure 3.7). The one following right afterwards (with an elision on the high D in the baritone) restates 1P (Figure 3.8). The last two and a quarter beats of measure 39 are also derived from two reordered five-note segments (the last five and the first five) of 4I.

The phonemic repertoire is still confined to vowels. New features are numerous diphthongs, glottal stops, and frequent nasality.

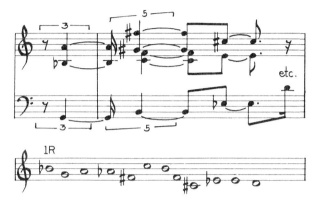

Figure 3.7

Figure 3.8

The pacing of the passage is of importance. The amount of time-lag between the utterances underscores the affects to be conveyed, and so does its absence. This is accomplished in a non-periodic, quasi-rubato manner, more comfortable to perform than the earlier hoquetus.

The total effect of the scene is of increased sophistication of expression. Each vocalist has asserted an individual personality before merging into a group expression again. Each of these changing profiles develops in response to, and unimpeded by, the other two. No one breaks into the utterance of another, but, instead, there is a lucid relay of vocal gestures, in which each protagonist takes her or his turn. Individual tempers, however intense, are under control. This structure shows the group moving towards increasing individuality, which is reconcilable with a similar gain in the cohesive force that holds the group together. The phonemic means (the vowels) so far employed may have been used to their maximum potential as to expressive load; consequently, the group is at the threshold of discovering new phonemic devices for expressing its thoughts at this heightened level of intellectual and social awareness.

Scene 6: 'Retrogression-Articulation' (measures 40–57)
As if exhausted from the great expressive effort of the preceding scene, the group seems to retrench into a collective, rapid, murmured, nervous stutter, punctuated by spasms of vocalized inhalings: perhaps a thought-packed marking of time, molto pianissimo, before the next spurt of sociolinguistic evolution is to take place (Example 3.7). We do not have to wait long for this to occur. It is initiated by the soprano (in measure 42) in a momentous event: the first utterance of a consonant ('t') in the work. The consonant is an unvoiced plosive, as all the other consonants that are to follow in this scene. This new device is immediately taken over by the baritone and the alto, reinforcing the gain. When the three realize what has been discovered, a pause of astonishment follows, interrupted by the baritone's comment in the shape of a secretive-conspiratorial question. Immediately after this, the three resolutely reconfirm the consonant vowel (CV) events of measures 42–3. Measures 45–50 constitute a gradual modulation from a texture still dominated by the stammering, coloured by tic-like gasps, interrupted by the occasional CV utterances, to a texture consisting exclusively of a polyphony of CV successions in all three voices. (This modulation is very gradual and takes about 12¾ seconds to accomplish.) The stammering is all done at the molto pianissimo level. The CV interjections are sung either at the piano or at the sforzato level. There is an invariant, register-specific ordering of the pitch-phoneme CV couples (see Figure 3.9).

Figure 3.9

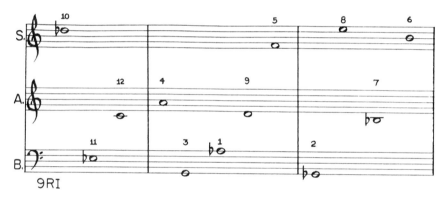

Figure 3.10

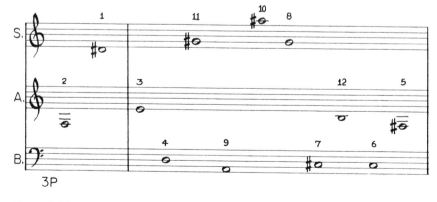

Figure 3.11

Two competing and contrasting states of mind seem to be fighting here for supremacy. One is a quasi-animal-like gasping-panting that culminates in measures 51, 53, and 55. The other is the carefully organized and articulated sequences of CV couples that reach their peak in measures 50, 52, and 54. It is as if articulated speech would emerge gradually in our presence. The strenuous panting-gasping sounds of measures 51, 53, and 55 may be understood also as expressions of excitement, and perhaps a kind of exhaustion, resulting from having accomplished this huge advance in language.

The phonetician reinforces our intuitive understanding of the importance of the introduction of the consonants. 'Ernst Jünger suspects that there exists between the consonants and the will a "mysterious relationship." In contrast to the free, unimpeded flow of vibrating air masses in the formation of vowels, the consonants are produced as a result of either narrowing the air passages or through a complete closure. If we equate the free flow of air with the free, unhindered flow of feeling (of pleasure and repugnance) we could perceive in the conscious restraining and directing of the gushing air masses a model for, and an archetype of, the manifestation of the will.'[19]

The deployment of the series here (Example 3.7) shows a reliance on reordered three-, four-, and five-note fragments (Figure 3.10 shows measures 42–7 and Figure 3.11 shows 47–8). This feature, as well as the retrograding process in measure 52 (restating bars 50, 49, and the end of 48), underline the thoughtful and controlled character of the scene.

The transition to the next scene takes the form of an expression-filled silence: 'a dumb show: as though articulating vowels with the mouth, quickly changing, utterly without sound. Mime: exaggerated, desperately excited, as though wanting to communicate something of great importance but unable to utter a sound.'[20] This temporary aphonia is probably brought about by the excitement resulting from an important discovery. The wish to communicate may be stronger here than the available linguistic competence of the group. Or, conversely, so many words want to spill out at the same time that a temporary bottleneck results. Measure 56 is one instance of Ligeti's eloquent use of what one may call coloured silence, a pause informed by events taking place before and after it. The impulse leading to a release from this occurs through the cello's 'virtually silent rapid' sequence, on the fingerboard only. This serves as a model for the patter-like speech of the next scene.

Scene 7: 'Gossipings' (measures 58–82)
Coincidentally with the violent tearing apart of a sheet of heavy paper, the baritone launches into a low-pitched, rapid, soft, but aggressive chatter, on a

monotone, using a series of CV couples with a single vowel, interrupted by a sequence of unvoiced plosives (Example 3.8). This gives way to other similar sequences by the soprano, the alto, and the baritone, in an uninterrupted relay. The passage may strike one as an exhibition of buccal virtuosity, accompanied by the pleasure derived from exercising such a newly acquired skill. It is difficult to say whether the thought governs the vehicle, or vice-versa; they may mutually influence and reinforce each other. The motion, and the sound, of tearing the paper apart may be understood as symbolizing the ripping apart of a binding, constraining, or inhibiting agent. There is thereby unleashed a not-too-subtle flow of logorrhoea. Apart from the affect of this chatter, there is a restatement in measures 63–4 of sounds from scene 1, unison singing by the soprano and alto on CV couples (as in the preceding scene), and an intricate series of vocal and instrumental echoes, as well as silences. New phonemic materials used here are voiced plosives, affricates (voiced, unvoiced), and unvoiced fricatives.

These materials may also be understood in the framework of Kenneth Burke's five categories of social interplay: the stage, the act, the roles, the ways in which communication occurs, and the kind of social order that is invoked as the purpose of the act (Duncan 1972: 16).

The implied stage, judging from the echoes, seems to be either a very large hall or a vast natural enclosure, bordered by echoing hard surfaces. (From the echo's delay, from measure 80 to measure 81, we may conclude that it must be at least one and a half miles wide.) The social act consists of exercising speech-competency and reacting to each other; we cannot identify the purpose of this activity because we do not understand the language in the semantic dimension. In the prosodic and paralinguistic dimensions, which we do understand, we may perceive such new affects as impatience, anger, bitterness, and a sort of amazement expressed through stone-like immobility. The protagonists are engaged in I-thou, I-me, I-they, we-thou, and we-they types of communication. (In the last two the audience's presence is implied: we are a part of the proceedings.) The roles shift rapidly as to who summons, who is addressed, who is dominating, who retreats, and so on. While we do not know the causes of the actions or the triggers of the affects, we have a clear enough understanding of their character and tendency. The social order is still evolving in an orderly way: the protagonists are willing to listen to each other, they are able to act in concert, they are capable of referring to past actions and thought processes, they can exhibit a common cause towards the 'outside,' they are aware of their physical environment, they agree, they quarrel, they respond to each other's rapidly changing moods, and they are capable of introspection. They are prone to extremes of affective behaviour (fear and anxiety on the one hand and aggression on the other).

No persisting alliances emerge between any two against the third or in all three against the 'outside world.'

The scene, together with our recollection of the previous scenes, gives us the impression that the members of the little group have achieved a great degree of psychic, social, and linguistic sophistication. They seem to be almost on the same level of linguistic competence as we are, and this impression is fully borne out by the next scene.

Scene 8: 'Communication' (measures 83–91)
In this scene the balanced deployment of the group's synergy reaches its highest state. The individual personalities and their collective syntality are in equilibrium. This condition is manifested through a soft, but intense conversation *à trois*, using quasi-ordinary, moderately inflected speech-like utterances, murmuring, and whisper. Their language now includes a wealth of fricatives, such as /θ/, /s/, /ʃ/, which, when performed as loudly as possible, are ideal sounds for the expression of such affects as an intensive, secretive whisper, a 'mysterious question,' 'restrainedly quarrelsome,' 'cryptic,' and the like (Example 3.9).

The distribution of speech (S), murmur (M), and whisper (W) show the following design:[21]

															S	M	W	TOTAL
Soprano	W	W	W		S	S	S		M	M	M	M	W		3	4	4	11
Alto	M	M	M		S	S	M	W	M	S	M	W			3	6	2	11
Baritone	S	S	S	S	S		M	M	M		W	W	M	W M M	5	6	3	14
															11	16	9	36

The tonetic curves show a considerable variety, most of them being in the normal speech register, and a few extending into the emphatic registers (see Figure 3.12).

In understanding the meaning of these tonetic curves, one would be helped by knowing what natural languages and dialects, if any, were consciously, or subconsciously, the composer's models.[22] But even if such information were available, it would be a very great and perhaps impossible task to identify these with precision, since the study of comparative tonetics is relatively underdeveloped.[23]

The tone colour is influenced by the condition that the vocalists speak, and so on, through tubes to make the voices sound unnatural, quasi-subterranean. The basically soft sounds are made to contrast with the effort

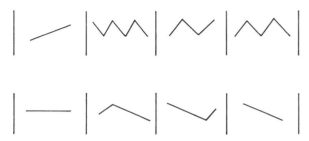

Figure 3.12

required (e.g. the production of a whisper at the fortissimo level), as indicated by Ligeti's instruction: 'The entire scene is played with inner, supressed excitement.'

The temporal correlation among the voices shows a situation often encountered when three persons familiar to each other are engaged in a natural conversation. There are rapid bouncings of the argument from participant to participant, with statements left half completed, overlaps, and the 'tearing the word from each other's mouths.' The conversation is almost totally uninterrupted, the longest interruption lasting about half a second. The passage has no formal 'ending'; the three suddenly break off after having reverted entirely to murmuring and whispering. (Perhaps the effort required from the production of the awkward consonant-chains induces a rest for the tongue.) The interruption is followed by a long pause of about twenty-five seconds, the most telling coloured silence in the work, in fact a musical event of the highest importance. It not only marks the mid-point in the piece, and provides a long pause for reflection by performers and listeners alike, but is also, as we shall see, a turning point.

Kenneth Burke, in *A Grammar of Motives*, refers to A. Korzybski and his 'almost mystical cult of silence.' According to Burke, Korzybski 'would systematically sharpen our awareness of that silent moment from which we may derive a truer knowledge in transcending the level of automatic verbalizations that hide reality behind a film of traditional misnaming. And the moment of delay which he would interpose between the Stimulus and the Response seems to derive its pattern from a sense of that situation wherein, when a person has been thinking hard and long about something in purely internal dialogue, words addressed to him by another seem to happen twice, as though there were a first hearing and a second hearing, the words being heard first by an outer self who heard them as words, and then by an inner self, who heard them as meanings' (Burke 1945: 239).

This pause for thinking enables us to summarize our impressions. While the three individuals were developing their linguistic competence and personality, they were also evolving an effective and cohesive routine for the group itself through a multitude of intricate patterns of interaction. Burke refers (237) to certain ideas of George Herbert Mead:

A social relation is established between the individual and external things or other people, since the individual learns to anticipate their attitudes toward him. He thus, to a degree, becomes aware of *himself* in terms of *them* (or generally, in terms of the 'other'). And *his* attitudes, being shaped by their attitudes as reflected in him, modify his ways of action. Hence, in proportion as he widens his social relations with persons and things outside him, in learning how to anticipate their attitudes, he builds within himself a more complex set of attitudes thoroughly social. This complexity of social attitudes comprises the 'self' (thus complexly erected, atop the purely biological motives, and in particular modified by the formative effects of language, or 'vocal gesture,' which invites the individual to form himself in keeping with its social directives).

This pause seems, then, to be one for taking stock. Alternatively, it could represent, symbolically, thousands of years in the evolution of this group, or other groups. When this silence is broken we shall hear and see new types of events. This 'stony silence,' a frozen posture, reminds one of those haunting moments of tense immobility in Alain Resnais's film *Last Year in Marienbad*. But ominous and frightening events will soon ensue, and we shall wonder, in retrospect, whether the germs of these new events already existed in earlier scenes.

PART TWO

The harsh double attack on the piano and the double-bass that breaks the long silence signals a radically different emotional climate. We instantly sense that we are being plunged into a new situation.

I might as well anticipate what is to come in part II (also see Examples 3.10–3.16). A series of longer and shorter combats among the protagonists, occasionally interrupted by sounds of exhaustion, satirical mockings, silences, the humming sound of a 'daemonic,' mysterious machine, and scratching, scraping, crumbling, and tearing noises (all sounds implying anxiety, damage, destruction) will lead to a situation characterized by dis-

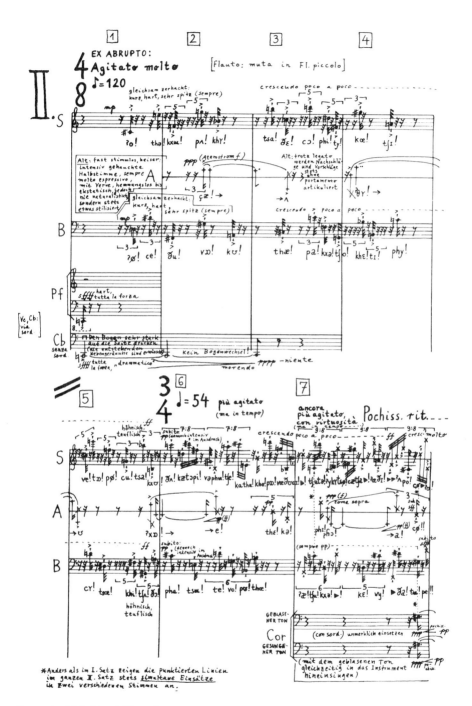

Example 3.10 Ligeti *Nouvelles Aventures*

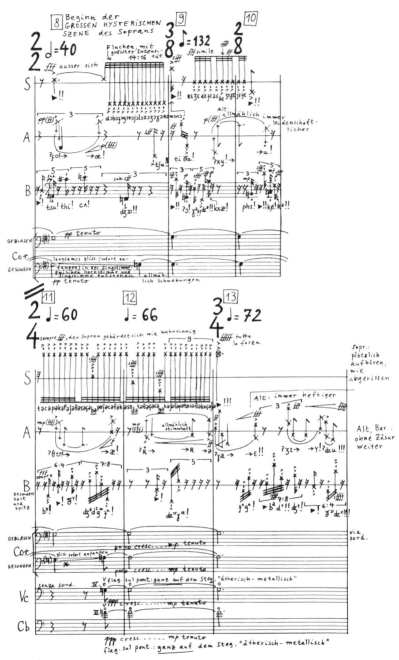

Example 3.11 Ligeti *Nouvelles Aventures*

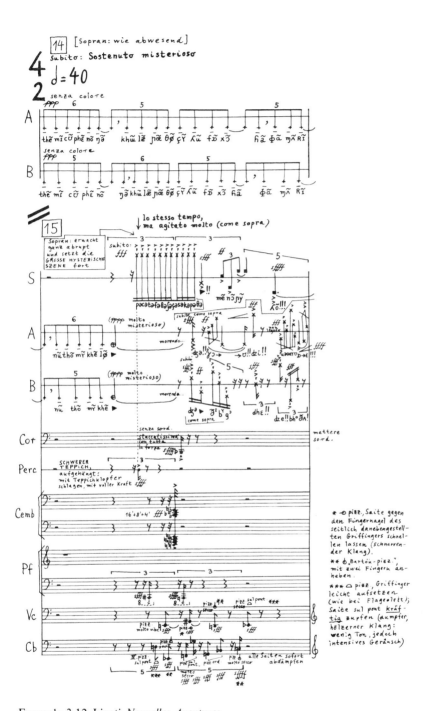

Example 3.12 Ligeti *Nouvelles Aventures*

Example 3.13 Ligeti *Nouvelles Aventures*

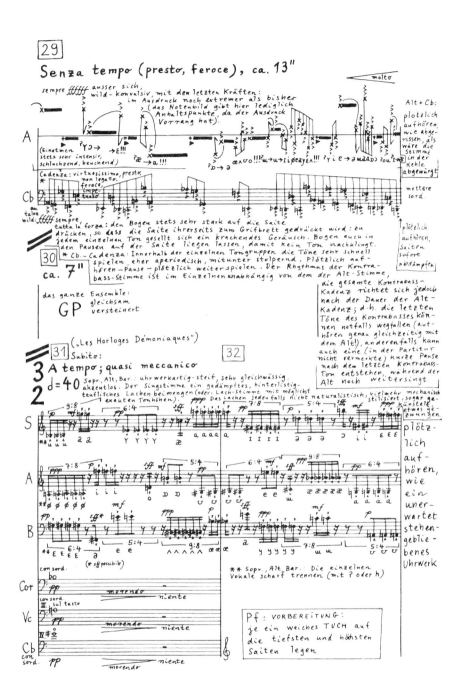

Example 3.14 Ligeti *Nouvelles Aventures*

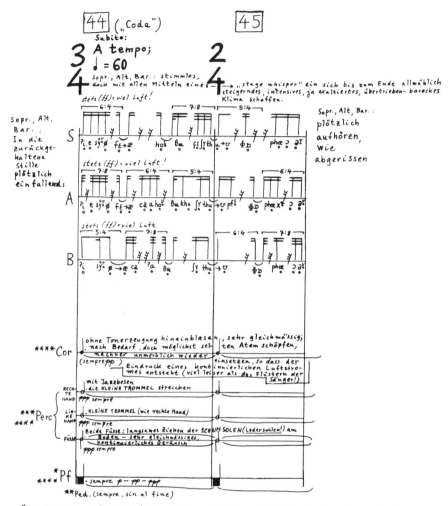

Example 3.15 Ligeti *Nouvelles Aventures*

Example 3.16 Ligeti *Nouvelles Aventures*

organization and fear of catastrophe and perhaps even of death. And at that stage, the piece fades away. Part II may be outlined as follows:

SCENES	MEASURES
1 'First Combat' – 'Beginning of the soprano's grand hysterical scene'	1–13
2 'First Interruption – An exhausted duo'	14–15
3 'Second Combat' – 'The grand hysterical scene continues'	15–17
4 'Second Interruption'	18–21
(a) 'Choking'	
(b) 'Chorale'	
5 'Third Combat' – 'The grand hysterical scene continues'	22–28
6 'Third Interruption'	29–40
(a) 'The hysterical alto'	
(b) 'Stony silence'	
(c) 'The daemonic clocks'	
(d) 'Stony silence'	
(e) 'Fricative sounds of fear'	
(f) 'Stony silence'	
(g) 'The daemonic clocks'	
(h) 'Stony silence'	
7 'Fourth Combat'	41
8 'Fourth Interruption'	42–43
(a) 'Stony silence'	
(b) 'An offhand remark'	
(c) 'Stony silence'	
9 'Coda'	44–57
(a) 'Intensive whisper'	
(b) 'Ambient sounds of fear'	
(c) 'Fifth combat'	
(d) 'Ambient sounds of fear'	
(e) 'Intensive whispering, breathing'	
(f) 'Ambient sounds of fear'	
(g) 'Stony silence'	

This progression from a sudden outburst of oral violence that for a while gains in intensity towards an end of annihilation – linguistic, social, and environmental – could sustain close study. It will receive but a summary comment here.

Scene 1: 'First Combat' – 'Beginning of the soprano's grand hysterical scene' (measures 1–13)

The fight is mainly between the soprano and the baritone, initiated by the former and taken up instantaneously by the latter (Example 3.10). As the baritone was the principal carrier of the tendency for stability in part I, so the soprano seems to be the cause and the dominating agent for dissension in part II. The scene is a contest between the two, who hurl at each other first sung monosyllabic quasi-swear-words (consisting of CV couples, of which the consonants are predominantly plosives and affricates) and later bisyllabic and polysyllabic spoken quasi-words. (There is a gradual changeover from a sung delivery to a shouted one.) In measure 8, the soprano is given an over-low, over-loud, over-fast monotone CV sequence of thirteen couples, of which all the vowels are /ɔ/, followed by a sudden ascending leap. Two similar sequences, one in the middle, and one in the very high register, follow in quick succession, with the performance instruction 'beside herself; cursing with the greatest intensity.' The baritone is angry, but still controlled: he does not indulge in compulsive over-rapid spurts of logorrhoeas but keeps to a 'chopped, short, hard, very pointed' staccato-like delivery, excited, but well articulated through interruptions of differing lengths. The alto, meanwhile, as if being a witness to this heated argument, intervenes with very intense and highly inflected grunts. The situation could be depicted by a net as in Figure 3.13 (Harary et al 1965: 20).

The soprano and the baritone are trying first to out-sing and later to out-shout each other. Gone is the considerate observation of the 'other person,' manifesting itself in patiently waiting until the speaker finished. Instead, there is a wild race of overlaps, making it quite clear that conflicting statements are made and the objective is no longer co-operation but domination of the other. The alto's 'almost voiceless,' 'hoarse,' 'breathy,' and 'impassioned' delivery does nothing to mediate the conflict between the soprano and the baritone. On the contrary, she seems to be inciting them. It appears that the little group suddenly finds itself torn apart by forces that menace it with as yet unknown, but ominous consequences. The hysterical outburst of the soprano is a reckless assertion of the self at the expense of the group. Moreover, we see that neither of the others is capable of assuaging the situation with a sobering or soothing tendency. A closer reading of this scene shows a residue of rationality in the earlier part of the competing duet of the soprano and the baritone (see Figure 3.14). The sung portion of this is based on an ascending row (see the bottom line of Figure 3.14). This derived row is deployed in the vertical arrangement of segments 1–5 and

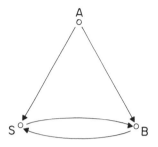

Figure 3.13

Figure 3.14

6–12, respectively, thus producing an ascending chromatic scale, which is ideal for depicting rising, unchecked tension. This indicator of a modicum of sanity soon disappears, though, as the two switch from sung tones to shouts.

Scene 2: 'First Interruption – An exhausted duo' (measures 14–15)
The soprano suddenly interrupts her long scream and there emerges a duo of the alto and baritone characterized by dragged-out, monotonous, low-pitched, pianissimo, CV couples, each with a nasal vowel. This 'colourless' (according to Ligeti's instruction) dialogue is a kind of weary mumble, a case of bradylalia. There is an agreement between the two speakers, but little to rejoice at in the content and expression. No lost social ground is regained and their agreement confirms only a jointly acknowledged fatigue and a fear of things to come (Example 3.12).

Scene 3: 'Second Combat' – 'The grand hysterical scene continues' (measures 15–17)
Without warning the soprano again bursts into her agitolalia, which instantly triggers similarly excited responses in the other two, as the 'self-other' is absorbed (Cottrell 1942). This continues until saturation is reached. By this time, the three voices seem to have lost all control. The soprano performs in a 'hysterical convulsion,' 'utterly beside herself.' The alto also is now 'utterly beside herself with excitement,' and the baritone shouts 'with anger,' 'in a state of great agitation, beside himself with fury.' During the last four and a half seconds of this outburst, the three seem to be determined, with all their force, to over-shout, to cancel out, the other two. The scene ends as if cut by a knife. All that remains is a suppressed over-soft, over-high sustained tone by the soprano, as if she were choking, matched as much as possible by a harmonic on the cello. This sound belongs already to the next scene.

Scene 4: 'Second Interruption' (a) 'Choking,' (b) 'Chorale' (measures 18–21)
What follows suddenly the choking sound constitutes one of the great surprises of *Nouvelles Aventures*. The alto and the baritone begin to sing a few phrases in a pseudo-chorale style (Example 3.13). If our hypothesis about the work's implication of a sociogenesis is to be sustained here, we must account for this chorale either as an anachronism or as poetic licence. It is a deliberate sham of a chorale, full of 'mistakes' (dissonant intervals in cadences, false chromatic relationship, 'poorly' resolved tritonus, 'direct' fifths, etc) and masterful in its satirical clumsiness. It is a rigorous construct, derived from the basic row, using the unordered hexachords of the 2P and

Figure 3.15

the 5I in the two voices (see Figure 3.15). Harmonically the two phrases show identical interval distribution:

NUMBER OF SEMITONES	FREQUENCY OF OCCURRENCE
1, 6, 7, 10	1
5	2

The overall affect is of a liturgical ceremony, all trappings and no substance. It is a rough caricature, abrasive by design. It suggests that a pseudo-harmony and an over-simple mode of synchronization have been substituted for the co-operation that prevailed during part I. The roles of the singers are quite clear: it is again the alto and the baritone who try, as in measure 14, to restore some degree of unanimity, but instead they succeed only in producing mockery and pretense. The soprano, perhaps the chief culprit of the situation, is vocally absent, waiting for an opportunity to disrupt this moment of faked respite. Ligeti suggests the desirability of exchanging the parts of the alto and the baritone; this blurring of sex roles is a long way from the characterization that prevailed at the beginning of the work.

Scene 5: 'Third Combat' – 'The grand hysterical scene continues' (measures 22–8)
The character of this phase of the struggle is similar to the previous phase (measures 15–17), but even more intense. The baritone at one point begins to 'curse wildly' (using the same monotone, over-high, over-loud, over-fast, series of CV couples, each containing the /e/ vowel, and the consonants being the same unvoiced plosives used in the 'Gossipings' scene (from measure 73) of part I. A feature not heard in the earlier duels between the baritone and the soprano is the repetition by the two of the 'word' /Ramaji/,[24] in a quasi-feedback chain, with which they are inciting each other towards an ever greater intensity of verbal brutality. This is underlined by the

thick clusters on the harpsichord and the piano, as well as by other sounds of tearing and breaking. The serial 'rationality' of the piccolo is helpless to offset this torrent of violence.

Scene 6: 'Third Interruption' (measures 29–40)
(a) 'The hysterical alto' (measure 29): From the preceding shouting match emerges the alto, who in bars 23–9 regressed to an exclusive 'vowel-stage.' Here she displays a wild array of register leaps, and diphthongal sneers, complemented by the ferociously performing double-bass, which plays a descending chromatic pitch-class succession, disguised through 'erratic' large leaps, mirroring the alto. The short passage conveys the feeling of vulgarity (Example 3.14).

(b) 'Stony silence' and (c) 'The daemonic clocks' (measures 30–2): This is a further return to a long inhibition of all body movement (including oral sound-making), only to be broken by another surprising construct: a simulation of an oddly ticking clock by the three singers, performed with 'an undertone of insidious diabolical laughter' (Example 3.14).[25] This seems to constitute an abrupt reversal into an orderly state, resembling some of the earlier occurrences in part I, where the soprano, alto, and baritone co-operate in the interest of creating one compound affect. But the mechanical nature of the construct, the laughing effect, its use of only a series of repeated vowels, and its pitch organization (the descending chromatic scale harmonically, and triads melodically) preclude hope that the tendency towards disintegration has been reversed.

(d) 'Stony silence' and (e) 'Fricative sounds of fear' (measures 33–4): This latest silence is exchanged for a doubly mocking echo of the preceding laughter, this time produced through the awkward devices of iterated, velar, uvular, and labio-dental fricatives. Each of these produce but a band of coloured noise. There seems to be a sort of unity in the group, not a unity likely to be conducive to a more complex and orderly state, but rather a huddling together in fear, in the face of an inexorably approaching disaster.

(f) 'Stony silence,' (g) 'The daemonic clocks,' and (h) 'Stony silence' (measures 35–40): After the silence, the instrumental ensemble imitates a smoothly humming machine, in contrast to the disintegrating human group. Its harmonic colour is influenced by the deployment of the initial $0+1+1$ chord throughout as a result of the identical melodic lines in all parts. It is ironical to hear this fragment of virtuoso musical engineering here; it is as if a well-

oiled piece of machinery would keep ticking away while its designers are about to give up the ghost.[26] This sound is suddenly broken off and another, very long silence ensues.

Scene 7: 'Fourth Combat' (measure 41)
Ligeti's performance instructions describe concisely the mental state of the vocal trio in this brief scene: 'profoundly shocked,' 'as if seeing something monstrous,' 'with the greatest horror,' 'with the greatest fear,' 'like a death-rattle,' 'suddenly crying out,' and 'weeping.'[27]

Scene 8: 'Fourth Interruption' (measures 42–3)
(a) 'Stony silence,' (b) 'An offhand remark,' and (c) 'Stony silence' (measures 42–3)
This scene consists of but a long silence, of about twenty seconds, interrupted briefly by a devil-may-care snort of the baritone.

Scene 9: 'Coda' (measures 44–57)
For its seven phases see 84. This scene is characterized by breathy whispering, and by scratching, shuffling, scraping, and other fricative instrumental sounds. The vocal sounds become more and more forced, almost painful to produce, as if the respiratory and vocal organs of the protagonists have deteriorated to the point where phonation itself becomes almost impossible (Example 3.15). The bands of coloured noise produced by the wind and percussion instruments provide an ambient background to the more and more intermittent vocal sounds. There is one more flare-up of collective energy that is translated into a very brief resumption of the last combat (measure 47). This is the last convulsion before the inevitable end, which is another long silence, lasting perhaps into eternity (Example 3.16).

The meaning of the conclusion of *Nouvelles Aventures* is all too clear in its terrifying pessimism. Ligeti, after offering us a compressed model for sociogenesis, ends with a show of social disintegration. Are the causes for the extinction of the group to be looked for outside or inside itself, or both? Is there an inherent conflict between personality and syntality, between personal freedom and group organization? Are there irresistible destructive forces embedded in the human brain, co-existing with the constructive ones? What are our chances of making the constructive forces prevail over the destructive ones?

For about seven years I have been intrigued by this work of Ligeti. Only recently[28] did I learn that Ligeti himself wrote a brief commentary about it

(Ligeti 1966a, 1967).[29] In this he makes observations that shed light on the work and have a bearing also on my analysis, which, in its outline, and in almost all its detail, was completed before I read Ligeti's words. I shall present here a few excerpts:

'All human affects, ritualized through forms of social intercourse, such as agreement and dissension, dominance and submission, sincerity and lie, arrogance, disobedience, the subtlest nuances of irony hidden behind a seeming consent, similarly high esteem that is concealed behind seeming disdain – all these, and still many more, can be exactly expressed through an a-semantic emotive artificial speech.'

'Such a text shouldn't be expected to define precisely any conceptual relationships, but ought to portray directly human emotions and modes of comportement, in a way that despite the conceptual meaninglessness of the text, scenic instances [*Momente*] and actions could be perceived as being meaningful.'

'An imaginary language, which makes human feelings and comportement communicable, must also be suitable for a work for the theatre, presuming that one regards the theatre as a pedestal for individual and social modes of comportement, as an essence [*Konzentrat*] of communication (and also that of isolation).'

'The point of departure for the composition was a conceptualization of relationships between affective modes of comportements, not an abstract structural plan.'

'... These groupings of vocal sounds and their transformations were determined first of all on the basis of their capacity to evoke contents of feelings through a speech-like channel.'

'Through the affective stratum of the text-sound composition [*Lautkomposition*], as well as through the gestures and mime that derive from it, the purely musical layer suggests the direction towards an emotively exactly defined imaginary scenic disposition that is yet undefined as to content. By listening to a performance of the concert version of the piece one experiences a kind of 'opera' with fantastic imaginary adventures [*Peripetien*] of imaginary persons on an imaginary stage. That is, the opposite happens to what we have experienced to date at a performance at the opera: the stage and the protagonists [*Bühnenhelden*] are evoked first of all through the music. One will not play the music for an opera, but the 'opera' comes to life within the music itself.'[30]

'Naturally, one can transfer this 'imaginary opera' onto a real stage as a real opera. There are numerous starting points as to content in the phonetic-kinesic-musical composition itself, which transpose the affective conditions and events that are expressed in the music, through concrete associations, into a real mise-en-scène.'

'One could question whether compositions such as *Aventures*[31] and *Nouvelles Aventures*, which already contain a many-layered scenic event in the music itself, would at all need a specific scenario. In view of the manifold possibilities that are already manifest in the music itself, is not a specific scenic realisation an impoverishment, and a limitation?'

'Certainly one can perform works like *Aventures* and *Nouvelles Aventures* as pure concert pieces complete in themselves without a scenic complement. Yet it seems to me, subjectively speaking, that to transpose precisely these pieces to the stage is not redundant.'[32]

'It seems significant to me that there is no "deeper meaning" hidden beyond the performed events. Despite the seeming absurdity and enigmatic character, the protagonists and the emotional and social situations are directly intelligible, and transparent. We don't find out what the story is about – and, in a deeper sense there is, of course, no story, yet we quite precisely find out how the persons behave and in what relationship towards each other they stand.'[33]

'The alienated presentation of human behaviour does not mean by itself a criticism of society. When aspects of "society" are treated ironically, are caricatured or daemonized, through the process of being recomposed [*Neu-Zusammensetzens*], this takes place without any bias. Precisely, the aversion to "deeper meaning" and to ideology makes for me any form of "committed art" impossible. The behavioural clichés of society are for my compositional work merely material for realistic formation and transformation; to project the work back onto society might take place unintentionally but it was never the object of my artistic reflections.'[34]

Ligeti, according to his own words, is a witness of, and a commentator on, society, and not an ideologue. He is not unlike the 'maker of images, the painter,' who, according to Leroi-Gourhan, 'always constituted, even in the Paleolithic times, a social exception, whose work remained incomplete because it needed the personal interpretation ... by the user of the image' (Leroi-Gourhan 1964). If so, each spectator and listener will probably want to provide that indispensable component: a personal assessment of the work's meaning.[35] One of the strengths of the work is an implicit 'pull' that draws out responses from hearers. It is, indeed, difficult to remain indifferent to *Nouvelles Aventures*.

4

Lutosławski's
Trois Poèmes d'Henri Michaux:
Voices of a multitude

At first impression this work appears as a statement of the collective soul of a community, an utterance pensive, aggressive, and distant in turn, supported by instrumental sounds of considerable complexity and of many hues. Repeated hearings, and a study of the score, bring out numerous details of such ordered intricacy that one's attention slips away from the broad expressive contours of the work, and one becomes occupied with the special nature of the component structures, with the composer's methods of work, and with the fascinating strategy required for the performance. However, as soon as a clear enough understanding of the details is achieved, all the elements come together again, and the original perception reasserts itself with force. All the techniques, materials, and strategies are then understood to be serving a unified affective whole, without losing their identity in the multi-faceted hierarchy of the work. There is a complementary relationship between the sharply etched contour and sculpted surface on the one hand and the richly diverse, and always appropriately crafted, detail on the other. This balance makes the work a statement that sounds right, is to the point, and is credible, articulate, timely, and timeless. It is composed so well that it appears spontaneous, easy, almost an improvisation in places. It is a work of grandeur, of bold strokes and large gestures, and may remind one of the allure of the murals of an Orozco or a Siqueiros, in as much as it exhibits a combination of raw strength and broadness of grasp with a capability for tenderness and subtlety. Lutosławski speaks in terms of sound-masses, and not in terms of individual melodies, polyphonies, or harmonic structures in which individual lines maintain their identity. His vehicles here are, almost exclusively, vibrant, multi-voiced choral and instrumental mass-sounds; thickly edged monorhythmic choral declamations; heterorhythmic structures, using from one to twelve pitch-classes, and their variants; and compound constructs consisting of combinations of these structures in a considerable variety of relationships. Even when the piece speaks in hushed tones, it implies large spaces or the depths of a collective subconscious. The entire work lives in a non-pulsing sound-time, a feature that contributes to its seeming spontaneity and elemental strength. Groups, and their individual constituents (which almost always remain submerged in the whole, except at the work's seams – the beginnings and the endings of certain substructures), have just the right length. How is this flexibility achieved? A glance at the score shows that Lutosławski not only had a clear conception of the total character of the piece, but also engineered an ingenious and economical notational scheme and a matching performance strategy to bring the work to life.

The principal features of the work are easy to relate. It lasts about eighteen minutes and consists of three contrasting movements. It employs a mixed choir in twenty parts, either of as many solo voices, or of forty to sixty singer-speakers, with each part being doubled, or tripled, and an orchestra of ten woodwinds, six brasses, four percussion, two pianos, and one harp, each of the two groups being led by its own conductor. The text consists of three poems by Henri Michaux, and these are set through singing, declaiming, and whispering, respectively. Each movement has a small number of dominant affects: the first, pensiveness, amorphousness, contourlessness, and a tendency for proliferation and dispersion; the second, the expression of raw force, aggression, menace, mob behaviour, which is gradually transformed into a stupefied retreat into fear and immobility; and the third, a kind of emptiness, a suggestion of being drained of emotion, of horror of losing control of one's own destiny, and of a final acceptance of a predicament in which one finds oneself. The movements are characterized by favoured choral and instrumental structures, timbres, and dynamics. In the first movement choral and instrumental mass-polyphonies, busy woodwinds, pianos, a celesta, a vibraphone, and orchestral bells dominate, and the dynamics range from very soft to moderately loud. In the second, spoken and whispered declamation dominates in the choir, and in the orchestra, the brasses and the drums. This is the loudest of the three sections. In the final movement the choir sings again, favouring structures beginning with monorhythmic unisons that open up into a multi-pitched state only to end again in unison, or in a solo. The orchestral stratum here is the thinnest in the entire piece; it is reduced almost exclusively to the use of the two pianos and the harp. It has the softest dynamics of the three movements.

Considering the power of Michaux's poems, Lutosławski's skill in word-painting, and the homage to the poet by the composer through the choice of the title, the listener may be justified in assuming that the work has been engendered by Michaux's poems. However, the information available about the genesis of the work negates this assumption; and this is on the authority of the composer himself. Lutosławski's two published comments on, or related to, this work (Lutosławski 1968; Nordwall 1968) that are known to me make it clear that the initial impetus was not derived from a reading of the poems, but came from a different source. This source is left unidentified by the composer, but seems by implication to be an interest in certain musical constructs, procedures, and performance conditions and an urge to experiment with these. While the poems imprinted their stamp on the work, I can accept the composer's statement that the anatomy of the musical language was determined by him before the choice of the poet or the poems to be used as vehicles. Yet this work has proven to be a fruitful meeting of the mind of a composer looking for a proper framework in which to express certain structural ideas and that of a poet whose poems provide the affective climate and the word-instruments that inform phonetically, semantically, and syntactically the field in which the composer was working. That formal considerations took precedence over the choice of the text indicates how much stress the composer wanted to lay on the structural features of the work. The finished composition is, however, so well integrated, that the primacy of inspiration claimed for either stratum seems to be of limited interest only. In the analysis that is to follow I will explore the morphology of the musical structures and comment on Michaux's three poems, which are now inextricably intertwined with Lutosławski's musical fabric in our mind, in six parts: additional large-scale formal features; the three poems of Henri Michaux; the morphology of the work's structures; a detailed description of a few characteristic middle-level structures; the affective impact of the formal procedures; and the strategy of performance and the notation.

ADDITIONAL LARGE-SCALE FORMAL FEATURES

The two strata of the work, the choral and the orchestral, exist in a half-autonomous, half-complementary relationship to each other. This relationship is suggestive of masses either pitted against each other or supportive of each other, but never totally merging their identities. The domains of the two strata remain under separate control, in a strategy inherent in the basic conception of the work, guaranteed by the notation, and realized through the physical separation of the two performing groups.

ORCHESTRA	CHOIR
○	○
The conductor of	The conductor of
the orchestra	the choir

While the 'formal weights' of the two groups are very well balanced, the choral group asserts a kind of emotive primacy over the orchestra in its first intervention and never loses its grip on our primary attention. The orchestra prepares and connects structural or affective events for the chorus, through modulation or through contrast; complements the chorus, by adding emphasis and colour; and contributes texture.

This triptych consists of two outer panels, the first pensive and the last somewhat subdued, and a central panel that asserts itself as a tense core. As we proceed from movement to movement this form reveals a double contrast, counterbalanced by two types of symmetry. One type is the symmetry inherent in the triptych structure itself and is caused by the affinity between the outer movements. The other symmetry resides in the similar designs of the three movements, even though each is realized at a different level of musical tension and through different devices. This design shows a relatively 'middle,' or 'low,' level of opening, as far as the structural tension of each movement is concerned. This progresses towards a climax at the mid-point, or a little later, in the movement. The design ends with a gradual fade-out in the choir, either unaccompanied or, as in the last movement, with a faint *laissez vibrer* in the pianos.

This simple design is complemented by strongly expressive choral writing and a series of imaginative and characteristic orchestral combinations in the three movements, adding up to a differentiated, yet somewhat redundant, construct.

THE THREE POEMS OF HENRI MICHAUX

The texts of the three poems of Michaux's that Lutosławski uses are brief:

'Pensées'

Penser, vivre, mer peu distincte ;
Moi – ça – tremble,
Infini incessamment qui tressaille.

Ombres de mondes infimes,
ombres d'ombres,
cendres d'ailes.

Pensées à la nage merveilleuse,
qui glissez en nous, entre nous, loin de nous,
loin de nous éclairer, loin de rien pénétrer ;

étrangères en nos maisons,
toujours à colporter,
poussières pour nous distraire et nous éparpiller la vie.

'Le Grand Combat'

Il l'emparouille et l'endosque contre terre ;
Il le rague et le roupète jusqu'à son drâle ;
Il le pratèle et le libucque et lui barufle les ouillais ;
Il le tocarde et le marmine,
Le manage rape à ri et ripe à ra.
Enfin il l'écorcobalisse.
L'autre hésite, s'espudrine, se défaisse, se torse et se ruine.
C'en sera bientôt fini de lui ;
Il se reprise et s'emmargine ... mais en vain
Le cerceau tombe qui a tant roulé.
Abrah ! Abrah ! Abrah !
Le pied a failli !
Le bras a cassé !
Le sang a coulé !
Fouille, fouille, fouille,
Dans la marmite de son ventre est un grand secret
Mégères alentour qui pleurez dans vos mouchoirs ;
On s'étonne, on s'étonne, on s'étonne
Et vous regarde
On cherche aussi, nous autres, le Grand Secret.

'Repos Dans le Malheur'

Le Malheur, mon grand laboureur,
Le Malheur, assois-toi,
Repose-toi,
Reposons-nous un peu, toi et moi,
Repose,
Tu me trouves, tu m'éprouves, tu me le prouves.
Je suis ta ruine.

Mon grand théâtre, mon havre, mon âtre,
Ma cave d'or,
Mon avenir, ma vraie mère, mon horizon,
Dans ta lumière, dans ton ampleur, dans ton horreur,
Je m'abandonne.

('Pensées' from Henri Michaux *Plumes* (©) Editions Gallimard, and 'Le Grand Combat' and 'Repos dans le malheur' from Henri Michaux *L'Espace du dedans* (©) Editions Gallimard; texts reproduced from the score of Lutosławski *Trois Poèmes d'Henri Michaux*)

The composer wrote: 'I chose these three poems, after I had already made a general outline of the entire work. The texts of the chosen poems then influenced the detailed development of the musical form. The verse, its sense and construction, and even particular words had to exert an influence on the music of my composition. This was, moreover, as I had intended. If I had proceeded otherwise, if the words of the text were to be merely one more sound-element of the music, this would be a misuse of the poetry and artistically false, and at any rate it would be a wrong approach.'

'As I have said, I had already made a general outline of my work when I chose the texts. On what did this choice depend and what influenced me in choosing these texts?' (Nordwall 1968: 75). Lutosławski does not answer these questions directly. Instead, he gives a brief account of the poems and an analysis and implies that he found them suitable for the task at hand: 'The first – "Pensées" briefly considers the theme of human thought. It is dominated by a sceptical tone from the first line.' 'The second movement of my work,' he continues, 'is in a sharp contrast to this introductory and reflective part. This part, because of its violent character and fast development leading to a dramatic climax, fulfills a role within the entire composition which is similar to that played by the development of conflict and the catastrophe in classical tragedy. Michaux's grotesque and macabre poem "Le Grand Combat" ... provides the text for this movement. ... [It] conjure[s] up an image of the shouts of an enraged crowd which ruthlessly follows the course of the great fight. The third movement provides a complete relaxation of the tension. Here the text is provided by a poem of resignation and a seeming acceptance of human fate' (Nordwall 1968: 75, 78). From this description it seems that Lutosławski probably had a formal outline in mind and was looking for three poems with certain stylistic characteristics and philosophical orientations that together would constitute a progression in thought and words similar to what he intended to realize through music.

The selection of these poems seems so right, the tone of the poems and their words matching so well the music, that I would surmise a deeper affinity between poet and composer than the brief, and tantalizingly ambiguous, account Lutosławski gives us. The little I know about Michaux indicates a mind and a sensibility close to the tone and structures of Lutosławski's music in *Trois Poèmes*. Michaux, on repeated occasions, has expressed a preoccupation with the perception of experiential rhythm and tempo, as well as a keen and open sensitivity to music. In words that mix the language of an experimental psychologist and that of a poet he has described his experiences with the sensations of time while he was under the influence of mescaline, or other drugs, taken precisely to experiment with the limits of his own perceptual powers. He is, furthermore, deeply interested in 'pure thought,' which occurs in a presumed pre-verbal mental act. This may be one reason why he has developed such a strong attachment to music. He calls this art 'opération du devenir, opération humaine la plus saine'[1] (the act of becoming, the most sane human activity).

One of his most dramatic descriptions of time-sensation under the influence of a drug is in the essay 'Dessiner l'écoulement du temps' (Depicting the Passing of Time), published in 1957:

Instead of a single vision, at the exclusion of the others, I wanted to depict the moments which, from one end to the other, constitute life, to give an insight into the phrase, the wordless phrase, a string that indefinitely unwinds sinuously and, intimately accompanies all that presents itself from the outside as well as from the inside ... I wanted to depict the consciousness of existence and the passing of time ... I, myself, had to learn about the horrible, shuddering experience of changing tempo, of suddenly losing it (in an experience with mescaline and lysergic acid), and of finding another in its place, unfamiliar, terribly fast, about which one doesn't know what to do, causing everything to appear different, unrecognisable, absurd ... an interior vision from which one is unable to detach oneself, luminous as the flash of magnesium, agitated ... as ... the carriage of a machine tool, vibrating trembling and zig-zagging, minute objects, caught in ceaseless Brownian motion ... images ... lines ... which have no upward end but continue rising indefinitely ... broken lines ... curves [that] are follies of loops ... infinitely complex laces ... or parallel lines and parallel objects indefinitely repeated. (Michaux 1950: 197, 203–4)

Some listeners may conclude that this account could also serve as a fitting description of many of Lutosławski's mass-structures in *Trois Poèmes*. Was Lutosławski familiar with this, or similar, statements of Michaux's about his use of hallucinogenic drugs?[2]

Other characteristics in Michaux's œuvre correspond to some of the stylistic features in this score. For example, there is almost no static moment in this music; as soon as an idea is posited, it is already changing. Similarly, Michaux seems to be attracted to the ephemeral, the instantly decaying impression, to the restless and slipping glance along the contours of the visible as well as the psychic horizons. He is a poet of the ambiguity of relationships.[3] He seems to have no interest in inductive or deductive thought processes, or in teleological argument; he observes life and gives account by accumulating data encompassing all that is encountered, right up to 'extreme states of consciousness ... and perceptual disorders' (Bowie 1973: 2).

The quasi-circular structures[4] of Lutosławski find their counterpart in Michaux:

Labyrinthe, la vie, labyrinthe, la mort
Labyrinthe sans fin, dit le maître de Ho.

Tout enfonce, rien ne libère
Le suicidé renaît à une nouvelle souffrance.   (Bowie 1973: 26)

('Labyrinthe ... nouvelle souffrance' from Henri Michaux *Exorcismes* (©) Editions Gallimard)

Michaux's search for the limits of reality led him to automatism in writing. There is something to be valued in the spontaneous invention, even though it might be polished subsequently. Moreover, to fix a thought in word forever is a little bit like betraying this thought. Words should be invented to suit specific occasions. (This indeed has happened in the writing of 'Le Grand Combat.') Bowie says: 'The frequency of Michaux's innovation might lead us to conclude that his ideal language would contain only nonce-words: each word would be so perfectly adapted to the complex and unrepeatable conditions of its first use that it could never be appropriately reapplied in any other conditions' (Bowie 1973: 160). Lutosławski, also, has been reluctant to fix his ideas in an immutable musical shape, led by the desire to liberate the often repressed creative potential of the interpreters – those powers that are needed to bring the special structures of this composition to life.

Michaux once observed how at times 'intonations emerge from words, from only certain ones, from only certain syllables' (Michaux 1957: 25). Isn't this one avenue in the process of language on the way to becoming music, the 'musicalization' of language? (Valery 1958: 159–68; Anhalt 1972). Lutosławski's structures, correspondingly, sometimes feature the colour of isolated syllables or of their phonemic ingredients in patterns of relative order, while at other times they are created to overwhelm us with an approximation of disorder and confusion.

Bowie has also observed: 'Michaux has long been fascinated by magical ritual and incantation' (Bowie 1973: 10).[5] It is not far-fetched to hear in the 'Le Grand Combat' movement a ritual, however gory it may be, concluding with the ever elusive quest for 'le Grand Secret.' 'The diffusiveness of the mental field' in some of Michaux's poems, such as 'Pensées,' and the phenomenon of the emergence 'within that field, [of] a single ordered ... image' (96) suggest a deep affinity between the mental and poetic processes of this author and the statistically conceived structures of Lutosławski with their ad lib beginnings and/or endings and their overall kaleidoscopic character, resulting from repeated use of mobile ostinato. Michaux's propensity for working with the accumulation of 'small structures' suggesting a 'fragmentary self' and a 'chaotic environment' (173) parallels the modular form-building method used in *Trois Poèmes*. But while, according to Bowie, Michaux's 'natural imaginative unit' (173) is the 'self-contained episode,' and while he is criticized for a certain shortness of imaginative impetus (173), Lutosławski's time spans are on a larger scale, and his ability to sustain a mood is considerable.

Michaux has a readily identifiable repertoire of favourite words. In 'Pensées' the key words are sea, infinity, tiny worlds, shadows, swimming, strange, dusts, distract, scatter, and indiscernible. There are no objects here with definite, hard-edged outlines, no abrupt decisive action, with identifiable beginning and ending; everything seems to be fluid, timeless, borderless, continuously gliding, coalescing into a view of an inner space, of a world of intimacy and immensity in which things often appear to float in a haze and weightlessness. The central image of the scene is that of the sea, the primeval symbol, the place where life has originated, and perhaps also the end of all matter and thought. The frame is vast and the medium that fills it presents little resistance to a soaring, perhaps aimless glance that is constantly being distracted by mementoes of past failures, perhaps also by the sediments of the periodically recurring failures of countless generations. It is also 'a flickering vision of the mental field: with shadow and sudden illumination, expansion and contractions, energies which surge and fade' (Bowie 1973: 101).[6]

'Le Grand Combat' tells a nasty story and suggests a bloody ritual, not unlike what may have taken place on the human slaughtering places that were the pyramids of Teotihuacan or Chichen-Itza. To tell about such horrors ordinary language lacks sufficient power. Special words, combining the destructive methodology of two or more types of savaging the human body, might be required. And Michaux has created these. A few examples will suffice:

emparouille
emparer = to catch, to size
ouille = an expletive of pain
rouiller = to rust, to make rusty
andouille = sausage, penis
fouiller = to look into one's guts

endosque
dos = back
que = a phonetic reinforcing expletive
il l'a dans l'os = beaten, with homo-
  sexual allusions
endosser = to flatten someone

rague
draguer = to drag
rager = to rage, to storm
raguer = to chafe, to tear, to shred

roupète
rouspéter = to protest
péter = to burp, to fart

drâle
atteler = to yoke
rateler = to rake
raté = bungled, botched

barufle
battre = to hit
barrer = to hit across
étouffer = to choke

libucque
ad lib = ad lib
bec = snout, beak
embuquer = to blow a horn

Professors P. Gobin and M. Surridge (Department of French, Queen's University) offered the following interpretations of the meaning of this poem: 'It is about combat and death, of which we are but spectators. Someone digs into another's guts looking, in a general confusion, for the secret of human existence' (Gobin). 'It begins in the manner of an epic. It proceeds to murder in order to be able to eat the enemy's guts to gain his power. The secret is in the guts ... This is about man's struggle against death' (Surridge).[7] I see relevance in both interpretations and can add to these that the poem suggests the violent part in the psyche of every one of us, our will to power, perhaps. The carnage is, accordingly, timeless and independent of locus or of ideology. The implication is that it definitely could happen time and again.

The mood of the third poem, 'repos dans le malheur,' is that of fatigue, resignation, and yearning, almost completely devoid of hope. Its 'repose' is a mixture of being vanquished and exhausted. The light that is left illuminates an implied scene of horror, and the commentator has no strength left to rise to make a challenge, not even to articulate a complaint. All that remains is to abandon oneself to the irresistible drift towards an unspeakable end from which, most probably, there is no return.[8]

The following are rough translations of the first and the third of these poems ('Le Grand Combat' is almost untranslatable):

'Thoughts'

To think, to live, an indiscernible sea;
I – the thing – tremble,
The forever throbbing infinity.

Shadows of tiny worlds,
shadows of shadows,
ashes of wings.

Thoughts of marvellous swimming,
which slides in us, between us, far from us,
far from enlightening us, far from penetrating anything;

strangers in our houses,
ceaselessly hawking,
dusts to distract us and to fritter away our lives.

'Rest in the malheur'[9]

Malheur, my great plowman
Malheur, sit down,
Rest,
Let us rest a little, you and I,
Rest,

You find me, you try me, you prove it to me.
I am your ruin.

My great theatre, my harbour, my hearth,
My golden cave,
My future, my real mother, my horizon,
In your light, in your spaciousness, in your horror,
I abandon myself.

THE MORPHOLOGY OF THE WORK'S STRUCTURES

Two form-building principles are dominant in *Trois Poèmes*: a realization of the idea of experientially non-periodic mass-structures,[10] and flexible interplay between two, and at times more than two, such structures. In this interplay the two structures, more often than not, maintain their identity, and at the same time are creating a third *Gestalt*, composed of the constituent sub-*Gestalts*. The elementary units no longer are 'lines' (melodies), or sufficiently steady-state simultaneities (chords), but bodies of homogeneous or heterogeneous, smaller or larger assemblies of lines, of such complexity (density) that the individual line is seldom perceived by itself, and when it is, this occurs only at the 'head,' or at the 'tail,' of an accumulating or disintegrating texture. As exceptions to this condition, the few brief solos that occur in the piece (the vocal ones in the third movement) have a surprising, almost jarring effect, like the unexpected emergence of a human face from behind an oversize mask in a play.

Structures resulting from form-building with distinct, individual melodies and chords require certain kinds of listening. Different listening modes are needed when one encounters dense masses of quasi-steady-state sounds, or when one tries to grasp brief, dense, and complex events (at times labelled gestures). For such structures the best, the most relevant, and often the only feasible, listening mode may be one that focuses on the outline, the density, the colour, and other relatively persisting features, if any, of the overall character of the event.

The problem of perceiving mass-structures is tied to the identity of such constructs. Lutosławski has commented on this problem by offering a hypothesis about the constituent features of such structures that lend these their individuality, making one sound unlike any other. His hypothesis is based on his understanding of what timbre is and on the way the colour of chords containing all the twelve pitch-classes (he calls these twelve-note-chords) is determined, or influenced by the intervalic configurations through which these are realized.[11] He suggests that the acoustic features of an instrument, together with the specific role given to it, creates the effect of timbre. (The same applies of course, to groups of instruments and the roles given them.) There is nothing startling in this understanding, and it rings true to me. However, those of his statements on this subject with which I am familiar do not add up to a hypothesis about a hierarchical model for the type of structures he is using.[12] These seem to have come to life through the good instinct, the inventiveness, and the musicality of a very gifted and experienced composer. An overwhelming majority of Lutosławski's structures work very well indeed – they have a strong identity. A few others are opaque by design.[13]

A glossary attached to this chapter contains a number of pertinent concepts about which Lutosławski has expressed a view. It contains other entries, the definitions of which, due to context, are somewhat unusual. Also included are a number of other terms (for example, coloured silence, interlock, pseudo-loop aggregate, and sweep) that I am suggesting in order to point out recurring formal features in *Trois Poèmes*.

What *type* of structures, and procedures, appear in this glossary? A few refer to processes that can also be found in the compositional styles of other composers and periods: accumulation, complementation, disintegration, convergence, divergence, etc. What makes these processes unique in the context of a work such as this is that they are almost exclusively applied to mass-structures; furthermore, many of these are realized in a partially aleatoric way. In the almost total absence of melodic, motivic, contrapuntal (that of lines) and harmonic (that of quasi-steady state aggregation) types of structures, the construction types mentioned assume, together with other variables, such as density, register-deployment, texture, and dynamic envelopes, a primary role, instead of being only gross features as in tonal and other musics. In Lutosławski's idiom a structure may be fully characterized, for example, by a woodwind timbre, a low-to-medium density, short attacks, rapid accumulation and disintegration, and a quasi-unison beginning that is followed by a modest expansion of range and concluded with a subsequent contraction into a unison, while the structure modulates registrally by the interval of an ascending minor sixth, in the middle of the total range of woodwind instruments.[14]

From the early 1960s the compositional use of chance assumed an important role in Lutosławski's output. This concept emerged in western music in the 1950s, chiefly through the initiative of John Cage. Here is what Lutosławski says: 'The phenomenon about which I am speaking is not simple and not so devoid of ambiguity that it could be either accepted or dismissed completely. It would be possible to define a composer's aesthetic and even, to a certain extent, his philosophic attitude to his task according to the role he designates to chance in his work' (Lutosławski 1968: 47). He adds: 'Those who make chance the actual author of the work ... [are] merely the initiator[s] of a play ... Consequently the sound result can, naturally, be foreseen only to a very limited extent' (47). About this approach, which he later labels 'absolute aleatorism,' he states that it is not 'a usable method in my work as a composer' (48). He holds a similarly negative view with regard to what he calls 'aleatorism of form.'[15]

What Lutosławski does find desirable for his music is an 'aleatorism [that] could be called "limited" or an "aleatorism of texture"' (49). He cites a definition by Mayer-Eppler: 'Aleatorisch nennt man Vorgänge deren Verlauf im Groben festliegt aber im einzelnen vom Zufall abhängt' (One calls aleatoric those events the courses of which are well defined in broad outlines, but whose details depend on chance). And then he says: 'Music defined in this way clearly belongs to the conventions and traditions typical of Europe' (49) (presumably as distinct from the practices of Cage and certain other American composers who employ aleatorism). 'The most typical form of "limited" aleatorism is collective ad libitum playing within an instrumental or vocal ensemble. The most characteristic feature of music performed in this way is the absence of a common division of time to which all performers must comply in the same way' (49). However, 'the dividing lines between the larger particular parts of the form are common for all performers ... Consequently ... the form of the work is fixed completely by the composer' (50).

We know why Lutosławski needed these formal procedures: he could not achieve in any other way the structures he was seeking, at least not with a comparable degree of economy of effort and rehearsal time. How does he control the results of such a 'limited aleatorism'? He devised for each structure what he calls a 'least advantageous version.' This idea reveals the extent of Lutosławski's ingenuity and practicality and his insight into performance practice and into the practical aspects of the phenomenology of perception. How does he devise this 'least advantageous version'? What kind of 'corrections' will be possible? What are the occurrences that are guaranteed to obtain even in this 'poor version'? What desirable features will appear and what undesirable features will be absent? He assures predictable results by designing structures that have a given minimum number of notes (the actual number depending on the effect wanted), with characteristic interval relationships, played by a minimum number of instruments, in a specified pattern of mutual time relationships (determined by the unit sizes and by the phase positions of the shorter or longer ostinato patterns, in the pseudo-loop-aggregates[16]) within a given duration. As far as corrections are concerned, the conductors can, given the flexible notation, easily change during the rehearsals the individual playing speeds, the phase distances, the number of repeats, even the number of performers, should it prove to be desirable to have a smaller, or larger, group to achieve the density sought. The procedures that are here labelled swarm (Example 4.2) or sweep (Example 4.1), or step-ladder (Examples 4.2 and 4.11), or interlock (Example 4.4) have a clear identity, if not always a differentiated colour. These processes, together with the others listed in the glossary (and probably with some additional ones as yet unidentified), constitute the middle level of the work's formal design. An example of a beautifully matched compound structure of well-defined identity and an unmistakable timbre is the passage in the second movement at 33. It is a chromatically saturated, heterogeneously compound bundle, consisting of a choral layer of female voices and an orchestral layer of woodwinds. The sopranos and the altos have a dense mono-textual, mono-intonational heterophony, performed according to the practice of limited aleatorism as a mobile group-ostinato, or, in other words, as a pseudo-loop-aggregate. The colour of this layer is influenced by the descent of each voice from a high, semi-cried/semi-shouted pitch, sampling a large expanse of the individual singers' total range, to a low, undefined pitch. The nature of its beginning – a rapid accumulation (Example 4.7) – and that of its ending – a sharp cut-off – also affect the character of this layer. The orchestral layer (Example 4.15) is a saturated interlock, spanning almost three and a half octaves and characterized by a constant crossing of instrumental timbres and by the use of large, and very large, intervals. (I am not considering the symmetries of this construct, because I am not certain whether they are identifiable by the ear alone.) It begins with a switch-on start and develops into a mobile-group ostinato, just as does the choral layer, and is characterized by widely differing unit lengths in the parts, thus producing complicatedly shifting relationships among the phases. The two component structures end at different times. As a result of both the similarity in register between the two layers and the timbral affinities, this bundle exhibits a very satisfying fusion. The effect is heightened by other elements, such as the attack characteristics of the winds, their rhythm (consisting of an almost even mix of longer and shorter notes), and the consonants used in the choral text.

The densest structures, and the least easy to resolve aurally, are the compound structures between 52 and 55 in the second movement (Examples 4.8 and 4.16). At 52 we have in the chorus a noise-like mass-structure in the

I. Pensées

Example 4.1 Lutosławski *Trois Poèmes d'Henri Michaux*

Example 4.1 (continued)

*) Kropki oznaczają możliwie najkrótsze nuty (staccatissimo). Przywiązanie kilku nut do tej samej kreski poziomej — legato. Każdy wykonawca powtarza swą frazę aż do następnego znaku dyrygenta. Linia falista oznacza, że zakończenie sekcji (lub przejście do następnej sekcji, jak np. w basach w nr 32) przypada nie na znak dyrygenta, ale po nim, gdy każdy z poszczególnych wykonawców dośpiewa do najbliższej cezury. Wynika z tego, że zakończenie sekcji (lub przejście do następnej) nie następuje u wszystkich wykonawców równocześnie. Długości sekcji podane są w sekundach, co należy rozumieć w przybliżeniu.

Notes without tails indicate the shortest sounds possible. The binding of several notes on one horizontal line denotes legato. Each of the singers repeats his phrase till the conductor's next signal. The wavy line means that the end of one section (or the transition to the next, as for instance in the basses at No. 32) falls not at the conductor's signal, but after it, when each of the performers has reached the next caesura. From this it follows that the end of one section (or the transition to the next) does not occur in all the parts at the same time. The durations of the sections are given in seconds and are to be taken as approximate.

Les notes sans queues indiquent des sons aussi brefs que possible. Les notes reliées par un trait horizontal s'exécutent legato. Chaque exécutant répète sa phrase jusqu'au prochain signe du chef de chœur. La ligne ondulée indique que la fin de la section (ou le passage à la section suivante, comme p. ex. dans les basses au N° 32) ne se fait pas au signe du chef, mais seulement lorsque chaque chanteur a atteint la césure la plus proche. Il en résulte que la fin de la section (ou le passage à la section suivante) n'a pas lieu simultanément chez tous les exécutants. Les durées approximatives des sections sont indiquées en secondes.

Noten ohne Hälse bezeichnen möglichst kurze Töne. Die Bindung mehrerer Noten an einen horizontalen Balken bedeutet legato. Jeder Sänger wiederholt seine Phrase bis zum nächsten Zeichen des Dirigenten. Die Wellenlinie bedeutet, daß der Schluß des Abschnittes (oder der Übergang zum nächsten Abschnitt, wie z. B. in den Bässen in Nr. 32) nicht mit dem Zeichen des Dirigenten zusammenfällt, sondern danach eintritt, dann nämlich, wenn jeder einzelne Sänger bis zur nächsten Zäsur gesungen hat. Daraus ergibt sich weiter, daß der Schluß des Abschnittes (oder der Übergang zu dem nächsten) nicht bei allen Sängern gleichzeitig ist. Die Längen der Abschnitte sind in Sekunden annäherungsweise angegeben.

Example 4.2 Lutosławski *Trois Poèmes d'Henri Michaux*

Example 4.2 (continued)

Example 4.3 Lutosławski *Trois Poèmes d'Henri Michaux*

Example 4.4 Lutosławski *Trois Poèmes d'Henri Michaux*

Example 4.5 Lutosławski *Trois Poèmes d'Henri Michaux*

II. Le grand combat

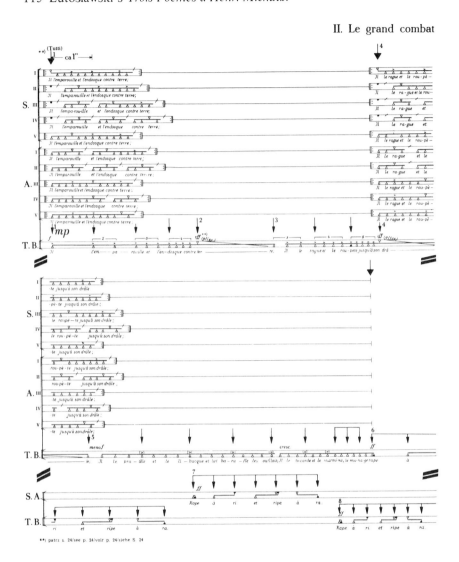

Example 4.6 Lutosławski *Trois Poèmes d'Henri Michaux*

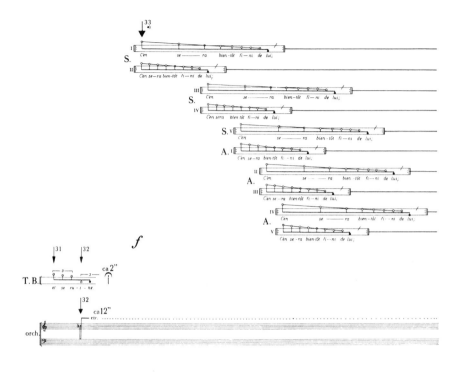

*) Krzyk wysoki opadający w 8-sylabowym *glissando*. Soprany III, IV, i V oraz alty I—V wchodzą kolejno według wpisanych do głosów „małych nut".

A high shout descending in an eight-syllable *glissando*. Sopranos III, IV and V and Contraltos I—V enter in succession as indicated by the cues in the parts.

Cri aigu descendant *glissando* sur 8 syllabes. Les entrées successives des Soprani III, IV et V et celles des Contraltos I—V sont signalées dans les parties par des «petites notes».

Hoch ansetzender, im 8-silbigen Glissando herabfallender Schrei. Sopran III, IV und V sowie Alt I—V setzen nacheinander mit den in den Stimmen angegebenen „kleinen Noten" ein.

Example 4.7 Lutosławski *Trois Poèmes d'Henri Michaux*

Example 4.8 Lutosławski *Trois Poèmes d'Henri Michaux*

III. Repos dans le Malheur

*) patrz s. 43/see p. 43/voir p. 43/siehe S. 43

Example 4.9 Lutosławski *Trois Poèmes d'Henri Michaux*

Example 4.10 Lutosławski *Trois Poèmes d'Henri Michaux*

Example 4.11 Lutosławski *Trois Poèmes d'Henri Michaux*

121 Lutosławski's *Trois Poèmes d'Henri Michaux*

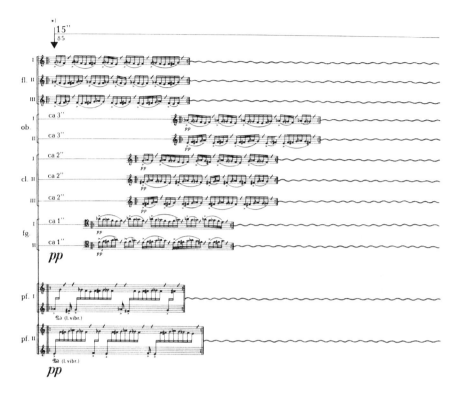

Example 4.12 Lutosławski *Trois Poèmes d'Henri Michaux*

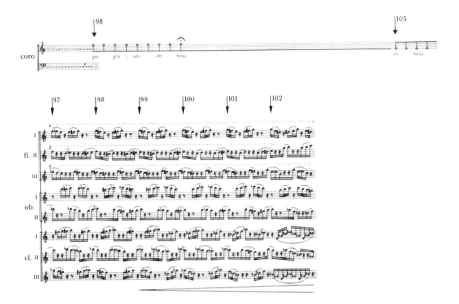

Example 4.13 Lutosławski *Trois Poèmes d'Henri Michaux*

Example 4.14 Lutosławski *Trois Poèmes d'Henri Michaux*

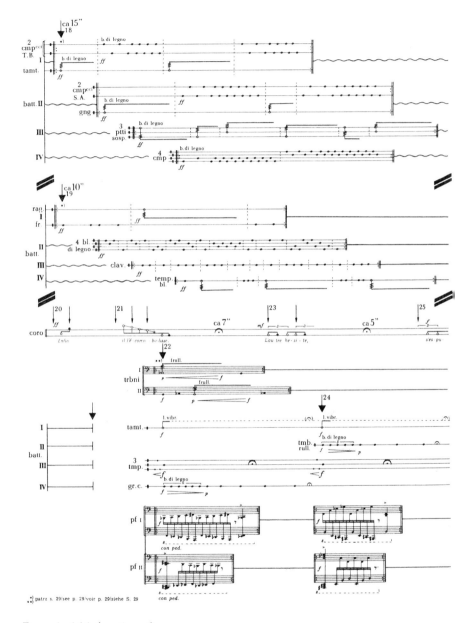

Example 4.14 (continued)

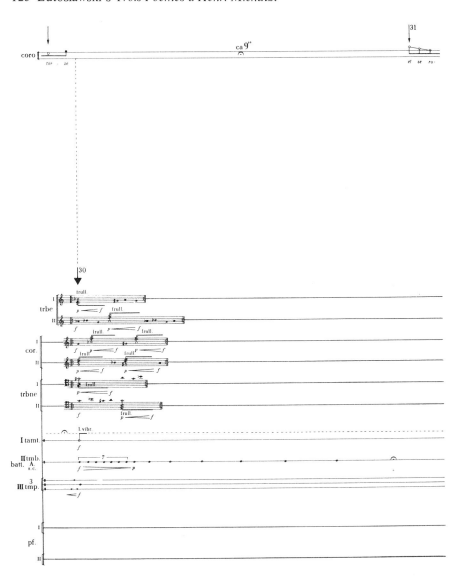

Example 4.15 Lutosławski *Trois Poèmes d'Henri Michaux*

126 Alternative voices

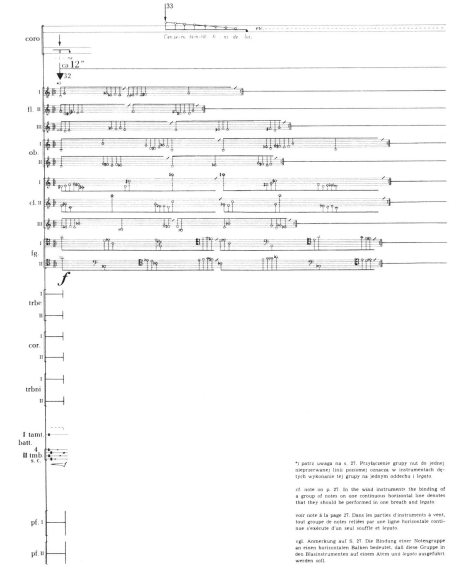

*) patrz uwaga na s. 27. Przyłączenie grupy nut do jednej nieprzerwanej linii poziomej oznacza w instrumentach dętych wykonanie tej grupy na jednym oddechu i *legato*.

cf. note on p. 27. In the wind instruments the binding of a group of notes on one continuous horizontal line denotes that they should be performed in one breath and *legato*.

voir note á la page 27. Dans les parties d'instruments á vent, tout groupe de notes reliées par une ligne horizontale continue s'exécute d'un seul souffle et *legato*.

vgl. Anmerkung auf S. 27. Die Bindung einer Notengruppe an einen horizontalen Balken bedeutet, daß diese Gruppe in den Blasinstrumenten auf einem Atem und *legato* ausgeführt werden soll.

Example 4.15 (continued)

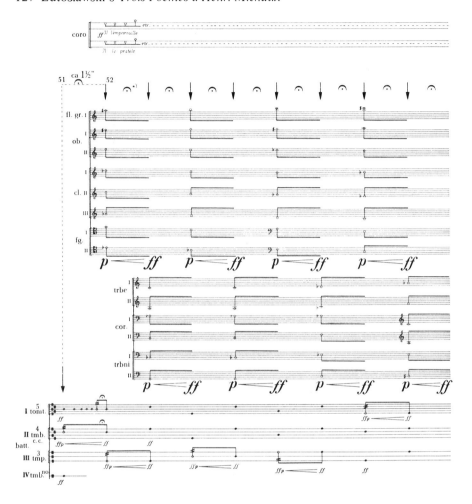

*) Fermaty winny być różnej długości, od 1 do 3 sekund.

The duration of the pauses should vary from 1 to 3 seconds.

Les points d'orgue doivent avoir chacun une durée diffé-
rente, variant d'une à trois secondes.

Die Fermaten sollen unterschiedliche Zeitwerte von 1 bis 3
Sekunden haben.

**) Sekcję tę (53—56) wykonywa się bez dyrygowania (wyjąwszy znaki na początek
i koniec, tj. 53 i 56). Bateria IV może otrzymać „potwierdzające' 4 znaki na początek każdej z interwencji. Pożądane jest wskazanie *cresc.* przed 56.

This section (53—56) is performed unconducted (except for the signals indicating
the beginning and the end, i. e. 53 and 56). Batteria IV may be given four "affirmative" signals to indicate the beginning of each intervention. The indication of
the *cresc.* before 56 is desirable.

Example 4.16 Lutosławski *Trois Poèmes d'Henri Michaux*

* *) patrz s. 38/see p. 38/voir p. 38 siehe S. 38

Cette section (53—56) s'exécute non dirigée. On donnera seulement les signes de départ et de fin (à 53 et 56). Pour la batterie IV on peut convenir de 4 signes «affirmatifs» marquant chacun le début d'une intervention. L'indication du *cresc.* avant 56 est à recommander.

Dieser Abschnitt (53—56) wird nicht dirigiert (mit Ausnahme der Zeichen am Anfang und Ende, d. h. bei Nr. 53 und 56). Der Schlagzeuggruppe IV kann man am Anfang jeder der 4 Interventionen ein „ermunterndes" Zeichen geben. Erwünscht ist das Anzeigen des Crescendos vor 56.

Example 4.16 (continued)

III. Repos dans le Malheur

Example 4.17 Lutosławski *Trois Poèmes d'Henri Michaux*

form of a poly-textual poly-rhythmic, poly-intonational mobile-ostinato-group layer for all singer-speakers, all of whom declaim in an over-high register, over-loudly, with numerous accents. The individual, repeating parts are so long, and the structure is so overloaded, that there is an assurance of the desired bedlam, of mass-riot effect. Each component seems to be cancelled out as an individual utterance by the rest. All that matters is the overall busy din. There is very little, if any, differentiation possible in such a structure. And perhaps there is only one possible perceptual version for it, similar to the phenomenon of white noise. However, the orchestral complement possesses a strong profile. It consists of what one could call a double pump – a series of mutually eliding crescendos in the two wind sections:

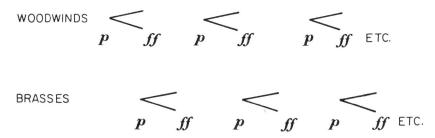

At 53 there is a sharp cut-off for the choir, and at the same time the orchestra (the winds, the pianos, and the percussion) launches into a noise-like mass-structure on its own. This consists of six different types of elements. Again, the density and the diversity are so great that only the total, the bedlam-like effect, is relevant.

The succession of the middle-level formal elements of the first movement of the work may be described in the following way:

The Choir
This stratum consists of nine groups of events.

Group 1 (28–9) is a tutti, that disintegrates gradually (Example 4.1).

Group 2 (29–34), a series of events of different timbral combinations, begins with a block of female voices and ends at the low end of the timbral spectrum (Example 4.2).

Group 3 (51–73), a series of three events, uses exclusively the sopranos (Example 4.3).

Group 4 (90–154) is a series of ten events. The first is the only loud SATB event in the movement (Example 4.4). The next six events consist of

THE CHORAL SCORE

(I, 90–154)

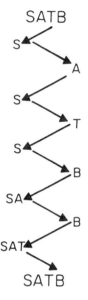

Figure 4.1

group dialogues between the sopranos and the other three groups, one by one, in descending timbral order (Example 4.5). The last exchange, S-B, is repeated, with the basses pitted in antiphony first against the SA pair, and then the SAT group appears. The buildup is completed with the full SATB group appearing at signal 154. Note the symmetrical features of this group (see Figure 4.1).

Group 5 (154–5) is an abbreviated reprise of the tutti of (28–9), which constitutes, with the preceding and subsequent groups an ABA + coda-like form.

Group 6 (162–3), a single event, is a further reduced version of the original 28–9. Group 7 (163–4) makes us recall the events of 51–73 (group 3). Group 8 (164–5) is a development of the idea first announced in 98–131, combined with elements of the previous section. Group 9 (165 to the end) is a residue of the event of group 8.

We see close connections within the following sets of groups: 1, parts of 4 (131–3 and 136–9+), 5, and 6; 2, 3, and 7; and 4 (98–131 and 133–6), 8, and 9.

We only have four different types of choral groups in this movement: the three listed below, plus the event 90–8 which is of a unique character. Groups 1, 5, and 6, and parts of 4, are of the character of a sweep. Groups 2, 3, and 7 are of the nature of a swarm (combined with sweep-like elements), consisting of legatos, descending glides, and very short, staccato notes. Groups 8 and 9 and parts of 4 are hetero-rhythmic unisons. One notes also the gradual modulation 127–39, from the hetero-rhythmic unison back to the opening sweep, which returns at 154.

This very economical, and almost classically deployed, timbral palette and structural plan create an easily perceivable form in the choral part.

The Orchestra

The orchestra has five groups of events.

Group 1 (1–28) is an event with the participation of woodwinds, brasses, and the two pianos. It begins as a chromatically saturated interlock that modulates (contracts) gradually into a swarm, still chromatically fully saturated, in the minimum range of a major seventh (Example 4.10).

Group 2 (35–84) consists of six pointillistic events. The first is an ascending single sweep. The second, third, and fourth are ascending step-ladders. The last two are descending single sweeps (Example 4.11).

Group 3 (85–90) consists of five events, each of which is a very dense interlock, using the woodwinds and the pianos (Example 4.12).

Group 4 (91–142) consists of a series of four antiphonal exchanges between two timbral groups: the woodwinds on the one hand, and the vibraphone, celesta, harp, and pianos on the other. Later the vibraphone is exchanged for the campanelli and the xylophone. The nature of the woodwind events is that of a sweep, and that of the other an interlock (Example 4.13).

Group 5 (143–65) is a fragmented and modified restatement of the closing portion of the structure that constituted group 1; thus there is a recapitulation also in the orchestra.

There are only four structural types in this orchestral fabric, namely the interlock, the swarm, the sweep, and the step-ladder.

The Choir and the Orchestra
Between the choral and orchestral strata we can observe the following types of relationships: temporal, registral, rhythmical-textural (density), timbral, typological, and dynamic (for some of these, see Figure 4.2).

Temporal relationships: We can hear the following patterns: elision (for example, at 28); overlap (between 51 and 53); both parts ceasing at the same time, followed by a pause (at 73); only one stratum active – it ceases to sound and, after a silence, the other stratum enters (at 155); a stratum sounding, while the other pauses – the sounding stratum ceases and after a brief pause begins again, with a new timbral configuration (142–3).

There is a clear complementary temporal relationship between the introductory orchestral passage and the first choral entry at 28. The series of overlaps between 35 and 73 are somewhat more complex. The double pattern of alternations in the two strata between 91 and 142 is still another construct with a clearly perceivable tendency.

Registral relationships: There are several registral modulations in the orchestra that function as preparations for a subsequent entry of the choir. These occur between 1 and 28 and 35 and 51. Registral contrast appears, for example, at 90; here the choir initiates a new registral distribution, which is followed by the orchestra at 91. The registral drop in the orchestra at 103, is mirrored two seconds later, at 105, in the choir. The immense registral drop from 142 to 143 is, of course, prepared by the vanishing dynamics between 138 and 142.

Rhythmical-textural relationships (density): There are no perceivable periodicities in either the choir or the orchestra. All that we have are densities of diverse magnitudes. The lowest orchestral densities occur between 35 and 84, while we hear only the sopranos. During the very dense orchestral passages between 85 and 90 the choir remains silent. The powerful and relatively dense choral entry at 90 is highlighted by the sudden cessation of the orchestra, which enters through accumulation between 91 and 98, by which time the choir begins a much simpler rhythm and texture.

Timbral relationships: There are beautiful timbral matchings in this movement, such as the combination of the pointillistic woodwind sweeps and step-ladders with the sopranos' swarms between 51 and 73 and the out-of-phase double alternations in the two strata between 98 and 143.

134 Alternative voices

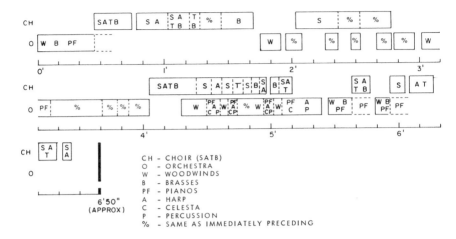

Figure 4.2

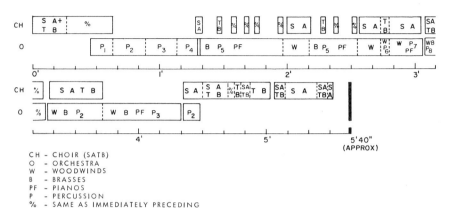

CH – CHOIR (SATB)
O – ORCHESTRA
W – WOODWINDS
B – BRASSES
PF – PIANOS
P – PERCUSSION
% – SAME AS IMMEDIATELY PRECEDING

Figure 4.3

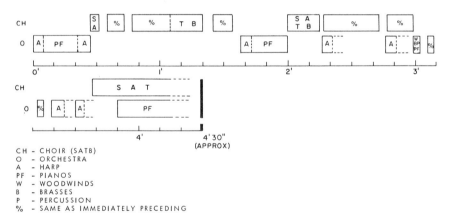

CH – CHOIR (SATB)
O – ORCHESTRA
A – HARP
PF – PIANOS
W – WOODWINDS
B – BRASSES
P – PERCUSSION
% – SAME AS IMMEDIATELY PRECEDING

Figure 4.4

Typological relationships: Examples are the combinations of different bidirectional, partly legato, partly staccato swarms in the choir, complemented by unidirectional, entirely pointillistic sweeps and step-ladders in the woodwinds between 51 and 73. Another compelling combination takes place between 98 and 131, where the choir intones hetero-rhythmic unisons, while the orchestra's structures are sweeps, swarms, and interlocks.

Dynamic relationships: The principal dynamic tessitura in the choir is the range below quasi-forte. Most of the time we hear piano or pianissimo. The loudest passage occurs in the central part, between 90 and 122.

The dynamics in the orchestra relate closely to those in the choir. The crescendo 89–90 prepares the loud choir entry at 90. The vanishing dynamics between 138 and 142 prepare the listener for the return of the opening materials at 143.

While the first movement is characterized by singing, soft dynamics, and the specific timbral combinations used, we are entering a new world right at the outset of the second movement (Example 4.6). This difference is readily perceivable in both strata. A major factor in their interplay (see Figure 4.3) is the sustained activity of the instruments (there are only four breaks in this stratum between its onset at 9 and its termination just before 58). This activity consists of a series of repeating ostinato groups and constitutes a violent ground to the declamation of the choir. The latter appears in a variety of structural types: mono-textual, mono-rhythmic, mono-intonational (6–32); poly-textual, poly-rhythmic, poly-intonational (52–3); mono-textual, poly-rhythmic, poly-intonational (1–3); mono-textual, hetero-rhythmic, mono-intonational (33–5); poly-textual, poly-rhythmic, monotone (57–63); and mono-textual, poly-rhythmic, monotone (65 to the end). The heavy use of the mono-textual, mono-rhythmic, mono-intonational group-declamation, either in the male or in the female voices, by itself, or in a two-sided antiphonal play, or over a background of a poly-textual, poly-rhythmic, monotone layer (see for example the passage 57–61) is characteristic. This type often occurs in brief bursts of quasi-expletives, or in other menacing words, the effect of which is heightened by the loud dynamics and by the broken-up manner of presentation. While the SATB structures in the first movement were homogeneous, we have here frequent opposition between the female and the male groups, either as antiphonies, or in the form of the women constituting a choral ground behind the aggressive utterances of the male voices. The clear intelligibility, and the direct, forceful, somewhat brutal character of this sub-group's vocal behaviour contrasts with the blurred, little understandable, and introverted choral character of the first movement. The poem's emphasis on certain affectively suggestive phonemes (allophones) in the second movement contributes to the overall drama. The orchestra powerfully complements the choir here. It performs the role of ground (see, for example, 52–3, Example 4.16), acts as an agent heightening the overall level of excitement by the device of accumulation (see between 19 and 31 the percussion and the brasses, Examples 4.14 and 4.15), provides a matching colour (such as that produced by the woodwinds, sustaining the women, between 33 and 34, Example 4.15), or adds yet another participating member to an antiphonal contest (such as the one that occurs between 49 and 52). The gradual descent from a high level of excitement, at the climactic passage of 52–3, to an ending in unaccompanied whisper prepares the way for the last movement.

The typological relationships, the expert deployment of resources, and the redundancies of design guarantee a compellingly dramatic result for the second movement.

The form of the third movement is the simplest of the three (see Figure 4.4). It almost appears to be an extended coda. As far as design is concerned, it has a strong identity, especially in the orchestra, and is different from those of the other movements.

Dominating the chorus is a fan-type structure that begins as a simultaneously attacked mono-rhythmic, mono-textual, monotone, sung recitation, that subsequently transforms itself into a swarm (Example 4.9). Implicit in such a structure is an allusion to the individual will, which seems to prevail over that of the collective, the latter being subsequently even stamped by association with the word *horreur*.

An austere ambiance is realized in the orchestra through the reduction of means, by the almost exclusive reliance on the harp and the two pianos (Example 4.17). The choir begins to recite on the words 'le malheur,' and this unison, mono-rhythmic, sung recitation, which opens most substructures here, is offered as a carrier of the affect. The clarity and the starkness of these unisons have the effect of an object bathed in the penetrating, almost painful illumination of a powerful light source. This impression is confirmed by the only instance in the work where the entire choir sings in mono-rhythmic unison and in the octave (between 27 and 29), and this occurs without turning this monotone recitation into a swarm, as in earlier instances. This extraordinary event is used to realize the words 'Dans ton horreur.'

The three brief orchestral multi-timbral interventions between 29 and 31 (the only places in the movement where we hear instruments other than the

Example 4.18

harp and the two pianos) repeat the note of the monotone F♯ of the preceding choral event in sharp co-ordinated attacks that rebound a few times like a ping-pong ball.

From some of the swarms mentioned earlier solo voices emerge; it is the first time this happens in the work. The passage 13–20 is a step-ladder with an accumulating opening and a disintegrating ending.

The choral passage from 21 to just before 24 is an interesting construct not hitherto deployed in the work. Its shape is that of an accumulating choral tutti. It begins, predictably, as a mono-textual, mono-rhythmic, unison, sung line in the tenors, who sing a rising diatonic five-note melody. In turn, the basses, the altos, and the sopranos enter – the altos with a rising four-note (two steps, one-third leap) melody, and the sopranos with another rising diatonic six-note melody, this time spanning a seventh (four steps, one-third leap); see Example 4.18. The chromatic saturation of this composite rise is underlined by the chromatic expansion of the structure in its remaining details. This also serves as a modulation to the climactic choral passage of the movement that begins at 24. This is a surprisingly unsaturated tutti with F♯ missing and with the design of an interlock. The missing note hardly makes a difference between this event and the busy, and dense structure at 90 in the first movement, of which this is perhaps a reminiscence. The reason for leaving out the F♯ pitch-class will be found, of course, in the passages to follow, 26–34, which are based exclusively on this note.

The instrumental stratum is very restrained here, both in timbre and in the materials played. We have here only the harp and the two pianos (that sound like one instrument), apart from those three brief, multi-timbral attacks between 29 and 31. The harp bisbigliando (always starting fast and slowing down like a gradually and rapidly attenuating small impact) prepares us for the choral monotone passages. The character of the first two of the three piano interventions is difficult to describe. As far as density is concerned, the beginning and end are at a low level. To, and from, the middle points of these structures there is a gradual increase and, in turn, decrease of density. The pitches begin as a series of un-hemitonic pentatonic structures that turn into chromatic events. The reason for the structure of the last piano

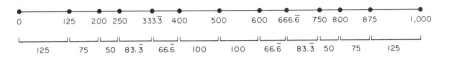

Figure 4.5

event must be considered when we focus on the last choral events. Each of the two strata uses the pitch-classes of two complementary, chromatically saturated clusters. The choral stratum is composed in the minimum range of a tritonus, while the piano stratum is registrally widely spaced. Both strata trail into nothingness, as the work ends.

The dominant temporal relationship between the choral and orchestral segments in this movement is non-simultaneity. This suggests the impression of a separation of the two groups that earlier in the work co-operated in so many ways. The impression of 'divorce' is further emphasized by frequent division of the choir into female and male voices, as if even the sexes got apart in the 'malheur' and the 'horreur' of the dénouement of this work. (The participation of the tenors, at the same register as those of the sopranos and altos, from 34 to the end does not alter this impression.)

A FEW CHARACTERISTIC MIDDLE-LEVEL STRUCTURES

The first orchestral section (1–28, see Example 4.10) is a constantly polymetric, periodically single-phase construct using the divisions 1/2, 3/4, 5/8. Within these schema we have the following note values:

METRIC UNIT LENGTH	NUMBER OF PHASE PLACEMENTS USED (SYNCOPATION, ETC)	CHRONOMETRIC DURATION (IN MILLISECONDS)
1	3	1,000
4/5	2	800
2/3	2	666.$\bar{6}$
1/2	1	500

The time points of note attacks during the 1,000-millisecond duration of the 'beats' are as follows: 0, 125, 200, 250, 333.$\bar{3}$, 400, 500, 600, 666.$\bar{6}$, 750, 800, 875, and 1,000. Note the palindromically symmetrical pattern of attack distances constituting this series (Figure 4.5). The complexity of the varying time distances between the attacks, the rhythmic density, and the fact that the 500-millisecond durations are *not* employed to mark the beginning of, and the half-way point between, the beats produces a non-periodic tissue of constantly middle-level density. This ground-type fabric is punctuated from beat 12 onwards by a series of *sfpp* in the brasses that gain in frequency of occurrence per unit time until 28.

The passage is constantly fully saturated chromatically. Its design is that of an interlock, spanning at the beginning the pitch limits c^1–e flat^3

and gradually shrinking, and descending, to the minimal frame of g–f sharp^1:

This procedure prepares us harmonically, registrally, and (through the *sfpp* of the brasses) dynamically for the first entry of the chorus at 29. This structure's sharp beginning and ending contrast with the accumulation/statistically steady-state/disintegration textural envelopes of other structures in this movement, such as the one between 35 and 45 in the orchestra.

The first choral event (Example 4.1), a sweep, exists in the minimal range that allows chromatic saturation. The joint attack on the first syllable of the word 'pensées' may allow for a measure of intelligibility, but in the rest of the structure we have but a swim of phonemes, which constitutes an appropriate word-painting, given the key words nage, mer, peu distincte, etc in the poem.

The overall character of structures such as 1, 29–30, and 51–60 (Examples 4.2 and 4.3) depends also on choices of timbre and register, overall density, the ostinato-character, the swarm-type structure, and the deployment of the text. In the first of these segments the phonemic saturation, by repeating the word 'moi,' imparts a nasal quality, further strengthened by the frequent repeats of /ã/ in 'tremble.' In the segment from 51 to 60, another swarm-like structure, the many repeats of the /d/ blend perfectly with the plosive sounds in the accompanying woodwinds. These brittle little cries sound as if emitted by small birds flying just over the surface of the sea – yet another instance of word-painting.

The effect of the mono-textual, poly-rhythmic, and monotone structures that begin at 98 in the first movement is quite different from that of structures in the last movement that begin in a similar manner. In the first movement these highlighted declamations float over the turbulence of the orchestra; in the last movement they are made to appear unaccompanied. The other difference is in the dynamics used: quasi-forte in the first movement, and pianissimo in the last.

In considering the entire work one observes that only a very few structural types are used. This imparts a sense of unity and a compactness of expression, while the numerous variants prevent one from feeling too much redundancy. This balance is highly satisfying and may help to account for the strong impact of the work. The balance, clarity, efficiency, and the perfectly suited text of the piece contribute to one's pleasure when one listens to or thinks of it. But will this reaction survive a longer acquaintance? Will a nagging feeling, a doubt, emerge about one's continuing interest in such an assembly of massed structures? How long will one sustain an interest in a form of such relatively simple outline? At what point will lucidity, ease of perception, and definiteness of affect slide prematurely into a feeling of experiencing a dearth of information? Are these massed structures going to gain in attraction by repeated hearings, revealing a hierarchy of harmonic and orchestral colour and tonal relationships as intricate as those of some works of other eras? Or shall we find that the capacity of these structures, as far as differentiation is concerned, is overly limited? Are we soon going to tire of them, as their internal grammar is forever hidden from aural comprehension by the very nature of the construct itself? I have no final answers to these questions.[17-19]

THE AFFECTIVE IMPACT OF THE FORMAL PROCEDURES

In describing the inspiration for the composition of his *Nuits* Iannis Xenakis referred (Souster 1968) to his experiences as a resistance fighter. While hiding he listened to the potentially menacing sounds of a rampaging mob in the streets. Lutosławski's background does not preclude, even makes likely, similar impressions. Thus it is not surprising that he reacted strongly to the text of 'Le Grand Combat.' The pensiveness, the abstraction of thought, and the allusive affective world of 'Pensées' is, of course, timeless, and independent of place, but its expression of massed choral sounds may be characteristic of time and place. The distantness of the setting of the 'Repos dans le malheur' has an existentialist starkness to it, which is best understood in relation to, or even as a consequence of, what was stated in the preceding movements. It could have been turned into a bleak statement; instead, however, Lutosławski speaks in it with the voice of a group that is at a certain kind of peace with itself. This does not contradict the poem, since it also allows for the co-existence of words such as malheur and horreur with others such as havre, cave d'or and âtre. One senses an ambiguity in the poem and, correspondingly, in the music – a feeling of having come to terms with a reality. This finds its most perfect allegorical representation perhaps in the word 'théâtre.' There is nothing better to do than to abandon oneself to an imaginary representation of an inexorable future and horizon.[20]

THE STRATEGY OF PERFORMANCE AND THE NOTATION

The performance strategy and the notation were devised by Lutosławski in such a way as to create certain structures and to do so with minimum effort.

The nature of the piece requires two, quasi-autonomously controlled groups; hence the decision to put each of these under a separate conductor who would be able to achieve a mixture of precision and flexibility.

There are various degrees of precision required in the work, depending on the structures concerned: mono-rhythmic non-periodic declamations; periodically conducted, but non-periodically sounding events; and shorter, or longer, *ad lib* structures that are only conducted when precise correlation is required, usually at the beginning and sometimes at the end. The performers are confident of getting a cue from the conductor when synchronous action is demanded and have no worry about the rhythm in the *ad lib* sections when they are on their own within the limits indicated in the score. This 'collective *ad libitum*' performance mode 'gives the performers the possibility of benefiting from all the advantages which in traditional music are kept exclusively for solo pieces ... The difficulties, which might possibly arise in the performance of this kind of music, merely consist of overcoming the performing habits of a long tradition. I am convinced (and many of my personal experiences support this conviction) that these difficulties are far less than those which sometimes arise in the performance of music, which has a division of time common to the entire ensemble' (Lutosławski 1968: 52).

The declamatory passages in the second movement, conducted by intermittent beating, could be easily accomplished, in part through rote-learning during rehearsals. Perhaps the most intricate passage of correlation can be found between 49 and 57 in the same movement. Lutosławski gives here a diagram of the conducting patterns in both scores.

The notation of this work, in two scores, with generous mutual cueing, is ingenious and practical. The two kinds of repeat signs (one with free ending, and the other with a simultaneous cut-off) are useful in the control of the materials to be repeated by the groups. The two kinds of arrows, the basic distance notation, the pauses, and the indication of the duration of the ostinato *ad lib* repeating groups in terms of seconds (where this is necessary) guarantee the precision required. Lutosławski has devised a practical notation for the work that was, most likely, in keeping with the competence of the performers he could count on at the time of the première.

The work was one of the first for large chorus to employ limited aleatorism and statistical structures. We saw earlier that Lutosławski has defined clearly his position in respect to Cage's ideas about chance operations. However, he made no mention of the work of Xenakis, to whom he and numerous other composers are indebted for the development of the idea of statistical structures. Lutosławski does refer to the body of complex and intricately notated works of the 1950s and early 1960s (for example, by Boulez and Stockhausen) that place inordinately heavy burdens on the performers. In an oblique way he speaks of this repertoire when he writes: 'The very concept of "collective ad libitum" can be considered as a reaction of composer-performer to the often absurd demands which some composers have made of performers in the last few years. Such demands are the result of a completely abstract approach to music considered exclusively as a series of acoustic phenomena occurring in time. I consider such an approach to music as being flagrantly one-sided. I understand music not only as a series of sound phenomena but also as an activity which is carried out by a group of human beings – the performers of the piece. Each of these persons is endowed with many far richer possibilities than those which a purely abstract score demands. I want to include into the repertoire of compositional means that wealth which is presented by the individual psyche of a human being – the performer' (Lutosławski 1968: 52).

Lutosławski has composed the details of this work in a manner congenial to the individual performer; by massing many such performer-individuals into groups, he has created a work that gives voice to the group as a whole. This voice has many shades of expression. At times it may even sound as the expression of the subconscious of a larger-than-life-size individual. Through this illusion the group and the individual merge into each other. The implication of this symmetrical relationship, which exists between a person and the groups to which he or she belongs, brings one to a deep stratum of the work, beyond notes and beyond other surface features. This is the level where the listener finds himself, face to face, in the most intimate contact with the composer.

GLOSSARY

Where no source is cited for a term and/or its definition, it is my own.

Accumulation: The gradual buildup of a choral or instrumental texture, its constituents entering one after another individually, or in groups

Bundle: 'In a complex construction of many layers [these] bundles fulfil a role similar to melodic lines of individual parts in the traditional orchestral polyphony. The appearance of one or more of such bundles or layers compels the composer to elaborate a special kind of counterpoint which is not a counterpoint of melodic lines but of their ensembles, i.e. of whole sets of melodic lines which cannot be split into single parts' (Lutosławski in Nordwall 1968: 109).

Choral declamation: Spoken or whispered, polyphonic or homophonic enunciation of a text. Its variables, apart from timbre and dynamics, are its rhythmic, textual, and intonational features.

Close, chromatically saturated bundle: A bundle of sweeps and/or swarms, the bands of which are contiguous with each other

Collective ad libitum: See *Limited aleatorism*.

Coloured silence: A silence characterized by the nature of the sound that preceded it and the one that follows it

Complementation: Relationship between simultaneous component parts. The two main types are, respectively, those where the components are of equal formal 'weight,' and where they are in figure-ground relationship to each other.

Compound structure: Two or more types of structures used simultaneously

Contraction: See *Disintegration*; *Fan*; *Saturation*.

Convergence: Dissimilar elements become similar.

Disintegration: The gradual termination of a texture by its constituents ceasing to sound one after another

Disturbance: The introduction into a steady-state or quasi-steady-state structure of a hitherto unused, contrasting element

Divergence: Similar elements become dissimilar.

Double pump: Two orchestral groups (A and B) performing a series of successively alternating crescendos in the following manner:

Envelope: This may be the dynamic profile of a sound (the customary meaning), or it may refer to the broad characteristics of a texture, consisting of its onset, steady state (if any), and termination. The onset may be by a sudden, simultaneous, switch-on of all the parts of the texture or by gradual accumulation (q.v.). The termination may be by a sudden switch-off of all the parts, or by a gradual disintegration (q.v.).

Expansion: See *Accumulation*; *Fan*; *Saturation*.

Fan: A unison opening up into a sweep, a swarm, an interlock, or other non-unison structures, and/or such structures closing into a unison. The two tendencies (q.v.) of a fan are those of expansion and contraction. (A.T. Davison used this term in *The Technique of Choral Composition* [Cambridge, Mass, 1955].)

Fusion: The merger of two, or more, dissimilar traits into a single compound trait

Hetero-rhythmic unison or octave: A layer of periodically, or non-periodically pulsing, out-of-phase lines of unisons and/or octaves

Interlock: A layer that uses a variety of intervals of any size. Its lines are often, but not necessarily, chromatically complementary to each other. The range exceeds the major seventh interval.

Interval types in twelve-note chords: 'Twelve-note chords constructed from one, two, or three types of intervals have for me a distinct, easily recognizable character while twelve-note chords comprising all types of intervals are colourless – they lack a clearly defined individuality' (Lutosławski in Nordwall 1968: 109, 112).

Layer: 'In the ensemble ad libitum technique, it is generally composed of several individual parts. These parts resemble each other in every respect and form a bundle of lines constantly intertwining with a characteristic contour: rhythmic, melodic and expressive' (Lutosławski in Nordwall 1968: 109).

Least advantageous version: 'In composing such a [collective ad libitum] sound picture I have in principle to foresee all possible versions which could result from my text, and to compose this text in such a way that all these versions would correspond to my intention. This can be done in a relatively easy way. Namely, it depends on composing only one version of a given section of the music which, with respect to the original intention, could be called "the least advantageous." In other words, of all possible situations which might arise from the combining elements of my sound picture, as the outcome of ad libitum playing, I choose that one which produces the result most divergent from my intention. By imagining the "least advantageous" situation which can arise from these elements, I can, if this is necessary, easily make the necessary corrections so that even this "least advantageous" situation will fulfil the required conditions. In doing this I can be completely sure that all other possible versions will be even more certain to fulfil the required conditions' (Lutosławski 1968: 51).[21]

Limited aleatorism: 'The most characteristic feature of music performed in this way is the absence of a common division of time to which all performers must comply in the same way. In my works this concerns only those phenomena which appear within the limits of the particular sections of the given musical form. On the whole, the dividing lines between the larger particular parts of the form are common for all performers, i.e. they fall at the same moments. Consequently, it follows that the form of the work as a set of the particular larger parts, is fixed completely by the composer' (Lutosławski 1968: 50).

'A particular sound picture, the essential features of which are to remain undisturbed despite the accepted method of collective ad libitum playing. Moreover this picture must be such that its nature cannot be changed by certain notes, and even groups of notes, not ultimately falling always in the same order' (50–1).

'This is exclusively the result of there being no common pulsation ... [It] leaves the performers the possibility of benefiting from all the advantages which in traditional music are kept exclusively for solo pieces ... In "collective ad libitum" all the variations of rubato playing are possible. The superimposing of several parts played rubato in a way quite independent of each other, is the most characteristic feature of the texture described above' (52).

Masking: Sustained or intermittent covering of one element (or groups of elements) by another or others

Mass-structure: A structure so complex, on account of the deployment of some or all of its dimensions at a large enough number of levels, that instead of inviting one to listen to the individual constituent parts, it invites listening to its entirety, as a *Gestalt*. Depending on its constituent parts it may be homogeneous or heterogeneous.

Mobile group-ostinato: See *Pseudo-loop-aggregate*.

Mono-intonational: Uses (in declamation) but a single notated intonation curve

Modulation: Gradual change, in one or more dimensions, from one condition to another, in such a manner that at, or close to, the point of juncture the (respective) pair(s) of conditions share at least one, but possibly more than one, structural feature(s)

Noise-like mass-structure: A homogeneous or heterogeneous mass structure of great complexity, in which the constituent parts seem to be competing with each other in a purposefully brought-about confusion

Poly-intonational: Uses (in declamation) two, or more, different intonation curves simultaneously

Predictable evolution: A process of structural change following along the lines of a recognizable tendency

Pseudo-loop-aggregate: A layer of, at least in part, out-of-phase lines that repeat, *ad lib*, shorter or longer phrases within a given time span; also: a bundle of such layers

Quasi-steady-state structure: A layer or bundle consisting of recognizably steadily recurring features

Register matching: The choral and orchestral strata are made to sound in the same register for an optimal mutual blending of the one into the other

Saturation: The fullest exploitation of a musical dimension in a given work (for example: a tutti, or all the brass instruments in the orchestra, the loudest dynamic level achievable, the fastest playing required in the work, etc). It may be absolute or relative; complete or partial.

Scatter: The opposite of convergence (q.v.)

Step-ladder: A bundle of sweeps and/or swarms, the bands of which are not contiguous with each other

Swarm: A layer using a variety of intervals of any size. Its lines are often, but not necessarily, chromatically complementary to each other. Its overall effect is that of a chromatically saturated interval (band).

Sweep: A layer consisting exclusively or predominantly of parts moving in semitone motion. The parts are, normally, out of phase with each other, due to the *ad lib* performance. The ascending and/or descending movement may be repeated. It is either uni-, bi-, or poly-directional. Its overall effect is that of a chromatically saturated interval (band).

Synchronization: The temporal relationship between layers, bundles, and compound structures may be that of simultaneity, alternation (one after another in different choral and/or instrumental groups), succession (one after another in one and the same choral and/or instrumental group), elision, or overlap.

Tendency: A presumptive course of the evolution of a given structural condition, whether in the process of change (see *Predictable evolution*) or in a steady-state, or in a quasi-steady-state

Timbre: 'I have always been of the opinion that the timbre of an instrument or of a group of allied instruments is not sufficient to create colour of full value. It is only the coupling of acoustic features of given instruments in the role they are going to play which makes it possible to attain this goal. Most sophisticated combinations of instrumental colours sound rather dull to me if the intervals and harmonic aggregations do not contribute to the colour effect' (Lutosławski in Nordwall 1968: 113).

PART TWO

5

Blurred boundaries

WHO IS A COMPOSER?

Of all the people who plan structures in the domain of vocal sound, or who cause such events to occur, only a few normally call themselves composers. The others profess to be working as vocal performers, playwrights, actors, stage-directors, poets, media sound-effects persons, clergymen, linguists, lawyers, Inuit shamans, sound-engineers, psychologists, announcers, advertising specialists, auctioneers, and so on. However, the work of these latter can and does at times bring the practitioner close to or into compositional activity.

WHAT IS A COMPOSITION?

A composition is an event, or a plan for such, in the domain of sound and silence, designated by one or more person(s) – not necessarily its creator(s) – as music. The acknowledgment that the same event or plan might have an additional function does not weaken its role or potential as music.[1] A composition may appear as any or a combination of the following: a work (more or less precisely defined in detail – notated or unnotated), an action-scheme, a procedure, a sequence, a situation, a segment of reality and its designation as a composition, or a plan for an action-scheme through which to obtain a succession of sounds. There might be other manifestations that warrant also to be called compositions. (See, for example, Schöning 1982.)

POETRY OR MUSIC? SPEAKING OR SINGING? THEATRE OR DANCE?

Sound-poets such as Charles Amirkhanian and composers such as Pauline Oliveros, by their creative practice, challenge the validity of the semantic distinctiveness implied by these pairs of expressions. Their position might be understood also as referring back to an Orphic period in which no such dichotomies existed and poetry and music constituted but a single expressive mode. But we do not have to travel so far back to find support for the idea that the implied contrasts in the subtitle might be due more to certain preferences acquired in the course of Western culture, than to objective criteria.

Numerous authors have studied the historical relationship between the spoken word and vocal music (Lach 1913; Steinitzer 1918; several of those included in Strunk 1950 and quoted in Duey 1951; Szabolcsi 1950; Van der Veen 1955). Most have commented on the transitional practices observable between the hypostatized states of speaking and singing. C. Høeg, for example, observed (after Aristoxenus) in *La Notation ekphonétique*, with respect to the *lectio sollennis*, that 'normal' speech or declamation turns into what we would call singing in the following way: 'Le *pathos* transforme la parole en chanson (Éléments 9), c'est-a-dire qu'on est amené par le *pathos* à donner aux intervalles de la parole un caractère nettement diastematique : car celle-ci a, elle aussi, sa mélodie determinée par la sequence des accents des mots dont elle se compose (Éléments 18) et cette mélodie de la parole ne diffère du chant qu'en tant qu'elle n'est pas diastématique' (Høeg 1935: 152).

That different cultures have developed different conceptual frameworks was pointed out by G. List: 'Certain cultures make a distinction between what is referred to as speech or talking and what is referred to as song or singing. Other cultures do not necessarily make this distinction. Other cultures distinguish forms other than speech or song which to us may seem to be intermediate forms. The nomenclature applied to these intermediate forms will vary considerably from culture to culture as will the social function of the form' (List 1963: 3).[2]

A frequently encountered formulation of the alleged difference between singing and speaking is 'that song exhibits pitches of greater duration than speech.' However, there are languages, such 'as those of the Australian aborigines, in which there is apparently greater sustenation of pitch in speech than in song' (List 1963: 2). P.R. Olsen demonstrated in a lecture given at Queen's University, Kingston, Ontario, in 1977 a 'vocal event' by a Greenland eskimo shaman, that fell between Western culture's categories of speaking and singing.

Some practices of contemporary poetry as well as composition seem to make certain divisions into categories inoperative. We are witnessing what appears to be a convergence of paths in certain works in the two fields. As far as poetry is concerned, I have in mind the work of such early-twentieth-century poets and poet-artists as Kurt Schwitters (Schwitters 1973–7, 1975), Hugo Ball (Ball 1974), Tristan Tzara (Motherwell 1951), Marinetti (Marinetti 1919, 1968), Giacomo Balla, Remo Chiti, Fortunato Depero, Mario Dessy, Fillia, Volt (Kirby and Nes Kirby 1971), concrete poets (Williams 1967), sound poets (Chopin 1967), practitioners of *lettrisme* (Isou 1947, Curtay and Gillard 1971), and authors of some scenarios (Kostelanetz 1980a) and of text-sound texts (Kostelanetz 1980b).[3]

As to musical compositions, works such as Oliveros's *Sound Patterns*, an amusing little piece of mouth-sounds children are apt to make, or Beckwith's *Gas!*, a delightful work (see chapter 8) that consists exclusively of a 'found poem,' assembled by the composer 'from various municipal and provincial traffic signs of south-central Ontario,' and 'onomatopoeic and imitative sounds,' recited by a small choir, seem to approach some types of recited poetry. Some works – Cage's *Mesostics* is an example – appear in both categories: as a published 'score' and as a performed text-sound piece.[4]

The influence of persons principally known perhaps as artists has also contributed to this confluence of media. 'When Roul Hausmann and Kurt Schwitters, two visual artists, began to give public readings of their abstract and nonsensical poems in the period following the First World War, an entirely new area of art activity was stimulated,' writes Charles Amirkhanian.[5] (Marinetti, of course, preceded them in this; Flint 1972.)

In concrete and lettrist poetry the selection of type and the page layout form intrinsic elements of the poem, suggesting interpretation. However, in reference to the former genre, Emmet Williams 'would place the emphasis on *poetry* rather than on *Concrete*' (Williams 1967: v). He continues with the questions: 'Concrete as opposed to what? Abstract? Analogies with the visual arts deemphasize the poetic element in favor of the visual, which is but a single (though consequential) aspect of the new poetry' (v). This element in the work of the poets working in this direction in the early 1950s 'tended to be structural, a consequence of the poem, a "picture" of the lines of force of the work of poets striving in this direction in the early 1950s 'tended to be completed or activated by the reader, a poetry of direct presentation' (vi). With this last comment, we find ourselves in the domain of performance, of articulated or silent (interior) soliloquy, which, depending on the nature of the text (and its degree of redundancy), as well as on the interpretation, might approximate the condition of music.

Isou's *Introduction à une nouvelle poésie et une nouvelle musique* (Isou 1947) is a seminal contribution pertaining to certain aspects of the rebirth of the Dadaist spirit and the merging of certain poetic and musical practices following the Second World War. *La Musique lettriste* (Curtay and Gillard

1971) includes an account of the brief history of this movement, beginning with *Dictature lettriste* no. 1, which included numerous poems and a semi-facetious 'lexique des lettres nouvelles' (67–70), assembled by Isou, François Dufrêne, et al, that contains 159 items such as entries for 'aspiration forte,' 'expiration forte,' 'gémissement,' 'claquement de langue,' 'crachat (une sorte de peuh-pouah-ptiou ensemble),' 'sifflement (simple non mélodique),' and 'applaudissement.' (We shall note in chapter 8 that several of these varieties appear also among the vocal sounds prescribed in some of the Graeco-Egyptian magical formulae that were used in thaumaturgic procedures during the early centuries AD, and probably even earlier.)

In some concrete or lettrist poetry there is an inherent synaesthesia that combines poetic idea with all the pictorial aspects of the poem. Some composers also show such a dual and related sensitivity. In the works of Schafer, this manifests itself in the unusual beauty of the graphic aspect of his musical scores, which complement fittingly, and often exquisitely, their musical character. The decorative, manneristic urge in Schafer's artistic personality (an influence of Asianism perhaps) seems so powerful that he is, at times, compelled to give it exclusive attention. This has resulted in three delightful poetical works of a lettrist character: *Smoke*, a short novel; *The Chaldean Inscription*, a short cryptic poem that is made to disguise itself through progressively more and more decorated and consequently less and less legible, repeated, scripts, that imitate the spirit of Arabic manuscripts; and the longest of the three, *Dicamus et Labyrinthos: A Philologist's Notebook*, a fictional account of the decipherment of a pseudo-ancient script, invented by Schafer, which he calls Ectocretan. The musical touches in at least some of these works is obvious: for example, *The Chaldean Inscription* has been composed in the form of a set of variations. *Dicamus et Labyrinthos* ties in with other works of Schafer's related to the person of Ariadne (*Patria II*, for example).

In *Not I* Samuel Beckett has reduced a person, a woman, to her mouth. She *is* called MOUTH. She is made to stand eight feet above floor level on a darkened stage, 'faintly lit from close-up and below, rest of face in shadow. Invisible microphone.'[6] In a 1977 television performance of the work on the BBC, only the woman's mouth was visible, in a 'near shot,' almost filling the entire screen. During the frenziedly rapid speech (approximately ten minutes long), interrupted only by loud gasps of air-intake, the notion of watching a *person* rapidly vanished, and was replaced by the puzzlement and awe of watching a strange yet somehow familiar creature, who performs a series of truly remarkably agile gymnastic feats. I was so taken by this virtuoso performance that I had hardly any attention left for the steady stream of speech that issued from that semi-dark, more than well-lubricated, sensuous cavity. The burden of her torrent of vocalizations was lost on me. All I was able to do was to concentrate on the dance of the tongue, on the flashing of the teeth as the lips parted and then closed shut again. This was a pity, I found out later, when I got hold of the text of the work. It includes the lines: '... imagine! ... whole body like gone ... just the mouth ... lips ... cheeks ... jaws ... never- ... what? ... tongue? ... yes ... lips ... cheeks ... jaws ... tongue ... never still a second ... mouth on fire ... stream of words ...' The sharp focus of light on this mouth, a symbol of language, which itself serves as a metaphor, nay a carrier, of being, is a *showing* of the soul in action. This, probably the most concrete possible presentation of speech, isolates it as a *showing* rather than as a saying. With this piece, a combination of poem, theatre, and acrobatic ballet, Beckett has reached into the very depth of language: he succeeded in *showing* us the very act of *showing* itself, with which Aristotle and Martin Heidegger, among many others, were concerned.

In 'On the Way to Language' (Heidegger 1971: 114) Heidegger quotes from Aristotle's 'On Interpretation': 'Now what [takes place] in the making of vocal sounds is a show of what there is in the soul in the way of passions and what is written is a show of the vocal sounds' (114). To this Heidegger adds: 'The letters show the sounds. The sounds show the passions in the soul, and the passions in the soul show the matters that arouse them' (115). Heidegger adds: '*The essential being of language is saying as Showing*' (123). Bruns, an astute student of the languages of poetry, said in this regard: 'The poet's concern ... is thus not with a language of signs but with what Heidegger calls "the language of being," which is ... the language of Orpheus.' In calling up Orpheus, Bruns of course makes an appeal for a unitary, spiritual, poetical, musical and mythical experience, the kind of passion certain poets, playwrights, and composers are striving to achieve. But we ought to recognize that passion resides in the very core of the word tone itself. Tone is derived from the Latin *tonus*, which means tone, sound. But *tonus* itself is derived from the Greek *tonos*, which means a stretching, straining, as well as raising the voice, pitch, accent, measure, and metre. In Sanskrit, *tana* means tone, fibre. St Augustine advises: 'Nor must we keep back the mystical meaning of the timbrel and psaltery. On the timbrel leather is stretched, on the psaltery gut is stretched; on either instrument the flesh is crucified' (Reese 1940: 64).

Stretching, straining – do not these words bring to mind the high-larynxed nasal voice of the typical young male rock singer standing, straining on a large stage, singing-shouting with all the vocal power he can muster? He might have begun his performance singing an intelligible text, but at a certain moment the words have become blurred, and one can only hear unbridled vocalizations and other unintelligible bursts of buccal noise, belonging to no scale, but to an extreme temperament. He seems to have overstepped a boundary of restraint and has entered a trance-like stage. What kind of 'mania' might have taken possession of him (Rouget 1980: 268–74)? Or is it only a 'show' instead of a Heideggerian 'showing'? Is it conceivable that he might be one of those gifted enthusiasts (in the original religious sense of the word) about whom Rabbi Schneor Zalman spoke when he said: 'For the song of the souls at the time they are swaying in the high regions to drink from the well of the Almighty King – consists of tone only, free and dismantled of burdensome words' (Werner 1959: 333).[7]

Is this gifted singer, who improvises phrase after phrase, only an interpreter of material composed by someone else? Or is he a composer? These questions bring us to yet another blurred boundary.

COMPOSERS AND INTERPRETERS

How is one to capture the nuances of a performance such as the one just described? What should we understand the word capture to signify in this context? Do we mean to listen concentratedly and savour as many details, besides the overall aura of the event, as possible? Or do we mean also the finding of a suitable and adequate symbolic (written) representation for it? If the latter is our objective, we must be aware that by such concretizations (which in Western music until recently normally denoted either the abstractions of steady states or processes) a more or less spontaneous event becomes a more or less precisely determined series of symbols.

Any notational system, whether it serves the purpose of analysis (hence descriptive), or that of reproducibility (thus prescriptive) (Seeger 1958), is based on anterior premises, measuring methods, and instruments. And these are all based on conceptual frameworks that hypothesize what is of primary and what is of peripheral importance. Thus reality is mapped into a system of templates in the mind and this system is then translated into perceivable representations. Nicolas Ruwet describes the transformation in a broader framework: 'L'homme n'accéde au réel que par la médiation d'un ensemble de systèmes significants (le langage, mais aussi le mythe, les rites, les systèmes de parenté, les systèmes économiques, l'art enfin) dont chacun, par le fait même de sa structure, et des conditions de son fonctionnement, impose sa marque au réel et y reste toujours irreductible, en même temps qu'il reste irreductible, à la limite, aux autres systèmes significants, malgré les rapports d'équivalence ou de transformation qu'on peut établir entre leurs structures respectives' (Ruwet 1971: 67).

In this respect, in Western musical practice a specific triangular relationship has developed in the course of several centuries, becoming a nearly exclusive usage by the early nineteenth century. It consists of the composer, the composition (notated in some form or other), and an interpreter, who has the know-how to reproduce the original invention from a symbolic script, with the help of a tradition that he shares with the composer, who, in turn, knows what he can expect from the interpreter. This way of making music is a kind of network for the storage and transmission of information for the specific purpose considered, but it is not the only one in existence in the world. Other cultures use different systems. Some have relied, for example, more on rote learning and/or 'on-the-spot,' controlled improvisation where composer and interpreter are frequently one and the same person (Emmert 1979: 67–9, Tamia 1981). Bruno Nettl has written about this matter: 'Manner of performance has been recognized since early descriptions of non-Western music as an essential aspect of musical style, but it has not always been adequately defined. The assumption has been that a musical performance, as an event, consists of the music itself, which possesses a certain degree of permanence and the way it is performed, which can be superimposed on the music itself. This idea, of course, stems from the Western cultivated music tradition, in which it is possible to separate what the composer has indicated in the notation and what is added by the performer. In traditional music this distinction exists only by conjecture' (Nettl 1964: 153).

Recent momentous changes in Western musical practice, including interest in non-Western musics, improvization, indeterminate procedures, vocal experimentation, and the use of various forms of technology, have cast doubt on the unconditional superiority of the triangular abstraction: composer-score-interpreter. It will suffice to remark that in current practice many alternative arrangements are being used: the identity of the composer is sometimes merged with that of the improvising performers, who interpret their own ideas in various degrees of co-ordination with those of their fellow interpreters; there can be several scores or no score at all; or the composer of an exclusively computer-generated piece is able to make his piece heard without the help of any performer. Much of the power of Cage's *4'33"* resides in its lucid showing of the individual roles of the constituent members of this triangle by the very expedient of not performing (*in the sense of preconceived sounds*) or of not providing a score, beyond indicating a soundless scenario.

How do the most creative interpreters achieve and convey great depth of psychological insight? Chaliapin, the great Russian basso of the turn of the century, was such a remarkable singer, best known for his operatic performances. He wrote that early in his career he spent his free evenings in the theatre, listening to actors, and learning from them about the infinite variety of voice modulation (Chaliapin 1932: 85). This might be one key to his much-admired interpretation of the role of Boris in Moussorgskij's *Boris Godunov*. He used a kind of demented *Sprechgesang* in certain passages. These paralinguistic sounds (a recording is still available) are not indicated in the score.[8] Has he violated the composer's intention by imposing without good reason his own notions on a fully and painstakingly notated, master-work? My answer would be no. He brought to life Moussorgskij's *intent* by realizing that the composer did not put down on paper all that he wished to evoke. We know that Moussorgskij was most sensitive to the rhythm, inflection, and contour of spoken language as a 'natural model for vocal music.' In a letter of 1868 he wrote: 'This is what I would like: my stage people should speak like living people ... My music must be an artistic reproduction of human speech in all its finest shades. That is, the *sounds of human speech*, as the external manifestations of thought and feeling must, without exaggeration or violence, become true, accurate *music*, but ... artistic, highly artistic' (Taruskin 1970: 440).

Yvette Guilbert, the celebrated French *diseuse*, whose career spanned more than fifty years, starting in the 1880s, commented on the necessity of commanding the technical as well as affective means for achieving a sufficiently broad interpretative range: 'La chanteuse qui a ce qu'on appelle "un registre unique" et normalement placé, ce qui est le cas de la plupart des chanteuses, ne peut pas espérer atteindre jamais l'art de bien illustrer la chanson ; sa voix serait-elle la plus belle du monde' (Guilbert 1928: 15–16). 'L'art de colorier, d'exprimer, de dire, "la chanson," implique la possession des moyens qui permettent de le faire. "Toutes les sortes de chansons" exigent toutes les sortes de registres ... Toute la *couleur* de cet art vient de là. J'emploie à dessein ce mot couleur. Nous sommes en effet des peintres, des imagiers, notre organe est notre palette, c'est avec la voix parlée melée au chant, la multiplicité des "nuances," que nous colorons, et mettons en lumière nos personnages, nos sujets, leur atmosphère, leur époque' (16–17).

The art of a Chaliapin, or a Guilbert, or, for that matter, a Janis Joplin, makes it clear that to penetrate beyond an intuitive understanding towards a reasoned comprehension of a work requires knowledge about acoustics, the physiology of the voice, phonetics, and the psychology of vocal utterance.

This supposition is strengthened by the frequent use of speech-like and paralinguistic sounds in recent works. If composers consider the entire domain of vocally producible sounds as, at least potentially, their domain then those who wish to understand this music might want to have some knowledge of the related conceptual frameworks. An understanding of vocal composition and performance benefits from a measure of linguistic knowledge. In the next section I shall briefly comment on some aspects of this relationship.

ASPECTS OF LANGUAGE STUDY: COGNATE AREAS FOR MUSIC

The aspects of language study I am principally referring to here are intonation and other prosodic phenomena, including those of paralinguistics; the physiology of the voice; speech pathology; and the semiotics of the voice.

The study of intonation in English, for example, has been pursued by students of this language for several centuries (Crystal 1969). Commentators analyse speech from the point of view of the function of the utterance and also the assumed social and attitudinal background from which it emerges. Kingdon, for example, identifies seven intonation patterns for questions: 'general, particular, alternative, asking for repetition, interrogative repetition, insistent, quizzical,' and ten for statements: 'straightforward, mocking or impatient, unfinished, perfunctory, implicatory, insinuating, insinuating with interrogative force, straightforward, with afterthoughts, enumerations' (Kingdon 1958: 208). He observes a similar diversity in the function of other types of utterance. E. Uldall has studied how meanings might be conveyed by intonation (Uldall 1960). She finds that there is little agreement as to the terms in which the meanings are to be described. Dealing with a somewhat broader repertoire, Fónagy and Magdics describe (Fónagy and Magdics 1963) in musical notation what they perceive to be the melodic patterns of certain emotions or emotional attitudes: joy, tenderness, longing, coquetry, surprise, fear, etc.

George L. Trager was perhaps the first to undertake systematic study of those aspects of language that he came to call paralinguistic (Trager 1958). He introduced the subject thus: 'For many years linguists and other students of language and communication as a whole have been aware that communication is more than language. They have known that all the noises and movements entering into the activity of people talking to each other and exchanging communications needed to be taken into account if a total picture of the activity was to be arrived at. At the same time it was known, by a sort of tacit consent that much of what went on was not accessible to study by "scientific methods" as had yet been devised' (1).

His classification of paralinguistic phenomena includes: voice set, which 'involves the physiological and physical peculiarities resulting in the patterned identification of individuals as members of a societal group and as persons of a certain sex, age, state of health, body build' (4); voice qualities, which are the results of the control of the vocal apparatus; vocalizations, which include vocal characterizers (such as laughing, moaning, crying); vocal qualifiers – the extreme registers of intensity, pitch, and extent (meaning probably tempo); and vocal segregates (*uh-uh*, *sh*, a *cough*, etc).

The dimension of voice quality, so important in both linguistic and musical communication, is one of the most complex. From the point of view of music, it has, until very recently, constituted an ambiguous situation: composers included relatively little information, beyond specifying certain broad voice-types (dramatic soprano, lyric tenor, etc) yet audiences tended to prize the art of this or that singer in large measure because of the special voice qualities he or she was able to produce.

Voice quality is determined by the phonetic content of the moment, physiological characteristics (societal, regional, due to shape of body organs, age, state of health, etc), and idiosyncratic features (such as a habitually retracted tongue position). Laver states: 'The quality of every speaker's voice is the product of two sorts of features – intrinsic features and extrinsic features. Intrinsic features are those whose quality is directly due to the invariant anatomy and physiology of the speaker's vocal apparatus. Extrinsic features derive their quality from long-term muscular adjustments, or *settings*, of the intrinsic vocal apparatus which were once acquired perhaps by social imitation, or idiosyncratically, and are now habitual, and outside the speaker's normal awareness' (Laver 1975).

All parts of the voice apparatus, the vocal folds, the larynx-position, the tenseness or laxness of the pharynx, and the personal, habitual use of the velum, the tongue, and all the resonant areas contribute to voice quality. Approaching the matter from the acoustical angle, one observes that both in speaking and in singing the relationship between the harmonic spectrum of the pitch-dependent complex tone of the vowel spoken or sung and the stable formant frequencies of the vowel in question plays an important role.

J.C. Catford, one of the most informative students of voice quality, has offered the view 'that phoneticians should be able to classify "voice qualities" and other phonatory activities in as systematic a way as they classify supralaryngeal articulation.' The starting point of his 'tentative' investigation was 'a systematic kinaesthetic-auditory exploration of phonatory activities, of a kind familiar to phoneticians: that is, an exploration starting from one or two known points of reference and proceeding from the known to the unknown by making minimal laryngeal adjustments, combining known phonation types, and so on' (Catford 1964: 29). To this he adds encouragingly: 'The larynx may not be well supplied with sensory nerves, but it is surprising how far one can go by "introspective" techniques.'

It is helpful for the understanding of such present-day works as Peter Maxwell Davies's *Eight Songs for a Mad King* and Dieter Schnebel's *AMN* or *Madrasha II* to be familiar with the categories of voice quality and their physiological correlates. These include, in addition to modal voice and falsetto, audible breath, whisper, raised larynx voice, creak, breathy voice, harsh voice, ventricular voice, and various compounds of these.

For a detailed description of the physiology of producing these voice qualities the reader is advised to consult related works by J.C. Catford, J. Laver, and others (Kaplan 1960; Catford 1964; Large 1973; Laver 1975, 1980). As an example of the type of description the reader may expect to encounter, consider Kaplan's description of the quality of harshness: 'Where the folds are drawn too tightly together during phonation rather than being lax, a shrill, harsh, creaking noise, which is called "stridency, or stridor" enters the tone. Some causes include general tension, spastic paralysis, or often a throat strain or "pinched throat." There is excessive constriction of muscles all through the vocal tract, and the tension is great in the external laryngeal muscles. The vibrations of the vocal folds are hindered and supraglottal friction noises are introduced' (Kaplan 1960: 167–8).

In addition to the simple phonation types already commented on, Laver identifies a number of compound ones in spoken English: whispery creak, whispery voice, whispery falsetto, creaky voice, creaky falsetto, whispery creaky voice, whispery creaky falsetto, breathy voice, harsh voice, harsh falsetto, harsh whispery voice, harsh whispery falsetto, harsh creaky voice, harsh creaky falsetto, harsh whispery creaky voice, and harsh whispery creaky falsetto (Laver 1975: 273–4).

As far as supralaryngeal settings are concerned, Laver lists three gross categories: longitudinal modifications (as a result of labial protrusion and/or vertical larynx position), latitudinal modifications (as a result of interlabial configurations; lingual articulations; tongue-body and tongue-root placements; faucal, pharyngeal, and mandibular conditions), and the presence or absence of nasality. Combining the degree of tenseness with a phonation type and with a specific supralaryngeal configuration, one comes up with compounds such as 'nasal voice with blade articulation and a protruded jaw' (Laver 1975: 271–2).

Considering the various simple and compound phonation types, and the just listed supralaryngeal settings, one can readily conclude that the number of different sounds the vocal tract can produce is likely to be very large, indeed. M.V. Mathews, in one investigation, has reported: 'A four-parameter articulatory model was used to describe the vocal tract shape. Frequencies of the first five formants were computed for each of 30,000 vocal tract shapes' (Mathews 1977). How many sounds, produced by these shapes, can a composer, or performer, differentiate from other sounds? How many of these can he remember, recall, and produce (or reproduce)? What kinds of musical structures do successions and/or simultaneities of such sounds make possible? Useful commentaries on these questions are provided by innovative composers through their works. These might also encourage experimentation, partly for its own sake and also as preparation for subsequent compositional activity.

As one gets ready for an experiment it is advisable to keep in mind that the control of the supralaryngeal and laryngeal parts of the vocal tract involves different degrees of verifiability. As Luchsinger and Arnold have pointed out: 'Owing to the logical and *conceptual definition of the phonemes* produced in the anterior oral articulator, its functional modulations can be readily associated with the resulting audible sound phenomena. This situation differs with regard to the pharyngeal resonator.' They find a possible reason for this 'in the fact that the influence of the throat on the voice has little to do with the logical conceptual levels of language. Instead, it is closely linked to the phylogenetically *older levels of emotional expression*. It follows ... that this interrelationship is of primary significance for singing' (Luchsinger and Arnold 1965: 115–16).

There are numerous manifestations of emotional, neurotic, or psychotic soul states in the vocal acts of speaking (coherently, or not quite so) and singing, with all the transitional forms between the two modalities. One only needs to think of such commonly occurring events in speech as break, self-correction, incompletion, repetition, distortion of various kinds, filled pause, retraced false start, stuttering, suppression, sudden interruptions, and non-verbal expressives to realize in how many different ways one indicates one's mental state (Mahl and Schulze 1964). Mahl and Schulze recognize five dimensions in which extralinguistic elements manifest themselves in vocal behaviour: language style, selection and diversity of vocabulary, pronunciation and dialect, voice dynamics, and the paralinguistic areas.

Among the writings of voice-oriented psychiatrists (working alone or in collaboration with linguists) two publications stand out: *The Voice of Neurosis*, by P.J. Moses (Moses 1954), and *The First Five Minutes – A Sample of Microscopic Interview Analysis*, by R.E. Pittenger, C.F. Hockett, and J.J. Danehy (Pittenger et al 1960).

Moses advises that 'Before attempting to analyze voice, one must divorce it from the message it seeks to convey ... we must subtract the content and retain the voice impression' (Moses 1954). (Isn't this what happens when we listen to commercials that return to the television screen night after night? Due to the repetition, the simple, often inane, text vanishes as a result of habituation, and what remains is but the tone of voice, the intonation, the prosodic and paralinguistic features that, for most persons, subliminally penetrate the mind and do the work of subtle persuasion that is the objective of the whole endeavour.) Elsewhere Moses observes: 'Lisping of the child is a ... continuation of infantile gratification. Playing with saliva, touching mucous membranes with the tongue are among the earliest sources of pleasure' (23). (The implication of this is clear when one hears an adult speaking in a slobbering manner.) Moses was also aware of the central role that speech, especially the rhythm of speech, played in ancient magical practice. He observed: 'Rhythm in ancient magic had three roles: to exercise remote control of the force to be subjugated by symbolic gesture and repeated invocations of its name, to create the concentration necessary for magic ritual, and to submerge the magician into a state of even greater antiquity where he could explore the unconscious for "inner voices," racial memories, Urgefühl' (53).

The First Five Minutes (Pittenger et al 1960) consists of a painstaking notation and analysis of a brief fragment of an interview between a therapist and his patient and an evaluation of the method used. About immanent reference the authors note: 'No matter what human beings may be communicating about or may think they are communicating about, *they are always communicating about themselves, about one another, and about the immediate context of the communication*' (229). They say about determinism: 'Any communicative act is ... culturally determined: the indeterminate or "accidental" residue is non-existent' (233). They observe: '*Anything anyone ever says is true* – the "truth" of a communication being what has caused it to occur' (234). They invoke the working principle of reasonable alternatives: 'The communicative value of a single received signal, then, lies not only in what it is but in what it is *not*' (237). They add that signal and noise are intimately connected: 'One man's noise is another man's signal'; however, 'in primary human communication one man's noise is the same man's signal' (239). Adjustment, for the authors, represents 'the recalibration of communicative conventions ... in transactions between human beings' (245). These observations refer to macro-strategies and/or to macro stylistic features in language use and can be readily transferred into the conception, performance, and analysis of musical structure.

We experience the use of simulations of pathological vocal expressions in Berio's *Sequenza III* and in Ligeti's *Nouvelles Aventures*, in Schafer's *Patria II – Requiems for the Party Girl*, in Schnebel's *AMN* and *Madrasha II*, in Kagel's *Phonophonie*, and in Maxwell Davies's *Eight Songs for a Mad King*. I shall return to these works later.

Aspects of the study of voice quality, as well as the matters treated by Moses and by Pittenger, Hockett, and Danehy, have led us directly into the field of the semiotics of the voice. Let us then pursue the discussion of voice quality, but this time from the point of view of the message it might convey. For example, why do promoters of rock concerts often select their vocalists from among young male singers who prefer to sing with an overly high-pitched, harsh, nasal, raised-larynx, strained voice, perhaps involving a severe pharyngeal constriction? What are the semiological implications of such voices? A. Lomax suggests that 'high-pitched, often harsh and strident voice quality is delivered from a tight throat with great vocal tension frequently with an effect of being pinched or strangulated' (Lomax 1959: 941). He notes that this voice quality exists in certain regions and countries that have a certain social structure and a certain attitude towards sex. He wonders if there is a 'correlation ... between a musical style and certain social factors, most especially the position of women, the degree of permissiveness toward sexual love, and the treatment of children' (941). He also asks: 'Is high-pitched, strident singing necessarily a musical symbol of the burning pain of sexual starvation?' (947). 'It appears to me that this is so, for people sing in this fashion in all the areas in which women are secluded, owned, exploited, and thus never can trust or be trusted completely by their men' (947).

Should Lomax be right,[9] one could understand the attraction that this type of voice might have for an adolescent with awakening sexual urges. Another semiotic connection may be found in the relationship between high-pitchedness and age. Luchsinger and Arnold comment on the descent of the larynx to a lower level in man, as compared to the laryngeal position in most other mammals. 'To this day the human embryo repeats the same physiological development in the course of ontogenetic growth. In the fetus, and even in the newborn baby, the laryngeal vestibule has a considerably higher position than in the adult' (Luchsinger and Arnold 1965: 115). We could possibly interpret the overly high-pitched, strangulated voice of the rock singer as a simulation of a desperate infant cry, full of urgent appeal due to some sort of frustration or other, and, as such, a symbolic regression into infancy.

At the other end of the voice spectrum is the very deep male voice. We shall find the most outstanding examples among the Buddhist monks of Tibet.

EAST COMES WEST ONCE AGAIN

Here we shall look at some of the more recent influences on Western composition by non-Western musics, many coming from the East but some also borrowed from the far South and other non-Western cultures.

The most striking use of the overly low male voice occurs in the chants of the Tibetan tantric rituals. In his notes, accompanying the record *The Music of Tibet*,[10] Huston Smith relates the choice of the extremely low register (of fundamental tones in the vicinity of 59 Hz) to religious thought. Extreme register, as a metaphor, is to show floundering men the extent of their truly extraordinary potential. 'If this much, how much more?' these chants with their especially strong fifth and tenth harmonics seem to suggest. The deep tones imply also 'plenitude' and, through 'fear and fascination,' a 'spiritual tension we call awe.' This religion does not 'neglect the dark side of existence.' Both Huston Smith and the anonymous author of the jacket notes on the UNESCO record *Tibetan Ritual*,[11] acknowledge the important demonic-magical element in Tibetan religion. The latter finds at the alleged 'basis of this religion' 'a prehistoric animistic and shamanistic stratum with its profound awareness of the constant presence of the supernatural world and the significance of rites and music as means of communication with the spirits.' Kaufmann (Kaufmann 1975: 1–25) also confirms the presence of demonic-magical elements in Tibetan Buddhist chant.

We find evidences for the influence of this chant in works by Ligeti, Xenakis, and Schafer. In Ligeti's *Requiem* (1963–5), for large chorus and orchestra, the opening movement, 'Introitus,' begins with similar very deep, sounds in two trombones followed by the entry of the basses, divided into four parts, singing slowly in the deepest register either sustained tones or small intervals, evoking the impression of a *rag-dung* drone of a Tibetan ritual (Kaufmann 1975: 16). Throughout the movement the initial subdued and mysterious mood is maintained: it suggests itself almost as a collective, very slow-moving exorcism ritual. Xenakis depicts a different kind of fear in his unaccompanied choral composition *Nuits* (1967–8). With it he commemorates (i.e. exorcises the memory of) the death and sufferings of political prisoners during the years 1946–1952. Xenakis himself, as we saw (141), knew the fear of persecution, experiencing it through sound (Souster 1968). The piece begins with loud wail-like shrieking, in high register, by the sopranos divided into three parts.[12] Following this, the basses, also divided in three groups, set in with loud, angry, gliding sounds on the unintelligible syllables 'YA, RA, SA' in the deepest register, somewhat like the 'rough,' 'roaring' style in certain Tibetan chants (Kaufmann 1975: 14), as if reciting the *yang-yig*, appealing to a 'terror deity' (2). The two choral gestures, the shrieking-wailing and the angry, quasi-menacing growling, recur in anti-phonal fashion five times.

Schafer's *Patria II* is a theatrical work of the genre that the composer calls 'theatre of confluence' (Schafer 1979: 30–48). Among the themes of the piece are mental illness, alienation, the absurdity in human relationships, and the merging of real experience into the dream image and vice versa. Even the identity of its heroine, Ariadne, is in doubt: at times she is a young woman, at other times a child; she also appears as a dead soul. All these help to create a surrealistic atmosphere. Schafer's extraordinarily wide grasp of the history of diverse cultures is in evidence. He uses, metaphorically, the word almagest to refer to the closed society of a mental asylum with its patients, nurses and psychiatrists and to the 'universe of activity' that takes place there, that includes in its manifestations 'convulsive' movement, cata-leptic stiffness, strained laughter, gurgles, moans, and other emotive vocali-zations. The movement entitled 'Almagest' (pages 11–17 in the score) precedes the one called 'Bardo Thödol' (18–33), which consists of the chorus *From the Tibetan Book of the Dead*, sung in Tibetan. The music begins with male chanting 'as deep as possible at first under the tape, then gradually louder. Pitch ad lib but following the speech contours, gliding very reso-nantly.' The character of this is, once again, that of the Tibetan Buddhist chant. The text begins with the words (translated into English): 'O nobly-born, the time hath now come for thee to seek the path.' Ariadne is about to experience 'the reality' of 'the clear light ... in the Bardo state.' She is being prepared for an initiatory 'spiritual exercise in order to anticipate the process of cosmic reabsorption that occurs at death' (Eliade 1969: 272). Schafer pre-served the authenticity of the text here, recognizing the belief in the power of certain mystical phonetic constructs – *mantras* and *dharanis* – in Buddhist as well as Śivaist tantric practice (212).

An earlier example of this orientation in choral music is Wladimir Vogel's *Wagadus Untergang durch die Eitelkeit* (1930) (Wagadu's Destruction on Account of Vanity), for solos, mixed choir, and five saxophones, based on fragments from the *Dausi*, the book of heroes of the Kabyles, edited by the Africanist Leo Frobenius. Certain parts of the work deserve attention on account of the measure of affinity it managed to achieve with its chosen milieu: for example, the plaintive, sung women's chorus[13] and the speaking chorus, repeatedly reciting the names(?) Agada, Dierra, Ganna, Silla, and Fasa, intact as well as fragmented, seemingly imitating some sort of ritual.[14]

I recall with particular vividness an attempt at transplanting an accompa-nied Javanese song into a Western setting. The piece was one of a group recorded by the German ethnomusicologist Eric M. Hornbostel and made public in the mid-1930s. A transcription of it, for a group of Western instruments (no vocalist was used), was made by Zoltán Pongrácz.[15] The most interesting feature was the choice of the medium to which the voice part, with its somewhat uncertain intonation, and child-like, innocent, nasal voice quality, was assigned. In a concert performance in 1942, which I attended, this part was played on a double-bass, throughout in a very high register on the G string, with a built-in uncertainty of intonation and precariousness of tone control and a good approximation of nasality throughout, in a vibrato-free playing, creating an analogue to child-like innocence.

Stockhausen's long-standing fascination with Eastern cultures is well known. His published statements and other manifestations of this affinity drew responses: some sympathetic, some uncomprehending, even suspicious or derisive. *Stimmung* (1967) appears to be the composer's first realization of a meditative state of mind through music. Its repetitive features find analogies in the *dhikr* practice of the Sufi orders of Islam (Trimingham 1971; Rouget 1980)[16] and the *nembutsu* of Chinese Buddhism in India (Suzuki 1950). The erotic aspects of the work, on first thought appearing incongruous in this context, subsequently fit well with the rest of the piece as soon as one realizes that Stockhausen probably derived his ideas from the mystical conception of eroticism that has existed in India since Vedic times. It included a view of 'conjugal union as a hierogamy' (Eliade 1969: 254) (sacred marriage), whereby the sexual act is transformed into a ceremony. 'The woman is first transfigured; she becomes the consecrated place where the sacrifice is performed' (255). Other features in *Stimmung*, the sequence of vowels, the control of their spectra and the transitions related to these, as well as the repertories of magical names, show the influence of Graeco-Egyptian magical papyri of the early centuries AD, with their arcane vowel series and lists of god and demon names.[17] Stockhausen's '*Am Himmel wandre ich ...*' (1972) ('In the sky I am walking ...'), a series of settings of American Indian songs, is a part of a larger work, *Alphabet für Liège* (1972), but can be performed separately. It consists of twelve duos for unaccompanied voices. The first piece uses but a single pitch; the second piece two pitches, and so on, concluding with a twelve-tone melos in the last movement. In addition to this controlled-pitch material, and the intelligible texts set in English, the performers also utter 'onomatopoeic articulations,' 'unusual calls,' and 'arbitrary names ... freely chosen by the interpreters: interjections, free intimate texts, a freely told fairy tale which is about sounds, also names, or purely tonal vowel and consonant formations.'[18] As we shall see in the next two chapters, most of these sound-types originate in other universes of thought and language use than the rational layer of our culture. We are dimly aware that this piece may be intended as a simulated ceremony of some kind. We shall consider this matter in detail later in this study (203–5); for the time being one might refer usefully to some of the numerous publications that mention rhythmic repetition and the use of meaningless syllables, etc, and to the contexts in which they might occur, in non-Western cultures. (Sachs 1943: 31; Bowra 1962: 57–61; Eliade 1958: 213–14; 1964: 96–9). Malinowski, for example, commenting on 'the texts and formulas of primitive magic,' identifies the following 'typical elements associated with the belief of magical efficiency': 'There are first, the phonetic effects, imitations of natural sounds, such as the whistling of the wind, the growling of the thunder, the roar of the sea, the voices of various animals. These sounds symbolize certain phenomena and thus are believed to produce them magically. Or else they express certain emotional states associated with the desire which is to be realized by means of magic' (Malinowski 1954: 73–4).

Berio's *Coro*; Schafer's *Gita*, *Divan i Shams i Tabriz*, *In Search of Zoroaster*, and *Apocalypsis*; Somers's *Death of Enkidu: Part I*; and Nørgård's *Gilgamesh* are also works that explore some aspects of civilizations other than the Judaeo-Christian.[19]

The opinions of Stockhausen, Nono, and Kagel on this topic might be well worth examining. The strong interest Stockhausen has developed in Japanese music is well known. We should, however, take cognizance of certain problems he was prepared to face up to after the completion of *Telemusik*: 'I have the feeling that one ought to control very, very carefully what one incorporates of "old" into the "new," and whether one has the strength to make the "new," the unknown, so strong and clear that the "old" serves only as a bridge to our past, without becoming more important than the "new"; otherwise it would truly function as a regressive step, or an atavism' (Stockhausen 1978 IV: 457). In an exchange with an unidentified questioner, Stockhausen preferred not to appear as a purist when it comes to the integration of materials from Gagaku music into Western-type musical forms (461). Elsewhere, however, he seems to express a deeper commitment to authenticity in this respect: 'The great shock occurs then, when someone, following a harmless curiosity with regard to a foreign culture will be so much taken by an event, that one falls in love without restraint. One cannot take home live music, a temple-ceremony, a dance. Either one has to remain there, or the longing will appear in the most unexpected moments, when one is, once again, at home ... These are, then, discoveries of the innermost self, within which everything, whatever has taken place on this earth, lies dormant ... When this fundamental layer has been touched, the yearning for bringing the *whole diversity* alive, and wanting to experience it, will never again fall asleep' (472). But realizing an inherent problem in this, he adds, almost immediately, the caveat: 'Therein lies the great danger, constantly moving in all registers and thereby losing all the strength that, before, was anchored in the tremendous concentration and one-sidedness of specific music cultures and specific forms in these cultures' (473).

This ambivalence is understandable. An artist, however interested and confident, may feel dwarfed by the enormous weight of knowledge that would be necessary for approximating the fiction of a universal composer. Speaking about this problem from the vantage point of communities of composers, however, the collective attitude might well prove to be different.

Kagel's position is quite at variance with Stockhausen's (and is borne out by his output at least up to the mid-1970s): 'This turning-back towards Asia has something of the fruitless search, for solitary islands, for the Garden of Eden. Since I know that reality is infinitely harder, I am against such substitutes.' He professes, though, to be in favour of 'intensive and thorough' study of the East which, he hopes, will lead to 'folkloristic knowledge,' with which one can 'actually operate' (Kagel 1975: 137).

Nono gives an account of a broad interest in the human voice, 'free or freed from all "a priori" or artificial scale, extraordinary in its great technical, phonetic and semantic wealth, still more comprehensive in the contrast between singing and speaking.' 'The "bel canto" employs only a part of the technical and acoustical possibilities of the voice, similarly to the rhythmic speaking and speech-song [*Sprechgesang*]. An analytical and comparative research of the various parts of the vocal apparatus itself (such as the Italian or the Japanese for example), in conjunction with phonetics of various spoken languages, with the various technical, physiological-acoustical expressive means of the voice, is fundamental. Similarly fundamental is the comparative study of vocal usage according to the habits and practices in various societies and cultures. For the past several years I have been studying physical-acoustical texts from Japan, India, those of Gypsies of Andalusia, several synagogues, especially of the USSR and Poland, and of certain African peoples' (Nono 1975: 190). Nono's work has a communist-oriented ideological component, and includes also attention to linguistic features related to the working class.

Chou Wen-chung, in his article 'Asian Music and Western Composition' (Vinton 1971: 24–9), briefly mentions several works by present-day Western-born composers in which Asiatic vocal elements are, in his opinion, suitably integrated. He gives a positive assessment to the work of José Maceda, but denies this to works, with a 'similar use of phonemes,' by Nono, Berio,

Martirano and other Western composers. Most of the music he mentions is instrumental.

Robert Palmer's 'The Resounding Impact of Third-World Music,'[20] with a somewhat more popular orientation, is a useful complement to Chou Wen-chung's contribution and makes a few brief references to vocal music, but also concentrates on the instrumental kind.

Both authors have seen that instrumental borrowings from non-Western cultures have by far exceeded vocal transfers. It has seemed easier to a Western-educated musician to learn certain non-Western instrumental techniques than vocal techniques. As a result, when certain non-Western vocal techniques were seemingly borrowed the results frequently failed to have the ring of authenticity. The situation is improving, however. Such specially trained performers or composer-performers as Tamia, Ed Herbst, or Deborah Kavásch of the Extended Vocal Techniques Ensemble have mastered, to a virtuoso degree, certain non-Western performance techniques and, to a certain extent, compositional procedures. (I am thinking especially of Kavásch's *Requiem*, Tamia's *Senza tempo*, and Herbst's *From Pine Tree to Spring.*) But is the 'authenticity of reproduction' of such a model necessarily an indispensable criterion for the appropriateness and the musical worth of an invented vocal event? I do not think so. The degree of worth or appositeness would depend on the function the composer assigns to such an event, and the result achieved.

About fifteen years ago I became acquainted with a recording[21] of a *gidayu-bushi* recitation, which is normally a part of a Bunraku performance. In 1976, with the help of J.L.M. Trim and Francis Nolan and the evaluative assistance of John Laver, I made a spectrographic-phonetic analysis of a few fragments of that material. The special, characterizing features in this recitation seemed to include the consistent and frequent use of high, or very high, and low, or very low, positions of the larynx; pharyngeal constriction; harshness in phonation; and an expert use of the creak.[22] Some of the fragments also included modulations from one vowel sound to another with changes in the formant structure being quite perceivable, especially at slower-than-normal playback speeds (Example 5.1).[23]

I have noted apparent similarities between certain features of this fragment from a *gidayu-bushi* and some of the vocal techniques used in Maxwell Davies's *Eight Songs for a Mad King*. The latter is an important work in the new vocal repertoire because of its central idea, its vocal technique, its integration of vocal and instrumental layers, expressed in terms of a wide variety of stylistic elements, and its extraordinary expressive range and convincing formal design. Its use of the solo voice interests us foremost in the present

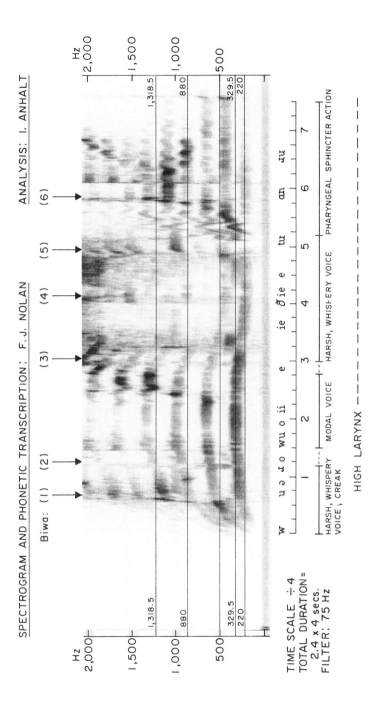

Example 5.1 Analysis of part of a *gidayu-bushi* recitation

context. I propose that we take a close look at the very first phrase of the baritone soloist sung to the following text:[24] 'Good day to your Honesty.' As notated (Example 5.2), the phrase consists of a chord, a descending glide from a very high tone onto which a rapid tremolo is superimposed, two modal tones with strong fundamentals and second harmonics, and a concluding loud breathy roar. In the recorded performance of this phrase by Julius Eastman,[25] made under the direction of the composer, the acoustic reality is at considerable variance with the intended model. These differences include the absence of the initial chord, the substitution of pitches different from those notated, and a host of voice quality modulations to which no references exist in the score. I have attempted to notate as much information as I was able to hear, in a form that allowed me to represent all the details that seemed relevant. The resulting format is a kind of score, showing the approximate fundamental-pitch line of the actual performance, with rough indications of the dynamics; a phonetic transcription of the performed text, showing that Eastman has changed 'your' to 'thy'; indication of the total duration (within which the distribution of the sub-events is given only in rough approximation); and my conjectures as to the voice qualities used and the sequence of their unfolding, through various compounds, transitions, and in relationship to the other parameters (Example 5.3).

Both the *gidayu-bushi* fragment and the phrase recorded by Julius Eastman use the voice qualities of harshness, creak, and modal voice as well as pharyngeal sphincter action[26] and high laryngeal position. In the expressive domain one also notes similarities, particularly when one compares the entire works of which they are but small parts. Maxwell Davies, I believe, was influenced by the great emotive range and intensity of the traditional *gidayu-bushi* narrator. Eta Harich-Schneider says that the *gidayu*-singer 'must have an extraordinary compass of voice – he sings the parts of all *dramatis personae* from the timid virgin to the awe-inspiring villain – but he must also be a great actor. His is an exhausting task' (Harich-Schneider 1973: 525). Maxwell Davies writes: 'The sounds made by human beings under extreme duress, physical and mental, will be at least in part familiar. With Roy Hart's [who probably sang the work at the première] extended vocal range, and his capacity for producing chords with his voice ... these poems of Randolph Stow presented a unique opportunity to categorize and exploit these techniques *to explore certain extreme regions of experience.*'[27] The respective idioms of both pieces require an extraordinarily wide effective range, and Maxwell Davies's work explores parts of the domain of the pathological expressions of the voice.

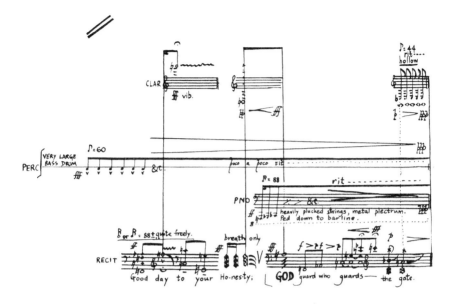

2

Example 5.2 Peter Maxwell Davies *Eight Songs for a Mad King*

Example 5.3 Analysis of Julius Eastman's performance of a phrase from Peter Maxwell Davies *Eight Songs for a Mad King*

There is nothing essentially new about cultural borrowing. Japan is one of the prime practitioners of this process. Writing about the gagaku, William P. Malm comments: 'When one views the overall history of ancient Asia, Japan can often be seen as a kind of cultural *cul-de-sac*. The traditions of the ancient Near East and India came across the trade routes to China and from there were passed over the sea to Japan. They could go no further. Asian cultures, so to speak, piled up in Japan like water behind a dam.'[28] Lawrence Picken gives other interesting examples for such migrations in his remarkable treatise, *Turkish Folk Music Instruments*. Even Tibetan Buddhist chant, a practice one would consider more isolated than most, allegedly shows traces of the influence of gnostic practices that supposedly originated in the eastern Mediterranean region about 2,000 years ago.

What do seem novel in recent years are both the rate and the variety of such exchanges. We shall encounter additional examples in subsequent pages.

6

Deep themes, not so hidden

'Cosmogony myth ... sacrifice ... mystical writings ... a ... totem ... a primitive initiation rite ... the symbolism of a temple ... ceremonial costumes and dances ... sacred stones ... agricultural ceremonies ... Each must be considered as a hierophany in as much as it expresses in some way some modality of the sacred and some moment in its history ... We must get used to the idea of recognizing hierophanies absolutely everywhere, in every area of psychological, economic, spiritual and social life. Indeed, we cannot be sure that there is *anything* – object, movement, psychological function, being or even game – that has not at some time in human history been somewhere transformed into a hierophany' (Eliade 1958: 2, 11).

'The question concerning the origin of the work of art asks about its essential source. On the usual view the work arises out of and by means of the activity of the artist. But by what and whence is the artist what he is? ... In the art work, the truth of being has set itself to work. Art is truth setting itself to work ... To be a work means to set up a world ... Art ... is the becoming and happening of truth' (Heidegger 1971: 149, 166, 170, 183).

In the works that constitute the repertoire we are studying, there appears to be a number of recurring themes. Each of them points either to a central or a characteristic aspect of our civilization.

We often find a theme or themes at varying depths below the surface of a composition; I suggest that we call these core topics deep themes. The purpose of this chapter is to identify at least some of these and to discuss briefly their nature, their provenance, and the ways in which they imprint their mark on the works concerned.

We shall consider the following as possible deep themes: hallowed names and cursed names; repetition as a mythical or mystical technique; the arcane again; magical elements in music and language; the hierophany of childhood; the hierophany of the victim and the substitute celebration of the absurd; performance of music as a spectacle or celebration; and the search for the past.

We can, of course, find examples for most (perhaps for each) of these themes in works that were composed in earlier periods. The recent repertoire, however, gives voice to these themes in a somewhat different manner from the way this was achieved earlier: the emphases, the means, and/or the contexts are likely to be different to a lesser or greater extent.

HALLOWED NAMES AND CURSED NAMES

Just as Dante needed the guiding hand of Virgil in his perilous descent, so most of us (Freud and Jung are among the exceptions) feel the necessity for supporting hands of a mentor or a psychopomp in our moments of uncertainty or questioning. The quotations at the beginning of this chapter help to set a course by invoking the ideas and the intellectual authority of their authors. As such, they function as *mezzuzahs*, fastened to a doorpost, to direct the passing spirits, some of whom might be ready to accept their guidance.

As previous periods, our time also has its public heroes, chosen according to values and beliefs groups of people share. (This, of course, does not preclude private shrines or pantheons for individuals.) For many contemporary artists, writers, and musicians, such figures as Mallarmé, Proust, Freud, Jung, Einstein, Wittgenstein, Joyce, Valéry, Picasso, Stravinsky, Schoenberg, Berg, Webern, Bartók, Kandinskij, Beckett, and Martin Luther King serve as guiding lights. There are also spirits of darkness around, some designated by their proper names, some by the names of places where they did their dreadful deeds. Among the latter are the demon without peer, Hitler, with his retinue of adjunct-demons, and places such as Auschwitz, Guernica, My-Lai, Coventry, Dresden, and Warsaw, where something bad of such magnitude has occurred that a group has committed the memory to its collective consciousness and, probably in time, to its collective unconscious.

As to their presence in music, first we look at Cage's *Song Books*, volumes I and II. In the general directions to the score, Cage gives an implied key to the whole work: 'Each solo is relevant or irrelevant to the subject: "We connect Satie with Thoreau."'

Anyone familiar with Cage's work knows of his deep and long-standing attachment to both Satie and Thoreau. He probably considers them among the most influential of his intellectual and spiritual ancestors. Satie offers a model for his whimsy, gentility, iconoclasm, and horror of everything that smacks even remotely of the officious or the pompous. From Thoreau he seems to have learned to accept and love nature, to live a life anchored in independence, guided by disdain for the normal instruments of material security; to lecture; and to collect (Cage is a gatherer, a mycologist, and a collector of bits and pieces of our technological environment, with some of which he makes sounds).

Several of the songs[1] have as their texts fragments, mixes, collages, and so on taken and assembled from Thoreau's *Journal*, nos. 3, 4, 5, 17, 20, 30, 49, and 85; words from the first paragraph of his *Essay on Civil Disobedience*, nos. 34 and 35; and fragments from unidentified source(s), nos. 52 and 53. In no. 5 the melodic line is to be derived by 'wandering over' the portrait of Thoreau himself. No. 81 calls for the projection of 'four slides relevant to Thoreau,' and no. 86 calls for twenty-two of the same. No. 15 calls for public typing (using a 'typewriter equipped with contact microphones'), thirty-eight times, of a statement by Satie. (Note also the deliciously mischievous opposition between the sentence in question – 'L'artiste n'a pas le droit de disposer inutilement du temps de son auditeur' – and the scenario that frames it.) No. 18 is an anagram of the syllables of part III ('Mort de Socrate') of Satie's *Socrate*. Nos. 21, 33, 43, 52, 53, and 56 also use texts of, or related to, Satie. The names and texts of Norman O. Brown, Marcel Duchamp, Merce Cunningham, and Marshall McLuhan also appear. (In another genre he calls mesostic,[2] Cage celebrates other names, including that of James Joyce.)

Schnebel's *Glossolalie* is composed in flexible form, consisting of twenty-six unbound pages of materials and instructions, on the basis of which any number of realizations can be made. In 1961, Schnebel composed one such realization for three (or four) speakers and three (or four) instrumentalists. The work is characterized by irony, mockery, a confusion of attitudes and values, castigation of sentimentality, displays of vulgarity, absurdity, the cacophonous interplay of voices oblivious of each other, and a gradual but predictable disintegration of language itself into gibberish.[3] Some of its logorrhoeas consist exclusively of names. To one group belong those of Schoenberg, Joyce, Helms, Malewitsch, Benjamin, Boulez, Proust, Webern, Freud, Pollock, Cage, Brecht, Heisenberg, Kafka, and others; to another those of Liz Taylor, Jurij Gagarin, Brigitte Bardot, and others of popular fame. A concurrent list of politically charged place names includes Laos, Kuba (sic), Algérie, and Berlin. Schnebel has still another list in close juxtaposition, containing concept words, such as oscillation and solar, denoting characteristic concerns of the times.[4]

The second movement of Berio's *Sinfonia* is a setting of the name of Martin Luther King, employing the phonetic elements of this name for the purpose. In the third movement, in a moment of rare serenity and peace, Berio makes the first tenor say the following words: 'The fact is I trouble no one. But I did. And after each group disintegration, the name of Majakowsky hangs in the clean air.' It is a beautiful moment, and the name of the poet rings with an echo of conflicting overtones for all who know about the role he played in Russian poetry and public life and about his tragic death.

Schafer's involvement with Ariadne resulted in several works in which she is a central figure (although, at least on the surface, she has little in common with the mythical saviour of Theseus).[5] The title of his *In Search of Zoroaster* is explicit with regard to the present theme.

Somers composed his opera *Louis Riel* partly as an atonement for what he regards as Riel's judicial murder. It is also a powerful statement about past and present tensions between the two dominant cultures of Canada.

At the outset of my *La Tourangelle*, the three solo sopranos intone the names by which the work's heroine, Marie de l'Incarnation, is known: 'La vénérable Ursuline de Tours,' 'Marie Guyart,' 'Marie Martin,' 'Mère spirituelle,' 'Supérieure des Ursulines de la Nouvelle France'; each phrase is an invocation.

The recurring enumerations of place names in Beckwith and James Reaney's *Canada Dash – Canada Dot* define, in an intermittent, quasi-ritualistic manner, a geographical area holy to some of its native inhabitants. Other lists include names given to the moon, to months (focusing on a cyclical rather than a historical conception of time), and to trees (perhaps a fragment of a native taxonomical system?); names of dead politicians (like faded pictures in a family album); and advertising slogans repeated surreptitiously (latter-day incantational formulas).

In *Stimmen*, Henze tries to exorcise the dark memory of the names of Guernica and Berchtesgaden, among others. He sets the words of Erich Fried in a dramatic arioso: 'What did the pupils of Mang Quang learn about the bombs? What did we learn from the pupils of Mang Quang?'

The magic names in Stockhausen's *Stimmung* bring us to a conception of music in which ritual of an unspecified sort merges with musical performance (to be discussed later).

It has been suggested that 'to know the name of a man means ... to know his real essence, and to grasp his soul ... To the view of early man, the name and the soul were one and the same thing' (Izutsu 1956: 22, 23). Izutsu enlarges on this, by asserting with Walter Porzig: 'To mean something by means of speech is no other than a weakened form of the intention of binding it magically ... Whenever and wherever man is moved by the desire to get possession of a specified piece of reality he gives it a name; the name once fixed, he can at will conjure up the thing designated and exercise over it whatever control he pleases by simply uttering the name' (50–1). The same appears to hold true for sacred names and for the names of demons, but these have to be handled with special care. One method for this may be to surround the powerful name with proper exclamations. Jules Combarieu, in his remarkable account (Combarieu 1908) of relationships between music and magic, gives the following example (a Pawnee text) for such an invocation:[6]

> Ho-o-o!
> I'hare, 'hare, ahe!
> I'hare, 'hare, ahe!
> Heru! AWAHOKSHU. He!
> I'hare, 'hare, ahe.

In this stanza there is but one word that is a name: AWAHOKSHU. All the other words are exclamations.

A.H. Fox Strangways reported an event experienced at a prayer ceremony conducted by the Kānika tribe in the Hindustan. It consisted of violent trembling spreading among a group of men upon hearing the repeated recitation (in no particular order) of the names of twenty or thirty divinities.[7]

Both of these examples are reported to involve repetition as an important structural or procedural device. In much of the music of the 1950s (especially of the serial kind) repetition was a procedure (structure) to be shunned;[8] in the 1960s and 1970s, more composers of both instrumental and vocal music resorted to this device, in some cases making repetition the central stylistic trait of their music.[9] We shall now consider this procedure more closely.

REPETITION AS A MYSTICAL OR MYTHICAL TECHNIQUE

Most of the compositions we shall consider under this heading show unmistakable affinity to meditative, religious or mystical attitudes and resemblances to magical techniques. This makes it necessary that we look at the practices upon which they might have modelled themselves. These will include the Buddhist *Nembutsu* practice (Suzuki 1950 II: 132–86), the Sufi way (*tariqa*) of Muslim ascetics, directed towards the goal of mystical understanding through recollection (*dhikr*) (Trimingham 1971: 194–217; Rouget 1980), and the discipline consisting of the use of the mystical syllable OM in Indian yogic meditative technique (Eliade 1969; Müller 1879: xxiii, 1–3).

Nembutsu means 'to think of the Buddha' or 'to meditate on the Buddha' (Suzuki: 1950 II: 141). It is based on the idea of substitution of the name for the Buddha himself. 'Name is as good as substance' (141). For some, 'the Nembutsu consists in intensely thinking of the thirty-two marks of excellence possessed by the Buddha, by holding them in mind in a state of concentration' (145). The practice involves 'the mechanical repetition of the Nembutsu, that is, the rhythmic though monotonous utterance of the Buddha name, 'na-mu-a-mi-da-bu' ... over again and again, tens of thousands of times [creating] a state of consciousness which tends to keep down all the ordinary functions of the mind' for the purpose of acquiring 'a most significant insight into the nature of Reality' (147).

Through the Sufi *dhikr* ceremony, the *murīd* (disciple) hopes 'to purify his *nafs* (the lower "self") as to attain union with God' (Trimingham 1971: 194). The first of its several parts consists of the repetition of each of three short formulas, thirty-three times. After a period of concentrated meditative breathing, aimed at the attainment of 'occult recollection' (201–3), and other liturgical exercises, there begin the 'recitals in congregation, known as the *haḍra*,' which might include the loud communal recitation of the *tahlīl* formula (Lā ilāha illā 'llāh, meaning 'There is no god but God') (201). This might last for about two hours, but with variations.

One of the Upanishads, the *Māṇḍūkya*, provides 'details concerning the four states of consciousness and their relations with the mystical syllable *OM*' (Eliade 1969: 122), in which 'four elements can likewise be distinguished ... the letters A, U, M, and the final synthesis, the sound *OM*' (123). According to the *Nādabindu Upaniṣad* 'the mystical syllable *OM*' is imagined as a bird' (132). 'Like the *Nādabindu*, the *Dhyānabindu* begins with an iconographic description of the syllable *OM*, which is to be 'contemplated' as identical with Brahman' (133). *Prāṇāyāma* (the disciplining of respiration in yogic technique) 'should be performed up to a hundred times ... with mental repetition of the syllable *OM*' (136). Eliade also reports that the study of the syllable *OM* 'designates techniques concerned with mystical audition, with repetition and "assimilation" of particular magical formulas (*dhāraṇī*), with incantation, etc' (151). '*OM* is the *mantra* par excellence' (212). Depending on the degree of contemplative sophistication of its user, a *dhāraṇī* can be thought of as a talisman to 'protect against demons, diseases, and spells' (213), hence an instrument of magic. 'But for the ascetics, the yogins, the contemplatives, *dhāraṇīs* become instruments for concentration' (213).

The reappearance of repetition as a central structural feature in music probably indicates the reappearance of the mystical, magical, and (in some instances) the mythical core of music, as a facet of a unitary Orphic language. I would ask the reader to suspend judgment on this question until a subsequent argument here. In the mean time, we shall look at relevant compositions from the point of view of repetition as a structural feature.

In Stockhausen's *Stimmung*, the tones of a single five-note chord, fashioned after the harmonic partial series, are repeated throughout the piece, which lasts well over an hour. While repeating the tones of the chord, the six solo singers sing or utter sequences of vowels (controlling with utmost care their harmonic partial constituents), words (such as hallelujah or Dienstag, and consonant-vowel pairs, interspersed with such other material as magical names (the names of gods or sacred words), laughter, and whispery whistling. Stockhausen says that *Stimmung* is 'certainly meditative music' (Stockhausen 1978: 109). In it 'time is suspended. Man listens to the innermost content of the sound (Klang) right to the inside of the harmonic spectrum, into the inside of a vowel, *into the essence* (*ins Innere*) ... In the beauty of the perceptible (Sinnlichen) gleams the beauty of the eternal' (109).

Philip Glass is one of the best known composers of minimal music, a genre that consistently draws on repetition as its major formal procedure. His recently premièred opera *Satyagraha*, 'which is a large-scaled three-act account of M.K. Gandhi's 21 years in South Africa' on a libretto based 'exclusively of excerpts from the *Bhagavad-Gita* recited in Sanskrit,' is reported to have a 'monumentally slow action and numbingly repetitive music.'[10] 'The music ... emulate(s) from start to finish the static whirring of a spinning wheel.' To this the critic has added that 'a trance, or a slowing down of the mind is likely crucial to the appreciation of Glass's art.'[11]

The original utterance of the phrase 'Come out to show them,' upon which Steve Reich based his tape piece *Come out*, was made by a man arrested and subsequently accused of murder and allegedly beaten by police. The tape layers (both containing the same sentence) gradually slowly separate from each other in the course of the piece, through differing durations, creating a sort of canonic ostinato, which functions with a hypnotic effect. After a relatively short time, the words begin to lose their semantic-syntactic meaning and fuse into a single acoustical-phonetical Gestalt. An identical effect is achieved in Charles Amirkhanian's text-sound piece *If in Is*, which is based on the repeated utterances of the words 'Inini, bullpup, banjo,' and his *Just*, which repeats the words 'rainbow, chug, bandit and bomb.'

The predictable neuro-biological effects of such repetitions seem to be part of the strategy of the composers and the sound-poet mentioned here. Barbara Lex (Lex 1971) has reported on fairly extensive recent research in this area. Citing E.D. Chapple, she writes: 'Regular and driving rhythms ... must synchronize the rhythms of muscular activity centered in the brain and nervous system' (122). She refers to 'a shift from the time-binding, verbal, linear mode of thought into a timeless, oceanic gestalt,' which, according to Neher's research on auditory driving, 'also provides an explanation for subjective reports of temporal distortion and unusual sensations – often inexpressible experiences – presented by persons who have undergone ritual trance' (125–6).

No. 64 in volume II of Cage's *Song Books* calls for 127 statements of the Japanese phrase 'NICHI NICHI KORE KO,' meaning 'Every day is a beautiful day' (Cage 1961: 41), which is to be shouted 'at highest volume without feedback like a football cheer-leader,' thus vulgarizing (at least for those who do not understand Japanese) the arcane and incantational effect of a repeated unintelligible phrase.[12]

In Somers's *Zen, Yeats, and Emily Dickinson*, a four-channel pre-recorded tape provides a repetitive spoken layer while a solo soprano sings vowel and unintelligible iterative phoneme-sequences, accompanied by two speaking voices, a piano, and a flute.

The repetitive elements in Schafer's *In Search of Zoroaster* and in Berio's *Coro* function at a different structural plane; we shall discuss these two works in chapter 8.

THE ARCANE AGAIN

Even the simple-sounding, repetitive pieces of Steve Reich or Phil Glass contain potential for transcendence in the direction of the mysterious, the arcane, as one shifts focus from the piece itself to the condition of the hearer. The arcane component is in this case in the human response, rather than in the stimulus.

The growth in appreciation of the music of Schoenberg, of Berg, and especially of Webern following the Second World War by a leading group of young composers (Boulez, Stockhausen, Nono, Berio) may reflect both a preference for something presumably untainted by certain former associations and an expression of an affinity to works that are complex and cerebral. The resulting short-lived extension of the serial idea, in a repertoire mostly of arid works, gave way to a multiplicity of orientations, including the one we are studying here. The fascination with the arcane – a part of all mannerist art and literature (Hocke 1959) – has remained, however, even after the waning of the serial mirage.

Cage's diverse, arcane ways of transforming order into disorder draw attention to certain forms of organization (linguistic, musical, social, and so on) by the very act of destroying them, especially when he does this in a graduated fashion as in nos. 3–5 in volume I of *Song Books*.

Kagel's *Anagrama* is based on a mediaeval palindrome: 'In girum imus nocte et consumimur igni' (We circle in the night and are consumed by fire). It refers to the nocturnal predicament of moths, but also has power as an allegory. Kagel submitted this text to an intricate disintegrative process, and the resulting debris spawned words and sentences (many of the latter surrealistic in character) in a number of modern languages, for example: 'numero hermetico,' 'consumir nuestro insomnio,' 'heresie incontinente.' Each of these involves the phenomenon of semantic absurdity, on account of what T. Drange calls type-crossing (Drange 1966). The three appearances of the word hermetico alludes to the hermetic tradition, and the appearance of a wing-shaped construct, containing all the consonants of the source palindrome (on page 9 in the score), confirms this orientation for a fleeting moment:

n
n g
n g R
n g R m
n g R m s
n g R m ʃ k
n g R m z (k) t
e e e e e e e oe (∅)[13]

Schnebel's :!, the work with the unpronouncable title (for which he supplies the alternative *Madrasha II*), has an arcane character that matches that of its title. Its overall character is that of a group of people who are trying to speak but cannot. Fragments of a language are still recognizably present, but the persons concerned are prevented from using it, probably not so much on account of an extraneous interdiction, but more probably as a result of an inhibition, derived from their individual and/or collective psyches.

Pousseur's *Mnemosyne I* and *Mnemosyne II* speak, in words borrowed from Hölderlin, of the loss of man's identity as well as his language. Michaux's conclusion for 'Le Grand Combat' is a search for the 'grand secret.' Nobody seems to know for certain the identity of the Godot for whom Beckett's two tramps (that is, a part of humanity) are waiting – it does not even seem to matter; what *does* count is waiting itself: 'as an essential and characteristic aspect of the human condition' (Esslin 1961: 17). Why does Claude Vivier in his *Chants* say 'airam,' 'nema,' 'atatacnasi,' and 'sibon,' instead of 'Maria,' 'amen,' 'sancta,' and 'nobis'? Why the concealment, or the play with words?

The repertoire of contemporary vocal and choral composition is saturated with works that use only unintelligible texts.[14] What are we to make of this trend? The identity of Schafer's Ariadne remains uncertain despite (perhaps because of) the several works in which she appears. A recent piece of his, *La Testa d'Adriane*, has an anagram of that name. Why does this Adriane appear only as a head placed on a magician's table in a circus setting? Perhaps the entirety of Cage's *Song Books*, which can be assembled into one piece any number of ways, is a kind of mad poem ('Irrgedicht') or a 'Carmen Labyrintheum,' which can be read from the left or from the right, from the top and from the bottom as well as diagonally.[15] (Aren't we reminded by this also of the way Berio 'read' Markus Kutter's text in *Sequenza III*?) Is there a key to this propensity for the arcane, for the concealed? If so, what might it be?

Jorge Luis Borges, perhaps the greatest living author of the arcane, quotes in 'The Mirror of Enigmas' one of his avatars, De Quincey (Borges 1964: 209): 'Even the articulate or brutal sounds of the globe must be all so many languages and ciphers that somewhere have their corresponding keys – have their own grammar and syntax; and thus the least things in the universe must be secret mirrors to the greatest.' A Muslim text reportedly dating from between 1246 and 1318 expresses the nature of the key in these terms: 'All secrets of God are to be found in heavenly books, the content of these in the Koran, that of the Koran in the 1st Sura, that of this Sura in the 1st verse, that of this verse, in the first letter of the same, and that of this letter in the point that lies at the bottom of it' (Dornseiff 1922: 134).

There is a familiar ring to these mystical formulations. Jacqueline de Romilly also heard them echoing from the fourth century BC, when, as she writes, irrational currents of thought began to contend with earlier, prevailing, rational ones. She sees a parallel to this also in the poetic outlooks of Baudelaire and Mallarmé (Romilly 1975). Frances Yates, in her turn, wrote about the inability of 'the late antique world(s)' 'to carry Greek science forward any further.' Consequently it 'turned to the religious cult of the world and its accompanying occultisms and magics' (Yates 1964: 449). Further on, she compares (after Festugière) 'the appearance of the Magus ideal in the Renaissance as similarly a retreat from the intense rationalism of mediaeval scholasticism' (449).

In our repertoire Stockhausen's real or apparent turning from the rational quasi-scientific conceptions in some of his earlier works (*Kontrapunkte*, *Studie II*, aspects of *Gesang der Jünglinge*) towards the arcane and the mystical and Schafer's longstanding affinity for German Romantic thought and literature and for Jung's work are but two manifestations of this trend.

What is behind this development? Does it indicate the most recent change of phase of the immense pendulum of Western civilization, which has, since the eighteenth century, defined successive phases: the Enlightenment,

Romanticism, scientific positivism, and now the emergence of a collective doubt about the idea of limitless and autonomous technological progress?[16] In what ways do composers give expression to irrational, mystical, magical, and other related tendencies of the mind? I suggest that the literature on vocal practices in Graeco-Egyptian magic, as well as reports on primitive magic, contain information relevant to these queries. To these we now shall turn.

MAGICAL ELEMENTS IN MUSIC AND LANGUAGE

E.M. Butler has stated: 'The fundamental aim of all magic is to impose the human will on nature, on man or on the supersensual world in order to master them' (Butler 1949: 3).[17] Frazer has reported the related apperception that 'the magician does not doubt that the same causes will always produce the same effects, that the performance of the proper ceremony accompanied by the appropriate spell, will inevitably be attended by the desired result, unless indeed, his incantations should chance to be thwarted and foiled by the more potent charms of another sorcerer' (Frazer 1922: 64). According to Frazer's definition the foundation of the magus's art (sympathetic magic) is the doctrine of correspondences, which are based on the two principles of similarity and contact (or contagion) (Frazer 1922: chapter 3). Of these only the first is operative in the oral and written devices of magic. From this, 'the magician infers that he can produce any effect he desires merely by imitating it' (14). His repertoire includes sound imitations, the deployment of names, and repetition.

Bowra in *Primitive Song* reports that, among the Yamanana, 'some of the shortest and simplest songs are charms or prayers' (Bowra 1968: 61) and observes that in certain songs of the bushman 'there is still some lingering element of magic,' but adds that they also 'show how the song moves from an immediately useful purpose to an element of art and pleasure' (62). Butler also points to 'evidence of creative instincts, poetical imagination and feeling for beauty and drama' in magical rituals (4). Combarieu observes that primitive 'magical chants contain, in an embryonic state, everything which later will constitute art proper' (Combarieu 1909: 12–3).

Frazer points out what he sees as the close analogy 'between the magical and scientific conceptions of the world' (Frazer 1922: 64). 'In both of them the succession of events is assumed to be perfectly regular and certain, being determined by immutable laws, the operation of which can be foreseen and calculated precisely' (64). In the light of this, the abstract vowel structures, and the manipulations (permutation, notation, retrograding, and so on) of the same, assume in Graeco-Egyptian magic a special signification. They appear as manifestations of the combinatorial-systematic propensity of the mind also involved in scientific speculation, in experiment, in certain kinds of musical construction (for which we shall shortly see examples), and even in play.

Where do these procedures and modes of thinking originate? Izutsu suggests that 'magical ritual must have been revealed to man in a number of subjective, emotional experiences, that, before being standardized into permanent forms, it must have long played its role as what may be best described as spontaneous ritual of emotional expression' (Izutsu 1956: 4). But what brought about such processes of standardizations? According to Izutsu's conjecture, 'we ought to assume that what is being perpetrated has been judged to have been efficacious, effective, on an earlier occasion' (4). But there is another complementary reason for the emergence of formulaic usage: this can be found, according to Izutsu, in 'the ... natural proclivity of the human mind towards ... symbol-making' (4). With this logical step we find ourselves having arrived at the thresholds of what we have come to call poetry, magic, and music. Repetition, attenuation of intensity and of feeling, formalization, and standardization might have been the major stations in the developments towards these practices.

Our primary written sources of 'savant' magic are the so-called Greek and Egyptian magical papyri, the first of which was transcribed and published before 1830.[18] I took the first example from such sources from papyrus XIII of *Papyri Graecae Magicae* (Preisendanz 1973 II: 86–131).[19] This is but a short fragment, lines 73 to 90, and constitutes what appears to be an invocation. I have selected it because it contains numerous oral and other sound devices: strange names of demons, vowel-assemblies, onomatopoeias that simulate animal 'language,' a paralinguistic sound (tongue-click), whistling, and clapping,[20] all of which have parallels in contemporary vocal music.

73 I appeal to you, Lord: appear to me in benevolent image, because I serve under
74 your world your angels Biathillarbar Berbir Schilatoyr Boyphroymtrōm and your fear Denoyph Chrator Belbali Balbith, 'Iaō. Through you did heaven and earth acquire order. I appeal to you, Lord, as to the gods, who have appeared on account of you, so that
79 they have obtained the power of Echebykrōm Hēlios, whose praise is: 'aaa ēēē | ōōō iii aaa ōōō, Sabaōth, Arbathiaō, Zagoyrē, Oh God Arathy Adōnaie.'
83 I appeal to you, Lord, in bird-language 'arai', in hiëroglyphics 'Laïlam', in Hebrew 'Anoch' Biathiarbath Berbir Echilatoyr Boyphroymtrōm, Egyptian 'Aldabaeim', as the dog-headed monkeys 'Abrasax', as the sparrow-hawks 'chi

chi chi chi chi chi chi, tiph tiph tiph', in the language of the priests 'mene-phōiphōth cha cha cha cha cha cha.'
89 Then clap three times, click a long time with your tongue, and whistle in a drawn-out way.

Our next example is from the same source; it consists of an invocation of a lord through imitating him, using the seven Greek vowels,[21] presumably as an instrument of sympathetic magic. Note the gradually accumulating character of the series:

207 Lord, I imitate you (follow your example) with the 7 vowels: come in and listen to me 'a ee ēēē iiii ooooo yyyyy ōōōōōōō, Abrōch, Braōch, Chrammaōth, Proarbathō, 'Iaō Oyaeēiōyō.'

The next contains a monster name (see also Hopfner 1974: chapter 3), in the form of a palindrome:

504 Her anagrammatical name is big and sacred and praiseworthy. It is very valu-able, a strong name 'Thoriobriti, tammaōrraggadōiōdaggarrōammatitirboiroth, 49 letters.

In the next example we can see the vowel series in various distributions:

856 Looking to the East say: 'a ee ēēē iiii ooooo yyyyy ōōōōōōō.
    I appeal to you, as the Southwind.' Looking to the South, say: 'ioo yyy ōōōō
    aaaaa eeeeee ēēēēēēē.
    I appeal to you as the Westwind.' Turn to the West and say:
861 'ē ii ooo yyyy ōōōōō aaaaaa eeeeee.
    I appeal to you as the Northwind.' Turn and look to the North and say:
864 'ō aa eee ēēēē iiiii oooooo yyyyyyy.
    I appeal to you as the Earth.' Looking toward the Earth say:
865 e ēē iii oooo yyyyy ōōōōōō aaaaaaa.
    I appeal to you as the Heaven.' Look towards the Heaven and say:
869 'y ōō aaa eeee ēēēēē iiiiii ooooooo.
    I appeal to you as the Cosmos:
    'o yy ōōō aaaa eeeee ēēēēēē iiiiii.

One example consists of the vowel series in three double wing-shaped figures (only two of the three are given here):

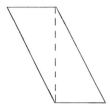

905 aeēioyō   aeēioyōō
    eēioyōa   eēioyōōa
    ēioyōae   ēioyōōae
    ioyōaeē   ioyōōaeē
    oyōaeēi   oyōōaeēi
    yōaeēio   yōoaeēio
    ōaeēioy   ōōaeēioy

A large klimata[22] from papyrus XVIII (Preisendanz 1973 II: 138), based on 'ablanathanalba' and 'akrammachamari,' is shown in Figure 6.1. Figure 6.2, from papyrus XIX (143), contains a giant grape-shaped vanishing palindrome, several wing-shaped texts, and other magical artifices.

Papyrus VII (lines 769–79) (II: 34) lists fourteen so-called unarticulated sounds (see also Hopfner 1974: 484), through which the magus expected to be able to impose his will on gods and other higher beings. The list contains the following (English equivalents translated from German): silence, tongue-clicking, sighing, whistling, shouting, groaning (moaning), barking, neighing, harmonious sound, ringing sound, wind-producing (breathy?) sounds, sound of coercion, strongly coercive outflow of consummation.

Sympathetic magic was supposed to be achieved by causing the letters of the name of the demon Schabriri to disappear gradually (Blau 1974: 79):

Schbriri
    briri
    riri
    iri
    ri

The structure of the palindrome, a device of retrograding, is allegedly related to the idea of sympathetic magic. Both are based on the belief that since one can undo a magic by reading the applicable formula backwards,

α	α
βα	ακ
λβα	ακρ
αλβα	ακρα
ναλβα	ακραμ
αναλβα	ακραμμ
θαναλβα	ακραμμα
αθαναλβα	ακραμμαχ
ναθαναλκα	ακραμμαχα
αναθαναλβα	ακραμμαχαμ
λαναθαναλβα	ακραμμαχαμα
βλαναθαναλβα	ακραμμαχαμαρ
αβλαναθαναλβα	ακραμμαχαμαρι
βλαναθαναλβα	ακραμμαχαμαρ
λαναθαναλβα	ακραμμαχαμα
αναθαναλβα	ακραμμαχαμ
ναθαναλβα	ακραμμαχα
αθαναλβα	ακραμμαχ
θαναλβα	ακραμμα
αναλβα	ακραμμ
ναλβα	ακραμ
αλβα	ακρα
λβα	ακρ
βα	ακ
α	α

Figure 6.1 A klimata from papyrus XVIII (Preisendanz 1973 II: 138)

אבגדהוזחטיכלמנסעפצקרשת א:
אבגדהוזחטיכלמנסעפצקרשא ב:
אבגדהוזחטיכלמנסעפצקראב ג
אבגדהוזחטיכלמנסעפצקאבג ד
אבגדהוזחטיכלמנסעפצאבגד ה
אבגדהוזחטיכלמנסעפאבגדה ו
אבגדהוזחטיכלמנסעאבגדהו ז
אבגדהוזחטיכלמנסאבגדהוז ח
אבגדהוזחטיכלמנאבגדהוזח ט
אבגדהוזחטיכלמאבגדהוזחט י
אבגדהוזחטיכלאבגדהוזחטי כ
אבגדהוזחטיכאבגדהוזחטיכ ל
אבגדהוזחטיאבגדהוזחטיכל מ
אבגדהוזחטאבגדהוזחטיכלמ נ
אבגדהוזחאבגדהוזחטיכלמנ ס
אבגדהוזאבגדהוזחט יכלמנס ע
אבגדהואבגדהוזחטיכלמנסע פ
אבגדהאבגדהוזחטיכלמנסעפ צ
אבגדאבגדהוזחטיכלמנסעפצ ק
אבגאבגדהוזחטיכלמנסעפצק ר
אבאבגדהוזחטיכלמנסעפצקר ש
אאבגדהוזחט יכלמנסעפצקרש ת:ו

Figure 6.3 A detail from a Samaritan phylactery (Gaster 1971: 453–4)

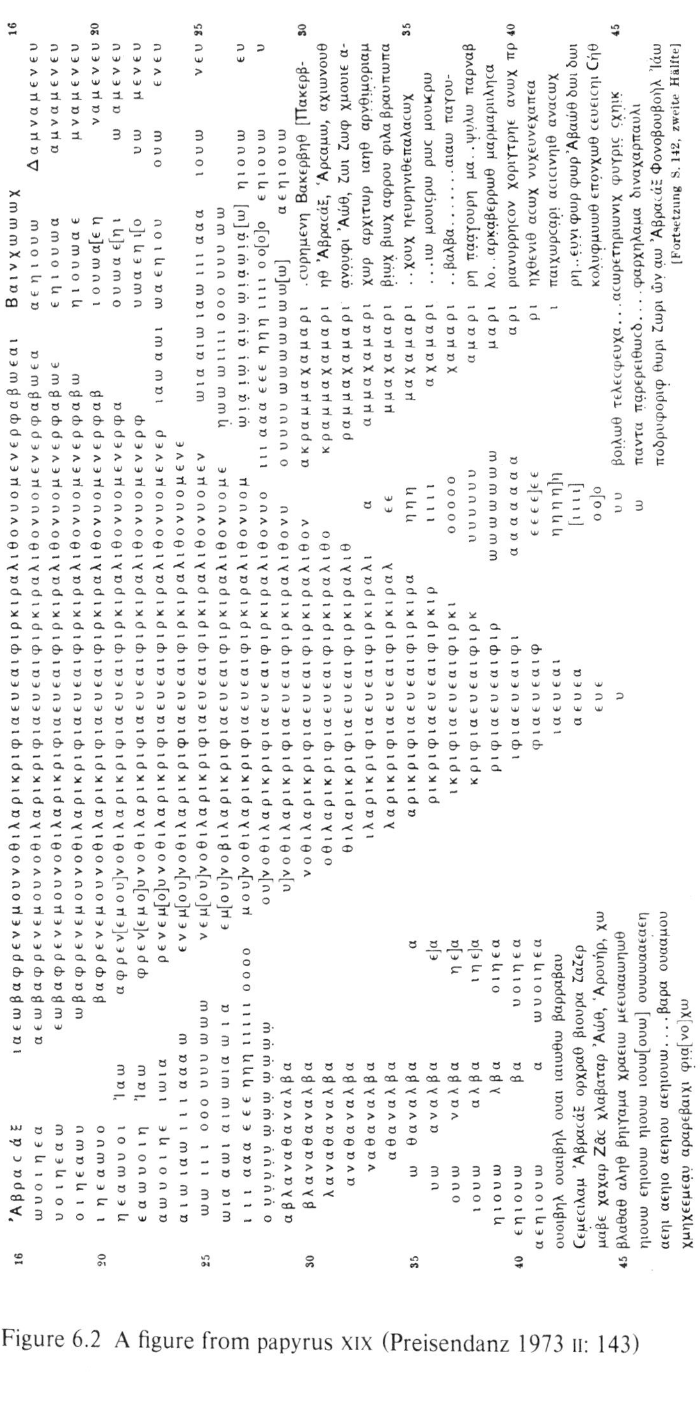

Figure 6.2 A figure from papyrus XIX (Preisendanz 1973 II: 143)

one could prevent this from occurring by using formulas that read the same way in both directions (Dornseiff 1922: 63; Kropp 1931: 122).

Yet another magical written-spoken device is the syllabary. Dornseiff's (Dornseiff 1922: 67–8)[23] first example for it is the following:

a ba ga da za ... psa
e be ge de ze ... pse [etc]

A second shows a magical recipe used against bleeding:

psa pse psē pse psē psa pse

The final example (Figure 6.3) is a detail from a Samaritan phylactery (Gaster 1971).[24] In it, 'the Hebrew alphabet is arranged in twenty-two lines of twenty-three letters in each in such a manner that the top and bottom, as well as left hand line should form a complete alphabet (I: 441). The construct constitutes a gradually decreasing alphabet on the right side and a gradually growing one on the left side, thus two concurrent wing-shaped constructs,[25] and possesses a symbolic meaning (Gaster 1971 I: 453–4).

Not only the words of the Bible and artificial constructs, such as the combinations of the *Shem ha-merforash*, but also the Hebrew alphabet alone was considered 'a divine instrument of creation which in its totality is the foundation of all things' (Poncé 1973: 39). As for a Kabbalistic mystic, such as Abraham Abulafia (Scholem 1954: 110–55), each word 'represents a concentration of energy and expresses a wealth of meaning which cannot be translated, or not fully at least, into human language' (Knowlson 1975: 83). With these 'abstract and non-corporeal elements the kabbalist develops a theory of mystical contemplation' (Scholem 1954: 132). The immediate objects of contemplation are the letters and their combinations. If they are lacking in meaning in the ordinary sense this is 'even an advantage ... as in that case they are less likely to distract us' (133).

What is the connection, if any, between a mystical attitude and the resulting practice, such as those of A. Abulafia's and Graeco-Egyptian magic? Scholem has an unequivocal answer to this. He refers to A. Abulafia as 'an eminently practical Kabbalist' (144) and adds: 'Practical Kabbalism means ... simply magic' (144) with the qualifier that it is distinct from black magic; 'this consecrated form of magic which calls out the tremendous powers of the names, is not very far removed from Abulafia's method' (144).

In the preceding examples of written and/or oral magical constructs we have seen the following devices: vowel series, wing- and grape-shapes (vanishing and/or accumulating series), retrograding, palindrome, names, monster (very long) name, unarticulated sounds, onomatopoeias (including the simulation of animal sounds), emotive sounds, and syllabaries, including vowel-gradation series (Ablautreihen). To this we should add mesostics that have been found in a Samaritan phylactery (see below). I shall now discuss appearances of identical, or similar, devices in contemporary vocal and choral music. Numerous additional examples will be discussed in the next two chapters.

Schafer's *Apocalypsis* is a monumental musical pageant with a pronounced gnostic-syncretistic character, on account of the combination in it of a Judaeo-Christian text with a setting that has non-Christian and at places magical undertones. The prominence given to percussion instruments in part I ('John's Vision'), many of which are metallophones, contributes significantly to the latter impression. The composer wrote for these instruments in full knowledge of the fact that percussion instruments (especially made of brass) were considered in the early Christian era as having an apotropaic (demon-averting) effect; the demons, allegedly, did not like their sound.[26] The other magical devices used in the first movement ('The Cosmic Christ') include repeats of invocation-like text-fragments by the leading solo recitant, speaking as John of Patmos; (invocation-like) repeats by the various constituent choirs; vowel sequences; a text consisting of words with decreasing (7, 6, 5, 4, 3, 2, 1) syllable-lengths thus constituting a wing-shaped construct; and identical constructs in the percussion ensembles, expressed through the numbers of attacks or attack-distances. Furthermore, the instrumental groups and the choirs exhibit additional features related to the number seven: divisions into that many parts per instrumental group and the selection of seven pitch-classes used here. These features cumulatively impart to the movement a strong mystical-cosmological, magical, deep meaning.

In *Empty Words*, Cage included several pieces in the form of what he calls mesostics. In 1971, he wrote *Mesostics* for unaccompanied voice, using microphone.[27] He defined the term (in relation to *Mesostics*) as follows: 'Row down the middle ... a given letter of the name does not occur between itself and the preceding letter of the name.' One may look at this procedure as it highlights an honoured (or hallowed) name, as a device for hierophany, or as 'theurgy.' Schafer, in a similar construct, combined a double palindromic structure with features of the mesostic, as well as with letter displacements that cause transformations between the words Theseus and escapes.[28] These devices have striking similarities to a construct M. Gaster has found in a Samaritan phylactery (Gaster 1971 III: 395–6).[29]

Stockhausen's '*Am Himmel wandre ich ...*' conveys the spirit of both primitive magic and the learned kind. Its pitch-structure shows a wing-shaped design (klimata):

MOVEMENT	PITCH
First	C
Second	CF♯
Third	CF♯G
Fourth	CF♯GE
Fifth	CF♯GED♯
Sixth	CF♯GED♯G♯
Seventh	CF♯GED♯G♯C♯
Eighth	CF♯GED♯G♯C♯B
Ninth	CF♯GED♯G♯C♯BD
Tenth	CF♯GED♯G♯C♯BDA
Eleventh	CF♯GED♯G♯C♯BDAB♭
Twelfth	CF♯GED♯G♯C♯BDAB♭F

For a 'very long version' of the piece the composer suggests (Stockhausen 1978 IV: 208) the following pattern for the succession of the songs: 1, 1+2, 1+2+3, etc. This is, of course, another klimata: 1, 1+2, 1+2+3, etc. Stockhausen uses, in addition to the borrowed, intelligible, texts, a large assortment of unintelligible interjections, bird-calls, onomatopoeias, etc. He, furthermore, cryptically remarks that the word Eagloo is 'one of the numerous bird-man names of the composer' (201). These features lend a shamanistic (that is magical) connotation to the piece.[30]

Stockhausen's *Stimmung* contains, apart from the many magical names, numerous repeating vowel-series such as

[ːi e Ɛ ae a d ɔ o u ʊ ∞ oe ø Yːi]

and repeating syllabaries such as

[ːni ni ny ny n oe nə nʊ nə noe ny ny niː]

which is also a palindrome. Both constructs also appear in magic.

Another ostensibly magical sound event occurs in the first movement of George Crumb's *Ancient Voices of Children*. We seem to be hearing, through a child's mind, a far-fetched anthropomorphic perception of cricket sounds: 'a-i-u-a-i-u-aiu-aiu-aiu-mm-ka-u-mm-ka-u-mm ...' They materialize through the voice of a woman, corresponding to the text of the Lorca poem: 'The little boy was looking for his voice. (The king of the crickets had it.) In a drop of water the little boy was looking for his voice.'

Kagel's *Staatstheater* contains many syllabaries, such as the following which appears in a solo part (the order of first appearance of its members is indicated in the brackets):

Pong (1)	Din (2)	Sching (3)	Xon (4)
Tong (9)	Kin (7)	Tsching (5)	Ton (8)
Xong (15)	Xin (11)	Xing (6)	Ron (10)
Tsong (21)	Tsin (13)	Ring (14)	Kon (12)
Song (23)	Tschin (32)	King (16)	on (17)
Kong (24)		Sching (18)	Tschon (22)
ong (25)		ing (19)	Schon (27)
Schong (28)		Ting (20)	
Bong (30)		Sing (26)	
		Ping (29)	
		Bing (31)	
		[etc][31]	

Somers's *Kyrie* also gives the impression of a pseudo-reconstruction of (or rather an artistic fantasy on the idea of) a gnostic ritual with magical undertones. The three basic vowels and the six consonants of the liturgical words and their permutations and combinations constitute the text of the work. Somers's attitude, characteristic of many composers who have disassembled texts into their phonemic elements, is expressed in the following note to the composition: 'It is my conviction that in words of ancient origin the inner meaning is revealed, not in semantics, but in their sounds and not necessarily in the order in which they have been handed down from generation to generation.' The work relies heavily on vowel sequences and has a double klimata-like structure between pages 5 and 21. The percussive sounds also contribute the impression of a magical component in a syncretistic whole.

Freud, in *Character and Culture*, acknowledges the connection between art and magic: 'In only a single field of our civilization has the omnipotence of thoughts been retained, and that is in the field of art. Only in art does it still happen that a man who is consumed by desires performs something resembling the accomplishment of these desires and that what he does in play produces emotional effects – thanks to artistic illusion – just as though it were something real. People speak with justice of the "magic of art" and compare artists to magicians. But the comparison is perhaps more significant than it claims to be. There can be no doubt that art did not begin as art for art's sake. It worked originally in the services of impulses which are for the most part extinct today. And among them we may suspect the presence of many magical purposes' (Freud 1963: 90–1). The new vocal and choral repertoire confirms unequivocally this interpretation.[32]

THE HIEROPHANY OF CHILDHOOD

In his *Ancient Voices of Children* Crumb shows the intense, mystical-magical, antropomorphic, animistic, inner life of a child. It is, however, childhood remembered, with layers of memory interacting, with time stretching during the reverie, rather than a representation of *being* a child, in the moment of experience itself. The work portrays the stage of childhood at which language skills have been more or less fully acquired: the child is perhaps eight to ten years of age.

Several other works of the repertoire also evoke childhood, and the implied age of the child in them varies. Of special interest are those works that use phonetic materials borrowed from the earliest stages of infancy or of the various other early stages of language acquisition. Roman Jakobson has very useful things to tell us in this regard: 'The actual beginning stages of language as is known, are preceded by the so-called babbling period, which brings to light in many children an astonishing quantity and diversity of sound productions. A child, during his babbling period, can accumulate articulations which are never found within a single language or even in a group of languages' (Jakobson 1968: 21). He then refers to A. Grégoire (Grégoire 1937) who wrote that 'the child at the height of his babbling period is capable of producing all conceivable sounds.' (This infant is a de facto composer-performer!) 'As all observers acknowledge with great surprise, the child then loses nearly all of his ability to produce sounds in passing over from the pre-language stage to the first acquisition of words, i.e. to the first genuine stage of language' (Jakobson 1968: 21).

As the child becomes ready for dialogue, according to Jakobson, phonemes appear, but these co-exist with 'exclamations and onomatopoeic formations' (25). Jakobson's examples for this stage include iterative structures such as *kra kra*, *gaga* (26), etc, but a little later, according to him, there appear series, such as *mama-papa*, *papa-tata*, *mama-nana* (48), and *papa-*

pipi-pupu (49), that might remind someone of the syllabaries discussed in the preceding section.

Towards the end of this study Jakobson, summarizing previously offered data, writes: 'The number of distinctive features in the phoneme [Jakobson et al. 1967] (or the number of phonemes in a phonetic system) and the maximum number of phonemes in the word as well as the number of their possibilities of distribution and the maximal number of phonemic distinctions within a word, increase by degrees in child language (or decreases by degrees in aphasia), *and this increase is aesthetically experienced and consequently practised by the child*' (my emphasis) (85).

Many sounds in Stockhausen's *Stimmung, Momente*, '*Am Himmel wandre ich* ...,' for example, and in Schafer's *La Testa d'Adriane*, have close relationships to sounds produced by young children in the various stages of language acquisition as described by Jakobson. The childhood image depicted by Cathy Berberian in her *Stripsody* is that of an older child conversant with the full spectrum of onomatopoeic sounds that enliven the pages of American comic books, or, as is the case with Oliveros's *Sound Patterns*, the American playground. Claude Vivier's 'child-remembered' in his *Chants*, probably a precocious and rebellious eight-to-ten-year-old, often expresses his recalcitrance, even opposition, by saying backwards (retrograding them) and thus neutralizing certain sacred words he might have been compelled to memorize. The syllabaries in Kagel's *Staatstheater* have not only the magical connotations, but also refer back to similar materials used in school curricula as early as Roman times.[33] Jolas's *Sonate à 12* contains a very large variety of phonetic sound sequences, which strongly remind one of Jakobson's description of phases in the child's acquisition of language. It contains many iterative sequences of short CV duplets.[34]

We have seen certain linguistic materials (abstract phoneme sequences, unarticulated sounds, etc) in the discussion of the oral aspects of magical technique and of the child's progress in the use of language. To the examples above, we can add the text of Colette used by Ravel in *L'enfant et les sortilèges* (The Bewitched Child), premièred in 1925. This text, and the work as a whole, show an animistic and anthropomorphic perception of reality by a child and a growing fear on his part of being unable to control this reality.

To understand a work that uses materials (vowel sequences, iterated, short phoneme-sequences, etc) that might convey simultaneously several connotations (magic, childhood, and/or psychosis, etc) one has to look at the entire piece. While *one* connotation might assert itself in an interpretation without ambiguity as dominant or unique, in other cases no such clear attribution is possible – the work might remain ambiguous. Several connotations might co-exist persuasively, precisely because the explicit or implied framework of the composition is ambiguous. For example, the first song in *Ancient Voices of Children* connotes a child who hears (or remembers someone imitating) cricket sounds (or just making strange sounds, that in no way resemble cricket sounds), and combines anthropomorphism and childhood. Repeated phoneme-sequences such as [ˈtakə dadaˑ], [ˈpiri bitsi biː] and [ˈtsi pətsi pəˑ]   in Stockhausen's '*Am Himmel Wandre ich ...*' are given shamanistic (magical) connotations by the context, while reminding one also of sounds of childhood. The circus or amusement park context of Schafer's *La Testa d'Adriane* prevents us from suspending disbelief and we take it for granted that the magic is only simulation, and the sounds the apparently detached head makes are a part of it.

More closely magical are probably the large rock festivals, such as that at Woodstock, New York, with their quasi-corybantic and bacchant complementary side events and with the shaman-sorcerer-magician performers high up on the stage, in their glittering attire, bathed in floodlights, their voices miraculously amplified thousand-fold, leading on the crowd.

An even more shamanistic performance – visually, vocally, and in other ways as well – was given by the celebrated Quebec chanteuse Pauline Julien, on 24 June 1981 at Quebec's Fête nationale. Dressed in a metallic bird-woman costume, and adorned with an Indian-style head-dress, she moved around in ways befitting the garb, singing, chanting, shouting, and emitting an assortment of shrieks, growls, and other buccal noises in a highly affective mixture, even simulating at times a state of ecstasy. At a high point in her act a large bonfire was lit in the background; at times it filled a large part of the television screen of viewers at home. As she stimulated the crowd to sing along with her, she truly acted as a *meneuse*, and viewers of the telecast could see alternately (or even together) the singer and her enthusiastic audience, with the roaring fire forming a suitable backdrop that contributed to the rising excitement.

We might then cautiously assert that some techniques of sympathetic magic are still with us in art and in music. These are still used (in advertising, for example) to try to gain control over people. To evaluate the effect in art and music of such techniques is difficult and cannot be attempted here in a synoptic fashion.[35] Each work in which such techniques can be identified is best considered in its own light, and its magical techniques related to the total context.

HIEROPHANY OF THE VICTIM AND THE
SUBSTITUTE CELEBRATION OF THE ABSURD

After the end of the Second World War, some composers felt the need to react to that experience. A number of works (Britten's *War Requiem*, for example) came into being to commemorate or give voice to its victims. Later works focused on other events – perceived injustices (collective or individual) such as political, racial, and religious persecution and social and economic oppression. The sombre tone of these works is at times tinged with anger, mirroring perhaps the brutality of the perpetrators or the outrage of the composers, and/or with fear, reflecting the frame of mind of the victims.

Other works, referring also to such sad or tragic aspects of human existence, are couched in irony or satire. Perhaps some composers were not able to speak directly about a specific tragedy[36] or about what they saw as the hopelessness of the human condition and have elected to express the absurdity inherent in a situation. This necessitates the recognition of yet another deep theme, complementary to the hierophany of the victim – that of the absurd.

Who are the victims? In our context, the answer is best sought in actual compositions. These indicate such a wide range of injustices that one wonders if any group or type of individual is to be excluded. If everyone can be victim, who are then the victimizers? The answer is both simple and complex. We all can be tormentors and victims.

One is able to identify the following types of victim in the repertoire we are concerned with:

(a) the political prisoner, the refugee, the 'displaced person' (DP), the concentration-camp inmate, the Jew, the slave;
(b) a person persecuted for creed, race, or other reason;
(c) the exploited worker, the 'guest'-worker;
(d) the mentally ill, who cannot cope with a social role;
(e) the 'faceless' man in the masses;
(f) those who find themselves implicated with crimes committed by others, including forebears;
(g) any other victimized individual (including child) or group;
(h) man himself, in an 'absurd' world.

Many of the composers who have written works on these themes are from countries whose populations suffered most during the Second World War or after: Xenakis (a former member of the Greek underground), Ligeti (a Rumanian-Hungarian Jew), Schoenberg (a German Jew), Schnebel (German), Lutosławski and Penderecki (Poles), and Dallapiccola, Nono, and Berio (Italians). A brief list of characteristic works includes (under the categories listed above):

(a) *Il prigioniero* (Dallapiccola), *Nuits* (Xenakis), *Red Bird* (Wishart), *Il canto sospeso* and *Ricorda cosa ti hanno fatto in Auschwitz* (Nono), *A Survivor from Warsaw* (Schoenberg), *Dies irae* (Penderecki), *Patria I – The Characteristics Man* (Schafer), *El Cimarrón*, *Stimmen* (Henze), and *Foci* (Anhalt);

(b) *El Cimarrón* (Henze), *O King* (Berio), *Threnody* (Schafer), *Aikichi Kuboyama* (Eimert), *Come out* (Reich), *The Visitation* (Schuller), *Coro* (Berio), and *Voices* (Henze), *Winthrop* (Anhalt);

(c) *Intolleranza*, *La fabbrica illuminata* (Nono), and *Stimmen* (Henze);

(d) *Sequenza III* and *Visage* (Berio), *Patria II* (Schafer), and *Eight Songs for a Mad King* and *Miss Donnithorne's Maggot* (Maxwell Davies);

(e) *Requiem* (Ligeti), *Trois Poèmes d'Henri Michaux* (Lutosławski), and *Nuits* (Xenakis), *Cento* (Anhalt);

(f) *AMN* and *Madrasha II* (Schnebel);

(g) *Die Teufel von Loudun* (Penderecki), *Passaggio* (Berio), and *The Raft of the Frigate Medusa* (Henze);

(h) *An Avalanche* (Hiller), *Glossolalie* (Schnebel), *Song Books I and II* (Cage), *Rezitativarie* and *Phonophonie* (Kagel).

The 'Kyrie' of Ligeti's *Requiem* is a powerful showing of a mass of human beings, swirling and twisting in so many vocal currents, adding up to a turbulent sea of voices in which the identity of an individual is painfully and irrevocably submerged on account of the number of concurrently used similar melodic designs and overlapping registers. The canonic structures here have a 'blind leading the blind' character, conveying the cumulative affect of a hopeless predicament for the whole mass; there is no appeal, perhaps because there is no being to whom one may appeal, and for the individual molecules there is nowhere else to go to. There are recurring features in these four- and five-part canons, such as the common onset and exit of the respective groups. The rhythmical differences in the individual voices of the groups are subtle and are designed to produce the desired harmonic and rhythmic density. The respective characteristic tonal territories of the groups are expressible through the identification of the band of frequencies, constituting a mobile cluster, occupied during a given canonic segment. The seemingly aimless ascending and descending motions of the group form larger structures, which are defined by frequency-band boundaries, as well as density and intensity, fluctuations. Also significant here is the contrast between the complex micro-structures and the easy perception of the outline, and the single affect, of the whole movement. Ligeti must have possessed a deep understanding of what takes place in the midst of a human mass, compressed into a relatively narrow space, based probably on his own experience.

For sources of inspiration of works such as this we might have also to look deeper. Ligeti has helped in this respect: he has related the Dies irae of the work to the desire to defeat 'the fear of death,' especially today, when 'in every minute, in every second our world might perish ... We could die, not only as individuals, but our entire civilisation' (Sabbe 1979: 23). About the whole work, he said that he had 'chosen the text of the *Requiem* for its imagining of anxiety of the fear of death, and of the end of the world' (17).

In Schnebel's *AMN* and *Madrasha II*, two very sombre works, the vocalists appear as individuals labouring under severe mental handicaps. In *AMN* one still hears snatches of intelligible speech in German: 'Help me,' 'Forgive me,' 'always worse,' 'That's the end,' etc, said in rushed, whispered voice, as if the speaker is being hounded and is bordering on a nervous breakdown. A recurring sound is that of gasping for air as if choking, interspersed with such religious exclamations as 'Um Gottes Willen' (Oh my God), 'Mon Dieu,' 'santissima,' and 'Kyrie eleison,' followed by frantic and repressed, hummed glides. The overall impression is that of a disoriented community that clutches, as at a last straw, at some verbal icons, which seem to have lost their sacred power to console and redeem. The individuals are left alone in their misery, to cope the best they can with the cause of their condition and their predicament itself. *Madrasha II*, in which some taped sounds – apparently a squealing pig, a crying baby, and a creaking door[37] – are added to the sounds of the eighteen vocalists, who exhibit an even more pronounced aphasic state than those in *AMN*. Heinz-Klaus Metzger has referred to this composition as being 'like a gnostic curse on the demiurge.'[38] In my understanding, these pieces have two additional connotations, the first substantive, the second more technical. Schnebel speaks through these works as if atoning for the crimes committed on behalf of official Germany during the Second World War. Two kinds of victims are depicted here: one kind killed during the war; the other, the tormentor and murderer, or a co-citizen, or descendant, suffering mental anguish for the crimes committed and remembered. Both works constitute desperate, yet courageous, statements of faith – belief in a redemption that can come only through the most thorough self-examination. Both compositions are also remarkably imaginative and virtuosic on the technical plane.

In March 1916, at mid-point in that slaughter that was the First World War, Hugo Ball expressed one of the most concise formulations of the Dadaist credo: 'What we are celebrating is at once a buffoonery and a requiem mass ...'[39] Following the end of that war the Dada spirit was shunted aside, repressed, drowned out for about thirty years, but not dead, because what gave it its raison d'être in the first place remained very much alive.

This spirit was reflected by Camus who came to regard man as 'a stranger ... an irremediable exile' in the universe.[40] The corollary of this was the view that 'this divorce between man and his life, the actor and his setting truly constitutes the feeling of Absurdity' (Esslin 1961: xix). Ionesco, one of the great dramatists of the theatre of the absurd, was ready to open the curtains on his workshop-window, showing a similar mental set operative in his work: 'I do feel that life is nightmarish, painful and unbearable, like a bad dream ... Wars, catastrophes and disasters, hatred and persecution, confusion, death, lying in wait for all of us, we talk without understanding one another' (Ionesco 1964: 110).

In music, Cage became the protagonist of a similarly dadaist-absurd spirit in the 1950s, with the introduction of chance procedures and with works such as *Imaginary Landscape No. 4*, for twelve 'live' radios (1951), and his 'silent' *4'33"* (1952). His earliest vocal work in this vein is *Solo for Voice I* (1958), a multilingual, disjointed, half-sung, half-recited monologue, suggestive of a pathological (perhaps a manic depressive) mind (Vetter 1970: 129–33).[41] His European tours of 1954 and 1958 made a notable impression on some younger composers – Kagel (newly arrived from Argentina), Schnebel, and the poet Hans Helms.[42] Helms's two works for small vocal ensemble, *Daidalos* (1961) and *Golem* (1962), Kagel's *Anagrama* (1957–8), and Schnebel's *Glossolalie* (1959–60) all show the influence of Cage and perhaps of contemporary theatre and literature.

Kagel has developed into the most imaginatively, consistently, and absurdly satirical and productive composer in Europe (Schnebel 1970). Who are the tenants in his house of many echoes, distorting yet truth-telling mirrors, and spotlights? The list includes an organist who, playing or silent, coughs, laughs, whistles, shouts, and claps (*Improvisation ajoutée*, 1961–2); a lady harpsichordist who absent-mindedly plays Chopin- and Bach-like fragments, over and over, while vocalizing a word-salad in a Sprechgesang (*Rezitativarie*, 1973); an anonymous singer-speaker, who is on the point of losing his voice (and perhaps his sanity), and who also acts as a ventriloquist, a mime, and an impersonator (*Phonophonie* 1963–4); singer-speakers in a choral piece, who also blow into organ-pipes and utter or sing a text in a semblance of pidgin Latin in a spiritless and mindless mock-liturgical routine (*Hallelujah für Stimmen*, 1967–8) (Schnebel 1970); and the vocalists in his absurd opera *Staatstheater* (1967–70), representatives of classical operatic roles: the Queen of the Night, Aida, Carmen, Erda, Ottavio, and others, singing in caricatures of the respective idioms, using pseudo-texts of nonsense words, coined with considerable combinatorial inventiveness.

Hiller's *An Avalanche*, for pitchman, prima donna, player-piano, percussion, and tape (1968), is a caricature of the solo recital and the contemporary cultural scene.

Ligeti's recent 'anti-anti-opera' *Le grand macabre*, a setting of Ghelderode's *Sprechstück*, appears to be a substantial addition to the repertoire of musical works expressing the spirit of the absurd (Sabbe 1979: 11–34). Comparing the theme of this opera with that of his *Requiem*, Ligeti said, 'Yes, it is the same theme of the end of the world, but treated with irony' (17).

Just as the theatre of the absurd turned language into a seemingly empty routine, to be able to make it say what it could not in its intact, earlier states, so works of the musical absurd broke earlier musical syntaxes into shards, making these function on the surface as debris, symbolic of decay and decadence, but on a deeper level as elements of a new, potentially still more complex, syntax, which can be more encompassing and accommodating and less predictable than its predecessors. In this process the visual element of musical performances often comes to the fore, carrying more and more information and claiming a correspondingly larger and larger portion of the listener-spectator's attention. This shift of the centre of gravity in what was hitherto a predominantly musical repertoire will now be considered further.

THE PERFORMANCE OF MUSIC AS SPECTACLE OR CELEBRATION

Certain developments in musical composition during the past thirty years have called into question the very primacy of sound in the art. Ives could ask: what has sound to do with music? Cage was able to compose a silent piece for a pianist sitting in front of an open keyboard. Cage, Kagel, and Cardew,[43] turning away from organized sound, proposed a new balance between the auditory and visual aspects of musical performance. One might argue that there is a more appropriate word than music for the presentation that is Cage's *4'33"*; but if not music, then what?

In 1957, referring to such developments in avant-garde music, Cage asked: 'Where do we go from here?' (Cage 1961: 12) And he answered:

'Towards the theatre. That art more than music resembles nature' (12), subsequently adding: 'Theatre takes place all the time wherever one is ... and art simply facilitates persuading one this is the case' (Kostelanetz 1974: 197), thus extending the idea underlying his *4'33"* in the visual domain. In 1955 he suggested, in a somewhat Wittgensteinian[44] and Beckettian appreciation, that 'relevant action is theatrical (music [imaginary separation of hearing from the other senses] does not exist), inclusive and intentionally purposeless. Theatre is continually becoming that it is becoming' (Cage 1961: 14).

The consequences of such perceptions resulted in new art-formats: mixed-media events (sometimes called multimedia or intermedia), total environments, happenings, out-of-doors celebrations, pseudo-rituals, ceremonies, and other contemporary manifestations of the *Gesamtkunstwerk* idea in new guises.[45]

One of Kagel's most elaborate works for the stage is *Staatstheater*, a large assortment of visual and auditory events, from which an actual performance can be assembled. Kagel compares the work to a peep-show ('Guck-Kastenbühne') (Kagel 1975: 89), capable of transmitting to the spectator the simultaneity and complexity of a multiplicity of actions and presenting a freedom of choice to focus on one or another event that is only illusory (89). Kagel calls the title of the work an 'analytical one' (95), referring to the 'object under study.' 'It is possible because there is a *state* theater, and there is also a *theater* of state ... The work contains very many elements that call the institution into question' (95).

Ligeti's surrealistic opera *Le grand macabre* consists of a succession of short tableaux, similar to a comic strip. The work contains several confusions of identity: the role of the chief of police is to be sung by a coloratura soprano, and that of a king by a child's voice. This and similar devices heighten the absurdity of the total impression (Sabbe 1979).[46]

Among works that have inventive and effective visual dimensions we must count two works by Maxwell Davies: *Eight Songs for a Mad King* and *Miss Donnithorne's Maggot*, both with texts by Randolph Stow. According to Stowe, the first of these is to be understood as George III's monologue while he struggles to teach his birds 'to make the music which he could so rarely torture out of his flute and harpsichord. Or trying to sing with them.' (The roles of birds are taken by the instrumentalists, with whom the singer interacts musically and visually.) The heroine of the second work is a strong-willed lady who was jilted on her wedding-day by the bridegroom-to-be. Her reaction to this had been to leave everything (wedding cake, dress, etc) 'forever' unaltered, with predictable results. When the piece begins, everything in it is in an advanced state of decay (even her mind, it seems).

Nono's *La fabbrica illuminata* and *Ricorda cosa ti hanno fatto in Auschwitz* are sometimes performed with a visual complement, consisting of effective slide-projections that help to bring out the political and ideological character of the first and the horror-protest character of the second work.[47]

Schafer's compositions in the *Patria* series are realizations of his ideas about what he calls the 'theater of confluence' (Schafer 1979: 30–48) and are also a kind of *Gesamtkunstwerk* 'conceived on all levels simultaneously. All the parameters ... *must* be elaborated coevally' (32). In this theatre 'the potentials of counterpointing the various arts one against the other might become a possibility. The rhythm of one medium may extend that of another medium or it may contravene it' (34).

We return to one of the initial concepts of this chapter when we read Peter Brook's statement: 'We do not know how to celebrate, because we do not know what to celebrate.' In his search for a new theatricality (a new celebration, perhaps) he has developed utterance into a process that aims in directions familiar to a Cage or a Kagel. He asks: 'Is there another language, just as exacting for the author as a language of words? Is there a language of actions, a language of sounds, a language of word-as-part-of movement, of word-as-lie, word-as-parody, of word-as-rubbish, of word-as-contradiction, of word-shock or word-cry?' (Brook 1968: 47, 49).

The mystical-ecstatic character of Vivier's opera *Kopernikus* became strengthened as the composer eliminated numerous intelligible passages of text and substituted for them sounds of a language created by himself. The work is ostensibly concerned with the after-life but in fact expresses, in a somewhat hieratic manner, the depth of mystery in human existence and relationships.

A sense of celebration can be experienced in the performances and compositions of singers such as Tamia, Ed Herbst, and Michiko Hirayama, as well as some vocalists performing non-Western music, such as the Iranian Parīsā, and the Mongolian Norovbanzad (Emmert 1979).[48] Schafer also is on a quest for the motivating spirit and circumstances of celebrations. His *Apocalypsis* has been modelled on the 'great dramatic pageants of the Middle Ages, which took place ... in cathedrals on festive occasions.'[49] The first part of the work ('John's Vision') is action-filled, turbulent, and colourful; the second ('Credo') is static, contrapuntally complex, mystical, monochromatic in timbre, and performed by twelve mixed choirs standing in a circle around the audience. The work depicts at a deep level a clash of creeds, a swirling cauldron of individual and group expressions of the spiritual, with Christianity (still tinged with Judaism) in the process of emerging victorious. It is one of the most telling of the new works that probe the past for an authentic experience of hierophany.

IN SEARCH OF THE PAST

Many of the topics discussed in this chapter have a bearing on this deep theme. I hope that by focusing on this aspect we may discover additional depth and perspective with regard to our general topic. Let us begin by looking at certain composers and works.

Beckwith, a composer with a very keen perception of a specific past, has a strong and felicitous gift for sensing the speech-and-life rhythms and reading the feelings and thoughts of turn-of-the-century rural Ontarians, and he depicts these through the eyes, ears, and mind of a precocious and observant boy of about twelve, who is obviously one with them. His operas, *Night Blooming Cereus* (1953–8), and *The Shivaree*, as well as his *The Great Lakes Suite* (1949), *The Trumpets of Summer*, *Canada Dash – Canada Dot*, and *Place of Meeting*, clearly show this child looking at the world around him and at its perplexities with wide-open eyes, intense attention, and fascination.

The whole of Crumb's *Ancient Voices of Children* is about remembrance, about trying to capture faint echoes of a childhood spent in Spain. The person from whose vantage point we hear the work manages to recall from the recesses of his aural memory passionate voices of a peasant woman, whispering voices of others, night sounds, a sustained chord, eerie glides, a phrase or so of familiar music played on a tinkly piano, a raw-sounding reedy wind instrument, a large assortment of percussive sounds – so many sounding icons from the past freely floating in more or less densely structured time-fields.

Jolas in *Sonate à 12*, Berberian in *Stripsody*, Oliveros in *Sound Patterns*, and Vivier in *Chants* all remember different kinds, and specific stages, of childhoods, their own and/or those of other children.

The many details of Schnebel's *Glossolalie* portray a society in disintegration. The burnt-out remnants of this civilization are still audible and in use by those who do not notice, or choose to ignore, the decay and dissolution. We can hear distorted, out-of-context, old turns of phrase, wise sayings, slogans, many pronounced in dialect for authenticity of effect; empty bandying about of names of famous people and quotations from 'sacred' authors, such as Schiller, Verlaine, Shakespeare; a fragment of psalmody, another from the *Niebelungenlied*; a few snatches of folksongs; and quotations from Schumann, Beethoven, and Wagner, all mixed together in disarray and confusion, compounded by the addition of fragments in a host of foreign languages. This mélange progresses to meaningless (but affective) phoneme-sequences, exclamations, and sundry noises, signalling a yet further state of disintegration. In his opera *Aus Deutschland*, Kagel probes the spirit and meaning of the German romanticism displayed in the poems put to music that constitute the repertoire of *Lieder*. He sets a large number of fragments from these texts in startling syntheses and situations. The work's dramatic realizations bring visibility and a novel aural identity to figures such as the organ-grinder, the two grenadiers, death, the girl, music, the nightingale, Mignon, Schubert, and so on. Some are made to appear as archetypes, others as allegories (symbols or even sacred figures, perhaps in a new light) 'as they come into contact with other protagonists of the piece' (Kagel in Kagel et al 1980: 6).[50]

When hearing the mystical, religious works of Stockhausen, Schafer, or Somers, one is led to think that perhaps these composers have a special sensitivity that enables them to pick up some faint echoes of long-defunct civilizations and liturgical practices. (Alternatively, perhaps they had the gift to uncover in current practice deeply penetrating roots.) This is perhaps the very ability that Eliade refers to when he says: 'In certain instances, the artist's approach to his material recovers and recapitulates a religiosity of an extreme archaic variety that disappeared from the Western World thousands of years ago' (Beane and Doty 1976, I: 127). Subsequently Eliade speaks about what he calls 'the two specific characteristics of modern art, namely the destruction of traditional forms and the fascination for the formless, for the elementary modes of matter' (128). He alleges that all these 'are susceptible to religious interpretation.' He uses a key expression to refer to all this: 'the hierophanization of matter,' which 'characterizes that which has been called "cosmic religiosity"' (128). This is perhaps the boldest and most profound reaching back into the 'past' that man (astronomer, theoretical physicist, artist) can conceive of.[51]

Gustav René Hocke regards 'archeologizing religiousness' as 'symptomatic for the ceaseless tension in all manneristic periods of Europe' (Hocke 1959: 130–1). He sees its concomitant 'reachings out for history and its push for the absolute' as deriving from an acceleration of decay and striving for a new 'unity and order.'

This reaching out involves also a search for the roots of literature, and even of language itself. Maurice Blanchot sees 'the language of literature' as being 'the search for the moment which precedes it' (Bruns 1974: 201), to which G.L. Bruns adds: 'the moment before speech' (201).

The question of why poets, artists, and composers would want to descend into the 'pit of time' (Thomas Mann's phrase) has now to be put. It seems that this urge derives partly from a cosmic quest and partly also from a man-centred wish to rediscover a supposed innocence, the ideal of a 'paradisiac stage of primordial humanity' (Beane and Doty I: 89), despite the knowl-

edge that this is 'an archetype never fully "realizable" in any human existence at all' (89). Is it possible that where the ideal of this dream is located
we might also find the image of the legendary speaker-singer Orpheus, himself? Or is Orpheus a more real figure than that other, idealized dream
image?

7

Orpheus resurgent ... perhaps

We shall focus in this chapter on some aspects of the use of voice and language by selected contemporary composers. We shall occasionally find it more apposite to speak about 'vocal-tract behaviour' than about 'language use,' when the acoustic material will not fit in the framework of language, however broadly defined. Depending on our focus of attention, we shall speak about a fragment of music as acoustical data, as a physiological process, and/or as a musical-semiotic event. The following themes will be discussed: audible breathing, various utterance modes and types, speech-sound concentrations, diverse abstract and other kinds of phonemic and phonetic constructs and processes, composition in terms of vocal-tract behaviour, and texts and text-settings.

AUDIBLE BREATHING

Breathing probably is the simplest of vocal-tract behaviours. Normal breathing in itself only, for our present purpose, constitutes a neutral configuration. The position of the lips is neither too spread nor too constricted, neither too open nor too closed. The rates and durations of inhalation and exhalation are neither too slow nor too rapid, neither too short nor too long, but resemble those processes that function in breathing when the body is in a state of repose. The volume of air used is neither more nor less than what is needed for this condition for a healthy adult, male or female. This inconspicuous kind of breathing, necessary for the sustenance of life, has no other expressive quality than to convey the sense of life in repose. All other kinds of breathings change this semiotic state and thus convey different meanings. By changing the person who breathes and the respective aspects of the breathing act in various combinations, one can convey a considerable number of different meanings, the magnitude and range of which have not, to my knowledge, been systematically and fully tested. While I am unable to cite examples of breathing types explicitly notated in scores of the *bel canto* period, different breathing types are implied in them (through choice of voice types, tempi, durations, rhythms, phrase-shapes, dynamics, registers, texts, and situation), and realized in performances. The sounds and characters of breaths, in the standard repertoire, are manifold and important carriers of affective meaning and fit the conceptual affective outlook of the periods.

We encounter audible breathing as an occasional, important, and characteristic expressive means in the new vocal and choral repertoire. But we often find specific instructions about the kinds of audible breathing the composers have in mind. Let us now look at a few examples.

Mégapneumes 67 by Gil J. Wolman[1] is a sound-poem that consists exclusively of breathing sounds of various kinds, conveying a spectrum of attitudes and feelings, including that of sensuality. So does *Solo for Voice No. 22* in Cage's *Song Books*, volume I, which calls for 'regular and irregular breathing (inhaling or exhaling as necessary) through the nose or mouth.' Cage is specific: 'Regular means: even or changing gradually. Irregular means: uneven or changing abruptly' (85–6). A number-series provides a plan for the successive events that constitute the piece. Somers's *Voiceplay* is a theatrical-musical work for a virtuoso solo vocalist and his or her 'accompanist.' The soloist assumes a number of roles (lecturer, demonstrator, actor, etc) and presents symbols of objective states (demonstration of vocal resources, etc) and of subjective states (fear, panic, anxiety, etc),[2] as well as performs a series of vocal events: exclamations, humming an assortment of linguistic sounds, phoneme-series, nonsense consonant-vowel (cv) duplets, isolated sibilants, short intelligible texts, and so on. Also included are various kinds of coloured audible breathings (exhalation, inhalation) using diverse supraglottal configurations, exercises aimed at freeing the flow of breath,[3] transitions from coloured audible breath to voiced events, panting, 'breath whisper on "huh" starting slowly, and softly, and then accelerating and crescendo, spasmodic breathing.'

Schnebel's *AMN*, after its opening short exclamation, has a series of well differentiated audible breathing types:

1. intensive inhaling, abruptly breaking off, with /f/ articulation,
2. shakily in- and exhaling with /ø/ articulation,
3. normal, but still continuously strongly blowing in- and exhaling with /ø/ articulation,

4. in- and exhaling, becoming gradually normal with /h/ articulation, intense but never exaggerated,

5. distinctly breathing with

6. /f/ articulation variants, produced through in- and exhaling, changing the mouth-configuration constantly between /i/ and /u/ and shifting the lower lip against the upper teeth in all directions; strong tongue movements; changes from fast to medium fast,

7. /s/ and /ʃ/ variants, produced while in- and exhaling: changing the mouth-configuration constantly between /i/ and /u/; moving the tongue between the teeth and the middle of the palate (right and left), opening and closing the teeth; changes fast to middle fast,

8. /x/ variants, produced while in- and exhaling: changing the position of the mouth constantly between /i/ and /a/; varying the attack of palatal sound production and the shape of the tongue. Take also into consideration the saliva in the sound production. Irregular breathing rate, changes from fast to middle-fast,

9. very deep, and strained in- and exhaling, softly, on /h/,

10. on the sounds /r/, /x/ softly and deeply in- and exhaling.

In measures 26–9 there are additional groups of rapid inhalings and exhalings of different kinds. All these audible breathing events appear affectively as variants of the expressions of anxiety, fear, and revulsion and as such contribute significantly to the dark overall character of the piece.

Earlier, in the analysis of Ligeti's *Nouvelles Aventures*, we noted the animal-like panting in part I (measures 51, 53, and 55), and the quasi-choking sounds in part II (measures 54–6), with which the piece comes to a terrible end. Similarly, we have noted the expressive audible inhalings ('gasps') in Berio's *Sequenza III*, one of the most telling paralinguistic effects in the piece.

A particularly depressive-sounding audible breathing sequence occurs in Schnebel's *Madrasha II* (8). It is a series of rapid inhalings and exhalings, on constantly changing pitch-levels (between medium and high), and with a great energy. Gasping, breathing, nervous speech occurs in Maxwell Davies's *Eight Songs for a Mad King*. Kagel's *Phonophonie* features at several places coloured breathing: HA HI HO HO HE. Haubenstock-Ramati's *Credentials* contains the instructions: 'audible in- and exhaling.'

The fourth movement ('Isaac') of my *La Tourangelle*, a ten-minute long, multi-layered, and tensely dramatic section, ends with a gradual dissolution of tension and a long, drawn-out sigh, performed by the three soprano soloists together, signifying an expression of relief, after the end of the turmoil.

A similar sigh occurs at the very close of Somers's opera *Death of Enkidu: Part I*.

In Schafer's *Patria II – Requiems for the Party Girl*, in editing unit 4 ('Almagest'), the tape brings 'heavy breathing,' which precedes the moment when the audience first perceives the outlines of the asylum with Ariadne's dead spirit and the other inmates 'slowly moving about' (11). In his *La Testa d'Adriane*, the instructions for the 'detached head' on the table at one point are the following: 'tongue suddenly in; suck in air loudly and fast at sides of tongue ... Exhaled hiss ... Inhaled hiss.'

From a related domain we should note scene 5 of *Mysteries and Smaller Pieces*, a collective creation of Julian Beck's and Judith Malina's Living Theater. It consists largely of the deep breathing of six actors, 'their bodies moving up and down with increasing rapidity, an orgasm of breathing.' After a period of immobility, 'one actor ... with a fierce expellation of air makes the sound "Z-Z-Z-z-z-z-z- ..."' ending in a burst of outraged rejection. Blackout. Intermission' (*The Living Theatre in Europe 1966*).

Stockhausen's *Atmen gibt das Leben* (Breathing Gives Life), a mystical work for chorus and orchestra, with cosmological connotations, begins with the choir very softly humming while exhaling and inhaling. Of course, the former would be only a variety of normal singing, but in the context of the latter, this slow succession of breathing becomes a foreground event, with the pitches themselves appearing as having only a background significance. This effect is strengthened by simultaneous half-whispered, half-whistled utterings of the duplet /py:/ while exhaling and inhaling, and a hiccup-like utterance, also while inhaling. All this takes place on a dimly lit stage, while most of the singers are 'squatting on the floor' in a prescribed posture, with eyes closed, immobile; some additional material with a similar character appears subsequently. This structure lasts about five minutes. The overall impression is of a meditative session in progress, with a quasi-ritual breathing playing a primary role.

To understand the full expressive spectrum of audible breathing we should remember that breathing, as a symbolic act, as well as a component of ritual, also plays a substantial role in a number of religions. This fact is incorporated into the very fabric of languages themselves. The word for breath is frequently 'synonymous with "soul," "spirit" and "life": "psykhē," "pneuma" in Greek, "anima," "spiritus" in Latin, "ātman," "prāna" in Sanscrit, "duh" in Russian, "rūah," "nephes" in Hebrew, and many others' (Izutsu 1956: 28).

In Yogic practice the disciplining of respiration (*prāṇāyāma*) 'is of very great importance. *Prāṇāyāma* begins with making the respiratory rhythms as slow as possible' (Eliade 1969: 55). '*Prāṇāyāma* is ... also identified with the three chief gods of the Vedic pantheon: Brahmā is said to be inhalation, Visnu suspension of breath, Rudra exhalation' (133).

According to the Kabbalistic doctrine of the *tsimtsum*, 'just as the human organism exists through the double process of inhaling and exhaling and the one cannot be conceived without the other, so also the whole of Creation constitutes a gigantic process of divine inhalation and exhalation' (Scholem 1954: 263). This doctrine seems to be related to a mystical formulation by Blavatsky: 'The appearance and disappearance of the Universe are pictured as an out-breathing and in breathing of the "Great Breath" which is eternal, and which being Motion, is one of the three symbols of the Absolute – Abstract Space and Duration being the other two. When the Great Breath is projected, it is called the Divine Breath, and is regarded as the breathing of the Unknowable Deity – the One Existence – which breathes out a thought, as it were, which becomes the Cosmos' (Blavatsky 1893: 74).

In Islamic Sufi mystical practice, 'the proper *dhikr khafi* (occult recollection) ... is based upon the rhythm of breathing: exhalation-inhalation. With closed eyes and lips using the basic *tahlīl* formula, *Lā ilāha illā 'llāh*,[4] the recollector (*dhākir*) exhales, concentrating on *lā ilāha* to expel all external distractions; then in inhaling he concentrates on *illā 'llāh*, affirming that all is God' (Trimingham 1971: 201–2).

There are suggestions that in Graeco-Egyptian magical practice, 'the effect of the invocation depends on the inhaling and exhaling' (Hopfner 1974: 479; also Bonner 1927: 171–2).

Izutsu observes: 'It is in the breath that the main virtue of all verbal magic is believed to reside ... Primitive people ... practically everywhere show a remarkable tendency to visualize the disembodied soul as something of breath-nature. The ideas of the soul and the breath are, to primitive reflection, so intimately interrelated that practically it is impossible to draw any sharp line of demarcation between the two' (Izutsu 1956: 28).

In the light of the foregoing one could attribute a somewhat different, and probably more appropriate, meaning to the long, drawn-out sigh that ends 'Isaac' in my *La Tourangelle*. During the ordeal Marie de L'Incarnation was compelled to endure as a result of the physical and psychic attacks against her, she might have, literally, held her breath at times – held on to her soul in danger of crumbling or of being taken away from her. Her tightly closed lips and blocked nose were causes, as well as symptoms, of her great inner tension. As she was bodily hiding behind the locked doors of the convent, so did she protect her soul behind the locked doors of those orifices through which it either could escape, or be snatched away. In this situation the metaphorical identity of soul and breath was transformed into a physiological process. With the outer and inner dangers subsiding, her breath could, once again, be allowed to resume its normal rhythm.

VARIOUS UTTERANCE MODES AND TYPES

Many composers have been trying to find alternatives to *bel canto* singing and to normal speech. These composers have got around the difficulty of specifying their objectives by using a combination of signs that include standard musical symbols, verbal descriptions, graphic notations, and other means to be discussed shortly.

The factors influencing utterance modes include the existence or absence of a recognizable tuning system, relative vowel lengths, statistical vowel-consonant ratio per unit time over a certain duration, degree of pitch stability, vocal resonance patterns, and patterns of voice quality. Depending on the nature of these criteria and their combinations we have a large variety of utterance modes to consider.

In surveying the repertoire, we find evidence of a considerable desire to be precise on the part of certain composers. Haubenstock-Ramati, in *Credentials*, indicates that in the solo voice part 'all possible nuances are needed, from singing (bel canto) to speaking, shouting and percussive effects.' After specifying graphic symbols for utterances featuring 'fixed pitch, approximate pitch, glissandi, bocca chiusa, bocca semichiusa (closed and half-closed mouth),' he specifies 'chanting,' which he defines as a 'mezza voce' utterance 'a middle stage between song and speech.' He lists 'speech declamation: mostly indicated by the appearance of the words (different heights and widths of the letters),' adding finally that this constitutes 'an attempt to suggest a whole scale of relationships and tensions between the single words and syllables.'[5] Roger Reynolds, in his *Blind Men*, uses the word '*intone*' to specify 'a technique combining the resources of singing and declamation.' He explains its meaning in these terms: 'It should involve a wider range of vocal colour than is allowed in normal singing and frequently a continuously changing pitch.' Then he adds: 'When several voices coincide on an intoned part ... they should avoid unison ensemble and simply relate their independent efforts to the same ideal.'[6] In Reynolds's *The Emperor of Ice Cream* 'the vocal notation gives: text; relative dynamics ... by means of thickness of letter.' Its modes of utterance include declamation, *Sprechgesang*, and 'the natural speaking intonation.'[7] In *Nouvelles Aventures* Ligeti prescribes, in addition to the 'singing voice,' 'speech-song ('Sprechgesang'), with fixed pitches, speech-song with changing, but not definitely fixed pitches,' four different kinds of speaking voices, three different murmurings, whisper, audible breathing sounds, as well as transitions from one to another mode of utterance.[8] In *Il Cantico delle creature* Lewkovitch specifies five modes: simple recitation, modulated recitation, singing on one or two tones, modulated song with free choice of interval and timbre, and unison recitation on a given tone and speech register.[9]

The degree of specificity of choice of pitch is controlled usually by a staff system, with or without clefs. From passages in an 'open field,' through the imposition of upper and lower limits or a central reference pitch (more or less precise), one arrives to a high-middle-low (three-valued) system, or to a system of five, six, or seven bands or levels (such as those in Helms's *Golem* or in my *Cento*), and finally to precise staff notation. Many works call for glides, and there is a passage in Schafer's *Patria II* that calls for a very wide vibrato (interval of the third or fourth) (score 49).

Concerning the difference between the respective resonance patterns in speaking and singing, we have the results of Johan Sundberg's studies, that indicate in the latter mode the presence of a special high formant (Sundberg 1977).

Composers of the scores studied indicate the desired voice qualities by the following means, or with combinations thereof: voice-types (dramatic soprano, etc), verbal labels, references to vocal-tract physiology, paralinguistic references, onomatopoeic references, and graphic means. The following list, while incomplete, gives a fair idea of what range of voice qualities one can expect to encounter in this repertoire.

The only specific reference to 'pharyngeal fricative' I saw appears in Schafer's *La Testa d'Adriane*. 'Whisper' occurs in a fairly large number of scores. 'Heavily aspirated whisper' can be found in Reynolds's *Blind Men*. 'Falsetto' appears in Helms's *Daidalos*, Maxwell Davies's *Eight Songs for a Mad King*, and others. Jolas specifies in her *Sonate à 12* a 'pinched throat voice, brassery (sic), somewhat acid.' 'Guttural' or 'very guttural' sounds appear in Helms's *Golem* and in Kagel's *Phonophonie*. 'Gargling' or 'falsetto gargling' is asked for in Beckwith's *Canada Dash – Canada Dot* and in Schafer's *La Testa d'Adriane*. 'Breathy' is included in *Eight Songs for a Mad King*. 'Throaty' sounds are specified in *Credentials* by Haubenstock-Ramati, in *Eight Songs for a Mad King*, and in Jolas's *Sonate à 12*. 'Nasality' is called for in Helms's *Golem* and in *Eight Songs for a Mad King*. Kagel, in *Phonophonie*, requires 'hoarse basic tone' and also 'brittle roughness.' Squeezed tone occurs in Schnebel's *AMN*.

Paralinguistic references in the repertoire include a wide assortment of directives; (a) as to voice set: like a child, imitate female vocalist, like a horse, ululate like a dog (*Eight Songs for a Mad King*), baby, commanding, sports reporter, drill sergeant, blues singer, asthmatically (Helms's *Golem*), laboured articulation of a deaf-mute, stammering, shaky voice (Kagel's *Phonophonie*), hysterical (*Eight Songs for a Mad King, Golem, Nouvelles Aventures*), in the manner of a salesman (*Credentials*), like a scat-singer, imitating trombone played with a mute (Schnebel's *Madrasha II*), speaking with disturbed articulation, stammering (Schnebel's *AMN*), garbled speech (Berio's *Sequenza III* and Schafer's *La Testa d'Adriane*); (b) as to dialects: 'oriental' (Helms's *Golem*), 'hurlement' of Algerian women (Berio's *Coro*), 'in the manner of South India singing' (Somers's *Zen, Yeats, and Emily Dickinson*), like a Spanish peasant woman's voice[10] (Crumb's *Ancient Voices of Children*), Provençal dialect (Constant's *St. Agnes*), 'hard-edged-Middle-Eastern' woman's voice (Schafer's *Apocalypsis*), Tibetan Buddhist chant-like chorus (Schafer's *Patria II*, etc); (c) as to vocal characterizers: laughing, crying, speaking-crying, shrieking, shouting, screaming, giggling, hiccuping, sneezing, etc; (d) as to vocal qualifiers: 'ps ps,' (for silence, perhaps) and 'brrrrr' (for indicating feeling chilly) (both in Schafer's *La Testa d'Adriane*).

Onomatopoeic references are also numerous. Beckwith's *Gas!* calls for an uncomplicated simulation of various traffic noises, his cycle *Canada Dash – Canada Dot* specifies Morse code, bird sounds, tree-cutting, and the noises of pulp-and-paper manufacturing; Kagel in *Phonophonie* asks for 'like a locomotive' and 'mechanical like a worn-out old disc,' 'flutter-tongue' is included in Oliveros's *Sound Patterns*, Haubenstock-Ramati's *Credentials*, and Crumb's *Ancient Voices of Children*. Berberian's *Stripsody* is a small compendium of such sounds: those made by a released coil, a dropped ping-pong ball, a toy airplane, eating, drinking, an alarm-clock, a telephone, animal (dog, cat) sounds, water dripping, kissing, and so on.

Stockhausen's *'Am Himmel wandre ich ...'* also asks for 'onomatopoeic articulations' and for 'unusual calls' and 'interjections.' Somers's *Voiceplay* begins with a judo exclamation, Berberian's *Stripsody* has a Tarzan-like call, and Jolas's *Sonate à 12* an 'Indian cry.'

Clicks, lip-popping, and a 'horse-trot' sound occur in *Sound Patterns*, *Sonate à 12*, *Sequenza III*, *Credentials*, and numerous other pieces.

Sound modification by placing the hand in front of the mouth and/or manipulating the lips with the fingers also occurs frequently.

Composers such as Schnebel (in *AMN* and especially in *Madrasha II* and *Mundstücke*) and Somers (in *Voiceplay*) have preferred to define sound-events in terms of phonetics and/or vocal-tract behaviour, either through indicating a desired phonetic-phonemic objective and/or giving a brief reference to physiology, primarily of the supraglottal aspects of it. These might include the sound made by the 'tongue darting in and out' (Schafer's *La Testa d'Adriane*).[11] A similar device in Jolas's *Sonate à 12* calls for 'lateral to and fro motion of the tongue.'

Haubenstock-Ramati (in *Credentials*), Schafer (in *La Testa d'Adriane* and others), Maxwell Davies (in *Eight Songs for a Mad King*), Reynolds (in *The Emperor of Ice Cream*), and Schnebel (in *Glossolalie*), among others, have relied on the suggestiveness of the graphic aspects of notation to indicate certain aspects of their vocal requirements. These graphic signs are, of course, complemented by other kinds of information.

All the above descriptions and references serve a predominantly prescriptive purpose: they are given to induce performers to reproduce the composers' intentions. As long as they accomplish this precisely enough to recreate the musical process or event envisaged by the composers, they have fulfilled their purpose. In certain cases (such as that of *Eight Songs for a Mad King*) the notation seems to be in part only suggestive of the event wanted. However, complemented by an authoritative recorded performance, it might be sufficient for performers to realize the composer's intentions.

The compositional shorthand, the compressed language of notation, that makes interpretation possible also includes a class of signs that pertain to expression.[12] A survey of our repertoire makes it clear that this domain also shows a significant expansion of its conceptual as well as its notated spectrum. Moreover, due to the great diversification of acceptable types and modes of utterance, the field of expression has become also increasingly differentiated. This can be seen, for example, in Ligeti's *Aventures* and *Nouvelles Aventures*, both of which contain a large number of expressemes and conturemes (Klüppelholz 1976: 164–5). This enrichment of the perception and portrayal of the psyche, from the most exuberant ecstatic state to the state of depressed immobility, has been the outcome of a correspondingly enriched understanding of that same psyche through new insights gained in related fields of endeavour.

SPEECH-SOUND CONCENTRATIONS

One frequently encounters repeated abstract[13] phoneme-sequences (vowels or consonants alone or the two combined into a single sequence) in the repertoire. Through repetition a normally meaningful phoneme-sequence (a word) might lose its referential function, its transparency, and, instead, its phonetic elements would come to occupy the foreground of our attention.

Sound sequences perceived phonetically (and not semantically) might then become elements in the compositional process. We might refer to this transformation as the 'musicalization of speech or of speech-like events.'

The nature of such events depends on phonetic content, type-token ratios, speed of utterance, the number of voices participating, dynamics, etc, as well as the possible simultaneous presence of other sounds that relate to them in the manner of masking, blending, contrasting, etc. It is easy to see that a very large number of different constructs are possible with these means, including some not used before in Western music.[14]

One of the most striking deployments of this compositional device occurs in section XIX of Berio's *Coro*. Here we shall be concerned only with those aspects that pertain to the topic under consideration.[15] The passage is written for a solo soprano, whose virtuoso part is intermittently complemented by a solo alto, who performs identical material. The instrumental layer features a virtuoso solo violin and a piano part. The latter consists only of a few isolated notes, chords, played here and there, punctuating twelve times in the course of the section the goings-on in the other parts. (The more active piano part at the very end of the section constitutes a transition into the very busy section XX.) The use of the word virtuoso refers to the very rapid singing and playing: six to eight notes per beat, at the speed of MM 116, are required from the vocalists and the violinist, amounting to a rate of between 11.7 and 15.6 notes per second (the upper speed limit of playability, and one wonders if it is possible to articulate vocally at that speed). A closer look at the score and a few listenings to a recorded performance[16] will show what takes place here.

The Navajo Indian text (in English translation) consists of the following:

It is so nice
a nice one gave a sound
it is nice
one gave a sound
it is the nice child of long happiness
a nice one just gave its sound
it's the nice child of ...

Its distribution in the setting shows a heavy emphasis on the words that form lines 1 and 2, and of these the word nice is further emphasized through repetition that subjects it to certain transformations. These include the notated phonetic-rhythmic shapes in figures 7.1–7.7, with the pitch of the recitation being indeterminate, hence free, and probably performed (as on the record) in a comfortable frequency range.

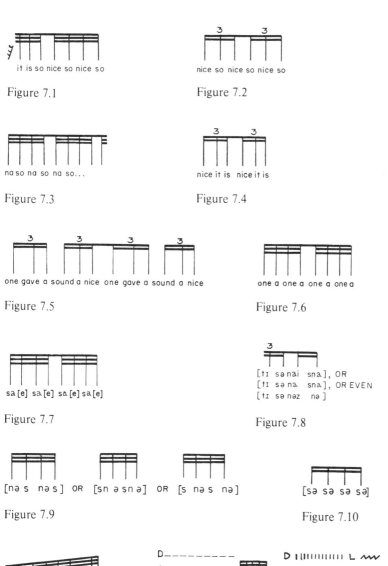

it is so nice so nice so

Figure 7.1

nice so nice so nice so

Figure 7.2

na so na so na so...

Figure 7.3

nice it is nice it is

Figure 7.4

one gave a sound a nice one gave a sound a nice

Figure 7.5

one a one a one a one a

Figure 7.6

sa [e] sa [e] sa [e] sa [e]

Figure 7.7

[tɪ sə nai   sna], OR
[tɪ sə na   sna], OR EVEN
[tɪ sə nəz   nə]

Figure 7.8

[nə s   nə s]   OR   [sn ə sn ə]   OR   [s nə s   nə]

Figure 7.9

[sə sə sə sə]

Figure 7.10

li wou li wou li wou......

Figure 7.11

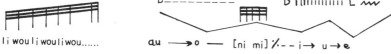

D———————   D ꓲꓲꓲꓲꓲꓲꓲꓲꓲꓲꓲꓲ L ∿

au ——→o — [ni mi] ⁒– – i→ u→e

vi de bi de bo de de

Figure 7.12

o ——→ ǎ ——→ i
vvv.......................

In the performance on the record of Figure 7.1, what I hear is, however, the sound shown in Figure 7.8. Figure 7.3, which is itself a fusion of 'nice so nice ...,' is performed as one of the three alternatives in Figure 7.9.

Similar reductions, simplifications, fusions, or substitutions occur with respect to Figures 7.4, 7.5, and 7.6. The notation of Figure 7.7 comes closest to the actual realization. But even there a fusion seems to take place: the diphtongue /ae/ is reduced to the single /ə/. Thus, what one hears is approximately the sound shown in Figure 7.10, which is difficult enough to perform at the speed specified, which requires four changes from voicing to non-voicing in 510 milliseconds.

The overall effect of all this amounts to the reality or illusion of a sequence of rapid productions of the phonemes /s/, /n/, and /ə/. Should the soprano be capable of conveying one or more meaningful *nice*s at the outset, the subsequent transformations of it will be taken as acceptable and, for a while, meaningful replicas of the same. But after a number of repeats (and transformations) the word dissolves into an abstract succession of the unvoiced alveolar fricative, /s/, the dental alveolar nasal continuant /n/ (note the closeness of the positions of the tip of the tongue for these two sounds), and the neutral vowel, /ə/, or into an even simpler reduction, as suggested earlier. The intermittently entering alto solo part increases, from time to time and for brief durations, the density level of this speech-sound concentration and further lowers an already very low type-token ratio. The accompanying solo violin part complements, rhythmically, registrally, and timbrally the phonetic-rhythmic concentrations in the voice parts. The rapid *detaché* bowings produce attack transients that blend exceedingly well with the high-frequency noise-bands of the /s/ sounds, and the somewhat slower legato groupings match well the spectral components of the /n/s and those of the few diphthongs. The stable repeated pitches, in turn, fuse well with the recurring vowel elements. The overall acoustical-musical effect is that of a timbrally highly unified, characteristical, and original tissue conveying exuberance and excitement, tinged with happiness and tension. From another point of view, the passage might be regarded as a realization of the idea of 'the sound' that 'the nice child of long happiness ... just ... gave' (score, 72), whatever that may be. This sentence has elements of wondrous and mythic quality, sustained by what preceded and what follows the section. The /tktk/ sequences in section XVIII, with their somewhat magical connotations (70–1), set the tone for the present section. The virtuoso, 'meaningless' phoneme assemblies, with their partial emphasis on hissing, which is well-known from magical practice,[17] might connote the abstraction of a magical operation here, perhaps, that of an incantation or spell for love or fertility.

The process of text-disintegration and phonemic-reconcentration just observed in *Coro* is also a principal structural idea in my *Cento*, a work for a live chorus of twelve recitants, complemented by a tape-recorded choir of equal size.[18] Two examples of it will illustrate the process used here. A segment of the work (from 6'58" to 8'02") is based exclusively on the word time, that is on the phonemic constituents of the word. Both choirs use various anagrams of the phonemes available. 'I'm,' 'tie,' 'tie time,' 'my,' 'might,' 'M.I.T.,' 'me,' 'am I?,' 'I.M.T.,' and 'T.I.M.' are used in combination with a variety of intonation curves and durations, accompanied by matching electronic sounds. In another concentration (from 4'10" to 5'23"), the rolled /r/, the flapped /ſ/, the plosives /g/, /k/, /p/, and /d/, and the fricatives /s/, /f/, /z/, and /ʒ/ predominate, conveying (that is showing) through their phonetic-metaphorical character the idea inherent in the text fragment:

... greyness
and confused improvisation
outrage and dispair ...
expanding

In this passage the choirs utter such speech-sound sequences as 'rrrage,' 'trrray, rrray,' 'gray progray dje ding dje,' and 'andes, doubt dje dim,' which are complemented on the tape by similar sequences and also 'crackling' and 'popping,' electronically generated sounds. The concentration on plosives and fricatives in this part, further enhanced by the setting, could remind one of two onomatopoeic buccal sounds referred to in the magical papyri, namely: *syrismos* (whistling, hissing) and *poppysmos* (tongue-clicking, or lip-smacking). The former was used for the attraction (control?) of snakes, the latter as an entreaty on the occasion of lightning (Hopfner 1974: 485). Is there perhaps an affective affinity (expressing persuasion, or even coercion) between this passage of *Cento* and these two very old incantational techniques?[19]

As a last example of phoneme concentrations, taken from a different context, I refer again to the *tahlīl* formula of the Sufi Muslims (see 181), with its emphasis on the phonemes /a/, /l/, /i/, and /h/. However, one has to keep in mind the reality of the *dhikr*, which was described by J.S. Trimingham in the following words: 'It commences very slowly ... with the tahlīl formula ... Then the measure is quickened, more stress being laid upon the last syllable ... With each change the voice is made more raucous until, at the final stage ... the words have degenerated to a pectoral barking noise or that of a rough saw' (Trimingham 1971: 210). This transformation affects the sonic character of the original concentration, but not the maintenance of the practice of concentration itself.

OTHER PHONEMIC AND PHONETIC CONSTRUCTS AND PROCESSES

Under this heading we shall consider examples from the contemporary repertoire, as well as examples from other contexts. I shall comment on certain details of Schafer's *La Testa d'Adriane*, Kagel's *Staatstheater*, Berio's *Circles*, Somers's *Voiceplay* and his *Zen, Yeats, and Emily Dickinson*, Jolas's *Sonate à 12*, Malec's *Dodecameron*, Schnebel's *Madrasha II*, and other compositions. The connotations of the elements of artificial languages used in these works are numerous. Some have been discussed earlier in some detail, and I shall consider more of them here.

As a first example we shall consider the concluding vocal passage from Schafer's *La Testa d'Adriane*. It consists of nine phases, in the following order: (a) 'very short burst of garbled unintelligible speech,' (b) 'hysterical laughter,' (c) 'laughter turning to sobs,' (d) 'laughter again,' (e) a seven-note melodic figure beginning with a six-vowel 'text,' stated six times, forming an isorhythmic construct, (f) the last three vowels of the six are repeated an indeterminate number of times on a three-pitch melodic figure (thus a sort of 'stability' sets in), (g) 'Ariadne continues to repeat this phrase gradually dropping it in pitch and fading away,' (h) gradually 'a kind of heavy breathing or soft sobbing takes over,' and (i) 'with a strange gurgling sound [she] expires.'

In (a), gibberish seems to be a simulation of a strange tongue; (b), (c), and (d) make up a succession of emotive sounds characteristic of neurosis; (e) and (f) show a kind of neurotically or psychotically compulsive propensity for order and repetition (see English and English 1958, 104); (g) brings forth perhaps the influence of a depressive tendency on the preceding compulsively repeating activity; and finally (h) and (i) bring her whole activity to an end – death? sleep? the machine run its course?. Thus, the passage is made up of elements of neurosis, or psychosis, artificial language formation, and ritualistically compulsive behaviour. As an analogy, we might think of a schizophrenic individual who engages in psychotic use of language. Vetter reproduces a report on a 'patient who, in response to the word 'Bett' spoken to him aloud, went through a process of 'senseless ringing of the changes on a syllable' in the following manner: 'Bett, Bett, Bett, dett, dett, dett, ditt, dutt, dutt, daut, daut, daut, dint, dint, dint, dutt, dett, datt. Wenn ich angefangen habe, fahre ich fort bis zu Ende' (When I have begun, I go on right to the end.)[20]

We have seen an example for the formation of artificial language in Ligeti's *Nouvelles Aventures*. In Kagel's *Staatstheater* we hear either one complex artificial language or numerous simple ones co-existing. Each of the sixteen voices of *Ensemble* and each of the sixty voices of *Début* has his or her own abstract text, some exceedingly simple, some quite intricate yet also redundant. Many of Kagel's texts here also show the tendency towards compulsively repeating short linguistic events. We have seen one such structure (195), and when we shall discuss the topic of setting texts, we shall look at yet another in detail.

The assignment of meaning to abstract phonetic and/or phonemic material is not new. It was known to grammarians (Nicomachus, who flourished about AD 100, and others) who 'perceived in the difference between vowels and consonants a symbol for the difference between Psyche and Hyle, soul and body, (Dornseiff 1922: 33). Pythagorean mysticism identified the seven vowels with the seven planets, thus ascribing to them cosmic signification and power (33). The mysterium of the Mithras liturgy also begins with reference to these: 'Open heaven, accept my speech-sounds, hear sun, father of the world. I appear to you with your name aōeyēoiaioēyeō' (42).

In addition to the numerous vowel series in the repertoire we are studying, one frequently encounters repetitive consonantal series also, namely: *tktk* or *dgdg* or *kada*. They appear in Berio's *Circles* and *Coro*, in Schafer's *La Testa d'Adriane*, in Somers's *Voiceplay* and *Zen, Yeats, and Emily Dickinson*, in Malec's *Dodecameron*, in Jolas's *Sonate à 12*, and in other works. In *Circles* the two *tktk* sequences (plus the three concluding kə sounds) (score, 28–9) are the only abstract phonemic events in the piece. All function as triggers that bring forth instantaneous mimetic responses on the part of the two percussionists and the harpist. The sonic resemblance between the plosives and the loud percussive and plucked sounds they elicit in response suggests cause and effect. The absence of an obvious transmission medium and the nature of the sounds involved suggest the simulation of sympathetic magic. Consonant series, indeed, are included in the magical papyri. Dornseiff gives one: 'ch ch ch   p p p p   ph ph ph ph ph ph ph   d d d d   e e e e' (Dornseiff 1922: 60). The *tktk* and similar, plosive series may be oral simulations of nature sounds (a kind of *poppysmos*) or of instrumental sounds (perhaps of the very *tktk* of tongueing on wind instruments and/or of sounds of small bells or drums). In all of these cases magical or mystical connotations are present. C. Sachs writes about 'the terrifying sound of the early trumpets associated with many magic rites' (Sachs 1940: 47). Flutes, according to

Cheyenne men, had the power of a love charm (45). The ritual-magical functions of drums are too well known to require additional documentation (Sachs 1940: chapter 1). Hopfner quotes Plutarch about the magical (apotropaic) effects of the sounds of bronze vessels and the sistrum. He also makes reference to the little bells that were sewn onto the garments of the Jewish high priests, for the same purpose (Hopfner 1974: 105, 353–4).

One of the most polished and virtuoso unaccompanied choral pieces using an abstract text in the repertoire is Jolas's *Sonate à 12*. It is a storehouse of abstract phoneme-assemblies that seem to have been composed with a close attention to phonaesthetic character, easy pronounciation at fast speeds, and compositional diversity. Many of the sounds also resemble mouth-games children like to play.[21] The piece divides into clearly articulated sections that are characterized by their respective phonemic-phonetic materials, including various clicks, tongue- and lip-tremolos (the latter with the help of fingers), in concentrations. It is subtly crafted in all its detail and expertly put together. The orthography used in the score is French. Two examples of micro-structures from individual voices in this score are shown in Figures 7.11[22] and 7.12.[23]

The following features characterize the micro-structures of this score: 1 Single vowels, vowel-series with legato transitions, and CV duplets are the most frequent events. 2 Voiced consonants are more frequent than unvoiced ones. The use of two or three different consonants in a micro-structure is preferred to the use of a single one. The largest number of consonants per micro-structure is three. 3 There might be as few as one, and as many as five different vowels in a micro-structure, or as many as six gradual transitions from one vowel to the next. 4 The textures include homophony, heterophony, polyphony, hocket, and a densely filled time-field in a structurally convincing succession.

The larger sections of the work are characterized by singing and harmonic considerations, by rapid bursts of phoneme-sequences with indeterminate pitches, by clusters of clicks and pops, or by various combinations of the three. The most complex of the texture types used is the one that contains phoneme-sequences. These display a considerable complexity and heterogeneity, which nevertheless allows for effects of blending and complexly fused clouds of phoneme-music. For example, the section on pages 7–17 shows a careful control of phoneme-modulation. One can observe in this section a predominance of /m/, /n/, and /l/ sounds, with a lesser concentration on /v/, /w/, and /j/, and only a sprinkling, here and there, of /b/, or /d/, or, towards the end of the passage, of /z/. This changes rather abruptly on page 18, where suddenly chains of /b/s, /z/s, /d/s, /j/s, /v/s and

/w/s appear, leading to a climax, containing a similar mixture of consonants, on page 20. There is a greater degree of vowel diversity than of consonantal diversity on these pages. However, even in this respect there is a constraint: close and half-close vowels are preferred, the others used but seldom. The overall structure of the piece suggests, in harmony with the title, that this is an abstract work for voices. The high degree and the type of virtuosity required in its performance convey the idea of exuberance, athleticism, excellent physical and mental health, and a general *joie de vivre*, tempered by serenity and the ability to remain calm. Despite the general, and almost instrumental, nimbleness required from the singers, the voices do *not* sound here as instruments, and on only one occasion, at the very end, does Jolas allow herself to produce the imitation of an instrumental attack.

In contrast to the Jolas work, Malec's *Dodecameron* features numerous events that appear as simulations of instrumental sounds by the twelve solo vocalists. Note for example the opening sextuple *ff* ('explosif') on the instrumental attack-like onomatopoeias: TRRR ... (twice), TCHE (twice), TEMM, and PEIN for the male voices; or the pizzicato-like D'n, T'n, P'm sounds on page 8 of the score. The familiar *dgdg* sequence, on the same page, he calls impulses, using the terminology and association-field of electronic music composition. In the last three measures of this page we have the simulation of the following electronic sounds: an attack transient, synthesized by a brief, filtered white-noise-like impulse; a sine-tone-like, rapid, ascending glissando (almost like one producible on a voltage-controlled oscillator); a steady-state sine-tone-like sound that divides up into a choral through a slow, soft, descending glissando (which Malec labels '"très électronique" et impersonnel'). In measure 3 of page 14, we hear the simulation of a voltage-controlled variable band-width filter. There are numerous similar effects in the piece, and these suggest that mimesis of electronic effects was a major compositional objective for Malec.

In contrast to the vitality of *Sonate à 12* and the machine-like precision of *Dodecameron*, the phonemic-phonetic abstractions of Schnebel's *Madrasha II* speak of a different world – that of depression, gloom, futile effort, hopelessness, and disintegration. The difficulty in producing the sound events corresponds here implicitly with similar psychic processes, a general relationship well-known to composers as well as to linguists and other students of the use of language.[24] Schnebel explains his approach in the following words: 'The piece is a composition of vocal sound-events: the departure is not from predetermined sounds, but from the processes necessary for their production.'[25] Schnebel indicates these processes, through phonetic-phonemic, prosodic, and descriptive data that the vocalists are expected to translate into action and sound. The prescriptions often include transitions from implied initial vocal-tract configurations, through a series of transformations, to a target configuration with which the event is to end. Schnebel prescribes a mandatory and persistently high energy level for the production of all these sounds. (Some, for example an aspirated, unvoiced, uvular fricative, need a big energy output just to become audible.) He puts it this way: 'In each event one should radiate a large, the largest possible quantum energy, generally that of a deep inhaling.'[26] Two characteristic examples will suffice here, to give an inkling of the nature of the sounds the piece is comprised of. The first of these demands the following:

A. A CONSONANTAL MODULATION: $\left[\text{ʒ} - \text{ʒ͜ʑ} - \text{j} - \text{ɣ} - \text{ʁ} \right]$

B. A VOWEL MODULATION: $\left[\text{e} \longrightarrow \text{i} \longrightarrow \text{a} \right]$

C. PITCH CHANGE: RISING–FALLING (HIGH → MIDDLE → LOW)

D. DYNAMICS:

E. DURATION: 3 3/4" (APPROX.)

This involves a gradual tongue-movement from the palato-alveolar position to the uvular position, while the half-closed position of the mouth becomes successively narrower, and then larger, until the maximal opening is reached. The overall effect is close to that through which one tries to bring up an unwanted object from one's throat.

The second example consists of the following:

A. A CONSONANTAL MODULATION: $\left[\text{ʁ} \longrightarrow \text{ɣ} \right]$

B. A VOWEL MODULATION: $\left[\text{æ} \longrightarrow \text{ɔ} \right]$

C. PITCH CHANGE: DESCENDING (HIGH → MIDDLE)

D. DYNAMICS:

E. DURATION: 4" (APPROX.)

The overall affect is again that of digust. The rather long duration given to these (simpler) transformations (modulations) might suggest ill health, lassitude, or depression. The simulation (in both instances) of the removal of an unwanted object from one's throat can also be looked at symbolically,

a.

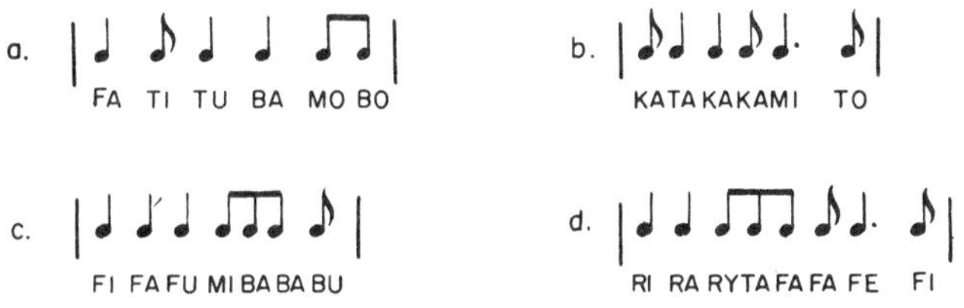

FA TI TU BA MO BO

b.

KATA KAKAMI TO

c.

FI FA FU MI BA BA BU

d.

RI RA RYTA FA FA FE FI

Figure 7.13

with the dynamics
also specified

SHEP HIS TRE GIR BA BO

Figure 7.14

meaning the desire to free oneself of an unpleasant memory, a cause for personal distress.

The abstract phoneme sequences in Nørgård's *Babel* (an interesting scenic work) are word-like and as such convey an impression of simple-mindedness and being comical. Figure 7.13 shows four typical sequences from this score. They are repeated, unchanged, by the performers.

A similar effect obtains also in the abstract words in Mellnäs's *Succsim*:

FOSI	RAFA POM	PUVAGIS	SHEP
SKE BA	AREUSA	SUVI	HIS
UDASPUT	FIPI	SEN	TREGIR
SESKUDO	KUGIPOBU	TREGI TROSKI	BABO

The pronunciation of these is ad lib (each to be said once); however the last one of these groups later becomes an ostinato, with the dynamics also specified (Figure 7.14).

After only a brief survey, one may become aware of the considerable connotative diversity inherent in the abstract vocal materials we are considering here. Abstract phoneme-sequences or phonetic events occur in many other cultures and periods. Some of the additional parallels that I am about to mention might have influenced some of the works we are studying. Even when there are no such connections, the pointing out of parallels, analogies, or resemblances might prove useful.

Several such connections between elements of this repertoire and elements of old Graeco-Egyptian magical practice have been already pointed out.[27] Yet another parallel might be the vocalization (glossolalia) produced during the trance induced during some religious ceremonies. This is alleged to replicate the occurrence described in the New Testament (Acts II: 1–4). F.D. Goodman, reporting on occurrences of glossolalia in Mexico, has transcribed such events in terms of phonetic content, syllable boundaries, intonation curves, stress, and duration. The example here has a descending

intonation curve in most lines (⟨∿⟩), primary (″) and secondary (′) stresses, and a duration of ten seconds:

```
hünda | hàndalanda
ʔïkala | hàndalanda | lòlolo
ʔ ïkada | hànda
ʔ àndalolololo | ʔ ihikada | hànda | lòlo lodi
ʔ ikada | ʔ ikada | hànda
    lù lodi | ʔ ikada | hànda
    lòkodu | hùnda
ʔ ikada handa                              (Goodman 1972: 108)
```

Goodman observes (1972: 108): 'Glossolalia is not productive. Once an audio signal has been internalized, it becomes stereotyped' (123). This reflects on abstract poems such as, for example, Kurt Schwitters's 'priimiitittiii':

```
priimiitittiii   tisch
tesch
priimiitittiii   tesch
tusch
priimiitittiii   tischa
tescho
priimiitittiii   tescho
tuschi ...                             (Motherwell 1951: xxii–iii)
```

and on Kagel's compulsively redundant texts in *Staatstheater* (see 195 and 238). One wonders if the psychic driving that seems to be indispensable for inducing some persons to produce glossolalia utterances (Goodman 1972: 52–60, 74–9, 90–2) has some aspects in common with what the Greeks called the poetic mania (Rouget 1980: 268–76). A similar trance-like state might have also existed in the process called automatic writing, which was practised by certain Kabbalists (Scholem 1954: 136–7; 1974: 188).

I referred in chapter 1 to the influence of Rimbaud, Mallarmé, and the futurist, dadaist, and surrealist poets on the development of music for the voice. To these names we have also to add those of certain Russian poets of the early twentieth century: Kruchenykh, Xlebnikov and Kamenskij.

Xlebnikov's *Incantation by Laughter*, one of his 'linguistic experiments with ... trans-sense language' (Barooshian 1974: 23), explores the field of word-transformation through prefixes and suffixes, creating in the process neologism, phonemic concentration, and, thus, the 'musicalization of speech' (23–4):

Oh, laugh forth, laugh laughadors!
O laugh on, laugh laughadors!
You who laugh in laughs, laugh-laugh, you who laughorize!
So laughly, laugh forth laugh laugh belaughly!
Oh, of laughdon overlaughly, laugh of languish laughadors!
Oh, forth laugh downrightly laughly, laugh of super laughadors!
Laughery! Laughery!
Belaugh, uplaugh, laughikins, laughikins,
Laughutelets, laughetelets!
Oh, laugh forth, laugh laughadors!
Oh, laugh on, laugh, laughadors!

One of Kruchenykh's early poems consisted solely of vowels (85):

	o		e		a	
i		e		e		i
a		e		e		e

It was one of his experimental quests for a universal language and 'served as an antidote to the paralysis of common language' (85).[28]

Kamenskij's 'verbal play also extended to the "breaking down" of words' (Barooshian 1974: 101) (which show a curious similarity to the wing-shaped constructs in the magical papyri):

Izlučistaja
Lučistaja
Čistaja
Istaja

Staja
Taja
Aja
Ja

However, this series of reduction does not produce meaningless debris. Each line has its own meaning:[29]

Bendy (river) (meander?)
Radiating
Clean
Very sincerely believing
Pack (or flock)
Melting
And me (?)
I

Writing about the new word-constructs of trans-sense language in Kruchenykh's poetry, Gorlow pointed out that it was effective only against the background of meaning as 'a semantic echo reflected in other words' (Barooshian 1974: 95). I find that this perception is compatible with Fónagy's account of the metaphorical content of phonemes.

Another early critic, Čukovskij, referring to the poets of the trans-sense orientation (defined as 'not a "language," but a pre-language, pre-cultural, pre-historical ... when there was no discourse conversation but only cries and screams' [95]) remarked that while he approved of the use of trans-sense in poetry, he found it discouraging that 'a whole generation of poets had given themselves up to it, by rejecting, therefore, all the higher forms of cultured human speech' (94). If these poets took delight in emotional belching, then it only reflected the poverty of the mental and spiritual life of the age. For this mode of 'expression was characteristic of wild shamans, idiots, imbeciles, maniacs, eunuchs, runners, jumpers' (94–5).

Čukovskij's criticism, an interesting amalgam of deep insight and fear of the unknown, could not, of course, stem the process that found expression in the works of the poets, artists, and composers whom we encountered on these pages. Closer to our time, lettrist poets and composers also experimented with abstract language constructs. The principle of speech-sound concentrations can be found also in their works. For example, Gérard-Philippe Brontin's poem (composition?) *L* features the phoneme /ℓ/, as does the *tahlīl* formula of the *dhikr* ceremony of the Sufi Muslims (Curtay and Gillard 1971: 95):

La llail ell llille, lélal el lai luloul lel lilles
Luil, lalal, luil le lell lue les oileaul loulilles
lelle lalli lélule illollue el lal lieul ...

Another example (77), Jean-Paul Curtay's *L'Étreinte ininterrompue*, shows a different pattern of phoneme concentration, and, thus, another instance of the musicalization of language:

hanahagnabongjifhahakssabongjifhahakssabongjifhahakssahagssonhaghanahagna-
bongjifhahakssahnagahanabigjifhahakssabibigjouha ...

COMPOSITION IN TERMS OF VOCAL-TRACT BEHAVIOUR

G.L. Bruns has reminded us of Elisabeth Sewell's understanding that 'one of the primary functions of language is to provide, in its words, small separate units for the mind to manipulate, convenient packets of experience which the mind can manage where it could not manage the chaotic multiplicity of total experience' (Sewell 1952: 131).[30] Poetry and music are but two of the means through which we can reclaim ground given up in the retrenchment implied by Sewell. This is perhaps what Bruns had in mind when he observed: 'It appears to be in the nature of poetry to call this "primary function" of language to which Sewell has referred to into question' (131). Through the musicalization of language, composers also have contributed to the further expansion of this process, as we have already seen. We shall look at other attempts to conceptualize oral utterance directly, through references to, or definitions of, physiological activity, without recourse to such linguistic abstractions as phonemes.

We have precedents in certain onomatopoeic words, such as sneezing or coughing, each of which suggestively denotes a specific physiological act. Other sound-making physiological acts are likely to be less common, and the signs by which one would want to evoke them might be less unambiguous and quite cumbersome.

Joan La Barbara, a singer-composer, has described her approach to the production of sounds in the following terms: 'I've tried to devise different situations that I can place myself in to not bypass the brain, but to not use intellect to make a sound. But rather to use another sense' (La Barbara 1976: 151–62).[31] Her explanations are complemented by verbal references to parts of vocal physiology and schematic drawings of the same. Her objectives include the investigation of various resonance areas, 'circular breathing,'[32] multiphonic octave singing, and electronic modifications of the voice.

The Center for Music Experiment and Related Research, at the University of California at San Diego, published in 1974 an *Index to a Recorded Lexicon of Extended Vocal Techniques*, which is accompanied by explanatory notes and tape-recorded demonstration.[33] It contains seventy-four different items, divided into three groups: monophonic, multiphonic, and miscellaneous sounds. One of the objectives of this research has been to amass 'a vocabulary of sounds ... many of which are unknown in Western music and some of which appear not to have been used musically anywhere' (Large 1977: 50–1 and Kavásch 1980). The other goals were to determine the generative nature of these new resources and whether these sounds can be produced without endangering the voice.[34]

Schnebel's article 'Sprech und Gesangsschule (Neue Vokalpraktiken) (Schnebel 1972: 444–57) (School for Speech and Singing [New Vocal Practices]), is one of the most insightful accounts of the post-Webern evolution of vocal compositional practices. In it he comments on the radical enlargement of the scope of music itself; the influence and function of improvization; the consequences of the use of phonetic signs; an increased awareness of voice production; the compositional use of unintelligible or meaningless speech events; transitional modalities between speaking and singing; speech features that suggest hysteria; decomposition and transformation processes related to speech events; sound production viewed from the point of view of the articulatory process; the role of the chest-cavity in sound production; and composition as the 'setting free of articulation' (455). He describes the evolution of his thinking about composing for, and with, the voice through references to his compositions *AMN*, *Madrasha II*, and *Maulwerke*. The first is 'a prayer composition' in which 'prayer-like events are created ... through interference with the process of articulation.' In addition to prayer-texts, the work also uses 'entirely arbitrary speech continuities' (455). The topic of *Madrasha II* is the 'genesis of praise' (455). Speech events here are totally rudimentary and manifest themselves through invocations and praise-formulas. Even these are 'broken up or hidden' (455). In *Maulwerke*, 'articulation itself is the final concern ... Here content no longer expresses itself through mediation, through the instrument of a however rudimentary text, but directly' (456). (The distortions of speech fragments and the obvious focal concern with vocal-tract physiology in much of *Madrasha II* put this work very close to *Maulwerke*, though the former has a clearly indicated referential context, while the latter does not.) Schnebel adds: 'In such a body-language not only the sounds that are emitted from the mouth have their meaning, but also the body organs themselves, that produce them, the parts of the mouth ... Perhaps it is that language which music was always aiming at' (456–7). With this comment he comes as close to implying the possibility of an Orphic language as one is likely to encounter among contemporary composers.

Schnebel has employed a number of notational modes for his pieces: a combination of verbal descriptions, phonetic signs, and musical symbols and some simple, suggestive, graphic elements – schematic drawings of supraglottal settings (lip-settings, mouth-cavity formations, and tongue positions). However, he expresses the hope that the person interested in such matters will find himself 'liberated' by the example of having heard and/or performed such experimental works. With his mind 'freed' and his vocal physiology 'unchained,' he might induce himself to engage in 'free' vocal-tract activity, following the inner promptings of his own mind and body. Schnebel refers to this type of music as a series of processes 'which are self-forming and on their part engender the formation of other processes. This has neither a precise beginning, nor a definite end' (457). He suggests that we regard this as no longer a work of art, but an instrument for the liberation of the self (457).

Wishart's *book of lost voices* has been written as a guidebook for his *Anticredos*, a work for six amplified voices. It is also a record of Wishart's research into extended vocal techniques over a period of three years. This catalogue, which contains 169 items, each described briefly, is a useful contribution to the field by an inventive composer, who is especially accomplished in the tape-manipulation of vocal materials.

Küpper's article 'New Possibilities of Vocal Music: Phonemes, Allophones, Phonatomes, Logatomes, Phonetic Microsounds' (Küpper 1975) presents phonetic and process composition in a broad theoretical perspective. It also makes reference to non-Western types of voice use, and to electro-acoustical possibilities of phonetic transformation.

The publication *La Musique lettriste* includes a 'lexique des lettres nouvelles' by Isou and others. It contains 159 different items, most of them vocal and some of which seem to be included for 'shock value' (Curtay and Gillard 1971: 67–70).

Additional information on this topic can also be found in Jensen 1979; in *Mouth Sounds*, by F.R. Newman (Newman 1980)[35] (which also includes a demonstration record); and in Schafer's *When Words Sing* (Schafer 1970).

Sir Richard Paget, about a half-century ago, wrote: 'Poetry is the art of pantomimic dancing with the tongue.'[36] This comes close to Schnebel's position. Johan Sundberg observes that 'there is a relation between the way the voice organs are used and the emotional content of the utterance ... A possible reason for this symbolic behavior in phonation and articulation may be a general body language of emotions which exerts its influence also over the behavior of the voice organs' (Sundberg 1980: 12–13).

TEXTS AND TEXT-SETTINGS

1 As far as the nature of text (should there be such) of a composition is concerned, the repertoire shows the following options: original text, poem, or scenario, composed for the purpose; a borrowed composed text; a collage, mix, etc of borrowed or found fragments, adapted for the purpose; abstract constructs; onomatopoeic constructs; composition in terms of vocal-tract behaviour (process composition); improvised indeterminate constructs; and various composites.

2 As to the nature of the language(s) used, the repertoire shows the following categories: a single natural language (dialect, sociolect or idiosyncratic); two or more natural languages; a single artificial language; two or more artificial languages; onomatopoeic languages, or similar constructs;[37] secret, mystical, unintelligible, magical, and other similar languages or constructs; infant and/or early childhood languages; and various composites.

3 The nature of the setting depends also on the prosodic, paralinguistic, stylistic, culture specific, dialectal, sociolectal, role specific, and idiosyncratic elements used, as well as on the degree of intactness or fragmentedness, the naturalness of delivery or distortion, and the degree of overall simplicity or complexity, of the whole and its parts. The character of a realization of a text (or a process composition) hinges also on many other compositional details, too numerous even to list, including those that contribute to the affective aspect of the work.

4 As to the number and nature of voices simultaneously employed, we find solo works and works for a smaller or larger group of voices. None, some, or all of these might be pre-recorded, which, in some instances, might be combined with live layers. Some compositions[38] have been conceived for, and are realized through, artificially generated voices.

5 The compositions concerned also display diversity in spatial deployment of the vocalists and in whether they remain in one place throughout a performance or are asked to move about.

6 Finally, the voice(s) may or may not be complemented by instrumental forces of various kinds.

Randolph Stow's poem 'The Sentry,' which constitutes the text of the first movement of Maxwell Davies's *Eight Songs for a Mad King*, shows a reasonable continuity of thought. It contains nothing that could not be accepted as a poetical expression of the thoughts and feelings of a rapidly, and at times metaphorically, associating person, under some stress, who yet manages to maintain a modicum of humour and is even able to express a touch of gentleness towards a young guard, who might still be in his adolescence. The setting changes this image drastically through the following features: an exceptionally wide vocal range with its extremities emphasized; frequent register changes; frequent changes of dynamics; a large diversity of unusual voice qualities; extreme vocalizations (shrieks, roarings); interruptions; impersonations (tyrant, child, woman, sqealing dog); stammering; child-like melos, combined with thick, harsh utterances, or squealings, etc, without sustained fundamental pitch; overall unpredictability (capriciousness) regarding the succession of the combinations of the various parameters. The text was left intact in the succession of its words but many distortions (deviations from norms) occur in the prosodic and paralinguistic parameters. The overall impression conveyed is the voice of a mentally ill person. This is sustained also by the complementing instrumental layers.

Cage's *Solo for Voice, No. 4*, in *Song Books* volume I, shows distortion of text, by the juxtaposition of non-adjacent fragments of an original text, that result in type-crossings (Drange 1966). *Solo for Voice, No. 18*, of the same work, features distortions of word order and syllable order simultaneously.

Reynolds, in his *The Emperor of Ice Cream*, composes with Wallace Stevens's poem by distributing it, at places word by word, among eight vocalists, thus creating a *Klangfarben* process. In addition, he fuses at places parts of words into new phoneme-combinations. These operations are complemented by changes of position on the stage by the vocalists. Nevertheless, the compositional objective of overall intelligibility of the text (coloured by the described disturbances) remains evident. In some aspects of this setting Reynolds follows the process pioneered by Nono in the mid-1950s in his *Il canto sospeso* and *La terra e la campagna*, but his achievement remains very much his own.

Sustained repetition of a short text, as in Steve Reich's *Come out*, tends to shift the focus of attention from the semantic-syntactic domain to the sonic one, thus resulting in the musicalization of the phonemic-phonetic content of the utterance, a kind of transformation.

In the Alto 1 part of 'Ensemble' in Kagel's *Staatstheater* the text unfolds to reveal a small number of root-syllables in an artificial language and a number of transformations, obeying a few rules. The root-syllables are /on/ and /in/, to which may be added one of a collection of prefixes and/or the single suffix /g/. This can be shown schematically as follows:

one of b, d, k, p, r, s, sch, t, ts, tsch, x optional as initial sound
one of i, o mandatory, as either initial or second-place sound
n mandatory, as either second- or third-place sound
g optional as ending sound

These rules produce the following collection: in, ing, on, ong, bin, din, kin, pin ... bon, don, kon, pin ... bing, ding, king, ping ... bong, dong, kong, pong ... (see 195) which resembles the abstract constructs encountered in the syllabaries (Dornseiff 1922: 67), as well as the compulsive generation of nonsense words by a schizophrenic patient, reported by Vetter (see 222–3 and n 20 to this chapter).

In poetry certain kinds of transformations are known under the names metathesis and anagram. In the Kabbalah, they are called *ziruf* (*tseruf*) (Dornseiff 1922: 136; Scholem 1941: 131)[39] or *gilgul*. Special Kabbalistic methods for exchanging one letter for another are indicated by the cipher words 'Atbash' and 'Albam,' both referring to the Hebrew alphabet's twenty-two letters.[40] Knowlson observes that Jonathan Swift's *Gulliver's Travels* shows a remarkable diversity of transformations: 'anagram, reversal, omission, substitution or transposition of letters and other more complex devices, with these distortions all operating upon material borrowed from numerous languages' (Knowlson 1975: 125). Perhaps the most systematically carried out succession of transformations occurs in Samuel Beckett's *Watt* (Beckett 1959: 164–8), in a passage which amounts to a sound-poem. It subjects short word-continuities to the following distortions: talking back to front, i.e. inverting the order of the words in the sentence; inverting the order of the letters in the words; inverting the order of the sentences in a period; and combining any two or all three of these rearrangements.[41]

Vivier's back-to-front transformations in *Chants* amount to disguising, or as I have suggested, to contravening the words retrograded.[42] Berio's setting of the text in *Sequenza III* portrays the workings of a mind.[43] The text of Pousseur's *Phonèmes pour Cathy* is developed from two sentences of Paul Claudel. During almost the entire first half of the piece the singer utters only abstract phonemic constructs, using the phoneme repertoire of Claudel's words. At that point intelligible fragments of the source-text appear, such as 'le temps est,' 'ce que l'invitation le cœur désir(e) à mourir peut à toute phrase de se décomposer toujours,' which in retrospect may suggest to the listener that the earlier process of using only unintelligible fragments was but a realization (a showing) of the very idea of decomposition that is central to the source-text itself. The work thus uses a dual, disintegrative-reintegrative process in its treatment of text. Another place where we can observe such a dual operation is in *Gesang der Jünglinge* by Stockhausen.[44] As we have seen, Ligeti's *Nouvelles Aventures* shows the evolution and disintegration of an imaginary language, a dual process that stands for the fortunes of a society. The process of linguistic disintegration in increasingly severe degrees that underlies the three works ($dt31_6$, *AMN*, and *:! (Madrasha II)*) in Schnebel's *für stimmen (... missa est)* is probably also an allegorical representation of the subject matter.

An interesting example of an artificial language serving as text occurs again in Kagel's *Staatstheater*, in the first half of the solo Tenor 4 part of 'Ensemble.' This language has four principal properties. 1 / It uses five consonants and four vowels, B, D, P, T, R and I, U, A, and A', of which the last occurs only four times, and only at the end of a word. 2 / These phonemes form CV duplets, chains of which constitute this language. The sample in question consists of eighty utterances (words), each of which is a chain. There are but two chains (each concludes a section) that consist of only two CV duplets; each of the others has four, five, six, or seven duplets. 3 / It is a selective system, which at each and every level uses only a part of the total number of combinatorial possibilities. For example: only two of the nine CV duplets used generate homogeneous chains (those that use only one type of CV duplet). 4 / Constraints include the following: in a given word there are never more than two different vowels and three different consonants. Events with two (different ones) of each predominate. Figure 7.15 shows the constituent elements, the actual words (underlined), as well as constraints, of this language.[45]

Another characteristic feature of our repertoire is the use of several languages in one and the same piece. This might be regarded as yet another manifestation of the increasingly and interactively global nature of our civilization. Berio's *Omaggio a Joyce* uses a single fragment from Joyce's *Ulysses*, read by a woman in English, French, and Italian. His *Passaggio* contains utterances in Italian, German, French, English, and Latin. In *Coro* he employs English, Spanish, German, French, Italian, and Hebrew, but certain texts from Amerindian and other languages are set to music in translation (almost in every instance in English). Stockhausen's *Stimmung* contains, besides its abstract texts, and words in German, foreign magical names. Cage's solos for

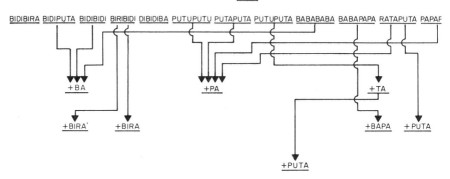

Figure 7.15

voice, nos. 12, 13, and 14 in *Song Books* volume I, not only contain a multiplicity of languages, but also there is such a constant changing from one to another that the effect created is of a high degree of dissociation. My own *Foci* contains sustained passages in English, French, German, Italian, Hungarian, Aramaic, Yiddish, Haitian, Byzantine, and modern Greek. Schnebel in his *Glossolalie* employs German (in several dialects), Italian, English, French, Czech, Spanish, Portuguese, Hungarian, Finnish, Turkish, Latin, classical Greek, Vietnamese, Khmer, Ewe, and Indonesian. Perhaps the greatest diversity can be found in Schafer's *Patria II*.

It is useful to recall the attitude towards the use of foreign words by the anonymous authors and/or scribes of some of the magical papyri written during the early Christian centuries, times when the spirit of syncretism was very much alive. We have evidence that the use of words in a foreign language was preferred in certain magical practices. Hopfner writes (Hopfner 1974: 433–5) of the favoured employment of Egyptian, Babylonian (Chaldean), Syrian, and/or Hebrew words. Kropp remarks that foreign names 'must not be translated into one's own language, lest they lose their magical power' (Kropp 1931 III: 120). Reasons for this (perhaps the weightiest ones) might have been the lack of necessity for translating a demon-name,[46] which might have been coined as an abstract or onomatopoeic construct in the first place, and the corollary of this, the recognition of the great importance of the sonic properties of such constructs. Both considerations bring us, once again, to the recognition of certain affinities between the vocal activities of the magus and those of the sound-poet, as well as the composer who works with all the possibilities of vocal utterance.

Also characteristic of our repertoire is the almost ubiquitous presence of the devices of text-distortions and disintegrations that frequently denote mental stress or alienation, dissociation, neurosis, or psychosis. Works in the latter category include *Eight Songs for a Mad King* and *Miss Donnithorne's Maggot* (Maxwell Davies); *Patria I* and *Patria II* (Schafer); *Sur Scène*, *Phonophonie*, *Rezitativarie*, and *Hallelujah* (Kagel); *Sequenza III*, *Visage*, and *Recital I. For Cathy* (Berio); *Nouvelles Aventures* (Ligeti); *An Avalanche* (Hiller); *AMN* and *Madrasha II* (Schnebel); and *Foci* (Anhalt).

Another less frequent influence on vocal utterances is erotic experience. Daniel Charles devotes to this topic considerable attention (Charles 1978),[47] referring to, among other subjects, the art of such singers as Jane Birkin, Donna Summer, Helen Merrill, and Cathy Berberian, to whose names we might add also that of Janis Joplin and those of many male 'rock' vocalists as well. Among works with erotic orientation, we should list Druckman's *Animus 2*, Schafer's *Loving*, and Stockhausen's *Stimmung*. Eroticism and mysticism are related in certain contexts. Eliade tells us that 'Tantric texts are often composed in an 'intentional language' (*sandhā-bhāṣā*), a secret, dark, ambiguous language in which a state of consciousness is expressed by an erotic term and the vocabulary of mythology or cosmology is charged with Haṭha-yogic or sexual meanings' (Eliade 1969: 249).

Should a thorough survey of the repertoire confirm the tentative assessment just made that works depicting stress, mental affliction, conflict, and disintegration are more numerous in our repertoire than works expressing love, eroticism, and other forces of creativity, one would have to ask why this state of affairs exists. Why do the forces of Thanatos seem to have a stronger impact on this group of composers than the forces of Eros?[48]

One way of securing in a work the presence of specific voice(s) performing in a precisely determined manner is the method of pre-recording voice(s) and including the recorded voice(s) in the composition. (A more recently developed version is the computer generation of artificial utterance.) This is used in Stockhausen's *Gesang der Jünglinge*, in Berio's *Omaggio a Joyce* and *Visage*, in Tamia's *Senza tempo*, in Kavásch's *Requiem*, and in my *Cento*, *Foci*, and *La Tourangelle*.

Some works for several voices (Stockhausen believes that 'many' begins at about seven) still allow us to feel that we are dealing with a group consisting of individuals. Whether this happens or we hear a group in which the members have surrendered their individuality depends not only on numbers, but also on the structural relationship among the voices. Thus *Nouvelles Aventures* and Helms's *Daidalos* are works for individual voices, as are my *Foci* and parts of *Cento*. But the twelve voices of Malec's *Dodecameron*, or those in Jolas's *Sonate à 12*, more often than not coalesce into an ensemble. It might be useful now to list the principal types of vocal groups from the point of view of their semiotic (pragmatic) connotations:

TYPE OF GROUP	TYPICAL WORK
Simulated collective meditation by a small group of individuals	Stockhausen *Stimmung*
Religious or quasi-religious action by a large group	Schafer *Apocalypsis*; Ligeti 'Introitus' from *Requiem*
Liturgical or quasi-liturgical recitation	Lewkovitch *Il Cantico delle creature*
Sea of humanity; a multitude or a mob under, or out of, control	Ligeti 'Kyrie' and 'De judicii sequentia' from *Requiem*; Lutosławski *Trois Poèmes d'Henri Michaux*
Group antiphonies	Xenakis *Nuits*

TYPE OF GROUP	TYPICAL WORK
Polychoral events	Stockhausen *Carré*; Globokar *Traumdeutung*; Schafer *Apocalypsis* and *In Search of Zoroaster*
Flexibly interacting individuals	Helms *Golem* and *Daidalos*; Ligeti *Aventures* and *Nouvelles Aventures*
An alternatingly cohesive or non-cohesive group of individuals	Schnebel *AMN*, *Madrasha II*, and *Glossolalie*; Kagel *Hallelujah*; Berio *Sinfonia* (third movement); Anhalt *Cento* and *Foci*
A middle-sized group of closely co-operating individuals who enact a unified text	Reynolds *The Emperor of Ice Cream*
A middle-sized group of individually and independently conceived vocal parts that can be assembled in any number of ways	Kagel 'Ensemble' from *Staatstheater* and *Hallelujah*; Cage *Song Books*
A large group of individually and independently conceived vocal parts that can be assembled in any number of ways	Kagel 'Début' from *Staatstheater*; Cage *Song Books*
Simultaneous, heterogeneous, yet interacting groups of voices, depicting a complex situation	Anhalt 'Isaac' from *La Tourangelle*
Onomatopoeic play (with or without other materials) by a middle-sized group, with or without an implied referential context	Oliveros *Sound Patterns*; Malec *Dodecameron*; Beckwith *Gas!*
Complex choral polyphony, using a broad spectrum of vocal utterance types, by a middle-sized group, with an intermittently implied referential context	Jolas *Sonate à 12*

Thus one could also think of these types of groups as abstractions of real-life agglomerations of people. The dynamics of such groups are usually complex. Describing a special kind of group consisting of a 'greater or lesser number of persons in ecstasy ('d'exaltés'),' P. de Felice perceives them as 'radiating around themselves their enthusiasm or their neurosis ... The intoxication of these psychically drunken people extends its influence further and further like a forest fire' (de Félice 1947: 357). William McDougall lists (McDougall 1921: 49–50) five conditions of 'principal importance in raising collective mental life to a higher level than the unorganized crowd': 'continuity of existence of the group' (awareness of each other's presence); an 'adequate idea of the group' (in the minds of the members); 'interaction'; a body of 'customs and traditions in the minds of the members'; and 'differentiation and specialization of the function of its constituents' (50). It would not be difficult to find a number of musical structures that one would be able to identify as abstractions or simulations of the conditions described by these authors. For example, Cage's, Kagel's, and Schnebel's choral structures often describe a lack of common purpose, while Ligeti portrays at times the ant-heap model of a human society. Quotations (like the Heinrich Schütz fragment in Schafer's *Gita*) can be symbols for common traditions reaffirmed. The same device in a different context (in Schnebel's *Glossolalie*, for example) denotes the rejection of a heritage or at least calls into question the sufficiency of relying exclusively on such. Many other examples could be given.

Erving Goffman, one of the most astute students of the ways in which people interact, in the chapter 'Alienation from Interaction' in *Interaction Ritual* (Goffman 1967) focuses on verbal interaction. He says: 'As a main focus of attention talk is unique ... for talk creates for the participant a world and a reality that has other participants in it. Joint spontaneous involvement is a *unio mystico* (Goffman's emphasis), a socialized trance' (113). Subsequently he lists several forms of alienation that can be observed to obstruct such interactions. I read this book only recently and, while doing so, was struck by the similarity between what he says about such hindering factors and the burden of the seventh movement, 'Definition 3,' of my *Foci*. The text of the movement is a definition of the word interaction (English and English 1958). The setting, for two (male, female) reciting voices (English and French) and a small group of instruments, expresses the lack of interaction between the vocalists and the repressed tension that results. The voices are impersonal, and each of their utterances is simultaneously punctuated by brittle electronic and instrumental sounds. Very soft, tonally unrelated, 'residue' chords 'result' from some of these and remain 'hanging in the air'; we are also reminded of the inexorable passing of time by a third voice. The setting uses the text as a vehicle (as a pretext, perhaps) to express its antonym and some of the human and social consequences that may ensue.[49]

G.L. Bruns, drawing from Paul Ricoeur, observes: 'It is in the act of speech that the sign is actualized as part of man's life in the world. The act of speech does not take place in a void of purely formal relations: it is not a hermetic act but an event in the world – an Orphic utterance in which world and word are brought forward as in a single presence' (Bruns 1974: 243). This is a familiar thought for those composers who seek to musicalize the word and to create for it a semiotically fitting habitat within a composition.

Beckwith is one composer whose works often speak lucidly and penetratingly of such interrelations (Anhalt 1981). An example is a short work of his entitled *Gas!* The locale of the piece is characteristically close to home for Beckwith, in south-central Ontario. But it could be situated at any place where there are streets and highways with cars and traffic signs. In the following chapter I shall endeavour to describe this piece and some of its connotations, as well as Schafer's *In Search of Zoroaster* and Berio's *Coro*.

8

Alternative voices

G A S !

I promised at the end of chapter 7 to comment on John Beckwith's *Gas!*. One is perhaps reluctant to bring to bear the paraphernalia of analysis on this short (barely four minutes long) and simple-sounding piece. Its sounds and surface structure are quite slight: a middle-sized group of vocalists recite in a low-key fashion a collection of words and texts taken from south-central Ontario traffic signs. These words could have come from almost anywhere and everywhere, from any locality or area in North America. For this reason, one is willing to accord a certain broad topicality and generality to the work. Anyone and everyone who ever sat in a car, or has crossed a street, finds that the piece strikes a familiar chord despite and perhaps especially because of the mildly unusual nature of that chord. One instinctively attributes to the composition a tongue-in-cheek quality and perhaps even something resembling the status of an in joke.

The piece appears to be based on a trivial, even cute idea – the recitation of found (verbal) objects,[1] those of traffic instructions and of onomatopoeically simulated traffic noises – and to bring out the humour inherent in placing these in a concert environment. In his notes to the score Beckwith suggests a historical parallel. Referring to the sound surface of the piece, he says: 'Once the novelty of producing the required sounds has worn off in rehearsal, they should be practiced as sounds and delivered in performance with a straight face. In this sense the composition is of course a successor to the 16th century "program chansons" with their humorous battle noises or bird-calls.' He expresses the hope that 'the piece will emerge ... as a vocal tone-poem with widely varied colours and images, and with levels of "message" that are both on the surface and deep under it.' To reduce whatever pathos he might have detected in this statement, which he allowed to surface in a moment of candidness, he quickly adds a countervailing remark to the effect that 'the ending should not be made *too* deep.' The work was intended as a serious piece of music, with several layers of meaning. We are, in effect, challenged by him to look for and find these strata.

The particular appeal of the found object becoming a part of a work of art resides in the tension between the respective semiotic worlds of the two. The former opens windows and even destroys walls, of the museum or concert-hall, enlarging the meanings of these institutions in the process. For found objects to be able to perform this function they must be treated with due respect, as if they would be precious commodities, or symbols thereof. Beckwith's performance instructions are given in this spirit: 'The participants should appear as serious disciplined performers rather than party cut-ups.' They should articulate with 'clarity' and 'complete naturalness.' What he wants them to avoid are the 'acting' of the lines, the playing 'for cheap laughs, by pseudo-comic inflections,' 'sing-song effect of pitch or regular rhythmic pulse.' The added onomatopoeic sounds are 'to be treated always as an accompaniment.' 'Their quality may be quite playful and they should involve whole-hearted muscular exertion (jaw, lips, mouth, tongue, teeth, etc.). But, while they may be exaggeratedly produced for purposes of sonority or projection they should be as "natural" in their way as the words they accompany.' And then again comes the warning that these sounds should not be produced as if 'showing-off by actors.'[2]

A second layer of meaning can appear either simultaneously with the first or following the first or a subsequent hearing of the work. One may become aware of the metaphorical character of some of the words or expressions: 'turning in one direction or in the other,' being 'given the green light'[3] of encouragement, being flashed a 'red light' of warning, being reminded that life is a 'two way street,' going with this or that 'speed' ahead, or encountering a 'detour,' a 'blind street,' or even a 'dead end.' For the time being, however, we are puzzled by the only dismantling and reassembling of words in the entire piece:

Railway, crossing
Rail/ing/cross/way
Rail/cross/ing/way

We also notice the funny juxtapositions (a few of which cause type-crossing [Drange 1966]) – 'Watch for falling rocks,' 'Watch for children,' 'Slippery when wet' – and the silly or senseless expressions – 'Bump soft shoulders,' 'Do not drive on paved shoulders,' 'Advanced green when flashing,' 'Right turn on green arrow only,' 'Ramp speed.' After a while we might begin to bristle at the surfeit of commands: 'Squeeze right,' 'Merge,' 'Yield,' feeling as if we are being 'pushed around.' We might even be wondering about the origin of these imperatives: who utters these commands, anonymously and ubiquitously? We have known how to cope with these one by one. But as Beckwith shows them to us, in an unrealistic yet truthful bulk, we suddenly feel the burden they cumulatively represent. They become symbols for all the kinds of commands, orders, interdictions, limitations, warnings, and general appeals that society imposes on the individual. The natural or impersonal delivery of the speaker-performers heightens our uneasiness, because they seem to have unquestioningly accepted these commands. We are a bit ambivalent about this, because, while bristling about the nature and implications of the language, we may also acknowledge the need for a body of rules that allows us to live together without collisions – literal or metaphorical. These simple traffic commands are twins of the moral judgments or ethical precepts that we live by all the time. C.L. Stevenson (quoted by Izutsu) puts it this way: 'There are close affinities between moral judgements and commands, indeed, a moral judgement, like a value judgement, is nothing else than a command in a misleading grammatical form' (Izutsu 1956: 36). Izutsu develops the idea further by saying: 'The ancient books of law ... are all collections of a great many minutest commands and prohibitions regulating the proper conduct of man in all the possible contingencies of individual and communal life. These rules are deemed by all to be divine in origin, but most of them especially prohibitions, are in reality but tribal taboos attired in new garments' (37). Perhaps *Gas!* is an allegory for the dos and don'ts of society. Has Beckwith's allegory a personal element? I think it might have one, and it might pertain to childhood, perhaps to the composer's own.

The very idea of *collecting* a text such as that of *Gas!* is somewhat analogous to the fun a child might have in collecting match-boxes or cheese labels or the sightings of men with beards. The act of recitation (naming) is analogous with possession. There are two overt references to children, and numerous hidden ones. The onomatopoeias are probably reminiscences of childhood mouth-games, rather than derivations from any other source. When a child imitates the sound of a car does he not, at the same time, imagine that he drives (controls) the car, or even *is* the car itself? If so, we have arrived at the level of sympathetic magic and thus reached the threshold Izutsu has taken us to via language forms and language use. The child may, indeed, practise vestiges of a very old method of control over parts of reality with which he is unable to cope in (what would appear to us) a more rational way. Moreover, a phrase as absurd as 'Don't drive on paved shoulders' may represent, through the perception of a young child, puzzlement with some aspects of reality as expressed through the use of language.

But now we have to attempt to get a little bit closer to the child, who seems to be playing hide-and-seek behind the screen of words constituting the text of *Gas!*. Perhaps the innocent combinational play with the words railway crossing might help us.[4] Beckwith created here the construct railing which can be a noun or a gerund. One can imagine a little boy confused by the language and behaviour of adults, both of which can appear to him at times as arbitrary and/or ambiguous. Along these lines of thought the three-fold presence of the word cross might be significant, especially in the construct crossway with its considerable poetic and religiously evocative appeal. The word cross can be a noun, a verb, or an adjective: the religious symbol, to cross (the street), to be cross (angry), and to cross someone (to counter someone's will). *Gas!* might speak of difficulties in coming to terms with rules.

The child-like perception and representation of a segment of reality (a major theme that runs through much of Beckwith's works) and the vocabulary and the noises of traffic (seen perhaps from the back seat of limited responsibility) might be a way of bringing a deep-lying layer of experience and feeling to the surface. The piece might also be an exorcism of resentments and fears (older, or more recent, ones) through metamorphosis into something humorous and through play with them. Beckwith perhaps asks us: isn't the whole thing really a 'gas'?[5]

All this Beckwith says with grace and wit, underlined by the understated attitudes and modes of speech (prosody, etc) of the tribe from which he hails.

IN SEARCH OF ZOROASTER

If we find in *Gas!* a dialogue between an individual and his community, here and now, the environment of R. Murray Schafer's *In Search of Zoroaster* is the Near East, some time between 1000 BC and AD 200–300.[6] This area and period constitute familiar terrain for the composer, who has written other works as well that relate to both.[7]

In Search of Zoroaster appears to be several things at the same time. In the notes to the piece Schafer says that it 'is not so much a performance as a perpetual rehearsal.' It is a 'coming together' of a number of groups that independently prepare the performance of certain assigned layers of the piece, for the purpose of performing the whole together in a kind of communal celebration. 'After each celebration the groups disperse, meditate on the performance, practice again in private, then come together again at a later date.' Earlier in the notes Schafer uses the word ritual to characterize the circumstances in which the piece is to be performed. His objective is to bring musical and religious experience into a single event: we are invited to help enact a simulated worship of Ahura Mazda, the Wise Lord. There is to be a struggle between the principal celebrant, Srosh, and Ahriman, the enemy spirit, the representative of all that is evil in the world, a counter-spirit to all the good that resides in Ahura Mazda.

Ahura Mazda and Ahriman appear only indirectly. The former is the subject of a search for his constituent ethical components and of numerous invocations and praise. The latter shows his negative powers by invading the body of the Srosh and by confusing and corrupting the procedures that aim at following what Schafer calls the 'true teaching of Zoroaster.' The six performing vocal ensembles (two solo quartets, two larger homogeneous groups, and two heterogeneous groups) are given the names of the six hypostases that constitute the central elements of Ahura Mazda's essence: Good Spirit, Right (the protector of fire, etc), War (also the defender of the poor), Water (also purification), Immortality (food, medicine), and Piety.[8] This allegorization is historically sound. In certain periods the followers of Zoroaster also considered these six 'Immortal Holy Ones' (*Amesha Spenta*) as archangels and placed them, somewhat confusingly, at a level identical to that of Ahura Mazda himself.

Schafer's source for the text is Max Müller ed *The Sacred Books of the East* vol V, XVIII, XXIII, XXIV, and XXXI. Some of the Graeco-Egyptian magical papyri we considered earlier also exerted an influence on the piece.

The score can be misleading in its stark simplicity. Its level of sophistication as to pitch-organization, especially for the individual parts, hardly ever exceeds that which an interested amateur is able to perform. Furthermore, most of the piece takes place in such a natural, unhurried, time-continuum that the synchronization of its various layers poses few problems. Most of the vocal materials consist of sustained or repeated tones and short figures, sung in unison or in the octave; indeterminate clusters; recitations on monotones; exclamations; shouts; chanting (in which only the direction of pitch-succession is indicated); onomatopoeic sounds; and simple chords and polyphonies, aided by pivot-tones. The instrumental parts consist almost exclusively of percussion instruments played by the vocalists themselves. (Towards the end of the work there is a held chord to be played on the organ.) The character of this instrumentation further sustains the overall religious (syncretistic, Near Eastern) character of the work. The instruments function as liturgical (praise-reinforcing and/or magical, apotropaic) implements and act as auditory cues, indispensable during those phases of the work that take place in complete darkness.

These elements add up to a very considerable stylistic diversity and structural complexity, which produce a strong dramatic and spiritual impact. The music rings with conviction and (in most places) authenticity. All this is accomplished with a remarkable economy of means.

The duration is about an hour. Its twenty-one sections (some only a few seconds long, while others last two minutes or longer) divide into ten larger groups: 1 / the 'cosmic sound'; 2 / sections A, B; 3 / C, D, E, F; 4 / G, H; 5 / I; 6 / J, K, L; 7 / M, N; 8 / P, Q, R, S; 9 / T, U; 10 / V and the exit. These groups may be characterized as follows: 1 / the cosmic sound in darkness; 2 / invocations; 3 / exclamations, invocations; 4 / self-dedication of the principal celebrant; 5 / praises of the sacred fire (light appears); 6 / a lesson and three hymns; 7 / interruptions – Ahriman's influence begins to assert itself; 8 / confusion; the exorcism of the principal celebrant; 9 / the epiphany of Ahura Mazda; and 10 / the return of the cosmic sound, and darkness.

The large-scale form is that of an enactment (or showing, epiphany) of a myth, framed by an opening ascent (anabasis) and a concluding descent (katabasis). The dynamic and rhythmic energy climax of the piece is achieved in the eighth group. The spiritual climax comes in group 9. The first and last groups balance each other. The schematic fever chart of the work is, thus: ⟋⟍ . We shall now look at some of the details.

At the beginning of group 1, the 'cosmic sound,' a hummed monotone, appears very faintly and is sustained as the performers file in, in darkness, very slowly and as silently as possible.[9] The audience, hearing (under the monotone) the soft shuffling of bare or stockinged feet, becomes aware of the large number of participants whose humming and quiet comportment suggests a community of purpose and a spiritual disposition. It is an evocative beginning, connoting discipline, submission, acceptance of constraint, perhaps even personal hardship and sacrifice. The complete darkness is also important. As Rudolf Otto has observed, the two most direct methods for the representation of the numinous are both '*negative*, viz., *darkness* and *silence*' (Otto 1923: 68). What happens acoustically is semi-silence, a condition analogous to what Otto has called semi-darkness (68).

Group 2 consists of a series of invocations by four soloists, who chant 'freely and rather rapidly' (score, 3), with the invariant pitch-objective of reaching the tone a perfect fifth above the cosmic sound, after which they individually return, through a descending glide, to the drone-sound. This 'freely chromatic' (3) melos, 'moving up and down in little glissando rips' (3) appears to suggest inflected (possibly liturgical) recitation which Schafer might have heard during his travels in the Near East.[10] After these solos the cosmic sound gradually ceases. The ensuing brief silence is broken by the sharp slap of the wood-block sound played by the principal celebrant, Srosh.[11] This ritual signalling is echoed by similar sounds coming from two other places in the hall. After these comes a long silence that is a temporary return to the numinous nothing I spoke of earlier. The beginning of the next part is indicated by the shattering of this calm by a very loud tam-tam sound.

In group 3, the loud tam-tam crash is the signal for a large group of voices to emit a broad-frequencied cluster of sustained exclamation, on the syllable 'Ta,' which is the first part of the invocation recurring several times, 'Tavo athro.'[12] The four exclamations of this expression are led by a solo soprano.

We should take note of the six kinds of events we have witnessed so far, each connoting a level of organization, or rank: the cosmic sound involving each and all, signifying perhaps that before Ahura Mazda all might be equal; the four solo chanters, perhaps 'officials, setting the stage' through invocations; the Srosh, with his wood-block, a central, commanding figure; those playing wood-blocks in the various groups, perhaps his surrogates in certain contexts; the players of the tam-tam crashes, who have the power and the duty to initiate, to set off, the 'Tavo athro' exclamations; and finally the soloists amid the groups of 'Those of Spenta Armati' and 'Those of Vohu Manah,' who control through their gliding chant the timings of these exclamations. Hence the outlines of a clearly defined pseudo-liturgical hierarchy begin to emerge through the musical features of the piece. Every sound seems to have a liturgical function that is clearly identifiable through its inherent character, but even more so, through its musical consequence. (We should also note that the initial darkness still persists unchanged.) In section E the first *tuned* metallophone sounds appear and trigger the first exactly pitched chanting. Both constitute new functions in the hierarchy. We also might begin wondering to what extent this hierarchy mirrors the profane, or civil, hierarchy of the society of the participating people.

The major new events constituting group 4 are the first sounds uttered by the Srosh himself[13] (they express a self-dedication to the sacred fire, which is a 'form of approach to the "Wise Lord"' [Moulton 1917: 146]), sounds by many small metallophone instruments, and whistling and hissing.

Schafer assigned to the symbols of fire and light important roles in the piece; the way he has accomplished this suggests a later, somewhat Magian (or perhaps even Manichean[14]) conception of Zoroastrianism. For the

Mani, light stands for god, and for everything that is good; while darkness is the birthplace of Satan and his demons. Man, an instrument of God, was sent to fight Satan and his cohorts. According to this understanding the light that the group wants to evoke represents gnosis (knowledge); but this has the prerequisite of vanquishing, or at least frightening away temporarily, Satan and his demons. The steps taken here for this latter purpose consist of sounding the brass instruments (Hopfner 1974: 104–5), the sounds of which were thought to be abhorrent to demons and to produce the hissing and whistling that purportedly have a similar effect. These are further strengthened by the vowel sounds, 'ai,' and 'a,' which lead finally to the lighting of the first candle, an act that coincides with the beginning of the next section.

This lighting up, at the beginning of group 5, is an indication that the preceding simulated apotropaic operation was successful. Soon various groups begin to sing in euphonous combinations the praise of fire, flame, and light, supported by the sound of many metallophonic instruments. To this is added a large assortment of groups of iterative onomatopoeic sounds, such as *taka, taka,*[15] *ping-ping, chou-chou,* and *ooli ooli.* This simulation of the sounds of certain instruments and thus a demon-chasing operation, brings on further light in the form of 'myriads of candles' lit in the hall.[16] The section ends with a protracted /ʃ/ sound commanding silence; a tutti /o̊:/ (a breathy 'oh') that might be close to what Rudolf Otto calls 'the long-protracted open vowel of wonder' (Otto 1923: 191). The passage ends with the commanding woodblock sound of the Srosh.

In group 6 we are offered a lesson, organized in the form of a statement-question-answer-type dialogue, followed by three hymns: one in two-part mirror form, with instrumental two-tone drone accompaniment; one in the form of a close two-part canon, with a pedal-point; and one that is monophonic and is repeatedly interrupted by evidence of the intruding presence of Ahriman, the 'enemy-spirit' (Angra Mainyu). Efforts at pseudo-exorcisms, by the use of ratchets and loud shrieks, seem to succeed only temporarily in averting this pseudo-presence; and despite what is made to appear as self-sacrificing efforts on the part of the Srosh, Ahriman seems to succeed in corrupting completely the whole assembly and that of which it is a symbolic representation. (This development might be an enactment by Schafer of the corruption of Zoroastrianism by members of the 'sacred' tribe of the Magi, reportedly a historical event.)

Group 7 shows this corruption at its worst, through a number of concurrent events that depict a high degree of confusion.

Group 8 consists of the pseudo-exorcism of the Srosh, who was lying prostrate during all the preceding section as a simulation of having been taken possession of by the spirit of Ahriman. A ratchet, maraccas, foot-stomping, and a drum, followed by metallophone sounds, as well as a long ascending vocal glide and shrieks, are assigned to perform a symbolic ceremony of purification.

Group 9 again contains harmonic sounds and constitutes perhaps the most complex structure of this type in the piece. It is the presentation of the epiphany of Ahura Mazda: the victory of the righteous one over the spirit of evil. With this having been accomplished, the participants may return to their homes.

In preparation for group 10, they extinguish, one by one, their candles. 'As each candle goes out, it is accompanied by a small bell sound' (score, 41). As the darkness returns, so does the cosmic sound, and 'after an interminable time' the participants slowly leave, one by one, the same way they came.

Some might label the means used in this work primitive. But they might just as well be called elemental. Whatever the designation, the piece is powerful. It has been wrought with a remarkable economy of means, with the right expressions for its various mystical references, and with much imagination and a clarity of form. The piece's performance logistics deserve special attention. With a minimum of visual cueing, this long, complex work unfolds as if it were a liturgical event of an ancient tradition.[17] The work seems to form a link in Schafer's extended *perpetuum carmen*, his continuous song (Szilágyi 1982: 32–3), in which he probes and poetically reconstructs past situations better to understand the present.[18]

CORO

The last work we shall look at is Berio's *Coro*, for forty vocalists and forty-four instrumentalists of whom forty pair up (one to one) with the members of the former group. The remaining four players – pianist, organist, and two percussionists – constitute a complementary group. There are numerous vocal solos that are assigned to members of the chorus, and there are instrumental solos as well. A special seating arrangement is defined for all. It is a substantial work in duration (almost an hour) and content. It is one of Berio's finest accomplishments and one of the most imaginative and powerful works of its kind in the repertoire.

The composer, in a commentary, gives us a number of clues for the understanding of the work. The work uses 'developments of folk techniques and modes,' although there are only two actual quotations in it. It might be looked at as a '*chorus* of different techniques from song to *lied*, from African heterophony (as analyzed by Simha Arom) to polyphony.' There are, of course, other than folk elements in it. It has an 'epic and narrative structure made up mostly of self-contained and often contrasting episodes' and is also 'an anthology of different modes of "setting to music."' Of its different structural dimensions, 'the harmonic one is perhaps the most important.' 'Two different and complementary levels' can be recognized in the piece: 'a folk level based on texts about love and work, and an epic level on a poem by Pablo Neruda.'[19]

I will describe briefly my first impression of the overall character of the piece and then consider its form; the texts; the nature of the major formal divisions; the deployment of the voices and instruments; and the musical language. I shall finally reconsider the overall character of the work and its connotations.

When I first heard *Coro* I thought it to be beautiful, complex, and forceful. Subsequent hearings suggest that there are likely to be numerous layers of referential meanings to the work that, similar to Lutosławski's *Trois Poèmes*, has the dimensions, thrust, and impact of a giant mural painting.

The piece is divided, in the score, into thirty-one individual sections. A number of these are close replicas, transformations, contractions, or expansions of section II, which is a prototype for this group, the members of which function as a refrain. The other sections, different in nature, relate to this refrain as episodes. The total form has some features of a very large-scale rondo. Not all the episodes have unique profiles, although cumulatively they contain much diversity. Several of them form sub-groups that share text and/or musical materials, in a pattern that invites detailed study. Sections II, IV, VI, VIII, X, XII, XIV, XXX, and XXXI form the refrain group, showing a big gap from about the central section onwards.

The refrains of *Coro* are set to the following line from the Chilean poet Pablo Neruda's *Explico algunas cosas*: 'Venid a ver a sangre por las calles' ('Come and see the blood in the streets'). (This is somewhat expanded in its last two appearances.) A few more fragments from Neruda's poetry are used in sections XXI and XXVIII. The other sections use folk poetry from Amerindian sources (Sioux, Peruvian, Navajo, Zuñi, Chilean) and (one fragment each) from Gabon, Persia, and Polynesia. Two fragments are of Croatian and Italian provenance, and the last episode uses verses 15–17 of chapter 1 of Song

of Solomon. All the Amerindian folk texts, as well as the African, Polynesian, and Chilean ones, are used in English translation. Some of the others
appear in French or in German. The biblical text, and Neruda's poems,
appear in their respective original languages.

Berio has chosen for *Coro* texts that, once again, avoid unequivocal deno-
tations, but are rich in connotations, related to certain environments and
interlocking fields of thought.[20] The very absence of precise references here
is conducive to an impression of broad applicability and universality. A case
in point is the text of the refrain itself. It makes it clear that somewhere,
some time, a tragedy has occurred. About its causes, the identity of its victims, and the perpetrators of the crime, we are left in the dark, and this lends
an even greater power to these few words. Through the settings (harsh, grat-
ing chords of many notes, often more than twenty) the words acquire an
ominous, at times brutal, character, and an epic function. Being intermittently reminded of the fact that blood has been spilled (perhaps in a recurring
fashion) in the streets, we are time and again shocked into feeling the horror
of it, and revulsion. Then come the episodes that temporarily distract us,
implying that life must, and does, go on parallel to death and grief. Thus a
pendulum is set up between these two facets: the life forces ('love and
work') here, and the recurring presence of sudden death there. This is, of
course, an over-simplification of a complex form, as shown by the absence of
the refrain between sections XV and XXX and by other features that we shall
soon see.

The Sioux text that begins section I creates an enigmatic and intense mood
(supported by the music):

Today is mine
I claimed to a man
a voice I sent
You grant me
this day
is mine
a voice I sent
now – here he is
today is mine
I claimed to a man
today is mine

It is an almost circular utterance, like a tape-loop, speaking of some unarticulated yearning, perhaps of personal freedom; yet one senses a binding depen-

dence on another, and a dim awareness of the inexorable onward march of time. Another text, this time Peruvian, conveys echoes of an ecstatic shaman-istic rite and the memory of the possession-state of a compulsive dancer (like a victim of tarantulism, or of St Vitus dance):[21]

> Wake up woman rise up woman
> you must dance
> comes the death
> you can't help it
> oh what a chill
> oh what a wind
> comes the death

The Polynesian fragment, used in four of the episodes, conveys the ideas of lament and of shamanistic practice, in the form of bird-symbolism. Eliade describes (Eliade 1964: 156–8) the importance of the ornithomorphic image of the shaman among certain Altai people and also among the Manchu. He writes: 'The Mongol shaman has "wings" on his shoulders and feels that he is changed into a bird as soon as he dons his costume' (157). He also reports that in Polynesia 'the hero Maui ... is famous for his ascents to the sky and descents to the underworld' (367). The posture referred to in the text might refer to a healing practice:

> Your eyes are red
> with hard crying
> I am carried up
> to the skies
> I put my feet
> around your neck

This text also is distilled to absolute essentials. No attempt is made to estab-lish links between its dimensions. All this would be unnecessary for the practitioners of the ceremony, and we are enlisted as initiated participants who have no need for further explanation. Through this and other texts we are experiencing the simulation of tribal appeals and are symbolically admitted to related, and possibly secret, ceremonies.

The poet-composer-shaman speaks through the words of the text of sec-tion XI, from Gabon:[22]

I have made a song
avaya
oh moon lying there
when will you arise?
tandinanan
oh mother moon hear my voice
I have made a song
I often do it badly
avavaya
It is so difficult
to make a song
to have wishes fulfilled
I often return to this song
I often try to repeat it
I who am not good at returning
to the stream
oh mother moon hear my voice
tandinanan

(Reproduced with permission of Universal Edition A.G., Wien)

This invocation (incantation), addressed to the moon, allows us to cast a glance into the workshop of a shaman (or medicine man, sorcerer or magician, etc) and to see him struggling while he works on an efficacious spell. He appears here as a candid practitioner of his art while harbouring some doubts about his capabilities, revealing himself in the process as being that much more human.

Several texts (those of sections XVIII, XIX, XXII, and XXIX) deal with the theme of love. Some of these are clearly love-spells (XVIII and XIX). A Croatian text speaks of spring and of the renewal of nature. The Zuñi text of section XXVIII is a prayer for rain (or a rain-spell). There are sections (XXIV and XXV, for example) that use several texts concurrently.

Even from this brief survey it is possible to conclude that numerous texts in *Coro* have ritualistic connotations, which include spells, charms, and so on.

The major formal divisions of *Coro* are realized through the settings of the words, which establish correspondences between the text and the music of the individual sections and between the sections (refrain and episodes, etc) themselves. As Berio points out in his comment on the 'self-contained and often contrasting episodes': 'It is not a question ... of an elementary contrast;

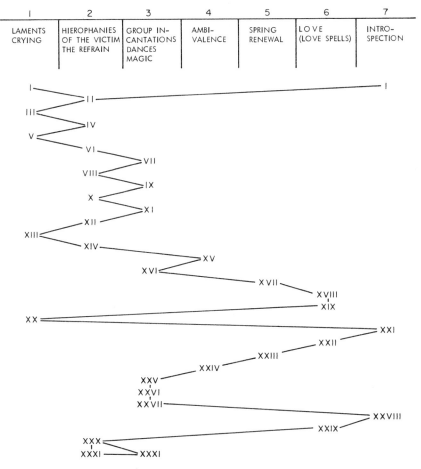

1	2	3	4	5	6	7
LAMENTS CRYING	HIEROPHANIES OF THE VICTIM THE REFRAIN	GROUP IN-CANTATIONS DANCES MAGIC	AMBI-VALENCE	SPRING RENEWAL	LOVE (LOVE SPELLS)	INTRO-SPECTION

N B   STREAMS   I, 3, 4, 5, 6, 'AND 7 ARE MADE UP OF EPISODES.

Figure 8.1

in fact, the same text can occur several times with different music, or the same musical model can, recur with different texts.' In the schematic outline of Figure 8.1, I have divided the work according to seven 'streams' of themes defined in terms of content and/or character or affect. However, no two-dimensional matrix can do justice to a work as complex as *Coro*. Yet the outline might serve a useful purpose at this stage of our discussion.

The seven streams of themes I was able to identify are the following:[23] laments and references to crying; hierophanies of the victims and expressions of horror, revulsion, and fear (the refrain); group incantations, with magical connotations; expressions of ambivalence; spring and the cyclical (annual) renewal of life; love, including love-spells; and introspection, with a focus on the chorus (sub-affects: anticipating the future, a great calmness, and a rising anguish and despair.)

Berio's simile, comparing *Coro*'s form to 'the plan for an imaginary city,'[24] which is open-ended (inasmuch as 'it could continue to generate ever different situations and relations'),[25] is helpful for the understanding of the piece. It provides a clue to the multiplicity of its affects and its diverse procedures, manifold rhythms, and differing textures. Within this overall framework, the sections that form stream 2 constitute what Berio calls the epic part of the work. These speak about the tragedy I have alluded to earlier. All the other sections refer to events, moods, occasions, ceremonies, and so on in the lives of various communities, which, at a deep level, share important attitudes and structures with each other and which are amalgamated by the cohesive forces in *Coro* into one imaginary composite community.

The thirty-one sections forming the seven streams of themes of *Coro* are well differentiated and well articulated. However, for the sake of continuity, Berio at times employs the device of overlap, through premature beginnings or delayed endings of sections. A pattern of structural invariances can be observed. All sections in streams 2 and 3 employ the full chorus and orchestra. In all sections belonging to streams 1, 5, and 6, as well as in section XV, solo voices are used either exclusively or predominantly. In all of these (with the exception of XX), a specific instrumental chamber group, or solo instrument, is used as a characteristic obbligato element. The initial portion of XXXI belongs also to this type. Both sections of stream 7 feature the whole chorus, supported by a chamber orchestra. Section XXIV is a hybrid; it begins with an emphasis on the soloistic character, but gradually changes into tutti.

Many of the melodies for solo voice begin with a small collection of notes, often, but not always, in a small ambitus. Immediate repetition, a frequent device, helps to create the impression of an incantation or a magic spell (sections VII and much of IX, XVIII, and XIX). Ostinatos play an important role in sections IX, XI, XVI, XXV, and XXVI.

Berio has successfully integrated a number of characteristic folk musical practices into a *savant* whole. Special voice qualities include: 'come una canzone andalusa' (section III), 'voce aperta senza vibrato' ('open' voice, without vibrato) (IX), 'as "hurlement"' (howling, wailing or ululating) 'of Algerian women' (XXVIII), and 'Yemenite' (XXIX). Rapid rhythmic speech is called for in XI and XIX and at the very end of XXXI.

Some of the instrumental melodic writing has folk-like connotations: the rapid piano arpeggios, which remind me of cymbalom figurations (for example, in section XVII); the heterophonic elaborations of the trumpets at the outset of IX; the many single, double, and multiple pedals (drones); and the numerous parallel motions, tracing a scalar construct (the strings in III and the violins, trumpet 1, and the clarinets in XXIV). The virtuoso, 'quasi-improvising' flute parts in XXIX remind one of the virtuosity of some Rumanian swineherds on their home-made instruments and the fast fiddling in XIX, of that of some country fiddlers. The percussion parts frequently make one think of Balinese or one kind or other of African percussion music, or of descriptions of the driving role of drums and other percussion instruments in ceremonies aiming at bringing about a trance (Rouget 1980).

Berio has made a special reference to African heterophony 'as analyzed by Simha Arom.'[26] It is likely that, among other materials, he has also seen Arom's paper 'Une Méthode pour la transcription de polyphonies et poly-rythmies de tradition orale' (Arom 1973), in which the author analyses a piece from Banda-Linda (Central African Republic) for eighteen trompe, as well as a chant for five voices, sung by the Aka pygmies (Central African Republic). The first of these uses a hocket-like technique, in which each instrument plays but one tone, in a fashion that shows a striving for precise repetition of the individual rhythmic patterns and of the relationships among the parts. A somewhat similar technique is used in most of the structures in sections IX, XI, XVI, XXV, XXVI, and XXVII. The second of these African pieces is more variable from performance to performance according to Arom. (For this reason we must look at the score given by Arom as only one of many equally acceptable performances of the same materials.) We see in this notation of an actual performance a certain degree of polyphonic strati-fication of melodic materials. A similar process is frequently used in *Coro* (measures 66–72 in section VIII, in the choir; 1–28 in XVI; 33–40 in XXIV, both in the choir; and so on).

The melodic organization of *Coro* shows three additional recurring traits. The first is the tendency to begin a melody with a small collection of notes (as observed above) and then to develop it by expansion, adding at varying rates new pitch-classes, until it reaches its saturation point with a total collection of nine, ten, eleven, or twelve pitch-classes. In the process the melody might follow any organizational principle. For example, the solo of alto 4, which has the vocal part in section XV, develops after a slow evolution into a total collection of ten pitch-classes.[27] Its organization shows three eliding tonal areas, of which the first is somewhat ambiguous (perhaps only on account of its notation), the second diatonic, and the third chromatic. The three areas are unified by the note A, which is one of two notes common to all three areas, begins and ends the song, lies almost exactly mid-way between the highest and lowest notes, and is, by far, the most frequently occurring note. The three collections are shown in Figure 8.2. We are dealing with a formally expanding organization which, in the course of its evolution, seeks new pockets of tonal stability and moves with subtle melodic modulations from one area to the next.

The second melodic device is the expanded scale passage that constitutes a kind of source material from which individual melodies are constructed. One such large design occurs in section XXIV and constitutes the basis for all the rapid figurations in the upper strings, trumpets and clarinets (see Figure 8.3).

The third melodic device is the variation process that generates, in a quasi-improvisatory way (but realized and precisely notated in the score), the changes rung on a relatively small repertoire of notes assigned to each of four choral parts, as in section XI. Underlying the whole (with the exception of the note B♭, which is added in the bass part) is the raga-like, ostinato melody (also at the basis of sections IX and XVI) shown in Figure 8.4. This is, of course, a diminution of its first appearance in the sopranos and altos at the beginning of section IX. In the variations in section XI, the notes of this pattern (plus the B♭) are distributed among the voices in the strata as shown in Figure 8.5. From about measure 44 these repertoires become even more specialized (see Figure 8.6). The missing notes, E♭, E♮, and F, occur in the instrumental complement.

There seems to be an interesting parallelism between the first type of melodic organization I was referring to (the one that exhibits an initial stability through a small repertoire of pitch-classes and that subsequently expands by the addition of new pitch-classes), and the way the thirty-one sections relate to each other, as shown in Figure 8.1. Of these seven streams of themes, streams 1 and 2 establish an area of stability during the first six sections. This is followed by a similarly structured, and similar-sized, group based on a different repertoire (streams 2 and 3). We should note, however,

Figure 8.2

Figure 8.3

Figure 8.4

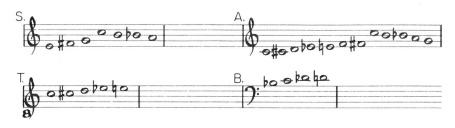

Figure 8.5

Figure 8.6

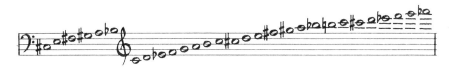

Figure 8.7

that stream 2 is common to both groups. Three additional sections (XII, XIII, and XIV) re-establish the character of the initial group (that of streams 1 and 2). The most diversified passage occurs in sections XV–XXIV, which constitute a considerable expansion, with only a single reference to the repertoires of the first two groups of stability (streams 1, 2, and 3). A pocket of stability can be observed in the three sections on the theme of love. It is difficult to assign a proper value to the retrograde symmetry (shown in the model – Figure 8.1) between the portions from XV to XXI and from XXI to XXV, respectively, due to the considerable differences between pairs of sections, such as those constituted by XV and XXIV. However, the interpolation of XX, close to the half-way point in this seeming mirror structure, helps to re-establish a degree of stability by reminding the listener of the theme of stream 1. There is little doubt about the new island of stability constituted by the three consecutive sections XXV, XXVI, and XXVII belonging to stream 3 and by the recurrence of the shift from stream 7 to 6 (XXVIII, XXIX). The piece ends with the reassertion of the theme of stream 2. Within it an agitated solo reminds the listener of the theme of stream 3.

This tempting idea of parallelism between a recurring micro-structural process and the macro-structure of the work might be verifiable in listening experience, or it may remain but the fruit of speculation. Either way, it describes a schematic process that begins with oscillations between pairs of streams, constituting sorts of persisting (quasi-periodic) motions. From section XV (almost precisely the half-way point in the work as far as the number of sections) onwards, the succession of the major themes becomes more complex as if the initial system would have been acted upon and displaced by some force. The final three sections return to one of the initial pairs (streams 2 and 3), but in a changed mood.

The harmonic language of *Coro* is probably its most intricate aspect. Its most important feature is the recurring succession of the giant chords that make up the refrain. It consists of the whole (or a part) of a core collection of notes that recurs time and again (Figure 8.7), often with certain changes, but nevertheless recognizable.

The following harmonic (contrapuntal) devices are used repeatedly: pedal-points (drones); parallel motions; harmonic or contrapuntal progressions, in which all the parts trace a given scale with register-invariance; verticalization of a melodic pitch-repertoire; complementation of strata or repertoires; and counterpoint saturated with a given motif and contrapuntal stratification.

The diversity and beauty of *Coro*'s instrumental and orchestral textures constitute further proof of Berio's extraordinary imagination and mastery of his craft. These features, through transformations and contrast and as complements to other structural dimensions, provide the links between adjacent sections. They also sustain and enhance the vocal and choral parts admirably.

The setting of the text and the vocal writing are intimately linked with each other and with the other features of the piece. One dominant characteristic is the use of the *bel canto* singing technique. With the exception of the very brief section IV, and of the parts where the few already mentioned dialectal voice qualities are called for, it is used in every section. Other vocal techniques (not yet commented upon) include highly inflected speech (section IV); screaming (VI, measures 6–7, tenor 1); rapid, breathy speech, almost whispering (VI, 7, tenors 2, 3, etc); rather fast, alternatingly voiced and unvoiced speech (XI, from 66); rhythmical, alternatingly voiced and unvoiced speech (XI, from 85); speaking with an exaggerated inflection as if parodying a dialect (VII); very rapid monotone speech (XIX); and colourless, senza vibrato singing (XXV, soprano 1, from 8). Combinations of some of these also occur.

The deployment of the texts shows the following modalities: quasi-neumatic solo singing (section I); simultaneous use of several texts in one language (I, measures 61–71, in the choir); 'one syllable to one note' distributions; very rapid repetitions of a text fragment (VI, 6–7, basses 3, 4, etc); fragmentation of words and rapid repetitions of a fragment (or fragments) (VII, 47–50); 'parole cavate' ('carved words'), meaning the use of only the vowels of a word (for example: a, i, and o from the word palido, in VIII, 20–5); vowel sequences (IX, 8–11, basses and tenors); repeats of unintelligible words (IX, 19–38; XI, 26–67 and from 83 to the end of the section); repetitions of a small number of words with pitches unchanged (XIV, 2–9); isolated vowel-hocket in the choir (XVI, 33–58); polyphonic inflected speech, all parts using the same text (XVIII); rapid repeats of the consonant pair *tk* (XVIII); phonetic disintegration of words, and single-voice or two-part rapid repetitions of the resulting fragments (XIX); uttering words according to a given pattern of inflection, with only the total duration of the event given (XXIV, 11, basses); sustained monotone singing of vowel series (XXVII, 1–26, soprano and alto); the simultaneous use of four different texts in three different languages (XXIV); and whisper (XXXI, from 43).

As already observed, *Coro* uses vocal solos extensively. In addition, we find the following types of simultaneous uses of two or more voices: two-part imitative polyphony (section I); four-part polyphony (I, measures 49–71); multi-voiced homophonies (II and XXIV, etc); four-part inflected polyphonic speech, precisely notated (IV and XVII); combinations of inflected speech and monotone singing (IV, 15–19); two-part heterophony (IV, 10–13); polyphony of singing and inflected speech (IX, 22–38); polyphony of stratified pitch-groups (XI, 19–21; XVI, 1–24); polyphony of monotone and two-to-three-recitations of unintelligible words (much of XI); forty-part polyphony of unmeasured, fast, alternatingly voiced and unvoiced speech (XI, 72–83); polyphony of inflected speech as complement to an accompanied *bel canto* solo (XVII); three-part homophony and four-part polyphony of *tk* iterations (XVII); intermittent, metrically indeterminate, two-part concentrations of rapid iterations of brief phonetic materials (XIX); seven-part sung clusters (XXI, 14–16 and 25–7); quasi-species counterpoint, using four texts in three languages (XXIII); sung polyphony with shrieking, imitating the 'hurlement' of Algerian women (XXVIII, 30–3); a solo voice imitating instrumental sounds (XXXI, 3–24); and, finally, rapid, intermittent, metrically determined recitation of words, chosen from a brief repertoire (XXXI, last two bars).

The preceding brief account perhaps will help to support the earlier assessment of *Coro* as a complex work, rich in musical ideas and crafted with great care and mastery. It could also allow one to observe that, in its materials and in the choice of its techniques, *Coro* is not so much an innovative as an integrative work: its manifold materials and languages were brought together for the sole purpose of serving the ideas that were to be expressed in the individual sections, which in turn were to be in the service of the overall conception of the work. However, when one comes to the appreciation of the total impact of *Coro*, the piece asserts itself as an original statement. One suspects that this effect might be due in part to the integrative skill of Berio, in bringing together the many disparate details into a unified conception, and in part to the very considerable connotative power the work radiates. This brings us back, full circle, to earlier concerns. It invites the question (probably in the background ever since I began to discuss the piece): what is *Coro* really about?

The key to *Coro* seems to be the text of the refrain, telling about some gruesome events (murders, most likely), the evidences of which still are visible in the streets. Or are they? Is it not conceivable that the fragments of the refrain refer to past events, possibly to ones that took place a long time ago? The group (or groups) of people cannot, do not want to, and/or are not allowed to forget the tragedy. The showing of the blood in the streets is in the process of becoming, or has already become, a ritualistic (i.e. sacred) event in the lives of the people concerned. If so, we are witnessing either a myth in the making (mythopoesis), or the re-enactment of the genesis of a myth, intertwined with all sorts of other details from the lives of the people.

Where does the witnessing of all this leave a Western urban listener? He might be well aware of his limitations as a potential participant in such a communal creative act. He might even tend to distrust the prospect of elevating a fellow human being, to the exalted rank of either hero or civic saint, on the way to becoming a central figure in a myth. But there appears to be an ambivalence in our minds about this. Martin Esslin has observed (in a language that suggests political preference): 'The world of myth has almost entirely ceased to be effective on a collective plane in most rationally organized Western societies' (it was most effectively in evidence in Nazi Germany and remains so in the countries of totalitarian Communism) (Esslin 1961: 248), but then adds, quoting Eliade, that 'at the level of *individual experience* it has never completely disappeared; it makes itself felt in the dreams, the fantasies and the longings of modern man' (Eliade 1966: 27). Is *Coro* Berio's answer to this paradox?

Perhaps Berio was persuaded of the existence of a truly tragic-heroic situation that demanded to be metamorphosed into a composition, a work that would demonstrate its mythic nature in an appropriate context. This very appropriateness would reside in the showing of the environment in which the tragic-heroic act came into being. From the point of view of a community, a heroic death and the renewal of communal life could well go together. According to Eliade, '*in illo tempore* a divine being, quite often a woman or a maiden, sometimes a child or a man, allowed himself to be immolated in order that tubers or fruit trees should grow from his body.' (Beane and Doty 1976 I: 254). We need not go very far to find contemporary examples for such self-sacrifice. One remembers the public self-immolations in Indochina during the Vietnam war, and at the very time of this writing the hunger strike–suicides of IRA men in a prison situated near Belfast, both politically motivated types of self-destruction, offered in the hope of helping the respective communities. Such sacrifices can be understood as means aiming at the strengthening of communal resolve. If so, they may have common motives with rain rituals. The maturing of good crops is the objective of the latter, and that of ideas of the former. The community's duty is to learn the lesson, to remember and retell the story, without failing, at regular intervals, at a fitting level of intensity. As Eliade formulates it, 'For all these paleo-agricultural peoples, what is essential is periodically to evoke the primordial event that established the present condition of humanity. Their whole religious life is a commemoration, a remembering ... What matters is to remember the mythical event, the only event worth considering because the only creative event' (255). And finally, Eliade touches on the didactic component in all this: 'It is in the myth that the principles and paradigms for all conduct must be sought and recovered' (255).

Are we right in considering *Coro* a kind of proto-drama, which enacts the transformation of an event (that has occurred yesterday, or a long time ago) into a myth, with numerous ancillary details supporting the central thread? I believe that many of our findings support this understanding, and I have not as yet recognized a feature in the work that would contradict it.

Coro's genre might also appear to be close to the process to which Nietzsche has referred in his *The Birth of Tragedy* as 'the *dramatic* proto-phenomenon: to see yourself transformed before your own eyes, and then to act as if you had actually taken possession of another body and another character' (Nietzsche 1927: 989). Such an identification with a group or with an idea is present implicitly in *Coro* and is, I think, an important part of the compositional objective that called the work into being. The listener is the addressee of these refrains that hammer out, with incantational force,[28] their terrible message.[29]

EPILOGUE

I am setting forth this book as an explanation for the words alternative voices. They denote a still expanding body of innovative (yet deeply rooted) compositions for the voice written since the mid-1950s. I regard this group of works as an important repertoire by virtue of the intrinsic merits of its best pieces and also on account of the insight it provides into many facets of the human personality and the human condition.

Science and philosophy have kept on redefining (and continue to do so) what reality and truth are. In the process man has achieved an ever-increasing degree of understanding of and control over diverse aspects of matter and life that have provided better circumstances for living for many, though by no means for all. This was accomplished at a certain cost, and it is clear to many that the price was considerable. With the growth of specialization and the mushrooming bulk of available information, man's perception of reality seems to have become more fragmented than ever before. Within this increased knowledge, science and philosophy have also shown to man the nature of his insignificantly minuscule corner in an unfathomably immense cosmos, which seems to be an overwhelmingly hostile environment for his existence. They have called into doubt a familiar, benevolent, and to a large extent anthropomorphic God, leaving man alone in the universe to cope with the cosmic defencelessness of his condition. As an individual, he has been urged to face up to the conflicts in the core of his mind and soul (or should I perhaps say: in the two halves of his bicameral brain?) and at the same time to knuckle under to the rules society imposes upon him in the name of an anonymous god – the 'common good' – although he might have done little to participate in the formulation of their principles. He has also been informed that the way he and others around him use their principal instrument, language, is suspect; it is more likely to give him a semblance of control over some trivial ingredients of his middle-sized world of things and relationships than real understanding. If so, some of our shared ills – loneliness, alienation, anxiety, unreasonable distrust – might be directly or indirectly related to these predicaments.

Could poetry, art, and in particular music help in this situation? If so, on the strength of what attributes, and how?

I think art, literature, and music are in a position to help. The latter can do so because it has the means with which to present holistic and graspable pictures of complex chunks of reality and, through these to provide for man a measure of understanding. Music can also be a picture of the mind's workings; it can portray an infinite variety of feelings and interaction; it can depict situations, and its ability to mirror abstraction is unlimited. The many existing and the yet-to-be-invented languages of music offer an inexhaustible potential for exercising the mind's propensity for combinatorial activity and its instinct for play. Music interprets, interrelates, and operates at a number of time-levels, including the various real-time speeds of the functioning brain. It engages the mind's capability for various types of memories and can simulate the workings of many of these memory layers (Laske 1977). Music can make one think in unique ways; it can make one travel in time – back into the past or forward into the future; it can elaborate on an ever-elusive present. Music (or access to music) can be purchased, thereby obtaining a sort of limited control over its products; one can learn how to make it, or do it, thereby achieving real control over it, for the pleasure and satisfaction of oneself and others. Music can simulate, represent, or evoke a host of things without menacing limb or soul. It can address itself to many serious questions and has the means to deal with the trivial ones as well. Music has as many facets as language, which is tantamount to saying that their number is infinite.

The innovative surge of music and art never ends, because man's need to create, to redefine, is unceasing. Every generation that sees the world in a different light than earlier generations will demand a mirror to reflect, clearly and sharply, that very new perception (which can, and at times does, contain very old elements freshly rediscovered). To provide that mirror is a task for poets, artists, and composers, along with scholars and scientists and creative thinkers active in other domains. Each generation is likely to have its own artists, poets, and composers.

These same inner necessities will cause man to want to keep on making music with his voice, still his most intimate musical means for expression.

He will continue using his voice in as many ways as he will be able and see fit to do.

A somewhat different conclusion from mine has recently been expressed about the prospects of innovative composition for the voice. Werner Klüppelholz, in the conclusion of his major study (Klüppelholz 1976), offers the view that 'despite all the imitators (Epigonen) following this direction of vocal composition the end to its authenticity can be perceived: it seems that everything unutterable has been said' (199). I believe this to be an unwarrantedly pessimistic view, one that seems to emanate from a mistakenly restrictive conception of what constitutes innovation and of the scope of inventiveness of the human mind, individually and collectively.[30]

The arts, as full partners to the other branches of the humanities, to the sciences, and to philosophy, have a unique, indispensable, and vital role to play in the sustenance and advancement of the human enterprise. They cannot but go on playing it, since man is inconceivable as such without his creativity, one of the outlets of which is the arts.

The compositions and the related ideas discussed in this book can be looked at as constituting but minute details from the broad, imperative perspective of man's struggle for survival and persistence. Even so, they have played a useful part and thereby have made a contribution.

Notes

1 The word innovative necessitates here the naming of its dialectical opposite, which, for our purposes, could be said to be the usual, that is *bel canto*-type, singing mode. With this definition, however, one encounters problems. As Philip A. Duey has pointed out (Duey 1951: 1–12) the term *bel canto* 'is not so easily defined' (3). An aspect of this difficulty resides in the difference between the notated form of music (and its realization in performances). This is expressed through the terms *cantus super librum*, *cantus a mente*, *contrapunto alla mente*, *chant sur le livre*, or *Verzierungskunst* (36). 'The English equivalent has been variously rendered as "art of ornamentation," "improvisation," "diminution," "coloration," or "embellishment"' (36–7). Idiomatic performances of pre-twentieth-century operas or other vocal works often show improvised vocal details that can be found in recently composed works as notated events (for example, laughter) or special features (modulations of vocal timbre, etc). These occurrences might not be new, then, but only have somehow changed their status in the act of transmission of information from the composer (or the composer-performer) to the listener. (See also chapter 5 in this regard; many other parts of the book deal also with this question.)

2 In the fall of 1969, at the invitation of Lejaren Hiller, I gave at SUNY at Buffalo a graduate seminar that focused on contemporary vocal and choral composition, in the course of which some of the problems discussed in this book first came to mind.

CHAPTER ONE: THEME AND RECENT BACKGROUND

1 In Canada younger composers who have produced interesting works belonging to this repertoire include John Hawkins, Alan Heard, David Keane, Bruce Pennycook, Clifford Ford, Barry Truax, and Keith Hamel.

2 I shall comment in some detail on Schafer's *In Search of Zoroaster* and on Berio's *Coro* in chapter 8.

3 It would be neglectful, even wrong, to omit consideration of the continuity that connects Schoenberg's, Berg's, and even Webern's sung melos with the vocal styles of the composers of the *Lied* and those of Wagner. I believe that one road to sung expressionistic melos leads through the works of Schubert, Schumann, Wagner, and Wolf. This connection deserves more study than it has received to date. (Klüppelholz [1976: 9–25] gives a concise account of Wagner's 'theory of vocal music' and its application in *Tristan und Isolde*.)

4 Varèse, who made an intrinsically musical and much more profound contribution to this development, knew Marinetti and Russolo. He resented being called the futurist composer, and regarded as shallow many futurist artefacts (Varèse 1972: 105–7).

5 Personal communication from Professor Roman Jakobson, dated 27 April 1981

6 I wish to thank Bengt Hambraeus for this information.

7 John Beckwith has called to my attention the fact that Mallarmé also anticipated the integration of typography and sense that one also finds in e.e. cummings.

8 Chassé writes regarding Mallarmé: 'This hesitation between mysticism and positivism is precisely very characteristic of men of his generation' (Chassé 1954: 15–16).

9 I wish to express my thanks to Dr F. Letemendia for drawing my attention to this book.

CHAPTER TWO: BERIO'S SEQUENZA III

1 I was advised that it is unlikely that any monologue would be entirely without appeal. The same commentator emphasized also the presence of an internal logic in infant babble. (See also 196–7.)

2 All these labels are of great help to the performer. They are suggestive, impressionistic. In some way they are often close to the paralinguistic categories listed by G.L. Trager (Trager 1958). A similar profusion of such labels is also observable in certain pioneering works of the German poet-composer Hans Helms (*Golem* and *Daidalos*) and in Ligeti's *Aventures* and *Nouvelles Aventures*. It is difficult to envisage how these, and other, composers could have brought forth certain complex affects without the use of such labels, which provide effectively suggestive and economical instructions to the interpreter.

3 For a thorough discussion of English prosodic, paralinguistic systems, intonation, and their notation, see D. Crystal 1969.

4 This and several subsequent definitions are taken (at times in an abbreviated form) from H.B. English and A.C. English 1958.

5 P.J. Moses in *The Voice of Neurosis* (Moses 1954) describes some of the characteristics of the schizophrenic voice. 1 / Rhythm is prevalent over melody. A rhythmic repetition of vocal patterns is characteristic. 2 / Registers are often separated: isolated head-register is used for long periods. 3 / There is a complete absence of melisms. This represents the inability to express appeal. 4 / There is decreased nasal resonance. 5 / Melody never glides but always jumps at intervals, often without any correlation to content. 6 / Mannerisms are used in histrionic excess. 7 / Accents are inappropriate to the content of speech. This is part of a constantly repeated rhythmic pattern that is maintained in an almost compulsive way. 8 / Words that are seemingly meaningless are interpolated regularly; other words are used over and over again.

It has been suggested to me that this list does not convey the full gamut of vocal usage observable in and characteristic of schizophrenia.

6 The English glossary of the notation of these affects accompanying the score (Universal Edition, ue. 13723) is misleading, because of an error in the vertical alignment. The German glossary is correct.

7 The affective sequence of the piece, of course, is more complex than that suggested by the structure of any one of these bi-polar series. A quick glance at the score will show lateral movements within a single series, and also jumps from one series to another.

8 Henri Pousseur is reported to have observed this characteristic: '[Il] montre, dans une notice de présentation, que la *Sequenza III* est rythmée par une oscillation régulière entre discours et chant' (Avron and Lyotard 1971: 41). This article came to my attention after I had completed this analysis. I found some of its linguistic and psychoanalytical references of interest. However, its political references seem to me forced. Berio has, indeed, composed several works with strong sociopolitical connotations, but I do not think that such are at the core of *Sequenza III*.

9 Berberian's interpretation of this and other works of Berio is of great importance. 'We almost composed together,' she was quoted as having said recently (Soria 1970: 5), in reference to their collaboration. This remarkable artist, indeed, created a new dimension for vocal technique. But beyond this, what makes her interpretation of *Sequenza III* so powerful is her controlled, even cool, virtuosity, with which she conveys both the gripping message of the piece and a sense of aesthetic distance.

10 This description of Berberian's is very close to my understanding. It seems much closer to the essence of the work than the cryptic allusion to the famous clown Grock by Berio himself, in the notes accompanying a recording of the

piece. I asked Berberian recently about the connection between this piece and Grock. At first she looked somewhat puzzled, and then she tried to document the analogy, but without full success. Perhaps an analysis of all the *Sequenzas* of Berio will shed more light on that statement by the composer. (A similar suggestion was recently made by John Beckwith.)

11 I was advised that symptoms similar to certain elements and procedures in *Sequenza III* can also be observed in the flashback experience, a delayed occurrence resulting from earlier use of hallucinogenic drugs.

12 For a discussion of cathartic cure see Ellenberger 1970.

13 Shortly before this book went to press, the psychiatrist Dr Felix Letemendia, of Queen's University, read and commented upon this chapter. In response to his remarks I altered the text in several places. While I wish to express my deep indebtedness to Dr Letemendia for his help, I retain full and exclusive responsibility for what appears in the text.

CHAPTER THREE: LIGETI'S NOUVELLES AVENTURES

1 'The nature of a social group as revealed by consistent behaviour of the group as such ...' (English and English 1958: 540–1).

2 I am grateful to Professor J.L.M. Trim for drawing this book to my attention.

3 I. Fónagy 1964: 18, quoting from Richard Mulcaster *The First Part of the Elementarie* (1582) (reprinted by E.T. Campagnac 1925: 132).

4 Quoting from Wang Li *Hah jü jin jün hio* (Peking 1956: 166)

5 Quoting from G.A. Wallin 'Über die Laute des Arabischen und ihre Bezeichnung' *Z. der deutschen Morgenländischen Ges.* 9 (1955: 10)

6 Quoting from Dionysios Halikarnasseus *De compositione verborum* ed Schaefer (Lipsiae 1808: 170)

7 Quoting from Estienne's *Deux Dialogues du nouveau langage françois italianizé* (Paris 1885)

8 A telling example for the concentrated use of such sounds is Henri Michaux's poem *Le Grand Combat*, which is the text of the second movement of Lutosławski's *Trois Poèmes d'Henri Michaux* (see chapter 4).

9 This utterance by the baritone brings to mind a statement by Merleau-Ponty: 'The point is that the first word was not what is commonly called a "conventional sign" (conventionality supposes a prior relation), that it did not represent a conceptual or terminal meaning, but presented primordially its gestural or psychical meaning (*sens emotionnel*), a spontaneous expression of lived meaning which we can recognize in an incantatory poem' (Lewis 1970: 20). It is worthwhile to compare this hypothesis with one advanced by C.F. Hockett and R. Ascher (1964) concerning the evolution of language. With respect to

the initial sound of the baritone, Cottrell's 'beginning or precipitating condition' comes also to mind.

10 These six trichordal patterns appear in 58 of the 113 trichords that comprise the passage; in other words, about 33 per cent of the 19 possible trichordal patterns take up more than 50 per cent of the material in the following distribution: 011 (9 occurrences), 022 (9 occurrences), 013 and 031 (15 occurrences), and 046 and 064 (25 occurrences).

11 The meaning of this brief agitated-repressed passage of melismas remains unclear to me. I have but one possible clue for it, and it is far-fetched. I mentioned earlier that Ligeti must have been in contact with Dr B. Szabolcsi at the Hungarian Academy of Music. In the first chapter of the book referred to earlier (Szabolcsi 1950), Szabolcsi posits some hypotheses about the possible common origin of speech and song that may have influenced Ligeti. 'Of the sounds of nature those have influenced him [early man] most which he had felt, experienced, and recalled, in his own immediate bodily reality: his own vocal sound, the human sound, with which he has conveyed his emotions despite his lack of a finer articulatory skill; the sound, which was hardly more, still, than half shouting and whimpering, but, in the same time, also half singing and half speaking.' If Ligeti, indeed, wanted an inarticulate, emotive half-song, half-whimper, he came close to this paralinguistic affect in this passage.

12 See in this regard Kubie 1967: 142.

13 The affinity of this hoquetus to post-Webernian pointillistic music is obvious. Does Ligeti engage here in a thinly disguised aesthetic criticism, or irony?

14 B. Malinowski: 'Phatic Communion' (in Laver and Hutcheson 1972: 146–52)

15 This process of information acquisition is described by Erving Goffman: 'When an individual enters the presence of others, they commonly seek to acquire information about him. [One may add that the reciprocal is true also; the individual, also, seeks information about the group.] ... During the period in which the individual is in the immediate presence of the others, few events may occur which directly provide the others with the conclusive information they will need if they are to direct wisely their own activity. Many crucial facts lie beyond the time and place of interaction or lie concealed within it. For example, the "true" or "real" attitudes, beliefs, and emotions of the individual can be ascertained only indirectly, through his avowal or through what appears to be involuntary expressive behaviour' (Goffman 1959: 1–2).

16 For further information consult Harary, Norman, and Cartwright 1965. I express my thanks to Professor David Easton for drawing this book to my attention.

17 D. Abercrombie: 'Paralanguage' (in Laver and Hutcheson 1972: 64–70)

18 J. Laver: 'Voice Quality and Indexical Information' (in ibid: 199)

19 E. Jünger: *Lob der Vokale* (Zürich 1954), quoted in Fónagy 1964: 82–3

20 The composer's instructions in the score (p 17, measure 56)

21 Is it a coincidence that there are 36 events in this scene, as there were 36 attacks in the hocket of measure 28, and similarly 36 vocal attack-points in scene 5? Or are these instances of a time-scheme that so far has remained undiscovered?

22 Ligeti speaks many languages, including Hungarian, Rumanian, German, English, and Swedish.

23 'Very little work has as yet been done in the vast field of Comparative Tonetics, which may be defined as the analysis and comparison of the intonation patterns that are used in different languages and in different dialects of the same language. The principal reason for this backwardness is probably the fact that there has been no detailed investigation and classification of elements of intonation which might serve as a basis on which comparative studies might be developed' (Kingdon 1958: 216). However, see Fónagy and Magdics, 1963, as well as the work of Professor Pierre Leon at the University of Toronto.

24 'The R comes to the fore at best when one deals with wild fights (quandoque exponuntur res acerbae ac vehementes)'; G.J. Vossins *Commentariorum Rhetoricorum sive Oratorium Institutionum libri sex* (= *Opera, III*) (Amsterdam 1597), quoted in Fónagy 1964: 83.

25 The composer's instruction in the score

26 Ligeti seems to be fascinated with clockworks going berserk. He once composed a work for 100 metronomes. In a statement written for *Music and Artists* 5 no. 7 (June–July 1972) 21, he said: 'My own music no harmony, no interval, no pitch, no rhythm, no meter, long sustained nothing enters imperceptively *pppppppp* pochiss. cres. to *ppppppp* microscopic polyphony threads webs blurring melting some pitch some interval some harmony disturbed clockwords lunatic sewing-machines fibrous perpetuum mobiles crumble away liquidize vanish silence.'

27 I have changed the English translation of some of these instructions, as they are given in the notes that accompany the score.

28 This was written in the fall of 1976.

29 I express my thanks to Professor Bengt Hambraeus for drawing these publications to my attention.

30 This would seem to encourage the imagining of a scenario such as the one that made up the body of this study of *Nouvelles Aventures*.

31 *Nouvelles Aventures*, composed 1962–5, was preceded by another, very similar work, *Aventures*, composed May–December 1962 and revised in 1963.

32 Ligeti wrote in 1966 a libretto for the two works; in that version they constitute a single stage piece (Ligeti 1966a and 1967). I have read this text, but
have never seen the works performed. I consider *Aventures* a musically less
effective work than *Nouvelles Aventures* and doubt that *Nouvelles Aventures*
would gain power by being performed together with *Aventures*, judging by the
libretto published in *Neues FORUM*.

33 There is significant information in this statement by the composer, and also
some ambivalence. The present essay could be regarded as a discussion of the
work as well as an attempt to clear up this ambivalence.

34 Concerning the qualified disclaimer that ends this statement: is it possible that
Ligeti, who had experienced persecution and hardship on political grounds, is
unwilling to allow himself to be drawn into a fixed political stance *definable in
words*, as distinct from the other kinds of stances that exist through the evocative power of *Nouvelles Aventures*?

35 This analysis has an interdisciplinary propensity. For it I have found some
support in the words of Leroi-Gourhan: 'If a paleontology of symbols risks
resembling more a psychoanalysis than a comparative anatomy, the principle
of its research must, at the least, be posited' (Leroi-Gourhan 1964 II: 88).

CHAPTER FOUR: LUTOSŁAWSKI'S TROIS POÈMES D'HENRI MICHAUX

1 In 'Un certain phenomène qu'on appelle musique' (Préface de *L'Encyclo-
pédie de la musique* Paris 1958); also in Michaux 1950: 184

2 He was not (letter from Lutosławski, 1 January 1977)

3 Michaux has a strong preoccupation with the loss inherent in having decided
on a definite text. He emphasizes the difference between thought and language and points to what he regards as the arbitrariness in making a unique
choice at the exclusion of all other, possibly equally valid choices. The core
issue of such a preoccupation is of course the search for essences below alternative surfaces: 'J'étais une parole, qui tentait d'avancer à la vitesse de la
pensée. / Les camarades de la pensée assistaient. / Pas une ne voulut sur
moi tenir le moindre pari, et elles étaient bien la six cent mille qui me regar-
daient en riant' (Henri Michaux *Qui je fus* © Editions Gallimard) (Bertelé
1975: 80) ('I was a word that attempted to progress at the speed of the
thought. / The friends of the thought helped. / Not one wanted to bet on
me at all, and there were at least six hundred thousand that looked at me
laughing').

Or let us consider the motto for *Passages*: 'Koyu, le religieux, dit : seule
une personne de comprehension réduite désire arranger les choses en series
complètes. C'est l'incomplètude qui est désirable. En tout, mauvaise est la

regularité. Dans les palais d'autrefois, on laissait toujours un batiment inachevé, obligatoirement' (*Tsuredzure Gusa*, by Yoshida No Kaneyoshi, fourteenth century) (Henri Michaux *Passages* © Editions Gallimard 1950) ('Koyu, the monk, said: "Only a person with little understanding wishes to arrange things in complete (fixed?) series. It is incompleteness that is desirable. Above all, regularity is bad. In olden days one always had to leave a room incomplete in the palace"').

4 See 'Pseudo-loop-aggregate' in the glossary of this chapter.

5 See also 186–93 in the present text.

6 Bowie's perceptive use of words depicting dynamic processes and their appropriateness when applied to some of Lutosławski's form-building processes deserve close attention.

7 Gobin and Surridge provided also most of the word analyses for this poem. I am grateful to them.

8 The forthcoming discussion of the musical setting of this poem suggests a somewhat modified, less desperate and bleak, conclusion than what is offered here. Is it possible that I have changed my mind about this poem, as a result of further thought about the piece, while I was working on this text? (See 'The Affective Impact' in this chapter, below.)

9 I failed to find an adequate word to translate malheur. I agree with Lutosławski that misfortune is not appropriate, if only for its rhythm, but sorrow is also flawed (Nordwall 1968: 78). For this reason I have decided to keep the French original, which is also unsatisfactory.

10 See the glossary for 'mass-structure,' 'layer,' and 'bundle.'

11 See in the glossary 'interval-types in twelve-note-chords' and 'timbre.'

12 Of course he is not expected to offer such a theory or hypothesis.

13 This understanding is sustained by a statement made by the composer in a letter of 1 January 1977.

14 See the orchestral part of *Trois Poèmes*, the first movement, from 35 to 45 (Example 4.11).

15 Lutosławski might be also referring here to a process that is called moment form by Stockhausen and others.

16 See the glossary for the definition of these terms as well as of those that will follow.

17 Upon reading an earlier, but essentially identical, version of this chapter, Lutosławski wrote to me: 'I share your doubts about the possibility of surviving the kind of music based on large masses of sounds. In some of my later scores you could see the reaction to it' (letter of 1 January 1977).

18 There has been, to my knowledge, no systematic study of mass-structures undertaken, either in a taxonomical sense or in a normative sense. While it

would perhaps not be too difficult to set up a hypothetical neutral taxonomy for the study of such structures, there is no guarantee that such a tidy ordering of notational data will be matchable with convincingly documented experimental observations regarding the various strategies of perception. While such experimental-psychological data remains unavailable I prefer to use (or should I say I have no choice but to use) an impressionistic commentary, employing a combination of labels and familiar terminology. The use of metaphors and apposite suggestiveness may have its justification in certain situations and may help towards a rigorous theory. (Consider in this respect chapter 7, 'Warum die Metapher?,' in Fónagy 1964: 101–17.)

19 Six years after writing the preceding paragraph I am of the view that mass-structures constitute a special and indispensable element in the potential vocabulary of a composer today. They are best thought of in terms of their appropriateness, their overall nature and quality.

20 The recent, and not so recent, history of Lutosławski's homeland puts the third poem and its setting here in a poignant light.

21 Commenting on his *String Quartet*, Lutosławski wrote about this idea slightly differently: 'In composing my piece I had to foresee all possibilities which could arise within the limits set beforehand. This, in fact, consisted of setting the limits themselves in such a way that even "the least desirable possibility" of execution in a given fragment, should nevertheless be acceptable. This guarantees that everything that may happen within the previously set limits fulfil my purpose' (Nordwall 1968: 88).

CHAPTER FIVE: BLURRED BOUNDARIES

1 There might be a dual possibility for focusing on a vocal event (either as speech or as music), somewhat analogously to the two interpretations possible for the Necker cube or the alternative meanings possible for an expression such as 'the shooting of the hunters' (Lenneberg 1967: 290–1, 297).

2 G. List's classification system (List 1963: 9) allows for in between or transitional utterance types, but is limited by the smallness of the corpus commented on and the paucity of the label repertoire suggested. List is aware of these limitations and concludes his article: 'The classification system presented here does not of course permit the placement of forms with a fine degree of accuracy. Much more data is needed concerning the intonational contours utilized in each language under consideration before a more exact classification is possible' (13).

3 For representative recordings see Schwitter's *An Anna Blume – Die Sonate in Urlauten*, Lord's Gallery, London; the record accompanying issue 33 of the

revue *OU*, Sceau, 1967; the seven records of text-sound compositions, Fylkingen Records, Sveriges Radios Förlag, Stockholm, 1968–70; and the record *10+2: 12 American Text Sound Pieces*, Arch Inc, Berkeley, Calif, 1974.

4 On the record *10+2: 12 American Text Sound Pieces*

5 See note 4.

6 From the stage directions of the play

7 Rabbi Zalman was, of course, echoing the thought of St Augustine: 'He who jubilates speaks no words: it is a song of joy without words.'

8 RCA Victor LTC 3

9 Professor Beverley Cavanagh has pointed out to me that this view of Lomax's has been contested.

10 *Anthology of the World's Music* AST-4005 St

11 Phillips 6586 007

12 One finds a similar expression in Berio's *Coro*: the very high shrieking in section XXVIII, which the composer characterizes as like the 'hurlement of Algerian women.' Thus, both composers may have wanted to recreate a kind of shrieking-wailing that may be an expression of grief for women in several regions along the rim of the Mediterranean.

13 64–5 in the choral score

14 67–75

15 *Contemporary Hungarian Composers* (1970) lists (99) a work by Pongrácz entitled *Gamelán Zene* (translated as *Javanese Music*) 1942.

16 A certain kind of contemplative, even mystical, state of mind appears to be an indispensable condition also for the singer of Iranian classical music. Jalal Zolfanun writes: 'The second aspect of the performance comes from within: the mind and the feelings of the performer, his overall personality, his virtues, the purity of his heart, his sincerity and other humanistic faculties ... His effort for the apprehension of divine qualities and their application in faith puts the performer in the right path for communicating with his listeners, to put his message across. In Iran we achieve this through Sufism ... Through Sufism we apprehend divine realities. We gain such enlightenment if we combine feeling and action and apply both in the practice of our performance' (Emmert 1979: 68). (I wish to thank Dr Beverley Cavanagh for drawing my attention to Emmert 1979 and to the films it comments on.) Tamia spoke with me after a performance that lasted more than an hour on 9 May 1982, at the festival Trois Jours de Musiques Vocales, held in Montreal. She referred to an inner urge that brings forth her many-faceted vocalizations that at times resemble elements of classical Iranian vocal music. Elsewhere (program notes for her performance at the festival) she was quoted as speaking of a quasi-natural urge to sing: 'In a certain moment I had the desire to sing. It was an urge to

be expressive. I felt like uttering a song, my song. One often speaks of uttering a cry [cri] to designate what I do; for me, it is singing.' This brings again Jalal Zolfanun to mind as he says: 'Persian singing is to some exent an imitation of the singing of the birds. Music has always been linked with the joys of life. For a Persian, listening to music is a means of rising to ecstasy, through whose portals ultimate reality can be reached' (Emmert 1979: 68).

17 These matters, as constituting analogies, and possibly also models, for certain contemporary compositional practices, will be discussed in some detail in the next chapter.

18 The composer's instructions, given on xii of the score

19 *Coro* and *In Search of Zoroaster* will be discussed in some detail in the final chapter.

20 *New York Times* Sunday 15 April 1979: 1, 21–2

21 The record was lent to me by the painter Yves Gaucher. It bore the Oiseau Lyre label, but I don't recall its number.

22 A word of caution is in order here. The voice quality labels indicated here and in Example 5.3 are derived from trying to imitate the sounds and attempting to find correct matchings between self-observation and perceived acoustic output, on one hand, and items on a list of voice quality labels in Laver (1975), on the other; hence they are only conjectural.

23 The word recited by the narrator means 'appeared.' I wish to thank Makoto Shinohara for the translation.

24 Page 2 in the score

25 Nonesuch H-71285 (stereo)

26 Although in different compound phonation types in each instance

27 From the composer's 'A note on the music,' in the score

28 Introduction by William P. Malm to Togi 1971: 6

CHAPTER SIX: DEEP THEMES, NOT SO HIDDEN

1 For a description of the general nature of this indeterminate work, consisting of ninety-two solos, see Gottwald 1975: 117–25.

2 See Cage 1979 for numerous works written in this genre.

3 For more detailed information on the work see Schnebel 1972: 257–61 and 386–7. The work is recorded on DG St 643 543.

4 Page 22 of the score, as realized by the composer

5 *Patria I, Patria II, The Crown of Ariadne*, the prose pseudo-archeological fantasy *Dicamus et Labyrinthos*, and perhaps also *La Testa d'Adriane*

6 Combarieu 1908: 321, quoting from Alice C. Fletcher 'The Hako, a Pawnee Ceremony' *Twenty-Second Annual Report of the Bureau of American Ethnology* I

371. I am including here only the first stanza. The structure of the others is almost identical to this one; the only change consists of the substitution of the names of other spirits (for that of AWAHOKSHU) who serve 'as intermediaries between men and Tira'wa the "great power."''

7 Sachs 1943: 22, quoting from A.H. Fox Strangways *The Music of Hindostan* Oxford, 1914

8 See in this respect the analysis of M. Kagel's *Anagrama* in Klüppelholz 1976: 117–22.

9 As in the cases of Steve Reich and Phil Glass, among others

10 From a review of the second of the initial three performances of the work, entitled 'Musical Hypnotism on a Grand Scale,' by Arthur Kaptainis, Toronto *Globe and Mail* 1 August 1981

11 Ibid. Kaptainis shows here a good critical sense and responsiveness. At its close he searches for a central theme in the opera. His conclusion is that in the work 'Glass intends to repeat assurances like Hare Krishna chanters, in a way that will allow sympathetic listeners to be further assured of the godliness of Gandhi's way.' I have not heard the work.

12 We shall soon begin to consider the use, function, and effect of unintelligible words in mystical, magical practices.

13 For a detailed analysis of this seminal work see Klüppelholz 1976.

14 Mellnäs's *Succsim*, Malec's *Dodecameron*, Jolas's *Sonate à 12*, Oliveros's *Sound Patterns*, etc

15 See also Hocke 1959: 230–1.

16 This broad-gauge metaphor ignores the immensely complex pattern of synchronicities and overlaps of the multiplicity of often clashing lines of thought that constitute civilization. I shall return to this topic in the concluding chapter. (See also Ellenberger 1970 for good summaries.)

17 Butler sees a parallel between this formula and Schopenhauer's conception of the role of the will in the scheme of things.

18 Preisendanz 1973 I: vi–vii. A considerable number of these are now available in annotated translations. Synoptic works such as Dornseiff (1922) and Hopfner (1921) as well as specialized monographs, such as those of A. Dieterich (1891, 1910) and L. Blau (1974), are also very informative. See other references in the bibliography.

19 The papyrus is in the Museum van Oudheden, Leiden, J 395(w). Preisendanz 1973 in his introduction comments that it is 'a collection of magical recipes. Amidst the magical action there is included, which is important from the point of view of the history of religion, a cosmogonic account, a cosmopoiia' (87). The papyrus is dated at AD 346.

20 My English translation of this text (and those that will follow) was made from the German translation that appears in Preisendanz 1973. Preisendanz indicates the magic words with the letters zw for *Zauberworte*. These I have transcribed from the Greek script supplied by him.

21 About the mystical and magical meaning of classes of letters, see Dornseiff 1922: 32–5. About the use of vowel series in magic see 35–51.

22 According to Dornseiff (1922: 63), klimatas are 'figures that are formed by writing the same word continuously under each other, but leaving out one letter on one side, each time, through which a right-angled triangle results ... or on both sides, through which a grape-like isosceles triangle results.'

23 Systematic combinatorial operations such as these could have been engendered by the hope that in the series one pair will eventually prove to be the right (effective) one for the purpose in question. (See, for an analogy, Dornseiff 1922: 54, regarding meaningless letter series.)

24 See III: 108–28 for the complete text, and I: 387–461 for the related commentary; see also I 441.

25 Practices of letter substitution such as the one here, and other similar manipulations, have become known through Kabbalistic Jewish writings. (For further information, see Gaster 1971; G. Scholem 1954, 1974; Blau 1974; Dornseiff 1922; and Poncé 1973.)

26 Hopfner 1974: 494. See also Sachs 1940.

27 Selections of this are included on the record *10+2: 12 American Text Sound Pieces* 1750 Arch Records.

28 'Jeu de Lettres' in 'Dicamus et Labyrinthos' (Schafer 1979: 93ff; the pages are unnumbered).

29 Gaster writes: 'It is well known that the Samaritans have invented a peculiar system of cryptography, the like of which has not yet been found among any other nation. It consists in picking out letters from the text in such a manner that they form a vertical column in the text, which now becomes divided into two large columns, and these letters in the middle form the name of the writer and the date of writing.'

30 Eliade writes about 'secret language' – the 'animal language' of the shamans. The shaman 'learns this secret language either from a teacher or by his own efforts, that is, directly from the "spirits" ... Very often this secret language is actually the "animal language," or originates in animal cries' (Eliade 1946: 96).

31 Kagel *Staatstheater* 'Ensemble' solo alto 1, full score

32 Instrumental music provides further allusions to the presence of this orientation: twelve-tone and serial musics and the coming to the fore of percussion instruments, to mention two.

33 Dornseiff 1922: 67. Dornseiff also refers here to a document from the fifth century BC.
34 See in chapter 7 a detailed description of the phonemic repertory of this interesting and beautiful piece.
35 See in this context Frye 1971: 327–8. I had read Frye's *Anatomy of Criticism* before even thinking of writing the present book. I was not ready for it at the time. While I was working on this book, not once did *Anatomy* come to my conscious mind, but, upon rereading it recently, long after completing the main body of this work, it became clear to me that unconsciously I must have been influenced by it, as well as by some authors (Jung, for example) who influenced Frye as well. I now see, of course, what an important and beautiful book *Anatomy* is.
36 T. Wiesengrund Adorno has given expression to this attitude by stating that after Auschwitz and Theresienstadt no poem should be written (Helms 1967: 118).
37 Perhaps symbols of an infant-like or animal-state reaction to pain, helplessness, neglect, and lost hope
38 Jacket notes to the recording of the work on DG St 643 544
39 Hugo Ball: 'Dada Fragments (1916–1917)' R. Motherwell 1951: 51
40 From *The Myth of Sisyphus*, quoted in Esslin 1961: xix
41 In 1970 he expanded this short piece into *Song Books*.
42 H.G. Helms told me in 1958 in Cologne about his admiration for Cage. However, less than a decade later he came to refer to these visits of Cage as constituting a 'natural catastrophe that broke over musical Europe' (Helms 1967: 128).
43 See his works for, and comments on, the 'Scratch Orchestra.'
44 I am referring to 2.012, 2.0121, and 2.0122 in Wittgenstein 1921.
45 See E. Salzman's article 'Mixed Media' in Vinton 1971: 489–92.
46 I have not attended a performance of, or heard, the work in its entirety or read the score. My comments are based on Sabbe 1979, on two reviews of performances, published in *Melos* and on listening to the record WER 60085.
47 Nono has described the unrealized plans for an open-air presentation of a piece that was to take place in Venice. The plans envisaged a prototype for an ideological-popular spectacle for a large number of spectators (Nono 1975: 96).
48 An introductory note to the program booklet of the festival Trois Jours de Musiques Vocales, held in Montreal in May 1982, stated: 'Un grand mérite de notre époque est sans doute d'avoir produit une ouverture sans précédent de la sensibilité musicale, rendant possible la rencontre d'expériences sonores, qui d'un côté, puisent aux traditions les plus anciennes et, de

l'autre, participent aux recherches les plus actuelles. La traversée des fron-tières n'a plus aujourd'hui le caractère d'une transgression' (A great achievement of our time is, without doubt, having opened doors to musical sensitivity, to a degree that is without precedent, making possible the coming together of those sonic experiences which, on the one hand, emanate from the most ancient traditions, and on the other, those that form part of the most recent researches. To step over boundaries no longer appears to be a transgression today). Accordingly, the organizers of this important event assembled a program that included Japanese traditional classical song, Mohawk chants, Inuit throat games, sonic poetry (by the Four Horsemen) and such performers and performer-composers as Tamia, Ed Herbst, J. Fleury-Coutu, P. Vaillancourt, P. Froehlich, Michiko Hirayama, and the Extended Vocal Tech-niques Ensemble (E. Harkins, D. Kavásch, P. Larson, and L. Vickerman).

49 From the composer's program notes for the première of the work in Lon-don, Ontario, on 1 December 1980

50 I have not heard the work. These remarks are made after reading the libretto and Kagel's comments in Kagel et al 1980. I wish to thank Dr H. Colpa for lending this publication to me.

51 Schafer has chosen this as a theme for the second part of his *Apocalypsis* ('Credo').

CHAPTER SEVEN: ORPHEUS RESURGENT ... PERHAPS

1 On a disc accompanying the *Revue OU* no. 33, Sceau, 1967

2 From the composer's notes to the score, 1

3 'These exercises ... were developed by the late Iris Warren for the training and development of her students of acting' (from the composer's notes to the score, 4).

4 It means: 'There is no god but God' (Trimingham 1971: 201).

5 Notes to the score

6 Notes to the score

7 Notes to the score

8 Notes to the score

9 Notes to the score

10 This is my characterization, arrived at on the basis of the 'heard' event.

11 Schafer adds in the score: 'The technique can be studied in Mauri war dances' (see 8).

12 For a brief and up-to-date survey of the linguistic literature in this regard see Klüppelholz 1976: 103–60.

13 That is, those that have no semantic denotata

14 For example: consonantal concentrations with as few vowel sounds included as possible. See Anhalt 1970 and 1972.

15 For a view of this section in the context of the whole work, see the last chapter, where the entire piece is analysed.

16 DG 2531270

17 'Syrismos' in the Graeco-Egyptian magical papyri (Bonner 1927: 172; Hopfner 1974: 484–5, 780)

18 For more detailed information on the work see Anhalt 1970: 81–9.

19 If there are such connections present, they were wholly unconscious on my part. I recall only responding to the strongly suggestive phonemic character of the text here. But this, in itself, is likely to be a superficial account of a compositional process.

20 Vetter 1970: 189. Upon reading this reference Schafer has suggested to me that one might compare this quote with the passage 'Tupfer – Hupfer – Huepfen – Sie Mal,' used in editing unit 2 of his *Patria II*. He added: 'The words came from a person undergoing brain surgery. I believe this involuntary reaction is called Foerster's Syndrome. The source is A. Koestler's *The Act of Creation*, New York, 1964, pages 315–16' (personal communication from the composer, 7 November 1981).

21 When speaking of games, I do not forget the possibility that some of these sounds (tongue-click, for example) can become the vehicles for compulsive action.

22 Page 15, measures 1–2, alto 2. (D ..., D ‖‖ , and ⟿ designate, respectively, finger and tongue tremolos.)

23 Page 18, measure 2, soprano 2 (both examples include gradual vowel-modulations).

24 See in this regard a recent excellent survey of the literature and other findings included in Sundberg 1980.

25 Notes to the score

26 Notes to the score

27 Iamblichus wrote in the second century A.D., in *De Mysteriis*: 'Even when they [the meaningless expressions and names] appear to us, men, as meaningless, they without exception, have their meaning, their idea-content, but naturally only for the gods' (Hopfner 1974: 440–1).

28 Quests for Adam's language, man's supposed original language, or for Orpheus's language, as well as for various universal languages, were made, of course, before the twentieth century, and these were engendered by diverse reasons and motivations. Jakob Böhme (1575–1624) believed in the existence of an onomatopoeic Adamic language (*The Works of Jacob Behmen*, London, 1764, I i, 204–6, quoted with marginal annotations by S.T. Coleridge, in Coleridge

1980: 606–8). During the seventeenth and eighteenth centuries a number of attempts were made in the direction of the construction of a conceptually logical, and expressive, 'universal language' that would be a fitting medium of communication for the new scientific society that was then in the process of emerging. (For details see Knowlson 1975.)

29 This translation, for which I wish to express here my thanks, was made by A. Lyubechansky.

30 Quoted in Bruns 1974: 161

31 She demonstrates some of the sounds she has produced on the record '*Voice Is the Original Instrument*,' Wizard Records, RVW 2266.

32 'Forcing air held in the mouth ... by means of cheek muscles while inhaling through the nose' (in the jacket-notes to the record referred to in note 31)

33 The Center for Music Experiment and Related Research, University of California at San Diego, La Jolla, Calif 92037

34 *Index* is complemented by a mimeographed paper written by R. Jennings, who comments further on the physiological aspects of the topic discussed. The members of the Extended Vocal Techniques Ensemble, E. Harkins, D. Kavásch, P. Larson, and L. Vickerman, who performed in the festival Trois Jours de Musiques Vocales, in Montreal, on 8 May 1982, have demonstrated a high degree of virtuosity in the use of many of the techniques listed in *Index*. Miss Kavásch told me that they have discontinued using those techniques that they came to regard as being demonstrably, or potentially, stressful, or harmful, to the voice. One is repeatedly advised by Kavásch that electronic amplification is desirable, at times even necessary, for the effective projection of some of the vocal devices of the Extended Vocal Techniques Ensemble (Kavásch 1980: 3, 4, 6, 8, 10, 12).

35 I wish to thank John Beckwith for this reference.

36 In his *Human Speech* (quoted in Schafer 1970: 202). This might remind us of Beckett's *Not I*. (See 154–5.)

37 Should one regard a piece that uses but a single bird-call type of utterance as having a language? The same question can be asked about a sneezing piece by Schwitters and of Wolman's *Mégapneumes 67*. I suggest an affirmative answer.

38 Such as some by Charles Dodge, for example

39 Here *ziruf* is defined as 'the science of the combination of letters.'

40 In the 'Albam' we have the following transformation:

$$\text{T:} \quad \begin{array}{ccccccccccc} 1 & 2 & 3 & 4 & 5 & 6 & 7 & 8 & 9 & 10 & 11 \\ 12 & 13 & 14 & 15 & 16 & 17 & 18 & 19 & 20 & 21 & 22 \end{array}$$

meaning that 'aleph' becomes 'lamedh' and 'beth,' 'mem,' etc. In 'Atbash' the transformation is:

1 2 3 4 5 6 7 8 9 10 11

T:

22 21 20 19 18 17 16 15 14 13 12

thus 'aleph' becomes 'tav,' and 'beth,' 'shin.'

41 Of great interest is Beckett's analytical commentary following the first of these transformations and also the sentence (or its variants) that follows each of the transformations: 'But soon I grew used to these sounds and then I understood as well as before ...' (165).

42 Pages 184 and 197 above

43 See chapter 2.

44 See Stockhausen's own description of the process in *Texte* II 51–68.

45 Beckwith has pointed out to me that this example is 'close to some actual Polynesian languages in which one finds a severely restricted number of consonants.' He further suggests that one might usefully compare this fragment 'also to the synthetic language used by Bergman in his film *Silence*.'

46 Bainchōōōōōōōōch, Baphrenemun, Barpharangēs, Chabantachōnēr, Chammanman, Damnameneus, Malamuri, Thalalmelal, etc (Kropp 1931 II: 257–73)

47 I wish to thank R.M. Schafer for drawing my attention to this book.

48 A recent example is Kagel's *Aus Deutschland*, the central idea of which is, avowedly, death (Kagel in Kagel et al 1980: 6).

49 This series of connotations could be pursued quite a bit longer still. Perhaps it is such a quasi-open-endedness what Umberto Eco had in mind when referring to an infinite regress in semiosis. (I cannot find where he wrote this.)

CHAPTER EIGHT: ALTERNATIVE VOICES

1 Similar to the placing of an inverted *urinoir* in an art gallery, as Marcel Duchamp did more than half a century ago

2 From the notes in the score

3 The word light is suppressed in the text (as is on traffic-signs), but remains in the metaphorical use of the expressions.

4 In an earlier, even more conjectural version of the two paragraphs that follow, I suggested at some length that the roots of this composition might reach into the composer's own childhood. The composer conveyed the following about the combinational play referred to: 'Because in Canada, these signs always

appear as an "x," since childhood I always dismembered the syllables in this fashion. No deeper significance was *intended*.'

5 Beckwith also made the following comment on the earlier version of the two preceding paragraphs, referred to in note 4: 'I had a happy upbringing in an environment with many restrictive rules in whose parental source I could readily equate authority with love. There was no "resentment" I had to overcome.' To this he adds: '*Gas!* in fact originated as a comment on my learning to drive a car. "Gas!" was a command from my Hungarian teacher whose qualifications had been gained in the Hungarian Army in World War Two. When I dawdled in traffic or tried while driving to subject my mistakes to reasoned analysis, I would hear "Gas!". I was forty, and clumsy – and there *was* indeed resentment at being unsuccessful, at first, in the role of pupil, to which I was unaccustomed after so many years: resentment at my own awkwardness, at my teacher, at those multiple commands rushing at my eyes from all the signs. I don't believe the exorcism was therefore of *old* resentments. (But I could be wrong.)'

6 For discussions of Zoroaster and Zoroastrianism see Moulton 1917 and the article 'Zoroaster' in *Encyclopaedia Britannica* 1960. References to these topics in the present section are taken from one or both of these sources.

7 *Divan i Shams i Tabriz*, and *Apocalypsis*.

8 According to Moulton (1917: 22) the six do not constitute a closed company. Later (95, 97) he lists additional qualities. Schafer employs some of these in the piece.

9 In his 'Ursound' (Schafer 1979: 83) Schafer's choice for the acoustical attribute of creation (if not that of Creation) is the recital of magic words, incantation, preferably in a language we do not understand, following examples in the magical papyri. (See Kropp 1931: section 200, p 120, for example.) Further on in the same article (90), Schafer writes about the 'memory of "Ursound," about a faint acoustic memory trace of God's ordering and creating presence.' Stockhausen, in an article entitled 'Mundstück' (*Texte* III 301), compares a modern artist to a 'radio-receiver,' who is 'conscious of himself in super-consciousness' (ein Radioempfänger mit Selbstbewustsein im Überbewusstsein). In writing about his *Sternklang*, which he labels 'spiritual music' (*Texte* IV 172), he says that the work constitutes music for 'concentrated meditative listening for the purpose of sinking the individual into the cosmic whole.' Both Stockhausen and Schafer, in their individual ways, seem to believe that music possesses powers that enable those who know how to listen to move, through it, into a heightened level of consciousness.

10 In the performance I attended on 8 February 1981, in Kingston, Ontario, this did not quite come off as it was probably intended. The young performers did

not possess (mentally) the model-sounds Schafer had in mind – a small detail, one might say, but perhaps not. It is really a manifestation of a deeper problem: namely, how to import from different cultures sonic events without importing at the same time also native-born, or -trained, interpreters.

11 According to Moulton 1917, *Sraosha*, in Zoroastrian terminology, means obedience, an angel or judgment. He also is considered to be part of Ahura Mazda's complex personality. Schafer in this score refers to him as a 'genius of hearing,' 'the mediator between Ahura Mazda and man' (1).

12 I was unable to locate this expression. In Christian Bartholomae's *Altiranisches Wörterbuch*, however, I have found the words 'tavah,' meaning fortune (or wealth), strength and power, and 'ātar,' meaning fire, which might provide clues for the understanding of 'tavo athro.'

13 The performance instructions indicate here that he 'sings in a quavering voice rising in glissando, like the voices of Japanese court theatre.' This constitutes an impressionistic prescription, the successful realization of which is predicated on certain assumptions.

14 Compare the attitudes of the Zoroastrians (as described by Moulton) and those of the Mani and his followers (as stated in the article 'Manichaeism' in *Encyclopaedia Britannica* 1960) to fire and light. See also chapter 13 in Eliade 1978.

15 Simha Arom (1970: 19) writes the following about the relationship between percussive instrumental sounds and the onomatopoeic sounds 'ti' and 'ki,' on which I commented earlier (223–4): 'The Ngbaka designate their recitations, whether or not they comprise sung passages, by the generic terms, SĪMOTI or SĪMOKI, of which the two initial elements literally signify: SĪ "song" or "tale," and MO "mouth"; TI or KI are idiophones, utilised as optional punctuation made at the expressed demand of the narrator, by a "respondent." The latter "either strikes a little bell (a traditional instrument or an improvised one), or sings the sound of the little bell, producing a ti ..., ti ..., ti ... ti ... or ki ... ki ... ki depending on the 'respondents,' on a high note"' (quoting from J.M.C. Thomas 1963 *Le Parler ngbaka de Bokanga. Phonologie, morphologie, syntaxe.* Paris and The Hague 3: 41).

16 Instruction given in the score, 18

17 I have a reservation about the work: most of the time it uses as text an English translation. One wonders why Schafer, one of the most sensitive of composers about language, chose to make do here with inauthentic phonetic material.

18 This might be regarded as a parallel to Jung's quest during the period 1913–18 (Ellenberger 1970: 719–26).

19 From the composer's notes accompanying a recording of this work on DG ST 2531 270.

20 The text of *Sequenza III* shares some of these features.

21 See references to these manias in Rouget 1980.

22 According to a note in the text accompanying the record referred to (see note 19), but *not* so indicated in the corresponding text-fragment given in the published score (UE 15044). Subsequently, from a letter from the publisher, dated 16 April 1982, I learned that the text of section XI is by Berio himself. I wrote the paragraph immediately following the poem before receiving this information about authorship.

23 Sections I and XXXI (the first and last ones) contribute to two streams, all the other individual sections to a single stream only. The individual streams contain a minimum of two, and a maximum of nine, different sections.

24 See note 19.

25 See note 19.

26 See note 19.

27 If we consider the D♯ as a different pitch-class from the E♭, then we have eleven.

28 J. Combarieu suggests that the device of the refrain grew out of the popular usage of the incantation (Combarieu 1909: 320).

29 One could raise the objection here about the use of many texts in translations that I raised concerning *In Search of Zoroaster*. These texts remain unintelligible more often in *Coro* than in Schafer's piece, and for this reason, at least, the translations are less (or not at all) objectionable. In both works this question might have posed the dilemma of a trade-off between sonic authenticity and easy intelligibility, assuming that there were practical options of using authentic texts.

30 Klüppelholz appears to have modified somewhat the view expressed in the statement I quoted in the preceding sentence. In his commentary on Kagel's opera *Aus Deutschland*, 'Schubert im Schosse Goethes in den Armen Freuds' (Schubert in the Lap of Goethe in the Arms of Freud), he wrote: 'In an environment that overflows with historical music he does not produce, in an emphatic sense, New Music, but instead Kagel articulates the certainty that these times require less new notes than new ears. Beyond blind belief in progress and lame decadence a new path was found which was no half-hearted middle course: Kagel's radical technique to transform composition into interpretation and creation into analysis. Neither the speech elements, nor the musical models are new, new is the resulting Lieder-opera, a sensuous reflection of Romanticism' (Kagel et al 1980: 11).

List of compositions

Dates immediately following the name of a work are year(s) of composition.

Amirkhanian, C. *Heavy Aspirations* 1973
- *If in Is* 1971
- *Just* 1972

Anhalt, I. *Cento* BMI Canada Ltd, Toronto, 1968
- *Foci* Berandol Music Ltd, Toronto, 1972
- *La Tourangelle* Berandol Music Ltd, Toronto, 1982
- *Winthrop* 1983

Arfid, D. *Catalogo Voce*
- *Maroon Bells*

Ashley, R. *In Sara, Mencken, Christ and…* 1972–3
- *She Was a Visitor* 1967

Babbitt, M. *Composition for Tenor and 6 Instruments* 1960
- *Philomel* 1963–4
- *Phonemena* 1969–70
- *Sounds and Words* 1960
- *Vision and Prayer* 1961

Baird, T. *Etiuda* Polskie Wydawnictwo Muzyczne, Warsaw, 1961

Ballif, C. *Phrases sur le souffle* 1958

Bark, J. *Nota* W. Hansen, Stockholm, 1964

Beckwith, J. *Canada Dash – Canada Dot* 1965–7
- *Gas!* Berandol Music Ltd, Toronto, 1978
- *The Great Lakes Suite* Canadian Music Centre, Toronto, 1949
- *A Little Organ Concert* 1982
- *Mating Time* Canadian Music Centre, Toronto, 1982
- *Night Blooming Cereus* Canadian Music Centre, Toronto, 1953–8

- *Place of Meeting* Canadian Music Centre, Toronto, 1967
- *The Shivaree* Canadian Music Centre, Toronto, 1965–78
- *The Sun Dance* Canadian Music Centre, Toronto, 1968
- *The Trumpets of Summer* Berandol Music Ltd, Toronto, 1964

Bedford, D. *Two Poems for Chorus. On Words of Kenneth Patchen* Universal Edition, London, 1967

Beecroft, N. *Two Went to Sleep* 1967

Berberian, C. *Stripsody* C.F. Peters, New York, London, Frankfurt, 1966

Berio, L. *A-ronne* 1974–5
- *Circles* 1960, Universal Edition, London, 1961
- *Coro* Universal Edition, Milan, 1976
- *Laborintus II* Universal Edition, Paris, 1965
- *Omaggio a Joyce* 1958
- *Opera* 1970
- *Passaggio* text by Edoardo Sanguineti, Universal Edition, Milan, 1963
- *Recital I. for Cathy* 1972
- *Sequenza III* per voce femminile, Universal Edition, London, 1968
- *Sinfonia* for eight voices and orchestra, Universal Edition, London, 1969
- *Visage* 1961

Birtwistle, H. *Orpheus* 1974–7

Blacher, B. *Abstrakte Oper Nr. 1* Ed. Bote and G. Bock, Berlin, 1953

Blin, J.-A. *Rapport sonore pour bande* 1983

Boulez, P. *'cummings ist der dichter ...'* Universal Edition, London, 1976
- *Improvisation sur Mallarmé. Le Vierge, le vivace et le bel aujourd'hui ... Une dentelle s'abolit* Universal Edition, London, 1958
- *Le Marteau sans maître* Universal Edition, Vienna, 1954
- *Le Soleil des eaux* 1948, Heugel et cie, Paris, 1959
- *Visage nuptial* Heugel et cie, Paris, 1946–7, rev 1951–2

Britten, B. *A Charm of Lullabies* Boosey & Hawkes, London, Toronto, 1949

Brooks, W. *3 Madrigals*

Bussotti, S. *Memoria* 1962, Bruzzichelli, Florence
- *La Passion selon Sade* G. Ricordi, Milan, 1966

Cage, J. *Mesostics* Henmar Press, New York, 1971
- *Solo for Voice I* Henmar Press, New York, 1958
- *Solo for Voice II* Henmar Press, New York, 1960
- *Song Books* I and II, Henmar Press, New York, 1970
- *The Wonderful Widow of Eighteen Springs* C.F. Peters Corp, New York, London, Frankfurt, 1961

Celona, J.A. *Micro-Macro* 1975

Chopin, H. *Audio-poème 'Le Ventre de Bertini'* 1967

Colgrass, M. *Best Wishes U.S.A.* 1976
- *New People* Carl Fischer, Inc 1969
- *Theatre of the Universe* 1975
- *Virgil's Dream* 1967

Constant, M. *Le Jeu de Ste Agnes* 1974

Crumb, G. *Ancient Voices of Children* C.F. Peters, New York, London, Frankfurt, 1970
- *Night Music* 1963–4
- *Songs, Drones, and Refrains of Death* 1968, C.F. Peters, New York, London, Frankfurt
- *Three Madrigals, Book I* 1965

Davies, P.M. *Eight Songs for a Mad King* Boosey & Hawkes, London, Toronto, 1971
- *Miss Donnithorne's Maggot* Boosey & Hawkes, London, Toronto, 1977
- *Missa super L'Homme armé* for voice and chamber ensemble, Boosey and Hawkes, London, Toronto, 1980
- *Revelation and Fall* Boosey & Hawkes, London, Toronto, 1971
- *Stone Litany. Runes from a House of the Dead* Boosey & Hawkes, London, Toronto, 1975

Dodge, C. *Speech Songs* 1973
- *Any Resemblance is Purely Coincidental*
- *The Story of Our Lives* 1974

Druckman, J. *Animus 2* for soprano (mezzo), two percussion players, and tape, MCA Music, New York, 1973

Dufrêne, F. *Crirythme 67 'Dédié à H. Chopin'* 1967

Eimert, H. *Epitaph für Aikichi Kuboyama* 1960–2

Ferrari, L. *Hétérozygote* 1963–4
- *Promenade symphonique à travers un paysage musical* 1978

Foss, L. *Fragments of Archilochos* B. Schott's Söhne, Mainz, 1966, and Carl Fischer, New York, 1966

Gaburo, K. *Antiphony III (Pearl-white moments)* 1962
- *Dwell:¹* Lingua Press 1976, reprinted in Kostelanetz 1980b: 229
- *Exit Music II: Fat Millie's Lament* 1965
- *Lingua I–IV* 1965–70

Glass, P. *Satyagraha* 1981

Globokar, V. *Traumdeutung* psychodrama for four choirs after *Traumdeutung* by Edoardo Sanguineti, Litolff's Verlag/C.F. Peters, Frankfurt, London, New York, 1968

Goehr, A. *Triptych* 1968–70

Hamel, K. *Land of Shades* 1982

Hanson, S. *Coucher et souffler* 1968

Harvey, J. *Mortuos Plango, Vivos Voco*

Haubenstock-Ramati, R. *Credentials, or 'Think, Think Lucky'* Universal Edition, Vienna, 1963

Hawkins, J. *Three Cavatinas* BMI Canada Ltd, Don Mills, Ontario, 1967

Heidsieck, B. *Biopsie V66 'Quel âge avez-vous?'* 1966

Helms, H.G. *Daidalos* Für 4 Sänger, 1961

- *Golem* Polemik für 9 Vokalsolisten, 1962.

Henze, H.W. *El Cimarrón Biography of the Runaway Slave Esteban Montejo* recital for four musicians, Schott's Söhne, Mainz, London, New York, 1972

- *Stimmen* Eine Sammlung von Liedern für zwei Singstimmen und Instrumentalgruppen, Schott's Söhne, Mainz, London, New York, 1974

Herbst, E. *From Pine Tree to Spring* n.d.

Hiller, L. *An Avalanche* for pitchman, prima donna, player piano, percussionist, and prerecorded playback, Theodore Presser Co, Bryn Mawr, Pennsylvania, 1968

Holliger, H. *Psaume de Celan* 16 voix solo, B. Schott's Söhne, Mainz, 1971

Hunt, J. *Volta*

Johnsson, B.E. *2/1967 (while)*

Jolas, B. *Mots* Heugel, Paris, 1969

- *Sonate à 12* pour choeur mixte à 12 voix solistes, Heugel and Cie, Paris, 1976

Jones, D.E. *Pastoral* 1977

Kagel, M. *Abend* Für Doppelvokalquartett, Posaunenquintett, Elektrische Orgel und Klavier, Universal Edition, London, 1975

- *Anagrama* 1957–8, Universal Edition, London, 1965

- *Aus Deutschland – Eine Lieder-Oper* 1980

- *Hallelujah für Stimmen* 1967–8, Universal Edition, London, 1970

- *Improvisation ajoutée* 1961–2

- *Phonophonie* 1963–4, Universal Edition, London, 1976

- *Rezitativarie* 1971–2, Universal Edition, London, 1973

- *Sonant* 1960–

- *Staatstheater* Szenische Komposition, 1967–70, Universal Edition, London, 1971

- *Sur Scène* chamber music theatre piece in one act, Litolff's Verlag/C.F. Peters, Frankfurt, London, New York, 1965

Karkoschka, E. *Homo Sapiens 1968* Moeck Verlag, Celle, 1969

Kasemets, U. *Wordmusik* 1973–4

Kavásch, D. *The Owl and the Pussycat* 1974

- *Requiem* 1978

- *Soliloquy for Solo Voice* 1981

- *Sweet Talk* 1977
- *Tintinnabulation* 1976

Keane, D. *Carmen tenebrarum* 1983

Küpper, L. *Aérosons* 1982
- *After Follows Before* 1971
- *Dodécagone* 1977
- *Electropoème* 1967
- *L'Enclume des Forces* 1974
- *L'Enfeu* 1981
- *Inflexions Vocales* 1982
- *Innominé* 1974
- *Kouros et Korê* 1979
- *Louanges d'Orient et d'Occident* 1980
- *Le Rêveur au Sourire Passager* 1977
- *Saint François d'Assise parlant aux oiseaux* 1975
- *La Vague Existence* 1981

Lachenman, H. *Consolation II* 1968

Levy, E. *3 Images* 1961

Lewkovitch, B. *Il Cantico delle creature* Wilhelm Hansen, Copenhagen, 1963

Ligeti, G. *Aventures* 1962, Litolff's Verlag/C.F. Peters, Frankfurt, London, New York, 1964
- *Le grand macabre* 1978
- *Lux aeterna* Litolff's Verlag/C.F. Peters, Frankfurt, London, New York, 1968
- *Nouvelles Aventures* 1962–5, Litolff's Verlag/C.F. Peters, Frankfurt, London, New York, 1966
- *Requiem* Litolff's Verlag/C.F. Peters, Frankfurt, London, New York, 1965

London, E. *Portraits of Three Ladies* 1967
- *Psalms of These Days* 1977

Lucier, A. *I Am Sitting in a Room* 1970, Source 7, reprinted in Kostelanetz 1980b: 109

Lutosławski, W. *Trois poèmes d'Henri Michaux* Polskie Wydawnictwo Muzyczne (Éditions polonaises de musique), Kraków, 1963

Mache, F.-B. *Danae* 1970

McNabb, M. *Dreamsong* 1977–8

Malec, I. *Dodecameron* pour 12 voix solistes, Éditions Salabert, Paris, 1970

Marsh, R. *Not a Soul but Ourselves* 1977

Martirano, S. *O, o, o, o, That Shakespeherian Rag* 1958
- *Underworld* 1959

Mather, B. *Madrigal IV* 1972
- *Madrigal V* 1972–3

Mellnås, A. *Succsim* per coro misto a capella 1964
Nono, L. *Il canto sospeso* Ars Viva Verlag, Mainz, 1957
– *La fabbrica illuminata* 1964
– *Incontri* Ars Viva Verlag, Mainz, 1958
– *Ricorda cosa ti hanno fatto in Auschwitz* 1965
– *Sara dolce tacere* 1960
– *La terra e la campagna* Ars Viva Verlag, Mainz, 1959
Nørgård, P. *Babel* Wilhelm Hansen, Copenhagen, 1968
– *Gilgamesh* 1971–2
Olive, J. *Mar-ri-ia-a* 1973
Oliveros, P. *Sound Patterns* Edition Tonos, Darmstadt, 1964
Orff, C. *Antigonae* B. Schott's Söhne, Mainz, 1949
– *Carmina Burana* B. Schott's Söhne, Mainz, 1956
– *Oedipus der Tyran* B. Schott's Söhne, Mainz, 1959
Otte, H. *Alpha-Omega* 1964–5, Peters edition
Papineau-Couture, J. *Paysage* 1968, Centre de musique canadienne, Montréal
Paynter, J. *May Magnificat* Oxford University Press, 1973
– *The Windhover* Oxford University Press, 1972
Pedersen, P. *An Old Song of the Sun and the Moon and the Fear of Loneliness*
  1973
Penderecki, K. *Aus den Psalmen Davids* Moeck Verlag, Celle, New York, 1960
– *Dies irae* Oratorium ob Memoriam in Perniciei Castris in Oswiecim Necatorum
  Inexstiguibilem Reddendam, Moeck Verlag, Celle, 1967
– *Dimensionen der Zeit und der Stille* Moeck Verlag, Celle, 1961
– *Passio et Mors Domini Nostri Jesu Christi Secundam Lucam* Moeck Verlag, Celle,
  1967
– *Die Teufel von Loudun* Oper in drei Akten, B. Schott's Söhne, Mainz, 1969
Pennycook, B. *Speeches for Dr. Frankenstein* Canadian Music Centre, Toronto,
  1980
Petersen, T.L. *Voices*
Pousseur, H. *Crosses of Crossed Colours* Edizioni Suvini Zerboni, Milan, 1974
– *Electre* Action musicale, Universal Edition, London, 1968
– *Mnemosyne I* Edizioni Suvini Zerboni, Milan, 1968
– *Mnemosyne II* Edizioni Suvini Zerboni, Milan, 1969
– *Phonèmes pour Cathy* per voce sola, Edizioni Suvini Zerboni, Milan, 1973
– *Votre Faust* 1961–7
Randall, J.K. *Mudgett: monologues of a mass murderer* 1965
Reich, S. *Come out* 1966
Reynolds, R. *Blind Men* C.F. Peters Corp, New York, London, Frankfurt, 1967
– *The Emperor of Ice Cream* C.F. Peters Corp, New York, London, Frankfurt, 1963

- *Voicespace* 1976

Rochberg, G. *Passions [According to the 20th Century]* 1964–7

Scelsi, G. *Canti di Capricorno* 1980

Schafer, R.M. *Adieu Robert Schumann* Canadian Music Centre, Toronto, 1976
- *Apocalypsis* 1977, Arcana Editions, Bancroft, Ontario, 1981
- *Divan i Shams i Tabriz* 1969–70, text: Jalal Al-Din Rumi, Universal Edition, 1977
- *Epitaph for Moonlight* BMI Canada Ltd, Don Mills, Ontario, 1969
- *Felix's Girls* nine settings of text by Henry Felix, Arcana Editions, Bancroft, Ontario, 1980
- *From the Tibetan Book of the Dead* Universal Edition, 1973
- *Gita* Universal Edition, 1977
- *Hear Me Out* published in Kostelanetz 1980a
- *Hymn to Night* chamber version, Canadian Music Centre, Toronto, 1976
- *In Search of Zoroaster* Berandol Music Ltd, Toronto, 1976
- and friends *Jonah* a musical-dramatic work, Arcana Editions, Bancroft, Ontario, 1980
- *La Testa d'Adriane* in Schafer 1979
- *Loving* Berandol Music Ltd, Toronto, 1979
- *Patria I – The Characteristics Man* Berandol Music Ltd, Toronto, 1978
- *Patria II – Requiems for the Party Girl* Berandol Music Ltd, Toronto, 1978
- *The Princess of the Stars – Patria: The Prelude* 1981
- *Ra* 1983
- *Threnody* for youth orchestra, speakers, chorus, and tape, Berandol Music Ltd, Toronto, 1970

Schnebel, D. *AMN* Für 7 Gruppen von Vokalisten (Sprechchor), facsimile of ms 1967
- *dt₆* Für 12 Gruppen von Vokalisten, Version für 15, 1956–8
- *Glossolalie* 1959–60
- *:! (Madrasha II)* Für 3 Chorgruppen, 1958–68

Schoenberg, A. *Die glückliche Hand* Universal Edition, Wien, 1920–3
- *Kol Nidre* 1938, B. Schott's Söhne, Mainz, Universal Edition, Wien, 1975
- *Moses und Aron* 1930–2, B. Schott's Söhne, Mainz, Universal Edition, Wien, 1977–8
- *Ode to Napoleon Buonaparte* 1942, G. Schirmer Inc 1944
- *Pierrot lunaire* 1912, Universal Edition, Wien, 1914
- *A Survivor from Warsaw* 1947, B. Schott's Söhne, Mainz, Universal Edition, Wien, 1975

Schuller, G. *The Visitation* Associated Music Publishers, New York, 1966

Searle, H. *Gold Coast Customs* 1947–9

- *The Riverrun* 1951
- *The Shadow of Cain* 1952

Serocki, K. *Niobe* Moeck Verlag, Celle, 1967

Shapey, R. *Incantations* 1961

Shields, A. *The Transformation of Ani*

Shinohara, M. *Personnage* für einen Mime, Beleuchtung und Tonband 1968–73

Somers, H. *The Death of Enkidu: Part I* Canadian Music Centre, Toronto, 1977
- *Evocations* BMI Canada Ltd, Don Mills, Ontario, 1968
- *Kyrie Exile* vol 1 no. 3, 1973
- *Louis Riel* Canadian Music Centre, Toronto, 1967
- *Voiceplay* Canadian Music Centre, Toronto, 1971
- *Zen, Yeats, and Emily Dickinson* Canadian Music Centre, Toronto, 1975

Stockhausen, K. *Alphabet für Liège* 1972
- *'Am Himmel wandre ich ... (Indianerlieder)'* Stockhausen-Verlag, Kürten, West Germany, 1977
- *Atmen Gibt das Leben* 1974–7, Chor-Oper mit Orchester (oder Tonband), Stockhausen-Verlag, Kürten, 1979
- *Aus den sieben Tagen* Universal Edition, 1968
- *Carré* für 4 Orchester und Chöre, Universal Edition, London, 1971
- *Für Kommende Zeiten* 17 Texte für Intuitive Musik, Stockhausen-Verlag, Kürten, West Germany, 1976
- *Gesang der Jünglinge* 1955–6
- *Licht* Stockhausen-Verlag, Kürten, 1977–80
- *Mikrophonie II* for choir, Hammond organ, and 4 ring-modulators, English version, Universal Edition, London, 1974
- *Momente* 1962–4, Universal Edition
- *Sternklang* Parkmusik für 5 Gruppen, Stockhausen-Verlag, Kürten, West Germany, 1977
- *Stimmung* Universal Edition, Vienna, 1969
- *Telemusik* Universal Edition, Vienna, 1969
- *Tierkreis* Stockhausen-Verlag, Kürten, West Germany, 1979
- *'Vortrag über Hu'* für 1 Sängerin oder Sänger und Beterstimme aus *Inori* für 1 oder 2 Tänzer-Mimen, Stockhausen-Verlag, Kürten, 1979
- *Ylem* für 19 oder mehr Spieler/Sänger, Stockhausen-Verlag, Kürten, West Germany, 1977

Straesser, J. *Herfst der Muziek* voor kammerkoor a capella, 1963-4, rev. 1966, agent: C.F. Peters, New York

Stravinsky, I. *The Flood* 1961–2, Boosey & Hawkes, London, 1962
- *Requiem Canticles* 1965–6, Boosey & Hawkes, London, 1967
- *A Sermon, a Narrative, and a Prayer* 1960–1, Boosey & Hawkes, London, 1961

Swayne, G. *Cry* for twenty-eight amplified voices, Novello, Borough Green, Sevenoaks, Kent, 1981

Tamia, *Senza tempo* 1981

Tavener, J. *Celtic Requiem* Chester, 1969

ten Holt, S. *I am Sylvia but somebody else* 1973

Tremblay, G. *Oralléluiants* 1975

Varèse, E. *Ecuatorial* Ricordi, New York, 1961

− *Poème électronique* 1957–8

Vivier, C. *Chants* Éditions Musicales Transatlantiques, Paris, 1975

− *Kopernikus* Centre de Musique Canadienne au Québec, Montréal, 1979

Vogel, W. *Arpiade* Ars Viva-Verlag, Zürich, 1954

− *Flucht* 1963–4, Bärenreiter Kassel

− *Jona ging doch nach Ninive* 1958, Bote, Berlin

− *Das Lied von der Glocke* 1959

− *Meditazione sulla maschera di Amadeo Modigliani* 1960, Ricordi, Milan

− *Thyl Claes, fils de Kolldrager* 1938–42, 1943–5, Ricordi, Milan

− *Wagadu's Untergang durch die Eitelkeit* Ed. Bote und G. Bock, Berlin, 1932

− *Worte* 1962

Weinzweig, J. *Trialogue* Canadian Music Centre, Toronto, 1971

Wishart, T. *Anticredos* 1980

− *Journey into Space Travelogue* an antiscore, Alfred A. Kalmus, Ltd, London, 1975

− *Machine − 2* 1970

− *Red Bird* 1973-7

− *Scylla and Charibdis* 1976

Wolman, G.J. *Mégapneumes 67* 1967

Wolpe, S. *Anna Blume* 1929

− *Cantata* 1963–8

Wuorinen, C. *The Politics of Harmony* 1967

Xenakis, I. *Nuits* Musique pour 12 voix mixtes, Editions Salabert, Paris, 1969

− *Polla ta dhina* 1962

Yuasa, J. *My Blue Sky in Southern California* 1976

− *Calling Together* Zen-On Music Co. Ltd, Tokyo, 1973

− *Questions* Zen-On Music Co. Ltd, Tokyo, 1978

− *Utterance* Zen-On Music Co. Ltd, Tokyo, 1981

Zimmermann, B.A. *'Ich wandte mich und sah an alles Unrecht, das geschah unter der Sonne'* Schott's Söhne, Mainz, London, New York, 1972

− *Die Soldaten* Schott's Söhne, Mainz, 1966

Bibliography

Abercrombie, D. 1967 *Elements of General Phonetics* Edinburgh University Press, Edinburgh

Abercrombie, D., Fry, D.B., MacCarthy, P.A.D., et al (ed) 1964 *In Honour of Daniel Jones* Longmans, London

Agulhon, M. 1977 'Fête spontanée et fête organisée à Paris, en 1848' in J. Erhard and P. Viallaneix ed *Les Fêtes de la Révolution – Colloque de Clermont-Ferrand (juin 1974)* Bibliothèque d'Histoire Révolutionnaire 3e série, no. 17, Société des Études Robespierristes, Paris, 243–71

Allen, R.F. 1974 *Literary Life in German Expressionism and the Berlin Circles* Verlag A. Kummerle, Göppingen

Altmann, P. 1977 *Sinfonia von Luciano Berio. Eine analytische Studie* Universal Edition A.G., Vienna

Anhalt, I. 1970 'The Making of "Cento"' *Canada Music Book* spring–summer 81–9

– 1971 'Foci' *Artscanada* 28 April–May 57–8

– 1972 'Composing with Speech' in *Proceedings of the Seventh International Congress of Phonetic Sciences*, ed A. Rigault and R. Charbonneau. Mouton, The Hague, Paris

– 1973 'Luciano Berio's "Sequenza III"' *Canada Music Book* 7 autumn–winter 23–60

– 1979 'Pâ spaning efter rösten i dag – reflexioner av en tonsättare' *Artes* 2: 58–74

– 1981 'John Beckwith' in H. Kallmann, G. Potvin, K. Winters ed *Encyclopedia of Music in Canada*, University of Toronto Press, Toronto, 70–2

Apollinaire, G. 1956 *Œuvres poétiques* Bibliothèque de la Pléiade, Paris

Appelman, D.R. 1967 *The Science of Vocal Pedagogy* Indiana University Press, Bloomington

D'Aquili, E.G., Laughlin, C.D., jr, and McManus, J. ed 1979 *The Spectrum of Ritual: A Biogenetic Structural Analysis* Columbia University Press, New York

Aristotle 1883 *De arte poetica* (Vahlen's text) with translation by E.R. Wharton and M.A. Oxford, Parker and Co, Oxford and London

Arom, S. 1970 *Conte et chantefables Ngbaka-Ma'bo* Société pour l'Étude des langues Africaines 21–2 and Centre National de la Recherche Scientifique, Paris

– 1973 'Une Méthode pour la transcription de polyphonies et polyrythmies de tradition orale' *Revue de musicologie* 59: 165–90

Artaud, A. 1958 *The Theater and Its Double* Grove Press, New York

Austin, W.W. 1966 *Music in the 20th Century* Dent, London

Avron, D., and Lyotard, J.-F. 1971 '"A Few Words to Sing" Sequenza III,' *Musique en jeu* no. 2: 30–44

Ball, H. 1974 *Flight out of Time* Viking Press, New York

Barbara, D.A. ed 1960 *Psychological and Psychiatric Aspects of Speech and Hearing* Charles C. Thomas, Springfield, Ill

Barcza, L. 1981 'Opera Is Once More a Contemporary Voice' *Music Magazine* July–August 12–17

Barooshian, V.D. 1974 *Russian Cubo-Futurism. 1910–1930. A Study in Avant-Gardism* Mouton, The Hague

Barron, S., and Tuchman, M. 1980 *The Avant-Garde in Russia 1910–1930 – New Perspectives* Los Angeles County Museum of Art, Los Angeles, Calif

Bartók, B., and Lord, A.B. 1951 *Serbo-Croatian Folksong* Columbia University Press, New York

Bauman, R., and Sherzer, J. 1974 *Explorations in the Ethnography of Speaking* Cambridge University Press, London

Beane, W.C., and Doty, W.G. ed 1976 *Myths, Rites, Symbols: A Mircea Eliade Reader* 2 vol, Harper and Row, New York

Beckett, S. 1931 *Proust* Grove Press, New York

– 1959 *Watt* Grove Press, New York; Evergreen Books, London (originally published by Olympia Press, Paris, 1953)

– 1973 *Not I* Faber, London

Bennet, G., Berio, L., Boulez, P., et al 1975 *La Musique en projet* Gallimard, Paris

Berg, A. 1929 'Die Stimme in der Oper' *Gesang*, Jahrbuch 1929 der Universal-Edition A.-G., Vienna

Berio, L. 1959 'Musik und Dichtung – Eine Erfahrung' *Darmstädter Beitrage*, 11: 36–45

– 1963 'Du geste et de Piazza Carità' in *La Musique et ses problèmes contemporaines, 1953–63. Cahiers de la Compagnie Madelaine Renaud-Jean-Louis Barrault XLI* Juilliard, Paris, 216–23

– 1967 'Commenti al rock' *Nuova Rivista Musicale Italiana* 1: 125–35

Bertelé, R. 1975 *Henri Michaux* Poètes d'aujourd'hui, 5, Editions Séghers, Paris

Blau, L. 1974 *Das Aljüdische Zauberwesen* (reprint of the 1898 ed) Akademische Druck u. Verlagsanstalt, Graz, Austria

Blavatsky, H.P. 1893 *The Secret Doctrine* I *Cosmogenesis* Theosophical Publishing House, London

Bolinger, D. ed 1972 *Intonation* Penguin, Harmondsworth

Bonner, C. 1927 'Traces of Thaumaturgic Technique in the Miracles' *Harvard Theological Review* 20: 171–81

Borges, J.L. 1964 *Labyrinths: Selected Stories and Other Writings* New Directions Publishing, New York

Boulez, P. 1958 'Son, verbe, synthese' *Melos* 25: 310–16

Bourguignon, E. ed 1973 *Religion, Altered States of Consciousness, and Social Change* Ohio State University Press, Columbus

Bowie, M. 1973 *Henri Michaux* Clarendon Press, Oxford

Bowra, C.M. 1936 *Greek Lyric Poetry. From Alcman to Simonides* Oxford University Press, London

– 1968 *Primitive Song* 3rd ed, Weidenfeld and Nicolson, London

Bremond, H. 1926 *La Poésie pure* Bernard Grasset, Paris

Breton, A., and Legrand, G. 1957 *L'Art magique* Formes de l'art 1, Club français de l'art, Paris

Briner, A. 1978 'Bericht – Ligetis "Le Grand Macabre" an der Königlichen Oper, Stockholm' *Melos/NZ* 4: 226–7

Brook, P. 1968 *The Empty Space* MacGibbon and Kee, London

Bruckner, F. 1904 *Georg Benda und Das Deutsche Singspiel* Inaugural-Dissertation der Philosophischen Fakultät in Rostock zur Erlangung der Doktorwürde, Breitkopf und Härtel, Leipzig

Bruns, G.L. 1974 *Modern Poetry and the Idea of Language: A Critical and Historical Study* Yale University Press, New Haven and London

Buchheim, L.-G. 1959 *Der Blaue Reiter* Buchheim Verl, Feldafing

Budde, E. 1972 'Zum dritten Satz der "Sinfonia" von Luciano Berio' in R. Stephan ed *Die Musik der sechziger Jahre* 128–44

Burke, K. 1945 *A Grammar of Motives* Prentice-Hall, New York

Busnel, R.G. ed 1963 *Acoustic Behavior of Animals* Amsterdam

Butler, E.M. 1949 *Ritual Magic* Cambridge University Press, Cambridge

Cadieu, M. 1967 'Luciano Berio' *Les Lettres françaises* December 24–6

Cage, J. 1961 *Silence* Wesleyan University Press, Middletown, Conn

– 1979 *Empty Words – Writings '73–'78* Wesleyan University Press, Middletown, Conn

Cardine, Dom E. 1970 *Sémiologie grégorienne* Abbaye Saint-Pierre de Solesmes

Carter, H. 1929 *The New Spirit in the Russian Theatre 1917–28* Bretano's, New York

Catford, J.C. 1964 'Phonation Types: The Classification of Some Laryngeal Components of Speech Production' in D. Abercrombie et al ed *In Honour of Daniel Jones* 26–37

– 1970 'The Articulatory Possibilities of Man' in B. Malmberg ed *Manual of Phonetics* 278–308

– 1977 *Fundamental Problems in Phonetics* Indiana University Press, Bloomington and London

Chaliapin, F. 1932 *Man and Mask – Forty Years in the Life of a Singer* Victor Gollancz, London

Chao, Yuen Ren 1956 'Tone, Intonation, Singing, Chanting, Recitative, Tonal Composition, and Atonal Composition in Chinese' in Morris Halle et al ed *For Roman Jakobson* Mouton, The Hague, 52–9

Charles, D. 1978 *Le Temps de la voix* Jean-Pierre Delarge, Paris

Chassé, C. 1947 *Le Mouvement symboliste dans l'art du XIXe siècle* Librairie Fleury, Paris

– 1954 *Les Clés de Mallarmé* Aubier Editions, Montaigne

Cheney, S. 1929 *The Theatre: 3000 Years of Drama, Acting and Stagecraft* Longman's Green, New York

Chopin, H. 1967 'Open Letter to Aphonic Musicians (1)' in a booklet accompanying the record OU no. 33, ed H. Chopin, Sceau, 11–23

Cogan, R. 1969 'Toward a Theory of Timbre: Verbal Timbre and Musical Line in Purcell, Sessions, and Stravinsky' *Perspectives of New Music* fall–winter 75–81 and eight (unnumbered) pages of illustration

Coleridge, S.T. 1980 *Collected Works* XII *Marginalia I* ed George Whalley, Princeton University Press, Princeton, NJ

Colton, R.H., and Hollien, H. 1973 'Physiology of Vocal Registers in Singers and Non-singers' in John W. Large ed *Vocal Registers in Singing* 105–36

Combarieu, J. 1909 *La Musique et la magie – Étude sur les origines populaires de l'art musical son influence et sa fonction dans les sociétés* Minkoff Reprints, Geneva, n.d. (first published 1909 by A. Picard, Paris)

Corbett, E.P.J. 1971 *Classical Rhetoric for the Modern Student* Oxford University Press, New York

Cottrell, L.A., jr 1942 'The Analysis of Situational Fields in Social Psychology' *American Sociological Review* 7: 370–82

Crawford, J.C. 1972 *The Relationship of Text and Music in the Vocal Works of Schoenberg, 1908–1924* University Microfilms, Ann Arbor, Mich

Crystal, D. 1969 *Prosodic Systems and Intonation in English* Cambridge University Press, Cambridge

- 1975 *The English Tone of Voice – Essays in Intonation, Prosody and Paralanguage* Edward Arnold, London
Crystal, D., and Davy, D. 1969 *Investigating English Style* Longman, London
Curtay, J-P., and Gillard, J-P. ed 1971 *La Musique lettriste* no. 282–3 of *La Revue musicale* (entire double number) Richard-Masse, Paris
Dahlback, K. 1958 *New Methods in Folk Music Research* Oslo University Press, Oslo
Deák, F. 1975 'Russian Mass Spectacles' *Drama Review* T-66: 7–22
Dibelius, U. 1972 'Szene und Technik. Zwei Aspekte einer Entwicklung' in R. Stephan ed *Die Musik der sechziger Jahre* 53–64
Dieterich, A. 1891 *Abraxas – Studien Zur Religionsgeschichte* B.G. Teubner, Leipzig
- 1910 *Eine Mithrasliturgie* Zweite Auflage, B.G. Teubner, Leipzig und Berlin
Dodge, C. 1976a 'Notes' on the jacket of the record *Synthesized Speech Music by Charles Dodge* (CRI SD 348) Composers Recordings, New York
- 1976b 'Synthesizing Speech' *Music Journal* 34 no. 2 (February): 14
Donat, M. 1964 'Berio and His "Circles"' *Musical Times* 105: 105–7
Dornseiff, F. 1922 *Das Alphabet in Mystik und Magie* B.G. Teubner, Leipzig, Berlin
Drange, T. 1966 *Type Crossings* Mouton, The Hague
Duey, P.A. 1951 *Bel Canto in Its Golden Age* King's Crown Press, New York
Duncan, H.D. 1972 *Symbols in Society* Oxford University Press, London
Eimert, H. 1965 'Vokalität im 20. Jahrhundert' *Melos* 32: 350–9
Eliade, M. 1958 *Patterns in Comparative Religion* Sheed and Ward, London and New York
- 1964 *Shamanism. Archaic Techniques of Ecstasy* Routledge and Kegan Paul, London
- 1969 *Yoga: Immortality and Freedom* 2nd edn, Bollingen Series LVI, Princeton University Press, Princeton, NJ
- 1978 *A History of Religious Ideas* I *From the Stone Age to the Eleusinian Mysteries* University of Chicago Press, Chicago
Ellenberger, H.F. 1970 *The Discovery of the Unconscious: The History and Evolution of Dynamic Psychiatry* Allen Lane, Penguin, London
Emmert, R. ed 1979 *Films of ATPA* [Asian Traditional Performing Arts] – *Explanatory Notes* Mitsu Productions, Tokyo
English, H.B., and English, A.C. 1958 *A Comprehensive Dictionary of Psychological and Psychoanalytical Terms* David McKay, New York
Ertel, S. 1961 *Psychophonetik. Untersuchungen über Lautsymbolik und Motivation* Verlag für Psychologie, Dr C.J. Hogrefe, Göttingen
Esslin, M. 1961 *The Theatre of the Absurd* Doubleday, Garden City, NY
Faltin, P. 1978 'Aesthetisierung der Sprache dargestellt an Dieter Schnebels Madrasha II' *Melos/NZ* 4: 287–94

Félice, P. de 1947 *Foules en délire, extases collectives* Editions Albin Michel, Paris

Fields, Victor A. 1973 'Review of the Literature on Vocal Registers' in John W. Large ed *Vocal Registers in Singing* 23–34

Flammer, E.H. 1977 'Form und Gehalt. Eine Analyse von Luigi Nonos "La Fabrica Illuminata"' *Melos* 44: 401–11

Flint, R.W. 1972 *Marinetti. Selected Writings* Farrar, Straus and Giroux, New York

Flynn, G.W. 1975 'Listening to Berio's Music' *Musical Quarterly* 61 no. 5: 388–421

Fónagy, I. 1964 *Die Metaphern in der Fonetik* Mouton, The Hague

Fónagy, I., and Magdics, K. 1963 'Emotional Patterns in Intonation and Music' in *Festgabe für Otto von Essen* Akademie-Verl., Berlin, 293–326

Forte, A. 1957 'Notes on the Historical Background of the Opera and on the Text' (notes accompanying a recording, Columbia Masterworks U3L-241, of A. Schoenberg's *Moses und Aron*)

Foss, L., Ligeti, G., and Schwartz, E. 1972 'Contemporary Music: Observations from Those Who create it' *Music and Artists* 5 no. 3: 11–12, 21–2

Frazer, Sir J.G. 1922 *The Golden Bough: A Study in Magic and Religion* abridged edn, Macmillan, London, Toronto (first published 1922)

Freud, S. 1963 *Character and Culture* Collier Books, New York

Froehlich, A.J.P. 1982 'Reaktionen des Publikums auf Vorführungen nach Abstrakten Vorlagen' in W. Paulsen and H.G. Hermann ed *Sinn aus Unsinn Dada International* Francke Verlag, Bern and Munich, 15–28

Frye, N. 1971 *Anatomy of Criticism: Four Essays* first paperback edn, Princeton University Press, Princeton, NJ

Füllöp-Miller, G. 1927 *Das Russiche Theater* Amalthea-Verlag, Berlin

Gaster, M. 1971 *Studies and Texts in Folklore, Magic, Mediaeval Romance, Hebrew Apocrypha and Samaritan Archaeology* I–III, KTAV Publishing, New York

Gengoux, J. 1950 *La Pensée poétique de Rimbaud* Nizet, Paris

Gillmor, A.M. 1972 'Erik Satie and the Concept of the Avant-Garde' PHD dissertation, University of Toronto

Goeyvaerts, K. 'Was aus Wörtern wird' *Melos* 39: 159–62

Goffman, E. 1959 *The Presentation of Self in Everyday Life* Doubleday Anchor, New York

– 1967 *Interaction Ritual: Essays on Face-to-Face Behavior* Anchor Books, Doubleday, Garden City, NY

Goldman-Eisler, G. 1958 'Speech Analysis and Mental Processes' *Language and Speech* 1: 59–75

Goodman, F.D. 1972 *Speaking in Tongues. A Cross-cultural Study of Glossolalia* University of Chicago Press, Chicago and London

Gottwald, C. 1975 'Éléments pour une théorie de la nouvelle musique vocale' and 'Fragments d'une analyse de "Song Books"' in *La Musique en projet* Gallimard, Paris, 95–125

Greer, T.H. 1969 'Music and Its Relation to Futurism, Cubism, Dadaism, and Surrealism 1905–1950' PHD dissertation, North Texas State University

Grégoire, A. 1937 *L'Apprentissage du langage. Les deux premières années* E. Droz, Paris

Greul, H. 1967 *Bretter, die die Zeit bedeuten* Die Kulturgeschichte des Kabaretts, Kiepenheuer and Witsch, Köln-Berlin

Gruhn, W. 1972 'Dieter Schnebels "Glossolalie," Ein Beitrag zum Thema Musik also Sprache-Sprache als Musik' *Musik und Bildung* 580–5

– 1974a 'Arnold Schönberg (1874–1951) Ein Überlebender aus Warschau op. 46 (1947)' in D. Zimmerschied ed *Perspektiven Neuer Musik: Material und didaktische Information* Schott's Söhne, Mainz, 128–52

– 1974b 'Luciano Berio (1925) Sequenza III (1965)' in D. Zimmerschied ed *Perspektiven Neuer Musik: Material und didaktische Information* Schott's Söhne, Mainz, 234–49

Guilbert, Y. 1928 *L'Art de chanter une chanson* Bernard Grasset, Paris

– 1929 *La Passante émerveillée* Bernard Grasset, Paris

– 1946 *Autres Temps autres chants* Robert Laffont, Paris

Gullan, M. 1929 *Speech Training in the School* Evans Brothers, London

Hamm, B., Nettl, B., and Byrnside, R. 1975 *Contemporary Music and Music Cultures* Prentice-Hall, Englewood Cliffs, NJ

Harary, F., Norman, R.Z., and Cartwright, D. 1965 *Structural Models: An Introduction to the Theory of Directed Graphs* J. Wiley, New York

Hardcastle, W.J. 1976 *Physiology of Speech Production* Academic Press, London, New York

Harich-Schneider, E. 1973 *A History of Japanese Music* Oxford University Press, London

Hausler, J. 1972 'Einige Aspekte des Wort Ton Verhältnisses' in R. Stephan ed *Die Musik der sechziger Jahre* 65–76

Headley, H.E. 1959 'The Choral Works of Arthur Honegger' PHD dissertation, North Texas College

Heidegger, M. 1971 *On the Way to Language* Harper and Row, New York

Heike, G. 1975 *Musik und Sprache in Der Neuen Musik* Institut für Phonetik der Universität zu Köln, Berichte, no. 4, Köln

Helms, H.G. 1959 *Fa:M Ahniesgwow* Du Mont Schauberg, Köln

– 1966 'Komponieren mit sprachlichen Material' *Melos* 33: 137–43

– 1967 'Voraussetzungen eines neuen Musik theater' *Melos* 34: 118–30

– 1968 'Über die Entwicklung der Sprache im 20. Jahrhundert' *Melos* 35: 365–70

– 1974 'Schönberg: Sprache und Ideologie' in U. Dibelius ed *Herausförderung Schönberg* Carl Hanser Verlag, Munich, 78–109

Henderson, E.J.A. 1977 'The Larynx and Language: A Missing Dimension?' in G. Fant and C. Scully ed *The Larynx and Language Proceedings of a Discussion*

Seminar at the 8th International Congress of Phonetic Sciences 1975, *Phonetica* 34: 256–63

Henius, C. 1975 'Erfahrungen mit Luigi Nonos "La fabbrica illuminata" Dokumente, Arbeitsnotizen und Berichte' *Melos/NZ* 1: 102–8

Herbert, E.W. 1961 *The Artist and Social Reform: France and Belgium, 1885–1898* Yale University Press, New Haven

Hocke, G.R. 1959 *Manierismus in der Literatur: Sprach-Alchimie und Esoterische Kombinationskunst* Rowohlt, Hamburg

Hockett, C.F., and Ascher, R. 1964 'The Human Revolution' *Current Anthropology* 5 no. 3

Høeg, C. 1935 *La Notation ekphonètique* Levin and Munksgaard, Copenhagen (Mon. Mus. Byz. Subs., I fasc. 2)

Hoenle, D., and Lanoix, A. 1974 ' "Circles" : Concordances' in *Motifs et Figures* Publications de l'Université de Rouen, Presses Universitaires de France, Paris, 85–107

Hoffmann, L., and Hoffmann-Ostwald, D. 1961 *Deutsches Arbeitertheater 1918–1933* Henschelverlag, Berlin

Hofstätter, H.H. 1965 *Symbolismus und die Kunst der Jahrhundertwende: Voraussetzungen, Erscheinungsformen, Bedeutungen* Verlag M. Du Mont Schauberg, Köln

Hollien, H., and Moore, P. 1960 'Measurements of the Vocal Folds during Changes in Vocal Pitch' *Journal of Speech and Hearing Research* 3: 158–65

Holroyde, P. 1972 *The Music of India*. Praeger, New York

Honikman, B. 1964 'Articulatory Settings' in D. Abercrombie et al ed *In Honour of Daniel Jones* 73–84

Hopfner, T. 1974 *Griechisch-Ägyptischer Offenbarungszauber*. Verlag Adolf M. Hakkert, Amsterdam (reprint)

Huelsenbeck, R. 1951 'En Avant Dada: A History of Dadaism' (first published 1920) in R. Motherwell ed *The Dada Painters and Poets: An Anthology* 21–48

Huizinga, J. 1949 *Homo Ludens: A Study of the Play Element in Culture* Routledge & Kegan Paul, London (reprinted by Paladin, London, 1970)

Hull, J.M. 1974 *Hellenistic Magic and the Synoptic Tradition* SCM Press, London

Husson, R. 1960 Gauthier-Villars ed *La Voix chantée* Paris

Iamblichus 1895 *On the Mysteries of the Egyptians, Chaldeans, Assyrians* translated from the Greek by Thomas Taylor, 2nd ed, Bertram Dobell, London

Index to a Recorded Lexicon of Extended Vocal Techniques 1974 Center for Music Experiment and Related Research, University of California at San Diego, La Jolla, California (demonstration tape included)

Ionesco, E. 1958 *Four Plays* Grove Press, New York

– 1964 *Notes and Counter Notes. Writings on the Theater* Grove Press, New York

Isou, I. 1947 *Introduction à une nouvelle poésie et une nouvelle musique* Gallimard, Paris

Istel, E. 1901 *Jean-Jacques Rousseau als Komponist Seiner Lyrischen Scene 'Pygmalion'* 'Publikation der Internationalen Musikgesellschaft' Breitkopf and Hartel, Leipzig

Izutsu, T. 1956 *Language and Magic – Studies in the Magical Function of Speech* Keio Institute of Philological Studies, Tokyo

Jacques, C. 1956 *Cent Ans de music hall : Histoire générale du music hall, de ses origines à nos jours, en Grande-Bretagne, en France et aux U.S.A.* Éditions Jeheber, Geneva, Paris

Jakobson, R. 1968 *Child Language Aphasia and Phonological Universals* Mouton, The Hague, Paris

– 1980 'Art and Poetry – An Interview with David Shapiro' in S. Barron and M. Tuchman ed *The Avant-Garde in Russia 1910–1930 – New Perspectives* Los Angeles County Museum of Art, Los Angeles, Calif

Jakobson, R., and Lévi-Strauss, C. 1970 'Charles Baudelaire's "Les Chats"' in Michael Lane ed *Structuralism: A Reader* Jonathan Cape, London, 202–21

Jakobson, R., Fant, C.G.M., and Halle, M. 1967 *Preliminaries to Speech Analysis: The Distinctive Features and Their Correlates* MIT Press, Cambridge, Mass

Janik, A., and Toulmin, S. 1973 *Wittgenstein's Vienna* Simon and Schuster, New York

Jarry, A. 1970 *Œuvres complètes* Bibliothèque de la Pléiade, Gallimard, Paris

Jensen, K. 1979 'Extensions of Mind and Voice' *Composer* spring 13–17

Jones, A.M. 1959 *Studies in African Music* I, Oxford University Press, London, New York, Toronto, Capetown

Josephson, M. 1962 *Life among the Surrealists, A Memoir* Holt, Rinehardt and Winston, New York

Joyce, J. 1939 *Finnegans Wake* Viking Press, New York, 1958

– 1949 *Ulysses* The Bodley Head, London

Jung, C.G. 1957 *Collected Works* Pantheon, New York

Kafka, F. 1935 *Parables and Paradoxes* Schocken Books, New York

Kagel, M. 1975 *Tamtam: Monologe und Dialoge zur Musik.* R. Piper and Co Verlag, Munich/Zürich

Kagel, M., Klüppelholz, W., Mayer, H., et al 1980 *Aus Deutschland – Eine Lieder-Oper* (a program booklet to the opera, with libretto, commentary, etc) Deutsche Oper, Berlin

Kaplan, H.M. 1960 *Anatomy and Physiology of Speech* McGraw-Hill, New York, Toronto, London

Karkoschka, E. 1965 'Musik und Semantik' *Melos* 32: 252–9

Kaufmann, H. 1966 'György Ligetis Szenische Abenteuer' *Neues Form* 13 November–December 773–4

Kaufmann, W. 1975 *Tibetan Buddhist Chant: Musical Notations and Interpretations* Indiana University Press, Bloomington, London

Kavásch, D. 1980 'An Introduction to Extended Vocal Techniques: Some Compositional Aspects and Performance Problems' *Reports from the Center* 1 no. 2, Center for Music Experiment, UC San Diego, La Jolla, Calif

Keller, H. 1956 'Two Schoenberg Problems' *Music Review* 17: 268–9

– 1965–6 'Whose Fault Is the Speaking Voice?' *Tempo* 75 winter 12–17

Killmauer, W. 1972 'Sprache als Musik' *Melos* 39: 35–41

Kingdon, R. 1958 *The Groundwork of English Intonation* Longman, London

Kirby, M. and Nes Kirby, V. 1971 *Futurist Performance – With Manifestos and Playscripts Translated from the Italian*. E.P. Dutton, New York

Kirchner, J.A. 1970 *Pressman and Kelemen's Physiology of the Larynx* American Academy of Ophthalmology and Otolaryngology, Rochester, Minn

Kluckhorn, C. 1944 *Navaho Witchcraft* Beacon Press, Boston

Klüppelholz, W. 1976 *Sprache als Musik: Studien zur Vokalkomposition seit 1956* Musikverlag Gotthard F. Döring, Herrenberg

– 1977 'Musik als Theologie zu Kagels Rezitativarie' *Melos NZ Neue Zeitschrift für Musik* 3: 483–9

Knapp, B., and Chipman, M. 1964 *That Was Yvette* Holt, Rinehardt and Winston, New York

Knowlson, J. 1975 *Universal Language Schemes in England and France 1600–1800* University of Toronto Press, Toronto

Kostelanetz, R. ed 1974 *John Cage* Allen Lane, London

– ed 1980a *Scenarios: Scripts to Perform* Assembling Press, Brooklyn, NY

– ed 1980b *Text-Sound Texts* William Morrow, New York

Krieger, G., and Stroh, W.M. 1971 'Probleme der Collage in der Musik – Aufgezeigt am 3. Satz der Sinfonia von L. Berio' *Musik und Bildung* 229–351

Kris, E. 1964 *Psychoanalytic Explorations in Art* Schocken, New York

Kropp, A.M. 1931 *Ausgewählte Koptische Zaubertexte* I–III Édition de la Fondation Égyptologique Reine Elisabeth, Bruxelles

Kruchenykh, A. 1971 *Victory over the Sun* translated by E. Bartos and V. Nes Kirby *Drama Review* T-52: 93–124

Kubie, L.S. 1967 'Social Forces and the Neurotic Process' in L.Y. Rabkin and J.E. Carr ed *Source Book in Abnormal Psychology* Houghton, Mifflin, Boston, 140–51

Küpper, L. 1975 'New Possibilities of Vocal Music: Phonemes, Allophones, Phonatomes, Logatomes, Phonetic Microsounds' *Faire* 4/5, G.M.E.B., Bourges, 31–6

La Barbara, J. 1976 'Conversation with Joan La Barbara' in W. Zimmermann *Desert Plants: Conversations with 23 American Musicians* ARC Publ, Vancouver, 149–62

Lach, R. 1913 *Studien zur Entwicklungsgeschichte der Ornamentalen Melopöie* Beiträge zur Geschichte der Melodie, C.F. Kahnt Nachfolger, Leipzig

- 1925 *Das Konstruktionsprinzip der Wiederholung in Musik, Sprache und Literatur* Hölder-Tischler-Kempsky, Wien/Leipzig

Lanyon and Travolga, W.N. ed 1960 *Animal Sounds and Communication* Washington, DC

Large, J.W. ed 1973 *Vocal Registers in Singing* Mouton, The Hague, Paris
- 1977 'Studies of Extended Vocal Techniques: Safety' (abstract) in *Program détaillé* IRCAM Symp. sur la Psychoacoust. Mus., Paris, 11–13 juillet 1977, 50–1

Laske, O.E. 1977 *Music, Memory and Thought* University Microfilms International, Ann Arbor, Michigan

Laver, J.D.M.H. 1975 'Individual Features in Voice Quality' PHD thesis, University of Edinburgh
- 1977 'Neurolinguistic Aspects of Speech Production' in C. Gutknecht ed *Grundbegriffe und Hauptströmungen der Linguistik*, (ed) Hoffmann und Campe, Hamburg
- 1980 *The Phonetic Description of Voice Quality* Cambridge University Press, Cambridge (with an illustrative cassette)
- n.d. 'Early Writings on Voice Quality and Tone of Voice: from Cicero to Sweet' unpublished paper

Laver, J.D.M.H., and Hutcheson, S. ed 1972 *Communication in Face to Face Interaction – Selected Readings* Penguin, Harmondsworth

Lenneberg, E.H. 1967 *Biological Foundations of Language*. J. Wiley, New York, London, Sydney

Léon, P.R. 1971 *Essais de phonostylistique* Didier, Montreal, Paris, Brussels

Leroi-Gourhan, A. 1964 *Le Geste et la parole* I and II Albin Michel, Paris

Lévi-Strauss, C. 1966 *The Savage Mind* University of Chicago Press, Chicago

Levy, E. 1971 'Text Setting and Usage' in J. Vinton ed *Dictionary of Contemporary Music* Dutton, New York, 734–41

Lewis, P.E. 1970 'Merleau-Ponty and the Phenomenology of Language' in J. Ehrmann ed *Structuralism* Anchor Books, Doubleday, Garden City, NY, 9–31

Lichtenfeld, M. 1972 'György Ligeti oder das Ende der seriellen Musik' *Melos* 39: 74–80

Liddell, H.G. 1901 *A Lexicon Abridged from Liddell and Scott's Greek-English Lexicon* 23rd edn, Economy Book House, New York

Ligeti, G. 1966a 'Libretto zu "Aventures" und "Nouvelles Aventures"' *Neues Forum* 13: 774–9
- 1966b 'Weberns Melodik' *Melos* 33: 116–18
- 1967 'Libretto zu "Aventures" und "Nouvelles Aventures"' *Neues Forum* 14: 86–92
- 1969 'Auf dem Weg zu "Lux Aeterna"' *Österreichische Musikzeitschrift* 24: 80–8

List, G. 1963 'The Boundaries of Speech and Song' *Ethnomusicology* 7: 1–16

The Living Theatre in Europe 1966 (a program booklet produced by Sigma Neder-
land, Amsterdam) Mickery Books, Amsterdam

Lomax, A. 1959 'Folk Song Style' *American Anthropologist* 61: 927–54

- 1962 'Song Structure and Social Structure' *Ethnology* 1: 425–51

- 1968 *Folk Song Style and Culture* American Association for the Advancement of
Science, Washington

Luchsinger, R., and Arnold, G.E. 1965 *Voice – Speech – Language* Wadsworth,
Belmont, Calif, Constable, London

Lutosławski, W. 1968 'About the Element of Chance in Music' in G. Ligeti ed
Three Aspects of New Music Nordiska Musikförlaget, Stockholm, 45–53

Lyons, J. 1969 *Introduction to Theoretical Linguistics* Cambridge University Press,
London

McDougall, W. 1921 *The Group Mind: A Sketch of the Principles of Collective Psychology with Some Attempt to Apply Them to the Interpretation of National Life and
Character* Cambridge University Press, Cambridge

McLean, M., and Orbell, M. 1975 *Traditional Songs of the Maori* A.H. and A.W.
Reed, Wellington, Sydney, London

MacMillan, K. and Beckwith, J. ed 1975 *Contemporary Canadian Composers*
Oxford University Press, Toronto, London, New York

Maconie, R. 1976 *The Works of Karlheinz Stockhausen* Oxford University press,
London, New York, Toronto

Mahl, G.F. and Schulze, G. 1964 'Psychological Research in the Extralinguistic
Area' in T.A. Sebeok et al ed *Approaches to Semiotics* Mouton, London, The
Hague, Paris, 51–124

Malinowski, B. 1954 *Magic, Science, Religion* Doubleday, Garden City, NY

Mallarmé, S. 1945 *Oeuvres complètes* Bibliothèque de la Pléiade, Éditions
Gallimard, Paris

Malm, W.P. 1959 *Japanese Music and Musical Instruments* Charles E. Tuttle, Rut-
land, Tokyo

Malmberg, B. ed 1970 *Manual of Phonetics* North-Holland Publishing, Amsterdam, London

Marcuse, H. 1955 *Eros and Civilization: A Philosophical Inquiry into Freud* Beacon
Press, Boston

Marinetti, F.T. 1919 *Les Mots en liberté futuristes* Edizioni Futuriste Di Poesia,
Milan

- 1968 *Teoria e invenzione futurista* A. Mondadori, Milan

Markov, V. 1968 *Russian Futurism: A History* Berkeley

Mathers, S.L.M. 1954 *The Kabbalah Unveiled* Routledge and Kegan Paul, London

Mathews, M.V. 1977 'Different Vocal Tract Configurations that Produce the Same
Sound' *Programme détaillé*, IRCAM Symposium sur la Psychoacoustique Musicale, Paris 11–13 juillet 1977, 50

Meyer, M.W. ed 1976 *The 'Mithras Liturgy'* Scholars Press for the Society of Biblical Literature, Missoula

Michaux, H. 1950 *Passages* Éditions Gallimard, Paris

– 1957 *L'Infini turbulent* Mercure de France, Paris

Mordden, E. 1978 *Opera in the Twentieth Century: Sacred, Profane, Godot* Oxford University Press, New York

Moses, P.J. 1954 *The Voice of Neurosis* Grune and Stratton, New York

Motherwell, R. ed 1951 *The Dada Painters and Poets: An Anthology* Wittenborn, Schultz, New York

Moulton, J.H. 1917 *The Treasure of the Magi: A Study of Modern Zoroastrianism* Oxford University Press, London, New York

Müller, F.M. 1879–1910 *The Sacred Books of the East* Clarendon Press, Oxford

Müller-Blattau, J. 1952 *Das Verhältnis von Wort und Ton in der Geschichte der Musik: Grundzüge und Probleme* J.B. Metzlersche Verlagsbuchhandlung, Stuttgart

Nattiez, J.J. 1975 *Fondements d'une sémiologie de la musique* Union Générale d'Éditions, Paris

Nettl, B. 1964 *Theory and Method in Ethnomusicology* Free Press of Glencoe, Collier-MacMillan, London

– 1966 'Zurich, 1914–1918' *Du* XXVI, special issue

Newman, F.R. 1980 *Mouth Sounds* Workman Publishing, New York (includes record)

Nietzsche, F.W. 1927 *The Philosophy of Nietzsche* The Modern Library, Random House, New York

Nketia, K. 1972 'Les langages musicaux de L'Afrique Sub-saharienne – Étude comparative' in *La Musique Africaine, La Revue Musicale*, no. 288–9: 7–42

Nono, L. 1975 *Texte Studien zu Seiner Musik* Atlantis Musikbuch Verlag, Zürich

Nordwall, O. ed 1968 *Lutoslawski* Edition Wilhelm Hansen, Stockholm

Noske, F.R. 1977 *The Signifier and the Signified: Studies in the Operas of Mozart and Verdi* Martinus Nijhoff, The Hague

Oesch, H. 1967 *Wladimir Vogel: sein Weg zu einer neuen musikalischen Wirklichkeit* Francke, Bern and Munich

Oncley, P. 1973 'Dual Concept of Singing Registers' in John W. Large ed *Vocal Registers in Singing* 35–44

Osgood, C.E., Suci, G.J., and Tannenbaum, P.H. 1957 *The Measurement of Meaning* Urbana, Ill

Otto, R. 1923 *The Idea of the Holy: An Inquiry into the Non-Rational Factor in the Idea of the Divine and Its Relation to the Rational* 2nd edn, Oxford University Press, London, New York, Toronto

Ozouf, M. 1976 *La Fête révolutionnaire – 1789–1799* Éditions Gallimard, Paris

Painters of the Brücke (a catalogue) Tate Gallery, London, 1964

Paulsen, W., and Hermann, H.G. 1982 *Sinn aus Unsinn Dada International* Francke Verlag, Bern and Munich

Pestalozza, L. 1974 'Luigi Nono – Musik, Text, Bedeutung' *Melos* 41: 265–70

Petri, H. 1965 'Identität von Sprache und Musik' *Melos* 32: 345–9

Piaget, J. 1926 *The Language and Thought of the Child* Routledge & Kegan Paul, London

Picken, L. 1975 *Folk Musical Instruments of Turkey* Oxford University Press, London

Pike, K.L. 1967 *Phonetics* University of Michigan Press, Ann Arbor

Pittenger, R.E., Hockett, C.F., and Danehy, J.J. 1960 *The First Five Minutes – A Sample of Microscopic Interview Analysis* Paul Martineau, Ithaca, NY

Poggioli, R. 1960 *The Poets of Russia, 1890–1930* Harvard University Press, Cambridge, Mass

– 1968 *The Theory of the Avant-Garde* Belknap Press, Cambridge, Mass

Poncé, C. 1973 *Kabbalah: An Introduction and Illumination for the World Today* Straight Arrow Books, San Francisco

Pound, E.L. 1977 in R. Murray Schafer ed *Ezra Pound and Music: The Complete Criticism* New Directions, New York

Pousseur, H. 1969 'Berio und das Wort' *Musik und Bildung*, 459–61

Preisendanz, K. ed 1973 *Papyri Graecae Magicae. Die Griechischen Zauberpapyri* I and II, Zweite, Verbesserte Auflage, Verlag B.G. Teubner, Stuttgart (reprint of the 1928 edn)

Pressman, J.J. 1942 'Physiology of the Vocal Cords in Phonation and Respiration' *Arch. Otolaryng.* 35: 355–98

Prieberg, F.K. 1965 'Imaginäres Gespräch mit Luciano Berio' *Melos* 32: 156–65

Proctor, G.A. 1981 *Canadian Music of the Twentieth Century* University of Toronto Press, Toronto

Reese, G. 1940 *Music in the Middle Ages* W.W. Norton, New York

Reinach, S. 1905–23 *Cultes, mythes et religions* E. Leroux, Paris

Renoult, C. 1980 'De la déclamation musicale à l'âge classique' *Musique ancienne* 8–9 février–mars 4–12

Rimbaud, A. 1972 *Œuvres complètes* Gallimard, Paris

Robbins, S.D. 1963 *A Dictionary of Speech Pathology and Therapy* Sci-Art Publishers, Cambridge, Mass

Rolland, R. 1901 *Le 14 Juillet* in *Théâtre de la Révolution* Albin Michel, Paris (1909) 1–151

– 1913 *Le Théâtre du peuple. Essai d'esthétique d'un théâtre nouveau* Albin Michel, Paris

Romilly, J. de 1975 *Magic and Rhetoric in Ancient Greece* Harvard University Press, Cambridge, Mass, and London

Rouget, G. 1968 'L'ethnomusicologie' in J. Poirier ed *Ethnologie générale* Galli-mard, Paris 1339–90

– 1970 'Transcrire ou décrire ? Chant soudanais et Chant fuégien' in *Echanges et Communications – Mélanges offerts à Claude Lévi-Strauss* réunis par J. Poullion et P. Maranda, Mouton, The Hague, Paris, 677–706

– 1980 *La Musique et la transe : Esquisse d'une théorie générale des relations de la musique et de la possession* Gallimard, Paris

Rouget, G., avec la collaboration de Schwarz, J. 1976 'Chant fuégien, conso-nance, mélodie de voyelles' *Revue de musicologie* 62 no. 1: 5–23

Russolo, L. 1916 *L'Arte dei Rumori* Edizioni Futuriste di 'Poesia,' Milan

Ruwet, N. 1971 *Langage, musique, poésie* Éditions de Seuil, Paris

Sabbe, H. 1979 'György Ligeti – Illusions et Allusions' *Interface* 8: 11–34

Sachs, C. 1940 *The History of Musical instruments* W.W. Norton, New York

– 1943 *The Rise of Music in the Ancient World East and West* W.W. Norton, New York

Salmenhaara, E. 1969 *Das Musikalische Material und Seine Behandlung in den Werken 'Apparitions,' 'Atmosphères,' 'Aventures' und 'Requiem' von György Ligeti. Forschungsbeitrage zur Musikwissenschaft* XIX Gustav Bosse Verlag, Regensburg

Samuel, R., and Thomas, R.H. 1939 *Expressionism in German Life, Literature and the Theatre (1910–1924)* W. Heffer, Cambridge

Schafer, R. Murray 1970 *When Words Sing* Berandol Music Ltd, Toronto

– 1976 *Smoke: A Novel* Arcana Editions, Bancroft, Ont

– 1978 *The Chaldean Inscription* Arcana Editions, Bancroft, Ont

– 1979 *A Collection, Open Letter*, 4th series, 4 and 5, fall, Toronto

Scherer, J. 1957 *Le 'Livre' de Mallarmé* H. Mondor, Paris

Schnebel, D. 1970 *Mauricio Kagel. Musik Theatre Film* Verlag M. Du Mont Schau-berg, Köln

– 1972a *Denkbare Musik: Schriften 1952–1972* Verlag M. du Mont Schauberg, Köln

– 1972b 'Sprech und Gesangschule (Neue Vokalpraktiken)' in D. Schnebel *Denk-bare Musik*, 444–60

Schoenberg, A. 1958 *Letters* Faber, London

Scholem, G.G. 1954 *Major Trends in Jewish Mysticism* 3rd edn, Schocken Books, New York

– 1974 *Kabbalah* Quadrangle, New York Times Book Co, New York

Schönberger, E. 1980 'Stockhausen: The Billy Graham of Contemporary Music' *Key Notes* 12: 15–16

Schöning, K. 1982 *Mauricio Kagel. Das Buch der Hörspiele* Suhrkamp Verlag, Frankfurt am Main

Schopenhauer, A. 1964 *The World as Will and Idea* Routledge and Kegan Paul, London (first published 1883)

Schuhmacher, G. 1967 'Gesungenes und gesprochenes Wort in Werken Wladimir Vogels' *Archiv für Musikwissenschaft* 24: 64–80

Schwimmer, H. 1968 'Die Musik in "Finnegans Wake"' *Melos* 35: 133–40

Schwitters, K. 1973–7 F. Lach ed *Das Literarische Werk* I–IV Du Mont Schauberg, Cologne

– 1975 *Merzhefte* mit einer Einleitung von F. Lach, Herbert Lang und Cie A.G., Bern und Frankfurt

Searle, C.L., Jacobson, J.Z., and Kimberley, B.P. 1978 'Speech as Patterns in the 3-Space of Time and Frequency' unpublished paper, Queen's University, Kingston, Canada

Searle, C.L., Jacobson, J.Z., and Rayment, S.G. 1978 'Stop Consonant Discrimination Based on Human Audition' unpublished paper, Queen's University, Kingston, Canada

Sebeok, T.A. ed 1955 *Myth. A Symposium* Indiana University Press, Bloomington

Seeger, C. 1958 'Prescriptive and Descriptive Music Writing' *Musical Quarterly* 44: 184–95

Serežnikov, V. 1923 *Muzyka Slova* Gosudarstvennoye Izdatel'stoo, Moscow, Petrograd

Sewell, E. 1952 *The Field of Nonsense* Chatto and Windus, London

Shattuck, R. 1961 *The Banquet Years* Anchor Books, Garden City, NY

Smalley, R. 1974 '"Momente" Material for the Listener and Composer' and '"Momente" Material for the Listener and Performer' *Musical Times* 115: 23–8, 289–95

Soria, D.J. 1970 'Artist Life: Cathy Berberian' *High Fidelity/Musical America* 20 July, section 2: 4–5

Souster, T. 1968 'Xenakis's "Nuits"' *Tempo* summer 5–18

Staempfli, E. 1967 'Musik, Wort und Sprache' *Melos* 34: 339–43

Starkie, E. 1938 *Arthur Rimbaud* Faber, London

Stein, E. 1953 *Orpheus in New Guises* Rockliff, London

Stein, G. 1980 *The Yale Gertrude Stein: Selections*, with an Introduction by Richard Kostelanetz, Yale University Press, New Haven and London

Steiner, G. 1975 *After Babel: Aspects of Language and Translation* Oxford University Press, London

Steinitzer, M. 1918 A. Siedl ed *Zur Entwicklungsgeschichte des Melodrams und Mimodrams* vol XXXV of *Die Musik*, C.F.W. Siegel, Leipzig

Stempel, W.-D., and Paulman, I. ed 1972 *Texte Der Russichen Formalisten* II Wilhelm Fink Verlag, Munich

Stephan, R. ed 1972 *Die Musik der sechziger Jahre: Zwölf Versuche* Schott's Söhne, Mainz

- ed 1974 *Über Musik und Sprache: Sieben Versuche zur Neueren Vokalmusik* B. Schott's Söhne, Mainz

Stevens, K.N. 1977 'Physics of Laryngeal Behavior and Larynx Modes' in G. Fant and C. Scully ed *The Larynx and Language, Proceedings of a Discussion Seminar at the 8th International Congress of Phonetic Sciences 1975, Phonetica* 34: 264–79

Stockhausen, K. 1960 'Music and Speech' *Die Reihe* 6: 40–60

- 1973–8 *Texte* I–IV Verlag M. Du Mont Schauberg, Köln

Stöckl, R. 1980 'Verschobener Weltuntergang. Ligetis 'Le Grand Macabre' in Nürnberg' *Neue Zeitschrift für Musik* March–April 138

Strunk, O. ed 1950 *Source Readings in Music History* W.W. Norton, New York

Sundberg, J. 1977 'The Acoustics of the Singing Voice' *Scientific American* March 82–91

- 1978 'Synthesis of Singing' *STM Swedish Journal of Musicology* 60 no. 1: 107–12 (with recorded illustrations)

- 1980 'Speech, Song and Emotions' an expanded and translated version of chapter 6 of the author's book *Röstlära* (Voice Science), Proprius Förlag, Stockholm

Suzuki, D.T. 1950, 1953 *Essays in Zen Buddhism* series 2 and 3, Rider, London

Szabolcsi, B. 1950 *A Melódia Története* Cserépfalvi, Budapest

Szilágyi, J.-G. 1982 *Paradigmák* Magvetö Kiadó, Budapest

Tamba, A. 1974 *La Structure musicale du Nô : Théâtre traditionnel japonais* Klincksieck, Paris

Taruskin, R. 1970 'Realism as Preached and Practiced – The Russian Opera Dialogue' *Musical Quarterly* 56 no. 3: 431–54

Thomas C., 1969 'Wege zu erklingender Sprache. Zu den Stücken für Sprechchor von Carl Orff' *Musik und Bildung* 1: 497–9

Tisdall, C., and Bozzolla, A. 1978 *Futurism* Oxford University Press, New York and Toronto

Togi, M. 1971 *Gagaku. Court Music and Dance* Vol V of *Performing Arts of Japan* John Weatherhill, Tokyo

Tomatis, A. 1962 'La Voix' *La Revue musicale* numéro special, no. 250: 39–57

Trager, G.L. 1958 'Paralanguage: A First Approximation' *Studies in Linguistics* 13 no. 12: 1–12

Trimingham, J.S. 1971 *The Sufi Orders in Islam* Oxford University Press, London, Oxford, New York

Tuchman, B. 1966 *The Proud Tower – A Portrait of the World before the War 1890–1914* Macmillan, New York

Uldall, E. 1960 'Attitudinal Meanings Conveyed by Intonation' *Language and Speech* 3: 223–34

– 1964 'Dimensions of Meaning in Intonation' in D. Abercrombie et al ed *In Honour of Daniel Jones* Longmans, London, 271–9

Usener, H. 1896 *Götternamen Versuch einer Lehre von der Religiösen Begriffsbildung* Verlag von Friedrich Cohen, Bonn

Valéry, P. 1958 *The Art of Poetry* Vintage, New York

Van den Berg, J. 1955 'On the Role of the Laryngeal Ventricle in Voice Production' *Folia Phoniatrica* 7: 57–69

– 1970 'Mechanism of the Larynx and the Laryngeal Vibrations' in B. Malmberg ed *Manual of Phonetics* 278–308

Van Riper, C., and Irwin, J.V. 1958 *Voice and Articulation* Prentice-Hall, Englewood Cliffs, NJ

Varèse, L. 1972 *Varèse – A Looking Glass Diary* I *1883–1928* W.W. Norton, New York

Veen, J. Van Der 1955 *Le Mélodrame musicale de Rousseau au romantisme : Ses aspects historiques et stylistiques* Martinus Nijhoff, The Hague

Vennard, W. 1967 *Singing, the Mechanism and the Technic* rev edn, Carl Fischer, New York

Vennard, W., and Hirano, M. 1973 'The Physiological Basis for Vocal Registers' in John W. Large ed *Vocal Registers in Singing* 45–58

Vetter, H.J. 1970 *Language Behavior and Psychopathology* Rand McNally, Chicago

Vetter, M. 1973 'Liebesspiele oder zur musikalischen Zukunft der Sprache' *Melos* 40: 270–3

Vinton, J. ed 1971 *Dictionary of Contemporary Music* E.P. Dutton, New York

Wagner, R. 1855 *Art and Revolution – Art-work of the Future* Kegan Paul, Trench, Trubner, London

Walker, D.P. 1958 *Spiritual and Demonic Magic from Ficino to Campanella* The Warburg Institute, University of London, London; Kraus reprint, Nendeln/Liechtenstein, 1969

Ward, W.D., and Burns, E.M. 1978 'Singing without Auditory Feedback' *Journal of Research in Singing* 1 no. 2: 24–44

Werner, E. 1957 'The Music of Post-biblical Judaism' in E. Wellesz ed *The New Oxford History of Music* I 313–35

– 1959 *The Sacred Bridge – The Interdependence of Liturgy and Music in Synagogue and Church during the First Millennium* Columbia University Press, New York

Westergaard, P. 1967 'Sung Language' American Society of University Composers *Proceedings of the Second Annual Conference* April: 9–36

Wiedman, R.W. 1955 'Expressionism in Music' PHD dissertation, New York University, available from University Microfilms, Ann Arbor, Mich

Williams, E. ed 1967 *An Anthology of Concrete Poetry* Something Else Press, New York

Wiora, W. 1962 'Jubilare sine verbis' in H. Anglès et al ed *In Memoriam Jaques Handschin* Martinus Nijhoff, The Hague

Wishart, T. 1979 *Book of Lost Voices* T. Wishart, or Philip Martin Books, York

– 1980 'The Composer's View: Extended Vocal Technique' *Musical Times* May 313–14

Withrow, G.J. 1961 *The Natural Philosophy of Time* T. Nelson, London and Edinburgh

Wittgenstein, L. 1921 *Tractatus Logico-Philosophicus* Routledge and Kegan Paul, London

Woroszylski, W. 1970 *The Life of Mayakovsky* Orion Press, New York

Wundt, W. 1965 *Elements of Folk Psychology: Outlines of a Psychological History of the Development of Mankind* translated by E.L. Schaub, George Allen and Unwin, London, Macmillan, New York

Yates, F.A. 1964 *Giordano Bruno and the Hermetic Tradition* Routledge and Kegan Paul, London

– 1966 *The Art of Memory* Routledge and Kegan Paul, London

Zeller, H.R. 1964 'Mallarmé and Serialist Thought' *Die Reihe* 6: 5–32

Index of names and titles

Index of subjects

absurd, effect of 11, 16–17, 18, 92, 154–5, 166, 177, 178, 184, 199, 202–3
accumulation 138, 140, 144
advertising, magical technique in 198
aleatoric, quasi-aleatoric structure 105–6
alphabet 192, 237
anabasis 249
anagram 4, 184–5, 221, 236, 280 n8, 285 n40
animism 194, 196, 197
anthropomorphism 266
antiphony 136–7, 240–1
apotropaic technique 193, 224, 249, 251
arcanum, music as 176, 183–6
assemblage 241
atonality 8
automatic writing 100–1, 228–9

bel canto 169, 210, 214, 263, 264, 269 n1
blurred boundaries, between media 11, 151–75
borrowing, intermusical 20, 206, 242

breath, breathing 3, 32, 161, 181, 209–14, 222; anima 212; ātman 212; circular 232, 285 n32; duh 212; nephes 212; pneuma 212; prāna 212; *prāṇāyāma* 181, 212–13; psykhē 212; rūah 212; spiritus 212; *tahlīl* 181, 213, 221–2, 230–1, 282 n4
breathy voice 4, 32, 85, 161, 172, 215, 251, 263

call, call signal 45, 55, 216, 250
centonization 221
chance 105–6
chant, chanting 165–6, 214, 248
chorale 80, 87–8
clapping 187
cluster 248, 250
collage 12, 178
collective ad libitum 146
communication 63, 163
compound structure 144
concept music 20
concrete music 19
convergence 144
cosmic sound 249, 252
creation, as theme 7, 287 n9